STRESS MANAGEMENT

Increasing Your Stress Resistance

Barbara A. Brehm

Smith College

LONGMAN

An Imprint of Addison Wesley Longman, Inc.

New York • Reading, Massachusetts • Menlo Park, California • Harlow, England
Don Mills, Ontario • Sydney • Mexico City • Madrid • Amsterdam

Editor in Chief: Priscilla McGeehon
Acquisitions Editor: Rebecca Dudley
Supplements Editor: Cyndy Taylor
Project Editors: Ann P. Kearns and Donna DeBenedictis
Text Designer: Karin Batten
Cover Designer: Wendy Ann Fredericks
Cover Illustration: © Alexandra Maldonado/SIS
Photo Researcher: Mira Schachne
Production Manager: Alexandra Odulak
Electronic Production Specialist: Joanne Del Ben
Manufacturing Manager: Hilda Koparanian
Printer and Binder: Courier/Kendallville, Inc.
Cover Printer: Phoenix Color Corp.

For permission to use copyrighted material, grateful acknowledgment is made to the copyright holders on p. 364, which is hereby made part of this copyright page.

Library of Congress Cataloging-in-Publication Data

Brehm, Barbara A.
    Stress management: increasing your stress resistance / Barbara A. Brehm.
        p.   cm.
    Includes bibliographical references and index.
    ISBN 0-321-01068-X
    1. Stress (Psychology)   2. Stress management.   I. Title.
    BF575.S75B73   1998

155.9'042—dc21   97-17767
                                                                    CIP

Please visit our website at http://longman.awl.com

ISBN 0-321-01068-X

12345678910—CRK—00999897

This book is dedicated with heartfelt gratitude to all my students,
whose teachings have enriched my understanding of stress
and whose words and lives fill these pages.

Brief Contents

Section I
The Nature of Stress

Section II
Direct Coping: Changing the Sources of Stress

Section III
Lifestyle and Stress Resistance

Section IV
Changing Your Perception of Stress

Section V
Changing Your Stress Response

Detailed Contents

Chapter 4
Stress and Your Life   67

Section II   Direct Coping: Changing the Sources of Stress

Chapter 5
Coping Strategies and Problem Solving   87

Chapter 8
Communication Skills   158

Section III Lifestyle and Stress Resistance

Chapter 11
The Pleasure Principle   229

Section IV *Changing Your Perception of Stress*

Chapter 12
Stress? It Depends on Your Point of View   255

Section V *Changing Your Stress Response*

Chapter 15
Relaxation Techniques: Decreasing Your Physical Stress Reactivity and Increasing Self-Awareness   317

To the Instructor

Stress management courses rarely engage students only in the cognitive realm. They often reach deeply into students' personal lives as well, encouraging student involvement to enhance learning. The layout, writing, and pedagogical features of this book support this active learning method and give it a framework.

Stress management courses are taught in many different contexts, from full-credit graduate courses in academic departments to noncredit workshops offered by student health services. This text has a strong research base and works well in an academic setting at any level. It also can be easily adapted to a workshop format, where the group leader may choose to put less emphasis on the psychophysiology of stress and more emphasis on the applications. No matter what the academic context or emphasis, students learn best when they are actively engaged with the material.

Stress Management: Increasing Your Stress Resistance takes a positive approach to stress management, encouraging students to build on existing strengths. It includes information I have found most relevant to college students of all ages. The material may be presented in any order that makes sense for you and your curriculum. The organization of this book reflects how I present stress management concepts to my students. Section I gives an overview of the psychophysiology of stress and the impact chronic stress can have on health. Section II covers topics associated with direct coping: problem-solving, values clarification, time management, study skills, and communication skills. Section III examines the relationship between lifestyle and stress resistance, and discusses topics such as nutrition, exercise, sleep habits, addiction, and recreation. Section IV delves into the important link between perception and stress resistance, a fascinating section for most students. Cognitive intervention techniques, self-esteem, and personality characteristics associated with strong stress resistance are covered here. Section V discusses the importance of the relaxation response and presents the relaxation techniques students have found most beneficial over the years. While this is the last section in the book, I actually begin introducing some of the relaxation techniques at the beginning of the semester, taking the entire semester to cover all the techniques. My two-hour class period combines conceptual material, class discussion, and relaxation practice.

This book has features that engage students and enhance their comprehension of concepts by having them draw on or relate to their own experiences and observations. Each chapter has the following boxed features that do just that:

- **Student Stress** sections provide case studies of college students coping with typical stressors. These case studies have all been drawn from students with whom I have worked over the past 12 years. (Names have been changed to protect the guilty and the innocent.)

- **Stress and You** sections give readers an opportunity to assess personal stress patterns. These boxes encourage students to think critically about chapter ideas in a real-life context.
- **Action Plan** sections at the end of each chapter (beginning with Chapter 4) give students an opportunity to analyze chapter concepts and incorporate these ideas into their own lives. The Action Plan format is based on behavior modification models that emphasize realistic planning and a problem-solving approach to behavior change. They are also based on the notion that small changes can make a big improvement in personal stress resistance.

Many chapters have additional special sections that enrich and broaden students' understanding of stress management:

- **Stress Research** sections highlight the work of historically important researchers and their contributions to our knowledge of the psychophysiology of stress. Instructors can use these sections to reinforce the importance of the research perspective and to increase students' awareness of science as process.
- **Exercises** and **Worksheets** present opportunities for students to apply and analyze chapter material or practice stress management techniques and relaxation exercises.

To further aid students in studying from this book, the following pedagogy is included in every chapter:

- Chapter summaries at the end of each chapter will help students organize, review, and retain important chapter concepts.
- Important terms are highlighted in bold in the text where they are defined, and these terms also are included in a glossary at the end of the book.

To aid instructors, this book is accompanied by an Instructor's Manual with helpful teaching ideas and test questions. This manual is available through your Addison Wesley Longman representative.

Teaching stress management has been one of the most interesting and personally rewarding experiences of my academic career—may it be so for you as well.

ACKNOWLEDGMENTS

I would like to thank everyone who has contributed to my understanding of stress and the creation of this book. Special thanks go to my students at Smith College, and workshop participants at Smith College, Kaiser-Permanente, and the Smith Management Program, to whom this book is dedicated.

Thanks also to those individuals who have supported my work teaching stress management, especially my colleagues Jim Johnson, Don Siegel, Chris Shelton, Lynn Oberbillig, and Tim Bacon. Special thanks to Michelle G. Finley, whose dedicated assistance allowed me to continue my work on this book even while I served as department chair, since she kept me organized and the office running smoothly. I am especially grateful to Smith College and its faculty support programs for funding my research and my terrific research assistants. I am grateful to Lisa Hoogesteger for signing me on as a stress management workshop leader for the health education department at Kaiser Permanente, and Lynn Bechtel for sharing her insights as a group leader. Gaynelle Weiss and the staff and participants of the Smith Management Program have added an invaluable dimension and breadth to my understanding of stress.

Three dedicated research assistants, all Smith students, provided countless hours of computer searching, article hunting, and photocopying. Thank you Jennifer Pearl for your incredible enthusiasm, Marilyn Finch for getting me organized, and Sharon Sears for expert sleuthing, and all three of you for great insights and discussions. It was truly a pleasure to work with each of you.

A famous choreographer once remarked that great choreographers never borrow; they steal. Writing this book of course brought me into contact with many wonderful people who gave me encouragement and new perspectives. Don Ardell, Tom Ferguson, David Castle, David Jenkins, Jon Kabat-Zinn, Barbara Reinhold, Randy Frost, and Anabel Prins were especially helpful.

I would like to thank Bonnie Roesch for getting me started on this book, and all of the people at Addison Wesley Longman who worked on this book, especially Mira Schachne for her good eye and great sense of humor, Ann Kearns and Donna DeBenedictis for pulling it all together, Patterson Lamb for seamless copyediting, Lee Paradise for proofreading and catching what was missed, Bernice Eisen for her indexing expertise, Joanne Del Ben for creating book pages from what was once a manuscript pile, Wendy Fredericks for an exciting cover design, Marjorie Mindell for all those details, and Becky Dudley for taking this project under her wing. Thanks also to the following reviewers for their helpful comments:

Cory Bates, *Ohio State University*

Carol M. Batt, *Washington State University*

John Curtis, *University of Wisconsin*

Joan R. Easton, *Emporia State University*

Martha E. Ewing, *Michigan State University*

Bill Hyman, *Sam Houston State University*

Darrel Lang, *Emporia State University*

Roseann M. Lyle, *Purdue University*

Charles Regin, *UNLV*

Barbara A. Rienzo, *University of Florida*

Roger Shipley, *Texas Woman's University*

Pamela Weisman, *University of Washington*

Terry Winfield, *University of Washington*

Denise E. Yeager, *Bowie State University*

I am grateful to the wonderful teachers of the Hartsbrook Waldorf School for teaching not only my children but also me. Thanks for your holistic body/mind/ spirit perspective and emphasis on the quality of life.

I would also like to acknowledge my parents, who taught me to follow my heart; my husband, Peter, who continues to be my soulmate uphill and downhill, in headwinds and tailwinds; and my children, Ian and Adam, who have given me an insider's perspective on the "full catastrophe" as well as love all around the universe and back again.

BARBARA A. BREHM

To the Student

This book is designed to help you understand the nature of stress, identify your personal stress patterns, and develop and implement strategies for increasing your resistance to the negative effects of stress by improving your ability to cope with stressful situations. An understanding of stress management will help you develop enjoyable and healthful ways to let go and relax. By increasing your understanding of stress and improving your stress resistance, you can make each day a little more joyful, meaningful, and personally fulfilling.

Stress management is the cornerstone of the wellness philosophy. This is the belief that in a given situation you make choices that determine and change the nature of your experience, thereby affecting the quality of both your daily life and your long-term health and well-being. Your stress response patterns interact with other wellness components: sleep, diet, and exercise habits; substance abuse and addiction; your sense of self-esteem; and your capacity to take responsibility for your own life. Learning to manage stress can help you perform better in college and in the rest of your life and to enjoy yourself more.

Coping with the stress of writing a term paper is a good example of how your stress management style affects your well-being, performance, and quality of life. Do you perceive term papers as a form of torture designed by evil professors to make poor students miserable? Best done in a frenzy at the last minute? On ten cups of coffee and no sleep? Or do you take the wellness approach: find an interesting topic, immerse yourself in the process of researching it, and enjoy the challenge of creating an interesting perspective as you synthesize your information into a paper? (Well, let's be real. Maybe two cups of coffee and a few well-chosen epithets when the paper gets jammed in the printer? Life is not perfect!)

An important premise of this book is that stress is a fact of life and indeed provides the spice of life. Not all stress is distress; often only habitual perception makes it so. Stress management classes let you get to know yourself a little better and help you use this self-understanding to design effective coping strategies, and ultimately to increase your resistance to harmful stress effects. You cannot and would not want to get rid of all sources of stress, but you can change or eliminate some of them. You can also change your physical and psychological response to stress. You can increase your stress resistance by strengthening your positive self-esteem, by developing an inner strength for challenging times, and by nurturing your ability to see life's changes as learning experiences.

Another theme of this book is that stress management does not always require hard work. Academicians often fail to realize that to some extent, the medium is the message. In our enthusiasm to teach, we assume that more is better. Teaching quality becomes measured in quantity: of notes, assignments, and topics. In addition, stress management classes and seminars are often guilty of creating more stress by focusing on what students are doing wrong. Professors teach the endless litany of negative stress effects and give mountains of advice on managing stress until the onslaught of information is overwhelming. Relaxation becomes a mechanized chore and successful stress management an unattainable goal. Many of the suggestions offered in this book are relatively simple to incorporate into your daily life. You are encouraged to build on the many ways you are already managing stress effectively. Specific goal-setting and action-plan exercises throughout the book help you design concrete lifestyle changes to increase your stress resistance.

Research on stress has blossomed over the past 20 years, confirming the significant impact excess stress can have on health and well-being. While research in this field can get somewhat esoteric, an introductory text need not be so. This text is research based, but the material is personal in orientation. In addition to published research, this text draws on my 12 years of experience teaching stress management classes and workshops for both traditional- and nontraditional-age college students.

Stress response patterns are as varied as the personalities they are a part of, and effective coping strategies must fit each individual's style. Some people respond to stress physically. A nervous stomach or tension headache lets them know they are on overload. Others experience stress in a more psychological way, feeling anxious, nervous, or depressed. Sources of stress also vary from person to person. Situations that can send a first-year student into a panic might be part of the routine for a senior. Nontraditional-age college students have sources of stress that are different from those of the 18-year-old still living at home. Consequently, there is no single magic method of stress reduction. What works for one person won't work for everyone.

For most students, the study of stress management is a personal journey. Research results help to illuminate the way, but in the end individuals must evaluate the information presented in a stress management text and incorporate into their lives whatever appears to be most relevant and useful. This text offers a variety of perspectives on stress management, a potpourri of suggestions for improving stress resistance, and encouragement for each student to discover what works best.

BARBARA A. BREHM

chapter 1

What Is Stress?

Ask a group of people "What is stress?" and you will get plenty of answers. Some people will talk about sources of stress: to them stress is writing a paper, having too much work to do, or getting into an argument with a friend. Others will describe emotions such as tension, anxiety, feeling out of control, or being overwhelmed. Some will add physical symptoms to the list: to them stress means a headache, painful muscle tension in the neck and shoulders, or sleeplessness. A few might talk about behavioral effects, things they do when stressed, like biting their nails, eating too much, or procrastinating.

Responses to "What is stress?" usually carry a negative connotation, although some people will acknowledge that stress motivates them to get their work done and even to perform better. A few will actually admit to enjoying the "adrenaline rush" of impending deadlines, or being in a high-pressure situation such as a job interview or an athletic event.

THE STRESS CYCLE

These answers are all part of the definition of stress. People generally use the word **stress** to describe that feeling of anxiety and physical tension that occurs when demands placed on them exceed their abilities to cope (Monat & Lazarus, 1991). Stress usually begins with some sort of stimulus, called a **stressor.** A stressor is anything that causes stress. Stressors may be real (a vicious dog), distortions of something real (a friendly dog that you perceive as vicious), or purely imaginary (fear of walking in a new neighborhood because a vicious dog might appear).

Your reaction to stressors is called the **stress response,** and it consists of physical and psychological components. Physically, your body responds to the source of stress by preparing to fight or run away—the famous "fight-or-flight" response. Your heart beats faster and harder, blood pressure rises, muscles brace for action, breathing becomes shallower and more rapid: it's almost like you're exercising while standing still.

Psychologically, your thoughts and feelings interact with your physical arousal. Words, phrases, and images may pop into your head. If they are negative ("I can't take it. Why me? I hate this job"), they may exacerbate your physical stress response. More positive thoughts ("I've done it before, I can do it again. I can work through this") may help reduce the fight-or-flight response. And sometimes you may be too busy coping to think! You may be immersed in what you're doing and not be aware of any thoughts at all.

Your stress response is made up of many feelings. Sometimes you may feel challenged, stimulated, excited, and even happy, especially if you perceive the stressor to be something you have some control over, and if you expect a mostly positive outcome (Dienstbier, 1991; Funk, 1992; Nowack, 1991; Sheppard & Kashani, 1991). When your stress reaction is more negative in tone, you are apt to feel anxious, frightened, helpless, or depressed. Your feelings and thoughts are inextricably intertwined (Lazarus, 1991). Positive thoughts create positive feelings. When you're feeling good, you're more apt to see things in a positive light and have positive thoughts. Thoughts and feelings affect, and are affected by, your physical response to stress as well. When your heart is pounding and your breathing is shallow, you may become more anxious. In other words, while teachers and researchers may separate physical and psychological responses in their discussions of the stress cycle, body and mind work together in real life (Moyer, 1993; Seaward, 1994).

Your perceptions of stressors and your perceptions of your abilities to cope with them are an important part of the stress cycle. Your perceptions can create sources of stress out of thin air, as in the fear of imaginary vicious dogs. They can also turn a minor source of stress, such as completing a school assignment, into a cause for panic; you may make mountains out of molehills. You may perceive the assignment to be more difficult than it really is and yourself as incapable of completing it. Sometimes you may worry for days about an assignment that, in the end, takes only two or three hours and isn't so difficult after all. On the other hand, you may overestimate your competence or underestimate the demands of a given assignment; you may not give the task the time or attention it truly demands, thus creating stress far beyond that inherent in the assignment.

COPING

Another important component of the stress cycle is **coping**—what you do to deal with the source of stress. Coping strategies may be categorized in several useful ways.

Direct coping, also called **problem-focused coping** (Monat & Lazarus, 1991), is always the first step in alleviating stress. When you try to eliminate or change the source of stress, you are using direct coping. Problem solving is the most common

I'm an old man and have known a great many troubles, but most of them never happened.

MARK TWAIN

Calvin and Hobbes   by Bill Watterson

When you do something to relax and feel less stressed, you are using palliative or emotion-focused coping.

form of direct coping. Suppose you're worried about a paper that is due next week. The best way to deal with this type of stress is to get started! Come up with some possible topics, and then go to the library and begin looking for some sources.

Sometimes you still feel stressed, even after you have done all you can to confront the problem. You've started the paper but you still feel worried. When you do something to relax and feel less stressed, you are using **palliative coping,** also called **emotion-focused coping.** Examples of palliative coping methods include talking to a friend, going for a walk, and listening to music.

Coping responses may have positive or negative effects on the source of stress and on the stress cycle in general. **Adaptive coping** responses have a generally positive effect and help reduce feelings of stress. **Madadaptive coping** strategies may help you feel better immediately but can create more problems down the road. Procrastinating in writing that paper might help you avoid feeling stressed tonight but may create worse stress in a few days. Dealing with stress by abusing alcohol might feel good initially but waking up with a hangover makes that paper look more difficult than ever the next morning.

Both direct and palliative coping responses may be classified as adaptive or maladaptive. Such categorization is almost always situational, as a response that proves helpful for one stressor might not work in another situation. A response that is usually adaptive, such as talking to a friend or exercising, can be maladaptive if it causes you to avoid confronting the source of stress or if it is done in excess. Nevertheless, let's consider a hypothetical stressor for the purposes of illustration. You're concerned about a paper you are writing, and would like some help to be sure you're on the right track. Possible direct and palliative coping responses, both adaptive and maladaptive, are listed in Figure 1.1 (p. 4).

HEALTH BEHAVIOR AND ENVIRONMENTAL INFLUENCES: THE CONTEXT OF STRESS

Have you ever lost control of yourself over something trivial, something that usually would not bother you very much? Maybe you spill your drink and fly into a rage or burst into tears. Something you can handle easily on a good day can be

FIGURE 1.1 *Categorization of coping responses*

	Adaptive	Maladaptive
Direct	Ask writing counselor or teacher for help. Talk to other students in the class.	Write professor a threatening letter. Plagiarize someone's paper.
Palliative	Take a walk. Go to a movie with friends. Call your mom. Go to the gym and work out.	Get drunk at a party and drive your car recklessly. Go to the gym and get in a fight with the monitor.

unbearable on a bad day. This is because your stress response is affected by many extraneous factors.

Some of these factors are **health behaviors**—things you do that affect your health. Eating, sleeping, and exercise habits are examples of health behaviors, as are cigarette smoking, drug use, and alcohol and caffeine consumption. All these affect your stress level. A given stressor might have a very different effect depending on whether you feel alert and rested after a good night's sleep or fatigued and strung out after staying up all night. You might drink several cups of coffee to stay alert to study but find you are merely stressed: tired and wired at the same time, unable either to concentrate or to fall asleep.

To a large extent, many health behaviors are under your control. Other less controllable factors also affect your stress cycle, illustrated in Figure 1.2. Health problems are an example. People usually feel less capable of coping with stress if they are battling a cold or a headache. An unexpected chore at the end of a long, hard day may seem impossible; the same task would be easy when you're full of energy and things are going well.

Many environmental factors influence your stress cycle as well: the type and level of noise in the room, the comfort or discomfort of your work area, the stress levels of those around you, and the current political and economic climate. Even too much cloudy weather can exacerbate stress for some people.

FIGURE 1.2 *The Stress Cycle*
The stress cycle involves the interaction of stressors, the physical and psychological response to stress, and coping behavior.

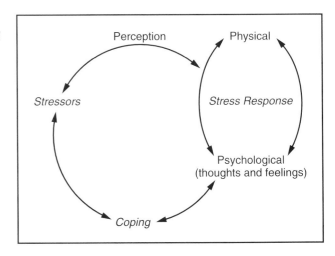

STUDENT STRESS

ANGELA'S STRESS CYCLE

Angela's first assignment in her stress management class was to complete a stress cycle diagram for a source of stress in her life and to categorize coping responses for that problem. Angela decided that the situation bothering her most wasn't a single event but an ongoing one that was starting to occur several evenings each week. Monica, a new friend, would drop by after dinner to chat. Sometimes they would just tell each other about the day, then get back to their schoolwork. That was fun for both young women. They found they had much in common and agreed about many things.

But lately Monica was staying longer and longer, sometimes for an hour or two. Monica's mother had just been diagnosed with breast cancer, and her family was experiencing financial difficulties as well. "Monica seems to be coping with her stress by talking to me," Angela thought to herself as she started completing her stress cycle assignment. "But what about me?" Angela, a hard-working and very conscientious student, was falling behind in her schoolwork and in her sleep, as she stayed up later and later to complete her assignments. Several evenings she had prepared herself to tell Monica she needed to cut down on her socializing, but inevitably Monica would burst in, upset about a phone conversation with her mother or other problems she was having, and Angela would not have the heart to interrupt. "I'll tell her tomorrow," she would think to herself, but tomorrow never came.

Angela decided to think about her response to Monica's visit the previous night, a particularly stressful one. Her stress cycle and coping response diagram are shown in Figure 1.3.

Angela found the assignment constructive because, as she categorized her coping responses, she realized that her only direct response, trying politely to wrap up the conversation, was not effectively addressing her problem. Her other coping techniques seemed to be prolonging her problem by making her a passive listener, behavior that Monica interpreted as that of an interested friend. Angela decided to discuss the problem directly with Monica, letting Monica know she could talk during dinner, but that on weeknights after dinner Angela had to spend more time studying. Angela also decided to go to the library to study, where there would be fewer interruptions.

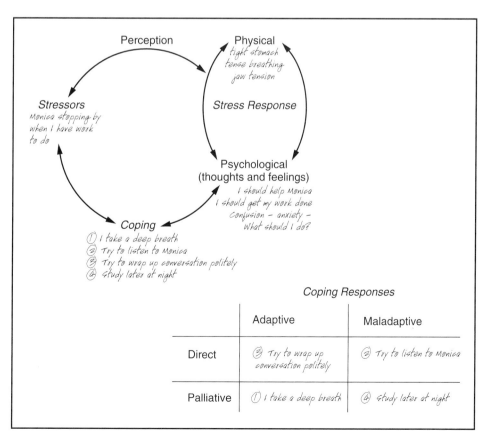

FIGURE 1.3
Angela's Stress Cycle

STRESS AND YOU

YOUR STRESS CYCLE

You probably have a fairly good idea about the kinds of things that cause you stress and about your stress response patterns. Take a moment to consider a recent event that caused you to feel stressed. How did you respond? Complete the stress cycle in Figure 1.4 to see how this diagram illustrates the stress in your life. Use the coping chart (Figure 1.5) to categorize your coping responses.

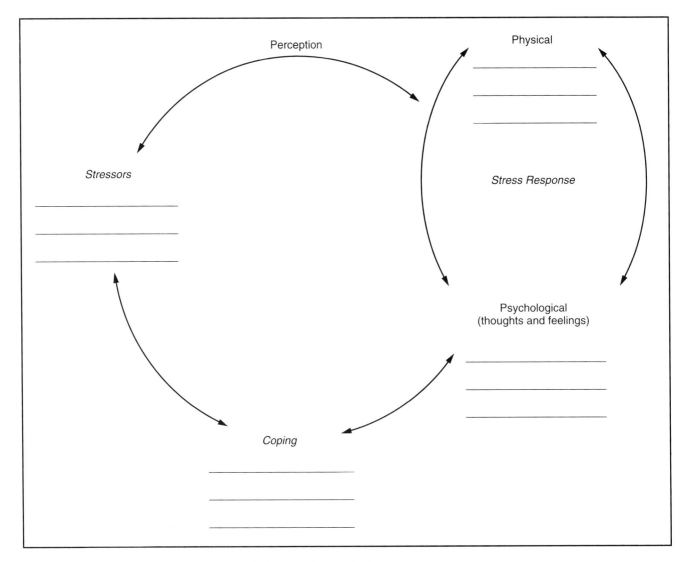

FIGURE 1.4 *Your Stress Cycle*

	Adaptive	Maladaptive
Direct	_____ _____ _____ _____	_____ _____ _____ _____
Palliative	_____ _____ _____ _____ _____ _____	_____ _____ _____ _____ _____ _____

FIGURE 1.5 *Your Coping Responses*
How do you cope with stress? Think about a significant source of stress in your life. Draw a chart like the one above. Can you think of direct and palliative coping strategies, both adaptive and maladaptive? Which are you most likely to use?

IS STRESS A BAD THING?

Most people associate the word *stress* with a negative context. They are more likely to think of *stress* in connection with getting fired than getting promoted, with getting divorced than getting married, with *distress* rather than **eustress** (positive stress) (Selye, 1974). Sometimes people use *stress* to mean excess stress: too much happening. Small hassles that in themselves might not be very bothersome become stressful when time or energy is in short supply (Kanner et al., 1981).

Given this association, it is easy to forget that an *appropriate* stress response is often helpful. Stress motivates you to produce works you are proud of, it helps you rise to meet challenges, and it inspires you as you write an exam or paper. The physical and psychological arousal of the stress response can be very useful, and unless you are overloaded and become chronically aroused and "stressed out," stress is not necessarily harmful (Kobasa et al., 1982). You'll hear more about the health effects of stress in Chapter 3, but most readers will be reassured to learn that unless you spend your time feeling angry, a moderate amount of stress does not appear to

▶ STRESS RESEARCH

Yerkes and Dodson: *A Question of Balance*

One of the earliest theories concerning the effects of stress is the Yerkes-Dodson Law, named after R. M. Yerkes and J. D. Dodson, the psychologists who proposed this model in 1908 (Yerkes & Dodson, 1908). They observed that a person's performance of a given task improves as physiological arousal increases until some optimal point, after which performance declines as arousal continues to climb. Yerkes and Dodson noted that the optimal level of arousal varies with the type of task being performed and that higher levels of arousal seem to be more detrimental as the complexity of the task increases. This theory is illustrated by the inverted-U curve in Figure 1.6.

Yerkes and Dodson based their theory on observations of laboratory mice. Arousal was created with foot shocks of various intensity. The psychologists

FIGURE 1.6
Yerkes-Dodson Law
The Yerkes-Dodson Law illustrates the relationship between arousal and performance.

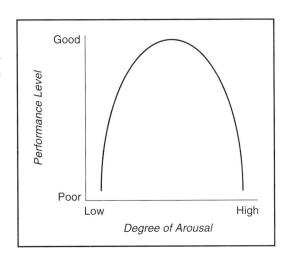

be hazardous to your health, as long as it is accompanied by some sense of control and expectations of primarily positive outcomes and is balanced by periods of relaxation (Williams & Williams, 1994).

WHAT IS STRESS MANAGEMENT?

Management implies that you have some control. The goals of **stress management** are to increase your understanding of yourself and your own stress cycle and to help you exercise what control you do have over this cycle. Classes in stress management help you develop techniques that will enhance your ability to cope effectively with stress and increase your resistance to its negative effects. Even small changes in the way you breathe, organize your day, or interpret events around you can significantly improve your sense of control and reduce your feelings of being overwhelmed by life.

found fewer errors in performance when mice received moderately intense foot shocks than when shocks were mild or strong. As the rats were asked to do increasingly complex tasks, the amount of shock resulting in optimal performance decreased. In the nine decades following these original experiments, many researchers have applied this theory of arousal and performance to a wide variety of tasks in humans as well as laboratory animals, with interesting results (Duffy, 1962; Eysenck, 1963; Oxendine, 1970). The types of performance studied in humans have included physical skills such as playing a musical instrument and mental tasks such as problem solving.

Many sports psychologists have studied and worked with athletes to further define the relationship of arousal and performance (Fenz & Epstein, 1969; Hatfield & Landers, 1987; Klavora, 1979; Landers et al., 1985; Lazarus et al., 1952). They have confirmed Yerkes and Dodson's original observation that the optimal level of arousal decreases as task complexity increases. Athletes performing complex sports tasks such as archery and golf putting give best results with low levels of arousal, while those in events such as short distance runs and swimming races have best times with high levels of arousal (Oxendine, 1984). Of course, arousal alone does not determine performance but interacts with many other factors, such as skill level.

What does the Yerkes-Dodson Law have to do with stress management? This relationship between arousal and performance exists not only for sports and other activities but for daily life as well. For everything you do there is a best level of arousal. Too little arousal produces boredom: stress. Too much arousal produces anxiety: stress. Find yourself on top of that curve, however, where you are stimulated and doing your best, and you reach that wonderful state called satisfaction. Finding the top of the Yerkes-Dodson curve becomes a parable for our stress management quest: finding just the right amount of arousal to get the most from the activity at hand, whatever that activity may be.

Stress management is about *intervention* (see Figure 1.7, p. 10). You will learn many ways to interrupt habitual stress response patterns that increase feelings of stress. After you step back and observe your own stress cycle, you will become aware of ways you can intervene at each point in the cycle, such as these:

1. By addressing stressors more directly—changing or eliminating sources of stress whenever possible and solving problems more effectively. Section II of this book presents a variety of approaches that can reduce and eliminate sources of stress common in the lives of college students. Included in this section are techniques to help you improve your problem-solving ability, clarify your goals, organize your time, and communicate more effectively. In Section III you learn how to develop a healthful, joyful, stress-resistant lifestyle.

2. By developing more accurate perceptions of stressors and your own abilities so that you do not blow things out of proportion or underestimate your own strengths. In Section IV you examine the way you look at life and try to tune

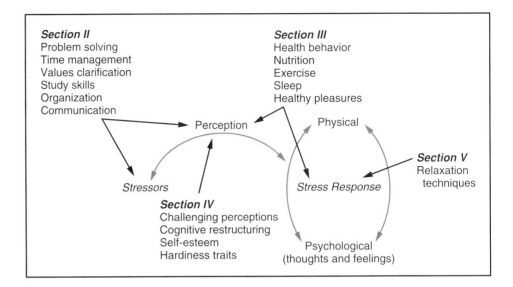

FIGURE 1.7   *Stress Management Interventions Discussed in This Text*
Stress management helps you develop skills to intervene in your stress cycle and reduce feelings of stress.

in to your automatic thoughts to uncover any habitual thought patterns that might be creating unnecessary stress. Self-esteem and personality styles are also discussed.

3. By changing your physical and psychological response to stress. Section V presents relaxation techniques to help you decrease feelings of stress and increase self-awareness. Relaxation practice helps reduce unwanted physical and psychological arousal that can lead to headaches, stomachaches, and other stress-related disorders. You can learn that you do not need to respond to perceived stress by hunching your shoulders, gritting your teeth, or tensing your forehead muscles. You'll be able to short-circuit negative thinking that leads to feelings of panic and anxiety. You will practice sensing an unnecessary stress response before it develops into a health problem.

As you come to understand your personal stress cycle, you will reinforce all those effective coping techniques that you currently use and use them more often. You will be able to make better decisions about health behaviors that influence your stress level and spend more of your time feeling good about yourself and satisfied with life.

WHAT STRESS MANAGEMENT IS NOT

Stress management is not a substitute for medical treatment. If you experience physical symptoms that you believe are related to stress, such as frequent headaches, stomachaches, or high blood pressure, check with your physician before you embark on your stress management program. Many symptoms may be indicative of something other than stress. If your physician believes your symptoms are related to stress, then stress management and relaxation techniques may be helpful. These techniques should always be used in conjunction with appropriate medical care.

Stress management may be a complement to, but not a substitute for, professional counseling. There are times when almost everyone can benefit from some sort of therapy. Psychologists, social workers, chaplains, and others can assist when you're having difficulty finding your way and help point you in a more productive direction. If you are experiencing a significant amount of stress, are unsure of how to cope with a particularly difficult situation, are feeling very anxious or depressed a lot of the time, you would probably benefit from some sort of therapy.

Many people feel that going to a counselor indicates that they have somehow failed, or that there is something "wrong" with them. We tend to believe we should follow the American model of the "rugged individualist" and be able to solve problems on our own. In fact, deciding to seek professional guidance does not mean you are mentally ill or impaired; it simply means you have decided to maximize your potential using the resources at hand. For many problems, short-term counseling is most beneficial. As few as six to ten visits may help you see a problem more clearly and solve it more effectively. At other times, long-term counseling may be desirable when you are dealing with more difficult issues.

Stress management is effective but it is not magic. Changing the way you view the world and yourself, your style of communication, and your organization and time management as well as reducing your physical responses to stress occur slowly and with practice. Stress management is not instant self-transformation. Some wishful students enroll in a stress management program to learn how to get rid of stress. They hope that after completing the program their lives will be totally stress free. This goal is neither feasible nor desirable. After all, stress is the spice of life. And no one, except perhaps characters in Harlequin romances, lives happily ever after. Real life is a mixture of good and bad, joy and sorrow. Tragedy is real (but hassles are often imaginary). While you cannot turn the world into a rose garden, you can reduce excess stress and find more satisfaction in life. You can enjoy more fully the roses that are there while learning how to deal more effectively with the thorns.

WELLNESS AND STRESS MANAGEMENT

Stress management is the cornerstone of a **wellness** lifestyle. The wellness philosophy supports the notion that the lifestyle choices you make throughout the years have an important influence on your mental and physical well-being. Wellness means doing what you can to maximize your personal potential for optimal well-being, and to construct a meaningful and rewarding life. It is a process rather than a product, a means rather than an end. You lead a wellness lifestyle when you live in a purposeful way that helps you achieve self-fulfillment.

While disease prevention is an important goal of the wellness lifestyle, wellness implies more than a state of good health. Wellness means taking responsibility for your health, preventing accidents and illness, and knowing when to consult and work with health care professionals. Wellness encourages consumer awareness and promotes the establishment of social systems and environments conducive to health-promoting behavior (Cowen, 1994). Paradoxically, disease and disability do not prevent a wellness lifestyle, for wellness simply means doing the best with the hand you've been dealt.

The wellness concept developed in response to the old notions that health has to do with a person's physical state and that people are healthy so long as they are not sick (Ardell, 1984). The word *wellness* was first used by a medical doctor, Halbert Dunn, in the 1950s. In his book *High Level Wellness* he used the concept of wellness to describe physical, emotional, psychological, and spiritual well-being, noting the interrelation of these areas (Dunn, 1961).

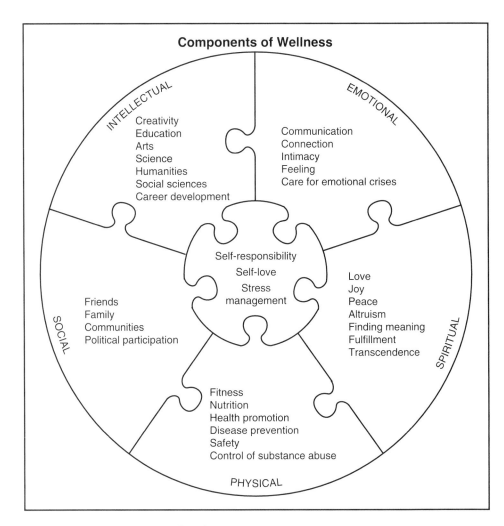

FIGURE 1.8 *Components of Wellness*
The wellness philosophy promotes a healthful, fulfilling lifestyle to maximize personal potential in all areas of your life. Stress management enhances your ability to make choices that promote personal growth and physical, emotional, occupational, intellectual, social, and spiritual well-being.

Wellness implies a state beyond the simple absence of sickness; in this context, people are viewed as holistic organisms. An illustration of the components of wellness is given in Figure 1.8. While this figure artificially separates wellness into sections, it portrays the idea that all parts of a person are important in the wellness concept. If you are not satisfied with your career (part of intellectual wellness), this dissatisfaction must be balanced by wellness in other areas or changed so that other areas are not thrown off balance. These components work together to create something greater than the sum of their parts.

Proponents of wellness believe that given appropriate information, people can make informed choices, directed by a sense of self-love and self-responsibility (Travis & Ryan, 1988). Wellness and stress management both involve a process of assessment, intervention, and reassessment. You might, for example, discover that trying to function on four hours of sleep per night is leaving you cranky, fatigued, sick, and stressed. You assess the way you spend your time and intervene by getting rid of certain obligations, minimizing "wasted" time, watching only your very fa-

Whatever you can do, or think you can, begin it. Boldness has genius, power and magic in it.

GOETHE

vorite television shows, and reorganizing your study schedule, trying to increase your night's sleep to a more reasonable length. After several days, you reassess the changes you've made and make other changes as necessary.

Many students with only occasional periods of problematic stress wonder whether stress management will benefit them. Like wellness, stress management is for everyone, the enlightened as well as the overloaded. Stress management is not only for dealing with problems; it also improves your ability to participate in life joyfully, to get the most out of each day.

Unlike many subjects, stress is familiar to us all. To most of us stress, if not a friend, is a constant companion. Almost every college student is an expert on stress. You are already handling many sources of stress very effectively. You are organizing your schedule, completing challenging assignments, getting involved with extracurricular activities, and developing friendships. Some of you are balancing the demands of school, families, and careers. Stress management will help you build on this success, expand your relaxation repertoire, and perhaps help others along the way. As you continue your stress management journey, remember that wellness is not a station at which you will someday arrive but a way of traveling.

SUMMARY

1. The stress cycle is composed of a source of stress (stressor) and your response to that stressor. Your stress response consists of physical and psychological reactions.
2. Your perceptions of stressors and your perceptions of your abilities to meet the demands placed on you by those stressors play an important role in your personal stress response patterns.
3. Coping is what you do to deal with stressors and your feelings of stress. Direct (problem-focused) coping methods attempt to eliminate or change the source of stress. Palliative (emotion-focused) coping methods do not directly affect the stressor but help you cope with your feelings of stress.
4. Adaptive coping responses have a generally positive effect on the stress cycle, either lessening the force of the stressor itself or helping you to feel less

stressed over both the short and long term. Madadaptive coping strategies may help you feel better initially but may create more problems down the road.

5. Health behaviors and environmental factors have an important effect on the stress cycle.

6. Stress is not always harmful. It can provide motivation and excitement as well as the appropriate level of arousal to help you perform well.

7. The goals of stress management are to increase your understanding of yourself and your own stress cycle and to help you change this cycle so that stress is a more productive and positive experience.

8. Stress management improves your ability to cope with stress by teaching techniques to help you (1) address stressors more directly, (2) develop a more accurate and positive perception of stressors and your abilities to cope with them, and (3) learn to relax and change your physical and psychological responses to stress so that they are less harmful to your health.

9. Stress management is not a substitute for medical treatment of physical or psychological problems.

10. Stress management is the cornerstone of a wellness lifestyle. The wellness philosophy states that lifestyle choices you make throughout the years have an important impact on your mental and physical well-being and your quality of life.

11. The Yerkes-Dodson Law states that for every task there is an optimal level of arousal for peak performance.

REFERENCES

Ardell, DB. The history and future of the wellness movement. JP Opatz (ed). *Wellness Promotion Strategies.* Dubuque, IA: Kendall/Hunt, 1984.

Cowen, EL. The enhancement of psychological wellness: Challenges and opportunities. *American Journal of Community Psychology* 22: 149–179, 1994.

Dienstbier, RA. Behavioral correlates of sympathoadrenal reactivity: The toughness model. *Medicine and Science in Sports and Exercise* 23: 846–852, 1991.

Duffy, E. *Activation and Behavior.* New York: Wiley, 1962.

Dunn, HL. *High Level Wellness.* Arlington, VA: RW Beatty, 1961.

Eysenck, HJ. The measurement of motivation. *Scientific American* 208 (May): 130–140, 1963.

Fenz, WD, and S Epstein. Stress in the air. *Psychology Today* 3(4): 27–28, 58–59, 1969.

Funk, SC. Hardiness: A review of theory and research. *Health Psychology* 11: 335–345, 1992.

Hatfield, BD, and DM Landers. Psychophysiology in exercise and sport research: An overview. KB Pandolf (ed). *Exercise and Sport Sciences Review,* Vol 15. New York: MacMillan, 1987.

Kanner, AD, JC Coyne, C Schaefer, and RS Lazarus. Comparison of two modes of stress measurement: Daily hassles and uplifts versus major life events. *Journal of Behavioral Medicine* 4:1–39, 1981.

Klavora, P. An attempt to derive inverted-U curves based on the relationship between anxiety and athletic performance. DM Landers and RW Christina (eds). *Psychology of Motor Behavior and Sport.* Champaign, IL: Human Kinetics, 1979.

Kobasa, SC, SR Maddi, and S Kahn. Hardiness and health: A prospective study. *Journal of Personality and Social Psychology* 42: 168–177, 1982.

Landers, DM, MQ Wang, and P Courtet. Peripheral narrowing among experienced and inexperienced rifle shooters under low- and high-stress conditions. *Research Quarterly* 56: 57–70, 1985.

Lazarus, RS, J Deese, and SF Osler. The effects of psychological stress upon performance. *Psychological Bulletin* 49: 293–317, 1952.

Lazarus, RS. *Emotion and Adaptation.* New York: Oxford University Press, 1991.

Monat, A, and RS Lazarus. Introduction: Stress and coping—Some current issues and controversies. A Monat and RS Lazarus (eds). *Stress and Coping*. New York: Columbia University Press, 1991.

Moyer, B. *Healing and the Mind.* New York: Doubleday, 1993.

Nowack, KM. Psychosocial predictors of health status. *Work and Stress* 5: 117–131, 1991.

Oxendine, JB. Emotional arousal and motor performance. *Quest* 13: 23–32, 1970.

Oxendine, JB. *Psychology of Motor Learning.* Englewood Cliffs, NJ: Prentice Hall, 1984.

Seaward, BL. *Managing Stress.* Boston: Jones & Barlett, 1994.

Selye, H. *Stress Without Distress.* New York: Lippincott, 1974.

Shepperd, JA, and JH Kashani. The relationship of hardiness, gender, and stress to health outcomes in adolescents. *Journal of Personality* 59: 747–768, 1991.

Travis, JW, and RS Ryan. *The Wellness Workbook.* Berkeley: Ten Speed Press, 1988.

Williams, RB, and V Williams. *Anger Kills: Seventeen Strategies for Controlling the Hostility That Can Harm Your Health.* New York: HarperCollins, 1994.

Yerkes, RM, and JD Dodson. The relation of strength of stimulus to rapidity of habit formation. *Journal of Comparative and Neurological Psychology* 18: 459–482, 1908.

chapter 2

The Fight-or-Flight Response: Survival of the Most Stressed?

Most members of the animal kingdom have three primary goals. The first is to find enough to eat. The second is to avoid becoming someone else's dinner. The third is to reproduce. To most animals, stress is a simple phenomenon. It usually wears the face of a predator or another animal competing for a mate or food source. Environmental conditions create stress as well: people, floods, and drought, for example, affect availability of nesting sites and food supplies.

Only a short while ago in geological time, our primitive ancestors were challenged by similar sources of stress. Nature favors survival of the fittest. Cavemen and women who were best able to escape predators, deal with disaster, and obtain food and mates were those who produced future generations who eventually produced us.

As you will learn in this chapter, the stress response produces physical changes that improve an organism's ability to cope with physical threats. It increases our strength and helps us run faster and farther. A strong stress response probably provided an evolutionary advantage for our prehistoric ancestors. The stronger their stress response, the better able they were to fight or flee predators, endure long journeys in search of food, and protect and provide for their children.

Civilization has changed, and the routine challenges we face rarely require a strong physical response; but human physiology is not so different from that of our ancient ancestors, and we still respond to perceived threats with the same fight-or-flight arousal. Such arousal is still quite beneficial when we must confront an attacker, rescue a child in danger, or even sprint to catch a bus. But what about the stress of feeling overloaded with work? Being consistently awakened by a noisy neighbor? Having to work with a difficult professor? By and large, your stress response is inappropriate for the challenges you face, as you rarely have an opportunity to fight or run away. This is the heart of the problem. A response that is sometimes advantageous is more often inappropriate and may ultimately cause physical strain and disease. Understanding the fight-or-flight response will enable you to better understand the health effects of chronic stress and the importance of stress management.

Students, especially those with little background in biology, have reported that this chapter causes more stress than any other chapter. Expecting this text to relieve rather than create stress, many are initially taken aback when faced with the intricacies of stress physiology. Read slowly, take notes, and then reread the chapter once again. Don't memorize anything you don't have to, but look for common themes and real life applications.

FIGHT OR FLIGHT?

Imagine you are walking along humming your favorite song to yourself when suddenly you hear a threatening growl behind some bushes. The growl turns into angry snarling, and a raging pit bull terrier emerges from the shrubbery, dragging a broken chain. Teeth bared, he rushes toward you in a frenzy. Fortunately for you, your immediate appraisal of this threat activates your fight-or-flight response and all systems are go, either to counter the attack or beat a hasty retreat.

Some of the manifestations of the fight-or-flight response are quite obvious: a rapidly pounding heart, shallow breathing, increased sweating, muscle tension, dry mouth, and stomach butterflies. Let's take a closer look at the stress response to see how these symptoms are produced and how they help you deal with that snarling pit bull.

The fight-or-flight response is orchestrated by your brain, which activates various organs such as your muscles by sending messages of arousal. These messages are sent in two ways. The first and fastest is by the **nervous system,** which activates the fight-or-flight response through direct communication with target organs via the nerve cells. The second is the **endocrine system,** which activates the fight-or-flight response through the action of chemical messengers called hormones that reach target organs through the circulatory system. Let's start with the nervous system to see how the fight-or-flight response is produced.

THE NERVOUS SYSTEM

The **nervous system** consists of your **brain, spinal cord,** and the **peripheral nerves** that travel from your spinal cord to all parts of the body. The brain and spinal cord make up the **central nervous system (CNS)** while all other nerves are considered the **peripheral nervous system** (see Figure 2.1). It is the job of the nervous system to coordinate all parts of the body so that they work together. The **afferent nervous system** consists of the nerve cells that receive information from the external and internal (inside your body) environment and conduct this information to the brain, where it is processed at both conscious and subconscious levels. In the example above, your ears send information about the dog growling, your eyes send information about the dog's movement, internal sensors (proprioceptors) send information about your body's position and muscle tension. Your brain integrates all this information, recalls past experiences and everything your mother ever told you about strange dogs, and decides what to do. Run as fast as you can! So the brain sounds the alarm and sends messages to all systems of the body via the **efferent nervous system.**

The efferent system is subdivided into two parts. The **somatic nervous system** sends impulses from the central nervous system to skeletal muscles. This is how the body produces movement. This system is considered to be at least partly under conscious control. You've decided to flee rather than fight the dog; your brain coordinates muscular contraction to produce a personal best in running time. The **autonomic nervous system (ANS)** sends information from the central nervous system to

FIGURE 2.1 *The Nervous System*
The nervous system includes the brain, spinal cord, and the peripheral nerves that carry messages to and from all parts of the body.

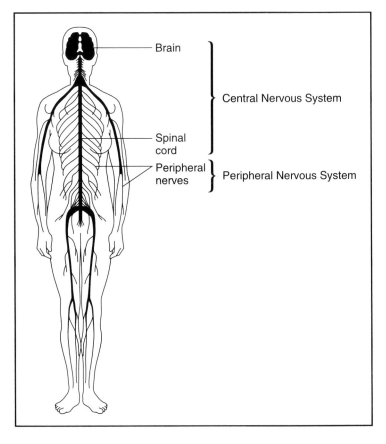

nonskeletal systems such as the circulatory system (heart and blood vessels), respiratory system (lungs and airways), digestive system (stomach, pancreas, liver, gallbladder, small intestine, large intestine), urinary system (kidneys, bladder), and endocrine system (glands). Scientists generally regard the activity of the ANS as outside voluntary control, although biofeedback research has shown people can learn to control many autonomic functions, including heart rate, stomach acidity, and blood pressure.

The autonomic nervous system can either speed up or slow down the activity of the organs and systems it innervates. The two branches of the ANS that perform these functions are the **sympathetic nervous system (SNS)** and the **parasympathetic nervous system (PNS)** (see Figure 2.2). In the fight-or-flight response, your brain activates the sympathetic nervous system, which speeds up those functions necessary for immediate survival. For example, the liver releases sugar into the bloodstream to fuel the working muscles, the heart beats faster and harder to circulate plenty of blood. The SNS suppresses such functions as digestion, which can be postponed. Following are some of the important physiological effects of the SNS response that help us fight or flee:

Sympathetic nervous system response	How it helps us fight or flee
Increases heart rate	Increases blood flow to active muscles,
Increases contractile force of the heart (heart beats harder)	lungs, and heart. Blood carries oxygen and nutrients needed by working
Dilates (opens) coronary (heart) arteries	muscles and removes the waste products generated by muscle
Dilates arteries to active muscles	metabolism.

Sympathetic nervous system response	How it helps us fight or flee
Constricts arteries to skin and abdominal organs	Reduces nonessential circulation.
Dilates pupils	Improves vision
Relaxes ciliary muscle of the eye	Improves distance vision
Dilates bronchioles (airways)	Increases flow of air to lungs
Releases glucose (sugar) from liver; releases fats from adipose (fat) tissue	Provides more fuel for working muscles

After getting safely away from the dog, you heave a sigh of relief and collapse into a chair. At this point, your brain decreases SNS activity while increasing parasympathetic output. This is the **relaxation response.** Heart rate and blood pressure return to normal, muscles relax, and your stomach and intestines resume the task of digesting your lunch. Some of the actions of the sympathetic and parasympathetic branches of the autonomic nervous system are listed in Table 2.1. In this table you can see that the actions of the sympathetic nervous system are balanced by the actions of the parasympathetic nervous system. For example, activation of sympathetic nerves causes the heart rate to increase, while activation of parasympathetic nerves causes the heart rate to decrease.

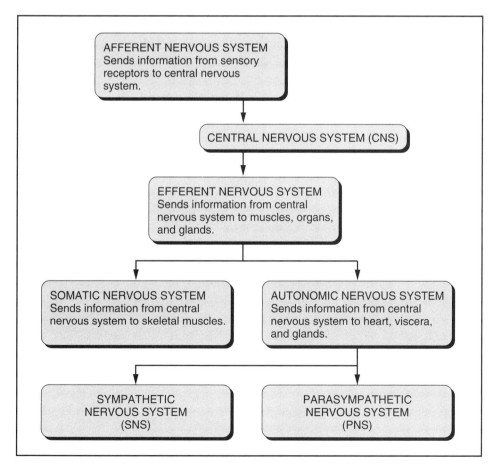

FIGURE 2.2 *Divisions of the Nervous System*
This diagram illustrates the way we categorize the nervous system.

TABLE 2.1 *Activities of the Autonomic Nervous System*

Site	Effect of Sympathetic Stimulation	Effect of Parasympathetic Stimulation
Eye	Radial muscle contracts and dilates pupil; Ciliary muscle relaxes to improve far vision	Sphincter muscle contracts and constricts pupil; Ciliary muscle contracts to improve near vision
Tear glands	—*	Tear secretion is stimulated
Arteries to skin	Arteries constrict	Arteries dilate
to skeletal muscle	Arteries constrict or dilate	—*
to abdominal organs	Arteries constrict	—*
to brain	Arteries constrict slightly	—*
Fat cells	Breakdown of fats and release of fats into bloodstream increases	—*
Heart	Rate and strength of contraction increases; coronary arteries dilate	Rate and strength of contraction decreases; coronary arteries constrict
Lungs	Airways dilate	Airways constrict
Liver	Conversion of protein and starch into blood sugar increases; bile secretion decreases	Synthesis of starch (glycogen) increases; bile secretion increases
Stomach	Motility and tone decrease; sphincters contract; secretion of digestive juices is inhibited	Motility and tone increase; sphincters relax; secretion of digestive juices increases
Intestines	Motility and tone decrease; sphincters contract; secretion of digestive juices is inhibited	Motility and tone increase; sphincters relax; secretion of digestive juices increases
Kidney	Constriction of blood vessels results in decreased urine volume	—*
Pancreas	Secretion of enzymes and insulin is inhibited; secretion of glucagon increases (raises blood sugar)	Secretion of enzymes and insulin increases, which decreases blood sugar

*No known functional innervation

At this point in our discussion of the physiology of the stress response, you may already have a glimmer of understanding about how the stress response becomes harmful. As long as a balance exists between arousal and relaxation, negative health effects from stress are less likely to develop. But suppose you are chronically aroused, your body continuously geared up to fight or flee. Continuous physiological arousal unbalanced by the relaxation response can lead to negative health consequences (Dienstbier, 1991; Woods, 1987). Among the primary goals of stress management and relaxation training are developing your ability to increase parasympathetic output, cultivating the relaxation response, and reducing the sympathetic fight-or-flight response, thus bringing the two systems into a more healthful balance.

BRAIN PHYSIOLOGY: THE BODY/MIND CONNECTION

Let's go back to one of the most important components of the nervous system: the brain (see Figure 2.3). As we examine how the brain participates in the stress response, you'll see why it's impossible to separate completely the psychological and physical responses to stress. This interaction forms the basis for an area of study known as **psychophysiology.** Psychophysiology is the study of the relationship between psychological and physiological functions; it provides much of the basic information we have concerning the physiology of stress.

The most obvious role played by the brain in the stress response is as the seat of conscious thought and awareness. Here is where you evaluate demands placed on you and your ability to respond. Here is where purely imaginary ideas and fears can trigger a full-blown stress response. Thought, judgment, and memory of past expe-

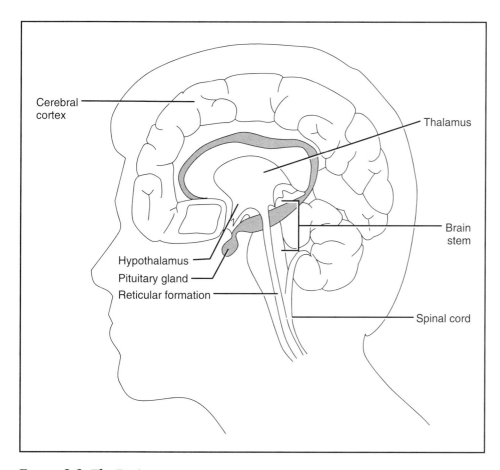

FIGURE 2.3 *The Brain*
The brain coordinates the nervous and endocrine responses to stress.

riences occur in the outer layer of the brain, the **cerebral cortex,** which is the largest area of the brain. Sensory areas in the cerebral cortex interpret sensory nerve impulses, motor areas control movement, and association areas are involved with emotional and intellectual processes.

Deeper areas of the brain participate in the stress response as well. An area called the **diencephalon** is made up of the **thalamus** and **hypothalamus.** The thalamus integrates and relays sensory information to the cerebral cortex. It helps interpret sensations of pain, temperature, and pressure; it is also involved in emotion and memory. The hypothalamus is an important control center for many physiological functions. It controls the autonomic nervous system, regulates the **pituitary gland,** and secretes several hormones and other chemical factors. The hypothalamus appears to be the center for the learned control of autonomic functions that occurs during relaxation and biofeedback training.

The thalamus and hypothalamus are part of an area of the brain called the **limbic system,** which also includes part of the cerebral cortex and other structures. It lies above and around the **brain stem** and is involved with motivation and emotion; it also contributes to memory. Because of its function in emotions such as pain, pleasure, anger, fear, sorrow, sexual feelings, and affection, the limbic system is sometimes refered to as the "emotional" brain (Tortora & Grabowski, 1993).

The deepest area of the brain is the brain stem. This is the "oldest" part of the brain, having been around for the longest period of our evolution. The brain stem contains structures that automatically regulate essential life functions such as breathing, heart action, and digestion through the sympathetic and parasympathetic branches of the autonomic nervous system. Although these functions are considered involuntary, psychological factors such as stress can affect them. An example is anxiety hyperventilation, in which breathing becomes very fast and interferes with the normal regulation of blood gas (oxygen and carbon dioxide) concentrations, resulting in dizziness, shortness of breath, pounding heart, and even fainting. Anxiety hyperventilation is uncomfortable and even frightening, and many experiencing this condition interpret it as an impending heart attack. Some research has suggested that breathing practice and relaxation are effective treatments for hyperventilation (Hegel et al., 1989). Rebreathing air in and out of a paper bag also works (by raising the carbon dioxide content of inspired air).

The nerve fibers of the **reticular formation (RF)** run through the middle of the brain stem up into the diencephalon and act as a major communication pathway between the brain and the rest of the body, an important body-mind connection. The RF scans the sensory information making its way to the brain and evaluates its importance. It alerts higher centers to critical information, thus stimulating arousal and consciousness.

The reticular formation *selectively* relays sensory information upward for further processing, sending on information deemed relevant and short-circuiting sensory information that seems unnecessary. This limits the amount of sensory information that actually reaches higher levels of the brain and keeps us from being overwhelmed with input. How does the RF "know" what is important? It receives information from higher brain centers responsible for emotion, motivation, and other associative processes that helps it "decide" what is relevant. For example, you may fall asleep while waiting for a friend to stop by. You snooze on, oblivious of the noise of traffic outside and the radio playing, but you awaken when you hear a knock on the door. The RF signals you that an important message is coming through. In our pit bull example, the dog's angry snarl need not be loud to be noticed above background noise such as traffic and construction. The RF knows this sound requires your attention.

An interesting application of this selectivity function of the RF is relaxation training for the treatment of chronic pain. The RF functions with the thalamus to control awareness of pain. Negative emotions associated with pain may increase sensory transmission of pain by the RF and thalamus, while relaxation training may

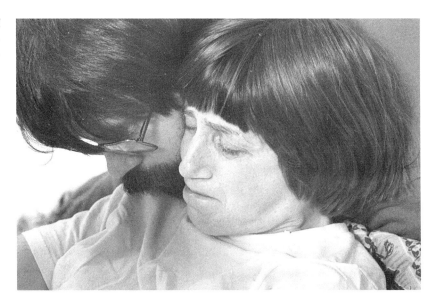

Breathing and relaxation exercises accompanied by reassuring, supportive labor coaches help reduce fear and sensations of pain during childbirth.

help reduce the transmission of pain impulses, thus reducing conscious awareness of pain. Childbirth is a good example. Feeling fearful and out of control increases a woman's pain during labor. Breathing and relaxation exercises accompanied by reassuring, supportive labor coaches help reduce fear and sensations of pain. Less medication is called for in these cases and labor is generally easier (Rosen, 1991).

The brain governs and coordinates the autonomic nervous system and endocrine system. Let's take a look at how the endocrine system complements the action of the ANS in the production of the fight-or-flight response.

THE ENDOCRINE SYSTEM: RAGING HORMONES

Raging hormones. Where do they come from? Hormones are chemical messengers produced by the **endocrine system** that, along with the nervous system, coordinates physiological functions so that all parts of the body work together. Messages from the nervous system reach specific sets of cells via nerve cell networks and take only milliseconds to transmit. The instantaneous response of the autonomic nervous system is why the fight-or-flight response occurs so quickly. The endocrine system releases hormones into the bloodstream, from where they reach and can affect virtually every cell in the body. Messages from the endocrine system may take from a few seconds to several hours or more to bring about their specific effects.

Why two systems? Many physiological responses, such as the fight-or-flight response, are so essential to survival that back-up systems have evolved. The immediate response of the sympathetic nervous system is backed up by the longer lasting action of several hormonal pathways, as you will see in this section. As you read about the actions of these hormones, you might anticipate why long-lasting stress, and long-term activation of these hormonal pathways, can lead to negative health effects.

The nervous and endocrine systems work closely together and are linked in several ways. The nervous system can stimulate or inhibit the release of hormones, while hormones can stimulate or inhibit the transmission of nerve impulses. Hormones have many functions, including the regulation of metabolism, reproduction, and growth and development (Mills & Chir, 1985). Let's take a look now at how they help us respond to stress.

Your brain has been alerted to the rapid approach of the snarling pit bull terrier. This message came from sensory information relayed by your eyes and ears up

Calvin and Hobbes   by Bill Watterson

through the reticular formation (no chance of this information getting short-circuited!) and to the cerebral cortex. The information has been processed with input from the limbic system, and a message has been sent to the hypothalamus to sound the alarm. The hypothalamus immediately initiates sympathetic nervous system arousal and the fight-or-flight response has begun. An endocrine response is initiated as well. Here are some of the pathways involved.

What a Rush: Hormones of the Adrenal Medulla

When responding to stress, the autonomic nervous system stimulates the **adrenal glands,** which sit on top of the kidneys like little caps (see Figure 2.4). The adrenal glands are really two glands in one. The outside layer is called the **adrenal cortex** while the inner portion is the **adrenal medulla.** The adrenal medulla is activated by direct nerve connection with the posterior (back portion) hypothalamus, and when stimulated secretes the hormones **epinephrine** (commonly called adrenaline) and **norepinephrine** (also called noradrenaline). These hormones are collectively referred to as the **catecholamines;** they are **sympathomimetic**—that is, they have effects similar to those listed for the sympathetic nervous system, as shown in the following list (Mullen et al., 1993; Tortora & Grabowski, 1993; Woods, 1987):

1. *Increase the heart rate and contractile force of the heart, thus also increasing blood pressure.* This increases blood flow to active muscles, heart, and lungs.
2. *Dilate arteries in the heart, lungs, brain, and skeletal muscles.* This increases blood flow to organs essential for fighting or fleeing.
3. *Constrict peripheral arteries (arteries in hands and feet).* This ensures good blood flow to the heart and is why, under stress, you get "cold feet." Hand temperature may also decrease.
4. *Dilate airways.* Increases air flow to lungs.
5. *Increase blood sugar level.* This is accomplished by signaling the liver to release stored sugar into the blood, which supplies more fuel for working muscles.
6. *Increase metabolic rate (speed up cellular metabolism).* This speeds up energy production to support emergency functions.
7. *Slow digestive processes.* This spares energy for essential fight-or-flight processes and avoids wasting energy on unnecessary functions.

FIGURE 2.4 *The Adrenal Glands*
The adrenal glands are composed of the adrenal medulla and the adrenal cortex; they are located on top of the kidneys.

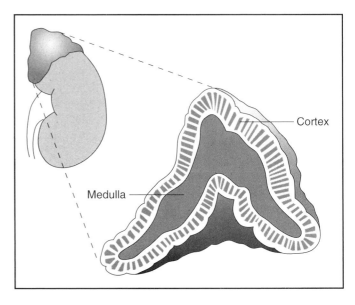

8. *Contract spleen.* This releases stored blood, which increases blood volume. Red blood cell production also increases.
9. *Speed rate of clotting.* This prevents bleeding.
10. *Increase sweating.*

Stressed Out: Hormones of the Adrenal Cortex

Even as it is orchestrating the autonomic nervous system response to stress and stimulating the response of the adrenal glands, the hypothalamus is secreting some hormones of its own. The anterior (front portion) hypothalamus secretes a hormone called **corticotropin-releasing hormone (CRH)** which stimulates the **pituitary gland,** located at the base of the brain, to release **adrenocorticotropic hormone (ACTH).** ACTH is carried in the blood stream, and soon reaches the adrenal glands. ACTH acts on the **adrenal cortex,** stimulating it to release two families of hormones called **glucocorticoids** and **mineralocorticoids** (see Figure 2.5). This sequence is known as the hypothalamus-pituitary-adrenal pathway.

Cortisol (*hydrocortisone*), **corticosterone,** and **cortisone** are three glucocorticoids involved with the-fight-or-flight response. Glucocorticoids affect several metabolic processes. Cortisol is the most abundant glucocorticoid and is responsible for about 95 percent of glucocorticoid activity (Tortora & Grabowski, 1993). Glucocorticoids do the following (Chrousos & Gold, 1992; Tortora & Grabowski, 1993):

1. *Mobilize energy sources by increasing the rate of protein breakdown in cells, especially muscles, so that the proteins may be used for energy or to make enzymes.* The glucocorticoids stimulate the liver to produce glucose from certain protein components if blood sugar is low.
2. *Make blood vessels more sensitive to agents promoting constriction, thus helping to raise blood pressure.* Since blood loss was often involved in fight or flight for our ancient ancestors, increased blood pressure was advantageous in maintaining adequate circulation despite a drop in blood volume.
3. *Glucocorticoids inhibit the process of inflammation.* Inflammation may make the inflamed area stiff. Preventing mobility limitations is helpful in the short run, but long-term effects include delayed healing.
4. *Cortisol also causes a decrease in the number of lymphocytes released from the thymus gland, located in the upper chest, and the lymph nodes.* Lymphocytes are an important component of the immune system defense against bacteria and

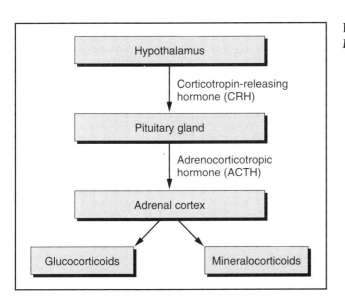

FIGURE 2.5 *The Hypothalamus-Pituitary-Adrenal Pathway*

other foreign invaders. This decrease in immune activity may be one of the "energy conservation" processes of the glucocorticoids. When facing the pit bull, you are not so worried about the cold germs in your nose. Of course, if you are under chronic stress and cortisol levels remain elevated, the negative impact of cortisol on the immune system becomes very important.

The adrenal cortex also secretes mineralocorticoids. Mineralocorticoids help control fluid and salt balance. The mineralocorticoid aldosterone is responsible for about 95 percent of the action of this hormone family. **Aldosterone** causes the kidneys to retain sodium and water, an action that increases blood volume and consequently, blood pressure—both helpful if blood is lost.

Nervous Energy: Thyroid Hormones

There's more. The busy hypothalamus also instructs the **thyroid gland** in its work. The thyroid gland is located in the throat (see Figure 2.6). It produces hormones that help regulate energy expenditure, growth and development, and nervous system activity. Here's how it works. The hypothalamus secretes **thyrotropin-releasing hormone (TRH),** which causes the pituitary gland to release **thyroid-stimulating hormone (TSH).** This hormone, TSH, then tells the thyroid gland to secrete the hormones **thyroxine (T4)** and **triiodothyronine (T3),** which are functionally similar and are commonly referred to as **thyroid hormones** (see Figure 2.7). This sequence of events is known as the hypothalamus-pituitary-thyroid pathway.

During the stress response, the thyroid hormones stimulate the breakdown of glycogen and fats in most cells of the body to increase production of sugar and fats to fuel metabolism. The thyroid hormones also stimulate protein synthesis. They increase the reactivity of the nervous system, heightening the autonomic nervous system stress response. Specific actions are (Greenberg, 1990; Tortora & Grabowski, 1993):

1. *Increase resting metabolic rate.*
2. *Increase **free fatty acids (FFA).*** These are produced from storage fat molecules called **triglycerides.** FFA can be used as fuel for energy production.

FIGURE 2.6 *Glands that Participate in the Fight-or-Flight Response*
Glands are organs that secrete hormones. The glands illustrated here play important roles in the fight-or-flight response.

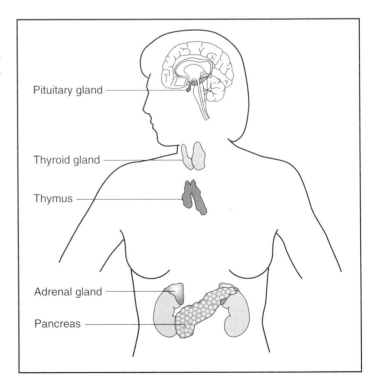

Pituitary gland

Thyroid gland

Thymus

Adrenal gland

Pancreas

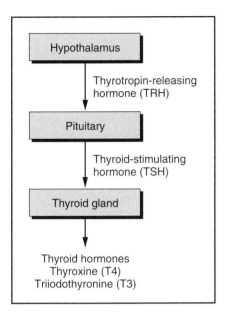

FIGURE 2.7 *The Hypothalamus-Pituitary-Thyroid Pathway*

3. *Increase rate at which liver converts protein into blood sugar (glucose).*
4. *Increase heart rate and contractile force.*
5. *Increase blood pressure and blood flow.*
6. *Increase rate and depth of breathing.*
7. *Increase gastrointestinal motility (may result in diarrhea).*
8. *Increase nervousness and alertness.*

Under Pressure: Antidiuretic Hormone

One final hormone important in the stress response and its health effects is **antidiuretic hormone (ADH),** also called **vasopressin,** which is secreted by the pituitary gland. An *antidiuretic* is anything that prevents urine production and water loss. This hormone, ADH, causes the kidneys to remove water from fluid destined to become urine and return it to the bloodstream—an action that increases blood volume and thus raises blood pressure. Antidiuretic hormone raises blood pressure by another mechanism as well: contraction of the smooth muscles in the artery walls. Many things influence the action of ADH. For example, alcohol inhibits ADH secretion and thus increases water loss. This helps explain why thirst accompanies a hangover.

Summary: Nervous and Endocrine Systems

Is this chapter starting to sound a little repetitious? It should be. At this point you are probably recognizing some common themes. Both the nervous and endocrine systems mobilize a person to respond to a stressor in some physically active manner. The hypothalamus activates the sympathetic nervous system response; it also stimulates the adrenal and thyroid glands through either direct innervation or stimulation of the pituitary gland to secrete epinephrine, norepinephrine, cortisol, aldosterone, and the thyroid hormones (see Figure 2.8). Sympathetic nervous system activation and the endocrine response have similar effects that reinforce each other. The combined actions of these systems increase metabolic rate and mobilize fuel for energy production; increase blood pressure, blood flow, and respiration; and inhibit systems not essential for immediate survival.

FIGURE 2.8
Pathways of the major stress hormones

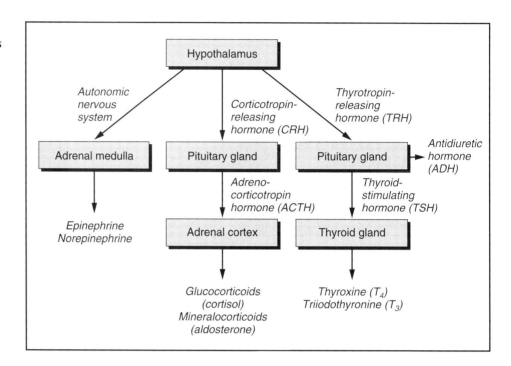

FIGURE 2.8
Pathways of the major stress hormones

▶ STRESS RESEARCH

Hans Selye: *Stress—A Response*

Probably best known of the early stress research pioneers is Hans Selye. Selye's work on laboratory animals in the 1930s and 1940s was some of the first to study the physical stress response (Selye, 1936). His research described in detail the stress response of the pituitary and adrenal glands, and the short- and long-term physical effects of stress throughout the body.

Selye created the first working definition of stress, describing it as *the nonspecific response of the body to any demand made upon it* (Selye, 1956). He called the response nonspecific because he observed the same physical response to a wide variety of "alarming agents" including bacterial infection, trauma, heat, cold, and psychological stimuli (Feuerstein et al., 1986). Selye believed that in humans, positive stressors, which he termed **eustress**—such as getting admitted to college, winning a scholarship, or taking a trip—caused a physiological fight-or-flight response similar to that caused by more disturbing change, which he called *distress*—such as getting a bad grade in a course, having an argument, or losing your wallet. He also noted that the same response occurred whether the threat was real or imagined (Selye, 1982).

Selye devised a theory about the health effects of chronic stress which he called the **General Adaptation Syndrome (GAS).** When exposed to chronic stress, such as continuous exposure to loud noise, an animal exhibits three stages of adaptation. Initially, the fight-or-flight response occurs, which Selye called the *alarm reaction.* Physiologists link the alarm reaction to the autonomic nervous system's immediate response to stress (Tortora & Grabowski, 1993). As exposure to the stressor continues, the animal will develop some resistance to the stressor. Selye referred to this period as the *stage of resistance.* Physiologists have characterized this stage as being supported by the various stress hormones that circulate throughout the period of stress, sustaining a

FIGHT OR FLIGHT: THE CARDIOVASCULAR SYSTEM RESPONDS

Now that you understand how the fight-or-flight response comes about, let's take a closer look at its effects. As you prepare to run away from that vicious pit bull terrier, your pounding heart signals that the cardiovascular system is ready for action.

The cardiovascular system includes the heart, blood vessels, and blood. This system circulates blood to every cell in the body, delivering oxygen, fuel, and hormones, and removing waste products. Physical activity dramatically increases the need for these services, which is why the cardiovascular system responds so strongly to stress.

Sympathetic stimulation causes an immediate increase in heart rate that is reinforced by the epinephrine and norepinephrine released into the bloodstream by the adrenal medulla. This response helps you retreat from the snarling dog but can be a distraction for stress that does not require a strong physical response. Perhaps you have felt your heart pound when called on in class, before giving a presentation, or when excited about a phone call. After a while, you relax, your heart calms down, and no harm is done. But in cases of extreme fright or for someone with an unhealthy heart, an overdose of catecholamines can be damaging and even fatal. The heart rate can become irregular and interfere with effective circulation; coronary arteries may spasm, cutting off blood flow to the heart muscle (Monagan, 1986; Turkkan et al., 1982). A catecholamine overdose may be responsible for

long-term stress reaction. The stage of resistance continues until the stressor stops or the animal's resistance is worn down. At this time it enters the *stage of exhaustion*, which, if the stressor continues, ends ultimately in the animal's death (Selye, 1982).

Selye's approach was typical of scientists working with laboratory animals in that its focus was on physiological response. Such a focus was convenient because it defined stress clearly and in a way that could be directly observed and measured in the laboratory. This early research laid the groundwork for the expanded definitions of stress to follow.

Selye continued to research and write about stress throughout his life. He theorized that each person possesses a finite amount of "adaptation energy," which he compared to "an inherited bank account from which we can make withdrawals but to which we apparently cannot make deposits" (Selye, 1982, p. 10). To Selye, eustress and distress both resulted in some degree of wear and tear, which accumulated to produce aging.

Stress researchers today have a deep respect for Selye's groundbreaking work, much of which continues to be supported by scientific investigation. Subsequent research has shown, however, that our responses to eustress and distress do differ somewhat, as do their health consequences. Psychologists also believe we probably can make deposits into our "inherited bank account" of adaptation energy, and this is what increasing one's stress resistance is all about. In modified form, however, Selye's adaptation energy theory holds much truth. We have all felt our adaptation energy run low when faced with excessive stress, and current research supports the notion that too much change increases one's likelihood of developing stress-related illnesses (Holmes & Rahe, 1967).

heart attacks caused by cocaine, which stimulates the sympathetic nervous system (Gawin, 1991; Isner et al., 1986).

Another major effect of the nervous and endocrine systems' stress response on the cardiovascular system is an increase in blood pressure. High resting blood pressure is called **hypertension,** and is caused by many factors, including too much stress. Blood pressure is a measure of the force exerted by the blood against the blood vessel walls. It can be measured using a blood pressure cuff (called a **sphygmomanometer**) and stethoscope, and is typically measured in the arteries of the upper arm. The pressure of the blood against the arterial walls is greatest at the moment blood is ejected from the heart as it contracts. This pressure is called the **systolic blood pressure.** The **diastolic blood pressure** is the pressure in the arteries while the heart is "resting" between beats. Pressure is measured in units called **millimeters of mercury (mmHg),** referring to the distance a column of mercury rises in a tube for a given pressure: the greater the pressure, the higher the column will rise. It is written as systolic/diastolic. Normal resting blood pressure varies from person to person but is usually about 120/80 for men and 110/70 for women.

During exercise, systolic blood pressure rises quickly as the amount of blood pumped by the heart increases. This is a healthy response and ensures an adequate blood supply to the working muscles. Blood pressure returns to normal after exercise. During the stress response, both systolic and diastolic blood pressures tend to rise. Diastolic pressure increases with the increased blood volume and increased peripheral resistance that results from the stress response. More fluid ejected with greater force in a smaller system means more pressure. (During exercise peripheral resistance decreases as peripheral arteries dilate to increase blood flow to the skin for cooling.)

The increase in blood pressure that occurs during the stress response does not appear to be harmful in healthy people. In fact, as you run from the pit bull terrier, it is quite helpful! You have a good supply of blood to your brain and muscles. The problem with blood pressure elevation during stress comes when you don't really need to respond physically to the stressor at hand, which is most of the time. When excess stress becomes a chronic situation, the nervous and endocrine stimulation may cause blood pressure to become chronically elevated if that stress response is not balanced with a healthy dose of the relaxation response (Benson, 1977).

THE SKELETAL MUSCLES: READY TO SPRING

The next time you watch a movie, monitor your level of muscle tension. You may find that high-energy scenes lead to a sympathetic response. As the protagonist breathlessly pursues the villain, you may brace for action as well. A loud noise and you jump!

Muscles are collections of muscle cells that are capable of contraction and relaxation. A muscle's strength of contraction is controlled by the number and type of cells that are activated, or recruited, by the nervous system. A stronger contraction is produced if more cells are recruited. Muscular contraction may or may not produce movement. Even resting muscles maintain some level of contraction. Your skeletal muscles are important actors in the fight-or-flight response. Their contraction creates the movement that enables you to fight or flee. As you prepare to respond to stress, your muscles contract in preparation for movement, much like a cat preparing to pounce. As the pit bull terrier lunges madly toward you, you might initially freeze as every muscle contracts before you spring into action.

As you relax after a successful escape from the pit bull's jaws, your muscles relax as well. But imagine an individual under chronic stress, and a muscle group that

■ STUDENT STRESS

CORY'S FIGHT-OR-FLIGHT RESPONSE

As Cory slugged his way through the stress physiology chapter of his stress management text, he could feel his neck and shoulders getting tighter and tighter. The tongue-twisting terminology was so foreign, and the effects of the stress hormones all sounded alike. "I hope the professor doesn't expect us to memorize all this!" he muttered aloud. An imaginary exam question began to take shape in his mind: "Describe in detail the physiology of the stress response. List the action of each hormone. Points deducted for incorrect spelling." Even though the stressor was imaginary, he could feel his breathing become shallower, and the tension in his neck and shoulders became painful.

As he read the section on muscle bracing, he recognized his symptoms immediately. "That's me," he thought. "Ready to respond at the least provocation." He could see himself hunched over like a boxer approaching his opponent, ready to throw a punch. Cory wondered whether he could change his muscle-bracing response to stress and decided to make it the focus of his work in the stress management course.

remains chronically contracted as it continually braces for action, unable to let go. This is the beginning of the muscle tension problems that commonly occur in the jaw, neck, shoulder, and back as posture muscles prepare you to face the worst. Muscle tension creates pain that creates stress and more muscle tension. Pain from muscle tension may be the result of a partially contracted muscle cutting off blood flow, leading to oxygen deprivation and a buildup of waste products in the muscle tissue. Pain may also be caused by muscle spasms that put abnormal pressure on sensitive joint areas, or lead to muscle tears from inflexibility (Girdano et al., 1997).

THE DIGESTIVE SYSTEM: PUT ON HOLD

Have you ever given a presentation and had a hard time talking because your mouth was very dry? Did you ever get into an argument during a meal and suddenly lose your appetite or develop a stomachache? Have you ever been unable to eat for a week because you had just fallen in love? These symptoms are a function of the effects the stress response has on the digestive system (see Figure 2.9).

The digestive system is responsible for converting food into molecules that can be used by the body. Food is ingested through the mouth, where it begins to be broken down by chewing and **saliva.** It is swallowed into the **esophagus,** which transports it into the **stomach.** There is a tight band of muscle called a sphincter (in this case it's called the **lower esophageal sphincter**) between the esophagus and the stomach that relaxes during swallowing but then prevents stomach contents from backing up into the esophagus. Heartburn occurs when this sphincter relaxes and allows the acidic contents of the stomach to enter the esophagus and produce a burning sensation.

In the stomach a number of chemicals, including hydrochloric acid, continue the process of digestion as the stomach contracts rhythmically to churn the food. The stomach contents exit the stomach through another sphincter into the **small intestine,** where they are further digested. The part of the small intestine adjacent

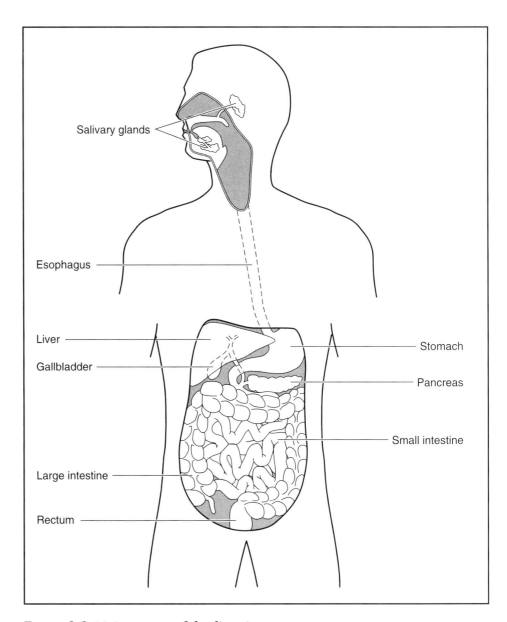

FIGURE 2.9 *Major organs of the digestive system*

to the stomach is called the **duodenum** and is a favorite place for ulcers. Useful molecules are absorbed or transported from the small intestine into the blood stream for use by body cells. The leftovers are sent to the **large intestine** and out of the body through the **anal canal.** The digestive system is composed primarily of **smooth muscle,** which conducts the food through the system by slow rhythmic contractions known as **peristalsis.** Other organs considered part of the digestive system include the pancreas, liver, and gallbladder, which manufacture and secrete substances that assist in the digestive processes.

We've seen that as you run away from the snarling dog, digestion of your lunch is put on hold as a strong cardiovascular response and contraction of skeletal muscles take priority. The normal flow of saliva decreases; stomach acidity may increase; peristaltic motion in the esophagus, stomach, and intestines may accelerate

STRESS AND YOU

FIGHT OR FLIGHT? OR SIT AND STEW?
YOUR EXPERIENCE WITH THE FIGHT-OR-FLIGHT RESPONSE

We have presented a rather generic version of the fight-or-flight response, simplified for easier learning, but of course the stress response manifests itself differently from person to person. It varies with the intensity and duration of the stressor. It may vary somewhat with fitness level (Sothman et al., 1991). And some studies suggest that there may be small differences between men and women, with men experiencing more deleterious cardiovascular responses (Johansson et al., 1989; Stoney et al., 1988). Most of all, it varies with one's degree of stress resistance (Dienstbier, 1991).

Take a moment to think about your own stress response. We have noted that the fight-or-flight response is very useful for situations requiring a physical response. This arousal is often helpful for mental activity as well. It sharpens the mind and is useful for giving good performances, writing inspired exams and papers, and energizing important conversations. It does not appear to be harmful as long as it is balanced by the relaxation response. But what about those days when you feel continually wound up, with one thing after another going wrong? Maybe at the end of one of those days you have gone to bed but been unable to sleep because your muscles were still tense and your heart was still beating more quickly than usual.

Try to recall one or two recent occasions when you remember the fight-or-flight response as inappropriate and obstructive. It could be something as simple as the alarm going off in the morning. Try to remember your physical response to those sources of stress. For each source of stress, try to answer the following questions:

What was the source of stress?

What were your physical symptoms?

How long did they last?

What did you finally do to relax?

---

or slow down. Noticeable symptoms include a dry mouth, stomach cramps or "butterflies," nausea, abdominal cramps, and even vomiting and diarrhea. These do not actually assist you as you fight or flee but are side effects of the stress response and can be annoying. Chronic stress can open a Pandora's box of digestive complaints from gum disease and esophageal spasms to ulcers and constipation; they are discussed more fully in the next chapter.

SUMMARY

1. A healthy fight-or-flight response provided an advantage to our ancient ancestors. Several physiological systems have evolved to ensure the function of this response that has, until relatively recently, been so important for survival.
2. The fight-or-flight response is controlled by the nervous and endocrine systems. The combined actions of these systems increase metabolic rate and mobilize fuel for energy production; increase blood pressure, blood flow, and respiration; and inhibit systems not essential for immediate survival.
3. The sympathetic branch of the autonomic nervous system initiates the fight-or-flight response.
4. Many areas of the brain coordinate our physical and psychological stress response as well as our conscious and subconscious responses to stressors. The hypothalamus and pituitary gland are especially important in the physiological regulation of the fight-or-flight response.
5. The organs of the endocrine system produce chemical messengers that help regulate the fight-or-flight response.
6. The adrenal medulla secretes epinephrine and norepinephrine in response to sympathetic stimulation. These hormones have actions that enhance cardiac and respiratory function, increase blood sugar level, increase blood volume, and speed clotting.
7. The hypothalamus-pituitary-adrenal pathway stimulates the adrenal cortex to release glucocorticoids and mineralocorticoids. These hormones raise blood sugar and blood pressure, and inhibit inflammation and immune function.
8. The hypothalamus-pituitary-thyroid pathway stimulates the thyroid gland to produce thyroid hormones. These increase resting metabolic rate, raise blood sugar, and enhance cardiac and respiratory function.
9. The antidiuretic hormone (vasopressin) increases blood pressure.
10. The fight-or-flight response causes an increase in heart rate and contractile force and an increase in blood pressure. Chronic stress can contribute to hypertension.
11. Muscles contract during the fight-or-flight response to prepare for action. Chronic muscle contraction can lead to muscle tension problems.
12. The fight-or-flight response inhibits digestive processes. Chronic stress can cause a number of gastrointestinal disorders.
13. Hans Selye defined stress as the nonspecific response of the body to any demand made on it. He believed that eustress and distress cause similar physical responses.
14. The General Adaptation Syndrome is composed of the alarm reaction, the stage of resistance, and the stage of exhaustion.

REFERENCES

Benson, H. Systemic hypertension and the relaxation response. *New England Journal of Medicine* 296: 1152–1156, 1977.

Chrousos, GP, and PW Gold. The concepts of stress and stress system disorders: Overview of physical and behavioral homeostasis. *Journal of the American Medical Association* 267: 1244–1252, 1992.

Dienstbier, RA. Behavioral correlates of sympathoadrenal reactivity: The toughness model. *Medicine and Science in Sports and Exercise* 23: 846–852, 1991.

Feuerstein, M, EE Labbe, and AR Kuczmierczyk. *Health Psychology: A Psychobiological Perspective*. New York: Plenum Press, 1986.

Gawin, GH. Cocaine addiction: Psychology and neurophysiology. *Science* 251: 1580–1586, 1991.

Girdano, DA, GS Everly, Jr., and DE Dusek. *Controlling Stress and Tension.* Englewood Cliffs, NJ: Prentice Hall, 1997.

Greenberg, JS. *Comprehensive Stress Management.* Dubuque, IA: Wm C Brown, 1996.

Hegel, MT, GG Abel, M Etscheidt, S Cohen-Cole, and CI Wilmer. Behavioral treatment of angina-like chest pain in patients with hyperventilation syndrome. *Journal of Behavior Therapy and Experimental Psychiatry* 20: 31–39, 1989.

Holmes, TH, and RH Rahe. The social readjustment rating scale. *Journal of Psychosomatic Research* 11: 213–218, 1967.

Isner, JM, NAM Estes III, PD Thompson, et al. Acute cardiac events temporally related to cocaine abuse. *The New England Journal of Medicine* 315(23): 1438–1443, 1986.

Johansson, GG, M Laakso, M Peder, and SL Karonen. Endocrine patterns before and after examination stress in males and females. *Activas Nervosa Superior* 31: 81–88, 1989.

Mills, FJ, and B Chir. The endocrinology of stress. *Aviation, Space, and Environmental Medicine* 56: 642–650, 1985.

Monagan, D. Sudden death. *Discover,* January 1986, 64–71.

Monat, A, and RS Lazarus. Introduction: Stress and coping—Some current issues and controversies. A Monat and RS Lazarus (eds). *Stress and Coping.* New York: Columbia University Press, 1991.

Mullen, KD, RS Gold, PA Belcastro, and RJ McDermott. *Connections for Health.* Madison, WI: Brown & Benchmark, 1993.

Rice, PL. *Stress and Health.* Pacific Grove, CA: Brooks/Cole, 1992.

Rosen, MG. Doula at the bedside of the patient in labor. *Journal of the American Medical Association* 265: 2236–2237, 1991.

Selye, H. A syndrome produced by diverse nocuous agents. *Nature* 138: 32, 1936.

Selye, H. *The Stress of Life.* New York: McGraw-Hill, 1956.

Selye, H. *Stress without Distress.* New York: Lippincott, 1974.

Selye, H. History and present status of the stress concept. L Goldberg and S Breznitz (eds). *Handbook of Stress: Theoretical and Clinical Aspects.* New York: Free Press, 1982.

Sothman, MS, BA Hart, and TS Horn. Plasma catecholamine response to acute psychological stress in humans: relation to aerobic fitness and exercise training. *Medicine and Science in Sports and Exercise* 23: 860–867, 1991.

Stoney, CM, KA Matthews, RH McDonald, and CA Johnson. Sex differences in lipid, lipoprotein, cardiovascular, and neuroendocrine responses to acute stress. *Psychophysiology* 25: 645–656, 1988.

Tortora, GJ, and S Grabowski. *Principles of Anatomy and Physiology.* New York: Harper-Collins, 1993.

Turkkan, JS, JV Brady, and AH Harris. Animal studies of stressful interactions: A behavioral-physiological overview. L Goldberger and S Breznitz (eds). *Handbook of Stress: Theoretical and Clinical Aspects.* New York: Free Press, 1982, 153–182.

Woods, PJ. Do you really want to maintain that a flat tire can upset your stomach? *Journal of Rational-Emotive Therapy* 5: 149–159, 1987.

chapter 3

Stress and Health

Life offers a succession of challenges and demands. Sometimes we find them stimulating and exciting; other times they seem depressing and overwhelming. We are continually responding to these challenges while trying to maintain our equilibrium. Sometimes the demands really seem to pile up or become very difficult to meet. It feels as though we are in a permanent fight- or-flight response and just can't relax. We may experience tension headaches, nervous stomachs, or sleeplessness. We may feel anxious or depressed. Realizing we are under stress, we do some active problem solving to deal with the demands and regain our equilibrium. We learn and grow from such challenges and develop our resources for meeting future demands.

But what happens when we get stuck, when the pressure is unrelenting and we seem unable to make headway against the winds of distress? There are times in almost everyone's life when the stress cloud hangs over us longer than usual, the fight-or-flight response becomes a way of life, and we tell our friends we are "stressed out." Prolonged periods of stress, especially negative stress, can contribute to a variety of stress-related disorders. Chronic activation of the nervous and endocrine systems' stress response can affect health in a number of important ways.

Heavy thoughts bring on physical maladies; when the soul is oppressed so is the body.

MARTIN LUTHER

CAN STRESS CAUSE ILLNESS?

Concern about the effects of long-term negative stress on physical and mental health is nothing new. In the fifth century B.C., Hippocrates, who has been called the father of medicine, counseled medical students to consider emotional factors in their diagnosis and treatment of disease. Aristotle, the Greek philosopher and scientist who lived from 384 to 322 B.C., believed that body and soul are inseparable and that the emotions play an important role in health and illness. Throughout history, people have observed that hard times and ill health often go hand in hand. We hear about people who become ill and die shortly after the loss of a spouse; we see middle-aged relatives and friends who live high-pressure lifestyles developing heart disease; and when ominous happenings loom on the horizon, we say we are "worried sick." Indeed, stress management students have commented that chronic negative stress feels so bad, it has to be bad for your body as well.

The relationship between stress and health is not simple. A certain amount or type of stress does not automatically cause a given health condition. The impact of

STUDENT STRESS

TAMARA'S STRESS-RESISTANT COPING

Jennifer and Tamara are both first-year students in the same academic program and have a similar workload. Both young women are on the tennis team as well and must attend practice or matches for at least two hours every day. With a heavy academic workload, athletics involvement, and weekend social engagements, they have both fallen somewhat behind in their studying. Exam alert! Midterms are approaching, three in the same week, with a lab report and paper due in another course as well. To top it off, many of the students in their dorms have come down with bad colds, and Jennifer and Tamara hope they will not get sick.

As midterm week approaches, Jennifer begins to feel panic rising in her throat. She feels tense, irritable, and distracted. She can often feel her heart pounding and her stomach getting tight when she thinks about what might happen if she doesn't get good grades. What will her parents say? Will she ever find a job? Will she lose her scholarship? Her study time is not always productive as she flits from one thing to another, stopping frequently to complain to her friends about all the work she has to do. Her tennis game deteriorates, and she even skips a couple of practices. A few nights before the first exam she can hardly sleep from worry, and her stomachaches are getting worse. "Just like Dad," she says to herself, thinking about her father's nervous stomach that always gets worse when he is under stress. Tired from missing sleep, Jennifer steps up her coffee intake; this irritates her stomach even more and makes it harder for her to sleep. The night before the first exam, Jennifer joins her classmates for an "all-nighter" that is filled with camaraderie (and more coffee) but leaves her nauseous and exhausted the next day. Jennifer looks at the first exam question with burning eyes; she swallows, feeling the beginning of a sore throat.

Tamara developed good study skills in high school, and although nervous about the upcoming midterms, does her best to prepare. Everyone else is in the same boat, she realizes. I'll just do my best and try to study the right stuff. She asks a senior classmate on her floor for some advice on what to study. Tamara enjoys the tennis practices and finds they provide a good study break and a little time to socialize, leaving her relaxed and alert. She continues to manage her time so that she gets enough rest, and turns down the invitation to the "all-nighter." She feels more pressure than usual during midterm week; she does her share of worrying but manages to find time for relaxation as well as studying. Although several of the women on her floor have caught the cold that's going around, Tamara doesn't get sick.

stress on health is mediated by a number of important genetic, environmental, and personality variables. The Student Stress box above illustrates how these variables affect the stress-illness relationship in two students experiencing similar stressors.

People respond in many different ways to stress. All the variables that make up the stress cycle introduced in the first chapter are important when you are considering the stress-illness relationship. Stress certainly has strong psychological and physical effects, and over time, these can interfere with your health. To add insult to injury, when under excess stress, people may engage in maladaptive coping behaviors, such as smoking and missing sleep, that increase their risk of illness. Illness itself is a

[T]here is no such thing as a purely psychic illness or a purely physical one—only a living event taking place in a living organism that is itself alive only by virture of the fact that in it psychic and somatic are united.

FRITZ MOHR

form of stress and can exacerbate other stressors (Cox, 1988). Writing a paper with a headache is much more stressful than writing a paper when you feel good.

The manner in which stress is perceived and experienced affects your stress response and thus your health. On the one hand, when a stressor is experienced as uncontrollable, and with an outcome that is expected to be negative, a chronic stress response is more likely to result in health problems (Fisher, 1988; Honzak et al., 1989; Strickland, 1989). When the emotional stress response is negative, you may feel fear, anger, hostility, or alienation; you might feel helpless and hopeless. Such feelings increase your risk of stress-related disorders (Powell et al., 1993; Williams, 1994). On the other hand, the negative effects of stress can be buffered by such factors as an optimistic outlook, some sense of control, a sense of social support, and positive health behaviors (Kobasa, 1979; Scheier & Carver, 1993). Recall the theme of this book—that you can increase your ability to buffer the negative effects of stress in many ways. Doing so can help you prevent or at least reduce the severity of stress-related illness.

Having qualified our "yes" response to the question of whether stress can cause illness, let's use the information from Chapter 2 to discover what happens if chronic sympathetic arousal is not balanced by the relaxation response.

THE CARDIOVASCULAR SYSTEM: HEART AT WORK

Artery Disease

Your cardiovascular system is hard at work when you are responding to stress. Sympathetic arousal and the stress hormones make the heart beat faster and harder. Blood flow is redistributed, blood volume increases, and blood pressure rises. With stress, the blood transports emergency fuel to muscles, so blood sugar, fat, and cholesterol levels increase. Blood clots form more easily. These effects contribute to the development of **atherosclerosis,** in which the inner walls of the arteries become thickened from deposits of fat, cholesterol, and other substances. (**Arteries** are the blood vessels that carry blood from the heart to the rest of the body.) Atherosclerosis may develop in any artery. It becomes life threatening when it develops in arteries supplying organs such as the heart or brain, which sustain irreparable damage if deprived of blood for even a few minutes.

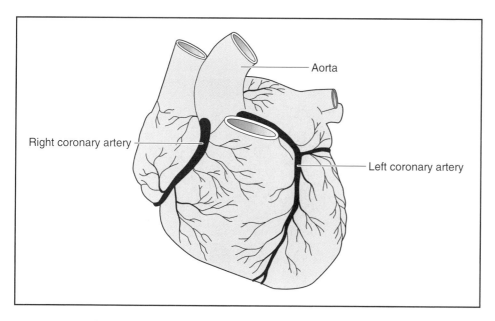

FIGURE 3.1 *The Coronary Arteries*

Although the heart pumps blood with each beat, it cannot obtain the oxygen and nutrients it needs from the blood that fills its chambers. Like every other organ, the heart has its own arterial system. These are the **coronary arteries** that "crown" the heart (see Figure 3.1). Their name comes from *corona*, the Latin word for crown. Most heart attacks result when blood flow in narrowed coronary arteries stops because of a blood clot or arterial spasm. **Coronary artery disease** is the leading cause of death in North America. Atherosclerosis in the arteries feeding the brain may contribute to **stroke,** which is caused by an insufficient blood supply to the brain.

The development of atherosclerosis and the role played by stress are only partially understood. Researchers believe that this disease begins with some sort of damage to the artery lining. The damage may be caused by many things, including high blood pressure, carbon monoxide from cigarette smoke, high blood cholesterol, and high blood sugar levels. Studies have shown that elevated levels of stress hormones may also damage the lining of arteries. Damaged cells in the arterial lining attract white blood cells that attempt to repair the problem. They move into the artery wall and begin to take up cholesterol from substances circulating in the blood known as **low-density lipoproteins (LDLs).** These lipoproteins contribute cholesterol after undergoing a process called oxidation, which somehow activates them to become targets for the white blood cells in the artery walls. As part of the repair process, artery cells proliferate and combine with the accumulated cholesterol to form an **atherosclerotic plaque,** a grayish-yellow mound of tissue inside the artery (see Figure 3.2). As the plaque continues to grow, its rough surface causes **platelets,** the blood cells that aid in blood clotting, to release hormones that lead to blood clots and more cell growth. Over the years the plaques grow and more blood clots form.

Atherosclerosis begins early in life; plaque formation has been observed in teenagers and young adults. It is a silent disease in its early stages. Once symptoms such as chest pain become apparent, the disease has already progressed to an advanced state. While atherosclerosis appears to be present in everyone to some degree, it progresses more quickly in some people than in others.

Atherosclerosis has no simple "cause," and researchers are unable to tell you whether you will have a heart attack because of it. But they can give you your odds.

FIGURE 3.2 *The Progression of Atherosclerosis*

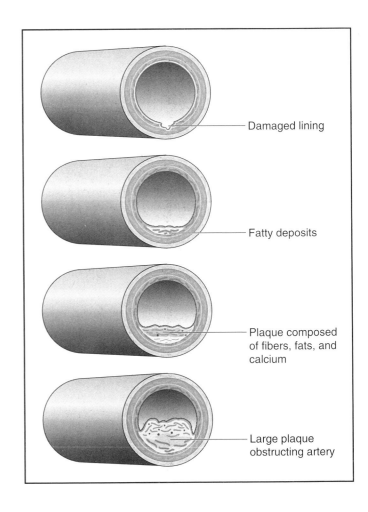

Scientists have been able to isolate **risk factors,** variables that affect your probability of developing coronary artery disease. Some of these risk factors are unchangeable: age (risk increases with age), gender (males at higher risk until they reach their 60s, when risk is similar for men and women), race (African-Americans have a higher risk), and family history of premature heart attack. Other risk factors can be modified by lifestyle change and appropriate medical intervention. The four strongest modifiable risk factors are high blood cholesterol level, smoking, hypertension, and a sedentary lifestyle.

What about stress? Does chronic stress contribute to atherosclerosis? Some research has suggested that chronic stress, as measured by the number of recent stressors in a person's life, one's perceived levels of stress, certain personality characteristics, and the nature of one's stress response are all related to risk of artery disease. Stress may contribute to the development of coronary artery disease in several ways.

Changes in Blood Chemistry

Blood Lipids Psychological stress has been shown to raise blood cholesterol levels (Dimsdale & Herd, 1982; Mattiasson et al., 1990). This elevation in cholesterol occurs within minutes of exposure to a stressor and lasts for over 30 minutes (Stoney et al., 1988; Muldoon et al., 1992). Although these increases in cholesterol level are not very large, if sustained over a period of years or a lifetime, they may contribute significantly to the progression of atherosclerosis.

Hemoconcentration and Clotting Part of the explanation for the increase in cholesterol following psychological stress is that the blood becomes more concentrated (Muldoon et al., 1992; Patterson et al., 1993). This effect is known as **hemoconcentration.** Blood is composed of water and formed elements such as red blood cells, platelets, and white blood cells. With hemoconcentration, there is a greater concentration of formed elements per unit of blood volume due to a loss of plasma (the watery part of the blood) volume. Hemoconcentration is potentially dangerous because it increases the "stickiness" of the blood and the chance of blood clot formation. It is associated with both hypertension and artery disease (Kiyohara et al., 1986; Sorlie et al., 1981).

Blood Sugar Levels Blood sugar levels increase when the body prepares to fight or run away. The effect of elevated blood sugar levels on artery disease is not well understood. Researchers do know that people who have diabetes, and thus poor blood sugar regulation, have an increased risk of artery disease. People with diabetes may be most vulnerable to the effects of stress on blood sugar levels (Goetsch et al., 1993). It is not clear whether such increases pose a risk for others.

Increased Blood Pressure

Hypertension is diagnosed by measuring blood pressure. Health scientists do not know exactly how high is too high, but hypertension is generally diagnosed when systolic blood pressure is greater than 140 mmHg or diastolic blood pressure is over 90 mmHg. About 10 percent of the time hypertension is symptomatic of an underlying disease. **Essential hypertension** refers to the other 90 percent of the cases in which the cause is unknown. Scientists in developed countries have observed for many years that blood pressure increases with age. At one time it was thought that this increase was a normal part of the aging process, and that a higher blood pressure was *essential* for adequate circulation in older adults—hence the term *essential hypertension.* We now know this is not true. People in many cultures do not experience this age-related rise in blood pressure, nor do they experience North America's high rates of heart disease. Hypertension is related to many risk factors, including age, genetics, obesity, alcohol intake, smoking, dietary factors, and a sedentary lifestyle. Stress appears to be a contributing factor as well (Markovitz et al., 1993). Hypertension in turn contributes to atherosclerosis and stroke, although the mechanisms responsible for this association are only partially understood. High arterial pressure may injure the arterial lining and thus initiate and accelerate atherosclerosis.

Several studies have found an association between stress and hypertension. One interesting study of 264 men examined the association between hypertension and job strain (defined by jobs that had high psychological demands but offered little personal control or decision latitude) (Schnall et al., 1992). The researchers found that job strain was significantly associated with blood pressure, even after they statistically controlled for variables such as obesity, alcohol consumption, smoking, and age. This result suggests that the effect of job strain on hypertension is *independent* of its effect on other important variables and that job strain has an effect on blood pressure in and of itself. This does not imply that the effect of stress on other variables is not important. If stress makes you smoke more, drink more, exercise less, and gain weight, these are still harmful effects. In the study above, researchers also found that job strain *interacts* with other variables. An interaction is

FIGURE 3.3
Interaction of Job Stress and
Alcohol Use on Blood Pressure

Reproduced with permission. Peter L. Schnall et al.,
Relation between job strain, alcohol, and ambulatory
blood pressure. *Hypertension* 19:488–494, 1992.
Copyright 1992 American Heart Association.

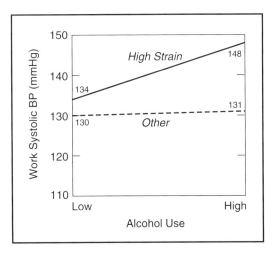

the change in one variable depending on another variable present. Stress had an even stronger effect on blood pressure in men who drank alcohol regularly. This interactive effect is illustrated in Figure 3.3.

Arterial Injury and Spasm

Stress hormones can damage the arterial lining, initiating and furthering the progression of atherosclerosis, at least in laboratory primates (Manuck, 1995). This finding may explain why some studies have found that stress contributes to artery disease even when other stress-related heart disease risk factors are statistically controlled for. In other words, stress contributes to artery disease in some way or ways in addition to its effects on blood pressure and cholesterol.

An interesting study from Sweden illustrates this point (Rosengren et al., 1991). This study placed middle-aged men into five groups based on self-reported levels of psychological stress, defined as feeling tense, irritable, or anxious, or having difficulty sleeping. Men in the category reporting feeling the most stressed were 50 percent more likely than the men in the other four groups to experience a heart attack in the following eight years. They were 80 percent more likely to have a stroke. This study is interesting for several reasons. First, stress was measured *before* disease occurred. You can imagine that a very strong link between stress and illness would be found if you asked people who had just had a heart attack how stressed they were! Second, this study followed 7,000 men—a fairly large sample. Last, the researchers statistically controlled for age and other risk factors such as smoking, hypertension, and high blood cholesterol. This manipulation allowed them to look more closely at the relationship between stress and illness. Their findings indicate that stress affects cardiovascular disease in some way (or ways) in addition to its effects on health behavior, blood chemistry, and blood pressure.

Stress hormones can also lead to the constriction of arteries damaged by atherosclerosis. Such constriction of already narrowed vessels causes a further decrease in blood flow, which can lead to chest pain, heart attack, or stroke.

One group of researchers studying this process monitored blood flow in both healthy and diseased arteries as volunteers counted backward by sevens from a three-digit number under time pressure (Yeung et al., 1991). Many subjects showed a typical stress response, which included increases in blood pressure, heart rate, and levels of norepinephrine. The researchers thought that people with a stronger stress response might have greater changes in arterial blood flow, but this was not the case; the intensity of a subject's stress response did not predict blood flow in coronary arteries. Arterial health did. Blood flow in the coronary arteries *increased* an average of 10 percent in healthy vessels, but *decreased* an average of 27 percent in diseased arteries. Healthy coronary arteries counter the effect of stress hormones, which tend to narrow arteries, by releasing a substance called **endothelium-derived relaxing factor (EDRF).** This substance makes the arteries expand so more blood can reach the heart during demanding times. Atherosclerotic plaques appear to interfere with this process (Yeung et al., 1991; Maseri, 1991). So once again we see stress interacting with other factors to cause illness. Combine stress with atherosclerosis and the result may be arterial spasm that causes a dangerous decrease in blood flow.

Irregular Heartbeat

The fight-or-flight response sometimes leads to irregular heartbeats. Most of the time these are not harmful, but in extreme cases, and especially in diseased hearts, these irregular beats can lead to a heart attack (Monagan, 1986). In a healthy heart, all parts of the heart work together in a synchronous fashion. The beat originates from an electrical impulse generated by a natural pacemaker called the **sino-atrial node.** The upper chambers, the **atria,** contract first, forcing blood into the two lower chambers, the **ventricles,** which then pump the blood out through large arteries to the rest of the body. A heart attack occurs when the heart loses this rhythmic beat. When the heart fails to contract in this synchronous fashion, its pumping ability is lost, and a heart attack results.

Changes in Health Behavior

Stress has a negative effect on health if it leads to negative effects on lifestyle. When people feel stressed, they are less likely to stick to their exercise programs, eat well, and get enough sleep. They may be more likely to eat too much and abuse substances such as caffeine, alcohol, and other drugs. The comparison of Jennifer and Tamara illustrates the importance of health behaviors. Although in our story Jennifer just caught a cold, 40 years down the line she would also be more prone than Tamara to high cholesterol levels, hypertension, and artery disease if she does not develop better ways to cope with stress.

[T]he high pressure at which men live, and the habit of working the machine to its maximum capacity are responsible for (arterial degeneration) rather than excesses in eating and drinking.

SIR WILLIAM OSLER, MD

STRESS, PERSONALITY, AND CARDIOVASCULAR DISEASE

Intriguing research on personality type and stress response suggests that the way you perceive stress (and life in general) has an important impact on your physical stress response, and your cardiovascular health. Research in the 1950s found that ambitious, competitive individuals who were always in a hurry trying to accomplish a poorly defined set of objectives were more susceptible to coronary artery disease than their easygoing friends (Friedman & Rosenman, 1974). Cardiologists Friedman and Rosenman, who conducted this research, coined the term **Type A behavior pattern** to describe this "coronary-prone personality." Subsequent research has confirmed that certain components of Type A behavior are especially harmful to one's health. Hostility and anger arising from a cynical distrust of others appear to be most strongly linked to artery disease (Alamada et al., 1991; Dembroski et al., 1989; Julkunen et al., 1994; Williams, 1989). People who score high on psychological tests measuring hostility seem to have higher elevations in stress hormones in response to aggravation and a weaker parasympathetic response; they recover from stressors more slowly. Such people tend to have chronic elevations in the stress hormones and cholesterol. This elevation appears to activate the macrophages, which

It is more important to know what sort of patient has a disease, than what sort of disease a patient has.

SIR WILLIAM OSLER, MD

▶ STRESS RESEARCH

Friedman and Rosenman: *Personality and Stress—Type A Behavior Pattern*

The concept of Type A behavior pattern was designed by two San Francisco cardiologists, Meyer Friedman and Ray Rosenman, in the 1950s. They had observed that their patients with coronary artery disease tended to share a number of traits that they began to call the Type A behavior pattern. These traits included a hard-driving competitiveness, hostility, a sense of time urgency, and a concern with achievement and acquisition of objects. Type B people were seen less frequently in the ward and were characterized by a lack of these qualities and a more easygoing attitude.

Friedman and Rosenman decided to test their theory. They came up with an interview technique, the Structured Interview, to categorize subjects into Type A or Type B groups. During the interview the investigator asked a number of simple questions designed not so much to bring forth information as to identify a Type A or B response style. People were categorized as Type A if they spoke quickly and loudly, finished the investigator's sentences, and exhibited impatient mannerisms.

The first study to show a relationship between Type A behavior pattern and artery disease was the Western Collaborative Group Study (Rosenman et al., 1975). In this experiment, Friedman, Rosenman, and their research team categorized 3,524 male volunteers into Type A and B groups. About half the men fell into each group. If these behavior patterns had no relationship to artery disease, one would expect that over time, both groups would show similar rates of artery disease development. This was not the case. The researchers kept track of these men for eight and a half years, during which more than twice as many men in the Type A group experienced coronary artery disease.

The Western Collaborative Group Study opened an enormously fruitful area of research that continues to this day. Subsequent research has focused on further refining the specific Type A traits most predictive of artery disease, the measurement of these traits, the physiological mechanisms through which these traits lead to artery disease, and possible treatment modalities for individuals with such traits. As mentioned in this chapter, some researchers believe that anger and hostility are the salient traits inducing arterial damage. Other researchers suggest that time urgency may underlie the anger and hostility, which may result when other people and events get in the way of the Type A person's highly valued "schedule" (Wright, 1991).

The hypothesized physiological mechanisms through which Type A's become vulnerable to artery disease all implicate chronic overactivation of the fight-or-flight response. They reinforce the notion that while a short-term stress response does not appear to be harmful, "hot reactors" who live life in a state of agitation, aggravation, and continuous sympathetic arousal are more prone to artery disease. Stress management techniques have helped many Type A's develop a stronger relaxation response to balance sympathetic arousal as well as a more serene approach to life in general.

in turn act with oxidized LDLs to promote the formation of arterial plaque (Williams, 1994). Elevated stress hormone levels are also associated with increases in blood pressure, plaque formation, and arterial spasms. Hostile anger leads to higher levels of testosterone as well. Elevations in testosterone decrease levels of **high-density lipoproteins (HDLs),** which are associated with slower rates of plaque accumulation and lower heart disease risk.

Depression is sometimes an effect of chronic stress. Likewise, stress may exacerbate depression that is already present. Depression is characterized by feelings such as hopelessness, helplessness, dejection, and guilt. It is often accompanied by symptoms such as loss of appetite, insomnia, a lack of interest in things that were previously enjoyable, withdrawal from social contacts, difficulty concentrating and making decisions, low self-esteem, and a focus on negative thoughts (Edlin & Golanty, 1996). One interesting study discovered that depression may make a person with other cardiovascular risk factors more prone to heart attack or stroke (Frasure-Smith et al., 1993). In this study, plaque buildup was measured in 1,100 men in Finland. Depression did not appear to increase atherosclerosis in men with no risk factors, but it amplified the effect of risk factors in others. For example, depressed smokers had on average 3.4 times the amount of atherosclerosis of nondepressed smokers. Twice as much plaque formation occurred in depressed men with high LDL levels than in nondepressed men with similar LDL levels. Such research underscores the importance of the body-mind-behavior interactions in the maintenance of health and the development of disease.

Personality variables also appear to be involved in how well people cope with and recover from cardiovascular disease. In an interesting study from McGill University, psychological tests were given to 200 men recovering from heart attacks; the men were then followed for five years. The researchers found that men who reported feeling useless or unable to "do things well" were almost four times as likely to have died during this period (Frasure-Smith, 1989). This study concluded that men with low self-esteem were less able to cope with the stress of heart attack. A subsequent study by the same researchers found that when subjects reporting high stress levels were given help in dealing with their problems, their risk was reduced to that of low-stress patients (Frasure-Smith, 1991).

Dean Ornish, a pioneer in the use of stress management and other lifestyle modifications for patients with artery disease, believes that psychological factors are important in both the development and treatment of this disease. His is one of several research teams (Hambrecht et al., 1993; Haskell et al., 1994; Schuler et al., 1992) to actually document a *decrease* in plaque buildup in patients undergoing rigorous programs of exercise, very low-fat diet, and stress management (Ornish et al., 1990). Stress management for Ornish's patients includes at least an hour each day of yoga, breathing exercises, meditation, and imagery. Group support and talking about feelings are an important part of the program. Ornish believes strongly that people's emotions play an important role in the disease process; he urges his patients to "open their hearts" to their feelings, inner peace, to others, and to their higher selves. He emphasizes that a sense of isolation may be the cause of the chronic emotional stress that can contribute to illnesses like heart disease (Ornish, 1990). Other research substantiates these beliefs (Chesney, 1993; Powell et al., 1993; Scheier & Bridges, 1995).

What is needed are ways of training ourselves and others to maintain diligence with pacing—that is, to run the race of life like a marathon and not a series of 100-yard dashes.

LOGAN WRIGHT

Summary: Stress and Cardiovascular Health

Stress seems to contribute to cardiovascular disease in many ways:

1. Stress may increase levels of blood cholesterol.
2. Stress leads to hemoconcentration and faster clotting rates.

3. Stress contributes to hypertension, which in turn increases cardiovascular risk.
4. Stress hormones damage the lining of the arteries, helping to initiate the process of atherosclerosis.
5. Stress makes unhealthy arteries more prone to spasms that occlude blood flow.
6. Stress may cause irregular heartbeats.
7. Stressful times are often accompanied by changes in sleep, eating, and exercise habits, and use of substances such as caffeine, alcohol, and other drugs.
8. Stress may interact with personality variables, such as hostility, feelings of isolation, and low self-esteem, and emotions, such as anger and depression, to increase artery disease.

THE DIGESTIVE SYSTEM: YOUR GUT RESPONSE

Stress and the Digestive System

If someone told you he had "butterflies" or a sinking feeling in the pit of his stomach, or that his stomach felt like it was "tied in a knot," you would know he was talking about the effects stress can have on the digestive system. Many people have abdominal sensations when experiencing a variety of emotions—from anger and hate to love and joy. These sensations are a reflection of our psychophysiological responses to both eustress and distress, which have a significant effect on digestive function and health. For most people, these "gut reactions" are a harmless response; but for some, chronic stress easily upsets the digestive system and can lead to a variety of health problems.

Recall from Chapter 2 that the digestive system consists of the **gastrointestinal (GI) tract,** which runs from the mouth to the anus and moves food through the digestive processes; and accessory structures that aid in digestion: teeth, tongue, salivary glands, liver, gallbladder, and pancreas. During the fight-or-flight response, digestion is a low priority; and digestive system function is neglected while the needs of the cardiovascular and musculoskeletal systems are tended to.

Not everyone develops a digestive problem during periods of chronic stress. Each of us seems to have our "Achilles' heel," our own special areas of vulnerability, in which excess stress manifests itself physically and psychologically. However, digestive complaints are some of the most common stress-related disorders. In addition, many people experience some sort of digestive disorder that seems to be caused by factors other than stress but which can be exacerbated by stress. For example, if you are prone to a "nervous stomach," irritable bowel syndrome, or colitis, a high-stress period can cause a worsening of symptoms. A number of symptoms, discussed next, have been associated with chronic stress.

Gum Disease

Let's start at the top. Many people, including dentists and hygienists, have noticed an association between stress and gum disease (**gingivitis**). Gum disease results when the gum tissue around the teeth becomes inflamed and bleeds easily. Inflammation is caused by the same bacteria that are responsible for dental caries, or tooth decay. As these bacteria act on sugars, they give off acids that penetrate the tooth's enamel. Other bacteria produce a sticky substance that combines with bacterial and other debris to form **dental plaque,** which adheres to the tooth surface, especially along the gum line. If plaque is not removed by oral hygiene procedures, such as brushing and flossing, it can build up and harden. Normally, saliva reduces acidity and protects the teeth, but plaque prevents saliva from reaching the surface of the teeth and providing these helpful actions. Plaque also provides a place for bacteria to thrive and inflame gum tissue.

Why should stress increase gum disease? A variety of hypotheses have been proposed: a reduction in saliva (which can result from stress as well as other factors) favors the growth of harmful bacteria and consequent plaque production; reduction in immune response (to be discussed later in this chapter) may mean a weaker defense against harmful oral bacteria; and oral hygiene and a healthful diet may be neglected during periods of stress. Cigarette smoke contributes to gum disease, so people who smoke more when stressed may experience more gum disease during stressful times.

Esophageal Spasms

Spasm of the smooth muscle of the esophagus produces pain in the chest, which many people mistake for heart attack. These spasms are the result of abnormal peristalsis and are sometimes initiated by gastroesophageal reflux, a condition in which stomach contents escape through the esophageal sphincter. Gastroesophageal reflux may also cause heartburn. Like other gastrointestinal symptoms, esophageal spasms may worsen during stressful times, even though they may be caused by factors other than stress.

Ulcers

Until the development of effective medication, ulcers were the hallmark of "success." Ulcers are sores. Early studies in animals, including those by Selye, found stomach ulcers to be a common stress response, especially when the animals had no control over the stressor (Selye, 1976; Turkhan et al., 1982; Weiss, 1972).

Why ulcers? The stomach produces a very strong acid, hydrochloric acid, that speeds up digestion by making food more vulnerable to the action of a variety of enzymes. Hydrochloric acid is such a strong acid that it would damage the tissue of the stomach itself if the stomach did not produce a protective mucous coating. It is possible that during stress, norepinephrine causes blood vessels in the stomach lining to constrict, decreasing mucous production. The stomach wall is then vulnerable to the destructive action of hydrochloric acid (Greenberg, 1996). Ulcers may occur anywhere along the gastrointestinal tract but are most common in the stomach and the upper portion of the small intestine.

It's important to acknowledge that stress is not the only or even the primary cause of ulcers. A bacterial strain, *H. pylori*, appears to be associated with the development of ulcers in many people. In these cases, ulcers may be treated effectively with antibiotics. An accurate diagnosis and appropriate medical treatment are essential for people with ulcers.

Nervous Stomach and Nausea

Many people experience nausea, a loss of appetite, and stomachaches when feeling stressed. Extreme stress can even lead to vomiting. These stomach symptoms are not necessarily indicative of ulcer development but are painful nonetheless. They may result from some of the same factors that cause ulcers, and in fact, many people with a nervous stomach develop ulcers later in life. These symptoms may also be caused by indigestion or strong spasms of the stomach muscle. Whatever the underlying cause, stomachaches and nausea are messages that something is wrong. People who find that stomach problems signal excess stress are likely to benefit from relaxation techniques that help reduce sympathetic arousal (Davis et al., 1995).

Irritable Bowel Syndrome, Chronic Constipation, and Chronic Diarrhea

Excess stress may alter peristalsis, the rhythmic contractions produced by the smooth muscles of the GI tract. Peristalsis may increase, to produce diarrhea, or slow down, leading to constipation. Symptoms of irritable bowel syndrome include abdominal pain and irregular bowel habits, including constipation and/or diarrhea. Indigestion and excess gas cause some of the pain. So do spastic contractions of the large colon. These conditions are best treated with a combination of diet, exercise, and stress management.

Inflammatory Bowel Disease

Inflammatory bowel diseases (IBDs) such as ulcerative colitis and Crohn's disease are characterized by an inflammation of the colon (large intestine) and do not appear to be caused by stress; however, most people who have IBDs find that their symptoms get worse when they are feeling stressed. Symptoms of IBDs are abdominal pain with blood (produced by bleeding ulcers present on the colon) and mucus in the stools. Inflammatory bowel diseases may be autoimmune disorders, in which the immune system inappropriately attacks healthy body tissue.

Health Behavior and the Digestive System

Sometimes maladaptive coping behavior provides an additional stress to the digestive system. Drinking countless cups of coffee irritates the stomach and intestines. Alcohol is also an irritant. Smokers have higher ulcer rates than nonsmokers, and their ulcers heal more slowly. When our intake of junk food, which is high in fat and low in fiber, is higher than usual, digestive function will reflect this change. Skipping meals means an empty stomach, which can exacerbate an already irritated stomach lining. Eating well can be a challenge during stressful periods, especially if you experience nausea, loss of appetite, or indigestion. If this is the case, you may need to experiment to find out which foods produce the least amount of symptoms; then vary your eating routine until you find one that works for you.

Summary: Stress and the Digestive System

The GI tract is especially vulnerable to chronic, excessive sympathetic response. Many GI symptoms are caused by stress, and stress can exacerbate preexisting problems and disease. Stress can interfere with peristalsis and other digestive functions, and with immune response. Gastrointestinal problems should be thoroughly evaluated before assuming stress is the culprit. Once a medical diagnosis is made, most GI problems respond well to stress management and relaxation practice, dietary therapy, and appropriate medication.

THE MUSCULOSKELETAL SYSTEM: STRESS IS A PAIN IN THE NECK

When you imagined the snarling pit bull charging toward you, you felt your muscles brace for action. Initially you froze, but only for a moment until you spun around to run as fast as you could. You may notice a similar bracing response when you face other sources of stress: giving a presentation, organizing a project, or maybe just hearing the phone ring. You probably even brace yourself for fight or flight when you watch an exciting play or movie. Some of the relaxation techniques discussed later in this book will help you learn to become more aware of and reduce excess muscular contraction. Excess muscle tension can cause or worsen several chronic musculoskeletal problems. The most common are discussed next.

Headache

Headaches were once thought to be caused by two different mechanisms. Tension headaches were attributed to excess tension in the muscles of the head and neck. Vascular or migraine headaches were thought to be triggered by changes in the blood vessels supplying the head. Medical researchers now believe most headaches arise from similar mechanisms involving both muscle tension and vascular changes. A headache is usually called a migraine if symptoms include nausea and vomiting; visual disturbances, dizziness, and confusion; or sensitivity to light, sound, and odor. While most headaches do not reflect serious underlying medical conditions, you should check with your doctor if your headaches are bothering you enough that you take medication more than twice a week, or if they change in frequency, intensity, or duration.

Headaches begin with some sort of trigger that seems to signal the hypothalamus to initiate the blood vessel and muscle tension problems that cause pain. People with chronic headaches are sometimes able to identify factors that trigger their headache, often with the help of a health behavior diary or stress log. Common triggers are substances in food and beverages, and over-the-counter and prescription medications. Headaches are sometimes related to health behaviors, such as smoking, alcohol and caffeine intake, and sleep deprivation. Stress is one of the most common headache triggers. Fortunately, headaches are very responsive to relaxation training (Sargent, 1982). You can learn to sense the very beginnings of a headache and instruct overactive muscles to relax. Relaxation also appears to change blood flow patterns as well.

Temporomandibular Joint (TMJ) Syndrome

The upper and lower jaw meet at the temporomandibular joint. Movement in this important joint is controlled by five muscles. Important nerves pass through this area. Problems in the functioning of this joint may cause **temporomandibular joint (TMJ) syndrome,** which is characterized by facial pain, headaches, earaches, and dizziness. The syndrome can be caused by many things: jaw misalignment, bite problems, and injury. The most common (and controllable) cause is teeth clenching and grinding. Stress management and relaxation techniques can help people with TMJ syndrome recognize excess jaw tension and teeth clenching, and assist them in changing their habits (Tasner, 1986). Other treatments include orthodontic adjustments to change jaw alignment and bite.

Back, Neck, and Shoulder Pain

A number of factors, including stress, contribute to back problems. Stress usually causes or worsens back problems by increasing contraction and spasm in vulnerable muscle groups. A spasm occurs when a muscle remains contracted, unable to relax. Excess muscle tension and muscle spasms may restrict blood flow; this leads to lack of oxygen and nutrient delivery and a buildup of waste products. This situation then irritates nerves, which send pain messages to the brain; muscles tighten up even more to "protect" the injured area.

Muscles in the neck, shoulders, and back are important anti-gravity muscles; during our waking hours they maintain some degree of contraction to keep our bodies from succumbing to gravitational forces (i.e., falling down). We brace these muscles when we move; they help hold us together. Excess tension in them is most likely to cause chronic pain when injury, poor posture, or muscular weakness and

tightness make muscles vulnerable to spasm. An overactive stress response often aggravates a preexisting problem. Relaxation training for back, neck, and shoulder muscles can help reduce pain and muscle tension (Lahad et al., 1994; Stoyva & Anderson, 1982). Posture education and exercises to stretch and strengthen postural muscles are also beneficial.

Stress and Injury

During periods of excess stress, people are more prone than usual to accidents and injury (Green, 1985; Williams et al., 1993). Our minds are on our worries, our concentration is poor, and we forget to attend to the task at hand, whether it is driving a car, going down a flight of stairs, or working out in the weight room. Too little sleep and low blood sugar from a poor diet compound the problem.

Summary: Stress and Musculoskeletal Problems

When muscles are continually braced for action, painful muscle tension may develop, and existing musculoskeletal problems may get worse. Areas most vulnerable to such problems are the muscles of the jaw, head, neck, shoulders, and back. People are more prone to accidents during periods of stress.

STRESS AND THE IMMUNE SYSTEM: THE WALL COMES TUMBLING DOWN

Psychoneuroimmunology

Subjects in a study designed to evaluate the effectiveness of a pain-killer experience symptom relief after receiving inactive "sugar pill" placebos. People with asthma suffer asthma attacks when they believe they are being exposed to allergens, even though the allergens are purely imaginary. Students experiencing the most psychological stress during exam period come down with more colds than their easygoing friends. Such observations illustrate the powerful connection between our thoughts and our immune system activity.

The **immune system** includes the lymph nodes and vessels that run throughout the body and carry immune cells; the spleen, thymus gland, and bone marrow that manufacture immune cells; and the various immune cells circulating in the blood and lymph (see Figure 3.4). At one time physiologists thought the immune system kept to itself, functioning independently without input from other physiological systems. Scientists now know that it communicates extensively with the nervous and endocrine systems (Dantzer & Kelly, 1989; Kiecolt-Glaser & Glaser, 1995). **Psychoneuroimmunology (PNI)** is the study of the interrelationships of the three body-mind systems that serve as communications networks in the maintainence of health: the nervous, endocrine, and immune systems. Mental states, such as the perception of stress, can affect the synthesis and behavior of various immune cells,

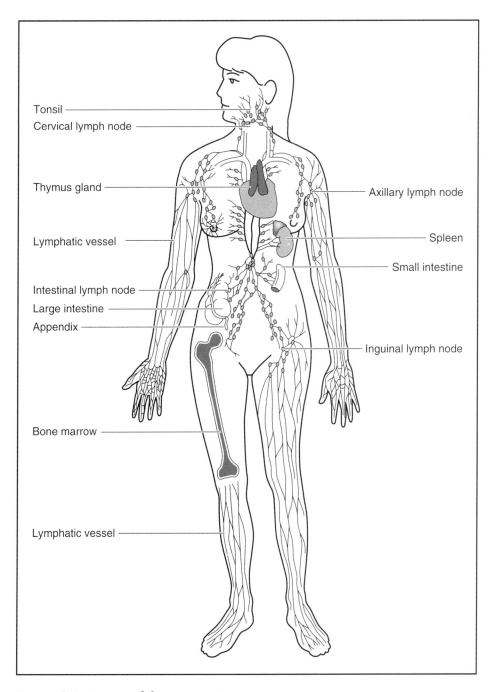

FIGURE 3.4 *Organs of the Immune System*

including **leukocytes** and **macrophages,** types of white blood cells that attack foreign invaders (Futterman et al., 1994; Mills et al., 1995). Immune cells respond to neurotransmitters and hormones and thus communicate with the nervous and endocrine systems. For example, at low concentrations, norepinephrine stimulates the immune system. Cortisol acts to inhibit immune system activity, perhaps one of its energy conservation effects. An elevation in cortisol has been observed in people with depression, so endocrine effects may help explain the link between depression and decreased immune response. Immune cells do not merely eavesdrop; they talk back. They manufacture substances called **cytokines** that are produced by the brain as well and are believed to act as or interact with central nervous system neurotransmitters (Dantzer, 1989).

The immune system appears to be the link between stress and a number of stress-related disorders. Some of these involve immune system suppression while others seem to involve an immune system gone awry.

Respiratory Infections

Why are students (and teachers) more likely to get sick around exam time? Research has shown that stress might be part of the problem. A depressed immune response means fewer bacteria- and virus-fighting white blood cells and an opportunity for the invaders to gain a foothold in the respiratory system. One group of researchers found that psychological stress was related to an increased risk of upper respiratory infections (colds) in a dose-response manner: more stress, more colds (Cohen et al., 1991).

Herpes

Herpes is caused by a virus, *Herpes simplex* virus or HSV. The virus can cause cold sores on the mouth, skin rashes, mononucleosis, and genital lesions. Genital herpes is most frequently caused by viral strain HSV-2, while oral herpes is usually caused by viral strain HSV-1, although both viruses can infect both areas. Once a person has been infected, the virus hangs around forever, and symptoms continue to recur from time to time. Herpes is caused by contact with the virus, usually exposure to someone who is "shedding" virus particles. But stress can contribute to the recurrence of symptoms. Some people with herpes have found that they are more likely to develop symptoms during high-stress periods, perhaps because their immune systems are less able to keep the virus in check (Glaser & Kiecolt-Glaser, 1994).

Allergies and Autoimmune Disorders

Allergies and autoimmune disorders occur when the immune system responds inappropriately to a harmless substance, such as dust, or to the cells of one's own body. One of the ways the immune system responds to injury and invasion is with inflammation. Several substances contribute to the inflammatory response—for example histamine, which we counter with antihistamines when we suffer from allergies. Inflammation begins with vasodilation of blood vessels and a leaking of fluid into the injured area. This produces redness, heat, pain, and swelling. You have probably observed inflammation if you ever sprained an ankle or other joint, or if you have ever had a skin infection.

Asthma, allergies, hay fever, rheumatoid arthritis, and many skin disorders, such as eczema and hives are examples of inappropriate immune responses. In asthma, inflammation occurs in the airways; allergic reactions can include inflammation in airways, nasal passages, the skin, and other areas. Rheumatoid arthritis is a chronic inflammatory joint disease and, as mentioned in the section on the digestive system, IBDs involve inflammation of the colon. Scientists do not know exactly what causes the onset of this immune system behavior, what triggers the inflammatory response normally reserved for foreign invaders. Stress does not appear to be the culprit, but it may exacerbate the inflammation in some cases (Farber & Nall, 1993; Fitzpatrick et al., 1990).

Cancer

One of the most controversial areas of psychoneuroimmunology research concerns the role played by stress in the causation and treatment of cancer. Cancer occurs when cells in some area duplicate without normal control and form a tumor that continues to grow, invading and destroying the healthy tissue around it. Many cancer tumors have the ability to spread, or metastasize, to other areas of the body. A few cancer cells will leave the original tumor and travel in the blood stream or lymph and find a new home, where they will initiate a new tumor.

Cancer begins when something changes a cell's genetic material. Such change is initiated by a carcinogen: a chemical, radiation, or a virus. Stress may trigger carcinogenic changes. Laboratory stressors such as shock have been shown to cause genetic damage in rats (Fackelman & Raloff, 1993).

How is the immune system involved? Some researchers believe mutant cells are relatively common but are destroyed by immune cells in the early stages before they have a chance to form a tumor. The immune system may also help prevent metastasis by recognizing cancer cells traveling in the blood stream or lymph.

Now the big question: does stress cause cancer? Although there have been some interesting studies suggesting a possible link, so far there is no clear evidence that stressful life events are associated with increased cancer risk (Cooper, 1988). Suppression of emotion and depression have also been suggested as possible factors that increase cancer risk, but the evidence is fairly tenuous at this point (Brannon & Feist, 1992; Grossarth-Maticek et al., 1982; Schmale & Iker, 1971). Some researchers have suggested that the effects of hostility on macrophages may contribute to cancer as well as artery disease. (The effect of hostility on macrophages was discussed in relation to artery disease.) A few studies have found some association between hostility scores and cancer incidence (Scheier & Bridges, 1995; Shekelle et al., 1983; Williams, 1994). Such research gives us one more reason to increase our stress resistance, but it is important to remember that factors such as exposure to environmental carcinogens (such as tobacco smoke) and genetic vulnerabilities appear to be much stronger as causative triggers than are emotional factors (Cassileth et al., 1985; Eysenck, 1988; Schultz et al., 1994). One review of the literature on stress and cancer concluded that stress may be a contributing factor in less than 10 percent of the cancers in 40- to 60-year-olds (Frank, 1981).

Now for the other big question: can stress management enhance the efficacy of treatment once cancer has been diagnosed? The use of stress management techniques to help treat cancer has been explored by many, with reports of success (Achterberg, 1985; Simonton et al., 1978). Two well-designed studies have found an association between stress management therapies and improved survival rates in patients with malignant melanoma (Fawzy et al., 1993) and breast cancer (Spiegel et al., 1989). One study found that women who reacted to the stress of a breast cancer diagnosis with resignation had a higher mortality rate than those who responded with denial and a fighting spirit (Greer et al., 1990). And even if stress management is not itself a potent factor in overcoming cancer, it can help people with cancer deal with difficult treatment procedures and make them feel more in control of their lives.

Human Immunodeficiency Virus (HIV)

Acquired immune deficiency syndrome (AIDS) is caused by the **human immunodeficiency virus (HIV).** The virus is acquired through contact with bodily fluids, such as blood or semen, containing the virus. It may remain latent for many years but eventually causes a decline in immune function, destroying important white blood cells known as **CD4 lymphocytes.** As the number of these cells declines, the body is less able to fight infections. Victims of AIDS usually die from "opportunistic" infections and cancers that take advantage of the body's weakened state of immunity. Stress is only indirectly implicated in the causation of AIDS if it leads to maladaptive coping in the form of risk-taking behavior such as intravenous drug use with shared needles or unprotected sexual contact.

Can stress management delay the onset of symptoms or slow disease progression in people infected with HIV? Some studies have suggested that stress management and emotional outlook may affect disease progression, especially in the early stages of infection (Barrett et al., 1994; Burack et al., 1993; Ironson et al., 1994). Increasing stress resistance can help people living with HIV infection cope more effectively with the difficult challenges presented by the illness.

Summary: Stress and the Immune System

Stress may decrease immune response and make people more vulnerable to viral and bacterial infections. Stress may also exacerbate allergies and autoimmune disorders. Stress may lead to cancerous genetic changes, at least in rats. Stress management may enhance the efficacy of medical treatment once cancer is diagnosed. While stress does not cause AIDS, stress management techniques may slow the progression of the disease, at least in its early stages, and help people with HIV infection cope with the disease.

STRESS AND MENTAL HEALTH

Where Does Stress End and Mental Illness Begin?

Like physical health, mental health is not an all or nothing deal but rather a continuum that runs from optimal mental wellness down to extreme mental illness.

Calvin and Hobbes   by Bill Watterson

There is no one point at which someone goes from being "stressed out" to "mentally ill." Someone dealing with schizophrenia or severe depression has an illness caused by something beyond what we commonly experience as stress and needs treatment beyond what stress management programs offer. Most of us, however, fall into that great gray area somewhere between optimal mental wellness and mental illness. All of us are striving to move toward the optimal mental health end of the continuum; stress management helps with this journey.

The relationship between stress and mental health is a complex one that involves all the components of the stress cycle. Stress interacts with mental health and contributes to several psychological disorders. A psychological disorder is characterized by inappropriate or maladaptive cognitive (thinking), emotional, and behavioral functioning (Brannon & Feist, 1992). Depression and anxiety are the two most common examples of psychological disorders.

Depression

Depression has been the most studied of all psychological disorders. Some studies have related stressful life events such as death of a spouse and divorce to subsequent depression. In general, however, life events alone are not a good predicter of depression. Other research suggests that factors such as vulnerability, perceived coping ability, and social support interact with stressful events to determine whether a person becomes depressed (Revicki & May, 1995). Such research suggests that the effects of stressful life events on mental health are buffered by feelings of control and social support. This should sound like an echo of stress effects on physical health.

Anxiety and Phobias

The relationship of stress to anxiety disorders has a similar echo. Anxiety is a feeling of apprehension. Anxiety disorders are divided into two groups: phobic neuroses and anxiety states. People with a phobic neurosis have an enduring and irrational fear of a specific situation or object, such as taking an exam or flying in an airplane. Anxiety states include panic disoders, generalized anxiety, posttraumatic stress, and obsessive-compulsive disorders. Research has shown a weak connection between stressful life events and onset of anxiety disorder (Brannon & Feist, 1992). Stress can certainly make anxiety disorders worse. Many types of anxiety disorders respond well to stress management techniques along with psychotherapy and medical treatment.

Addiction

Behavioral disorders characterized by addiction appear to be worsened by stress and poor coping skills. Such disorders include alcoholism, eating disorders, and drug addiction (Silvestrini, 1990).

Summary: Stress and Mental Health

Stressful events, a person's interpretations of these stressors, perceptions of vulnerability and the ability to cope with the perceived stressor, and social support variables interact with other psychological and physical variables and contribute to mental health and psychological disorders such as depression and anxiety. Behavioral disorders characterized by addiction, such as alcoholism, eating disorders, and drug addiction, worsen during periods of stress and are exacerbated by poor coping skills.

STRESS AND YOU

STRESS AND YOUR HEALTH

Stress Symptom Checklist

The following checklist contains common stress signals. Stress symptoms tend to get worse or become more pronounced when you feel more stressed. Of course, many of these symptoms may be caused by factors other than stress, so check with your doctor before assuming that stress is the cause. These signals can serve as personal stress barometers that help you recognize when stress is becoming a problem that may have a negative effect on your health. Check the symptoms that let you know when you are under excess stress.

Physical Signals

_____ Eye strain

_____ Tight neck or shoulders

_____ Backache

_____ Headache

_____ TMJ (temporomandibular joint) syndrome: teeth clenching; jaw tightness

_____ Muscle twitches

_____ Tightness in chest

_____ Heart palpitations

_____ High blood pressure

_____ Rapid, shallow breathing

_____ Hyperventilation

_____ Dizziness

_____ Sweaty palms and feet

_____ Skin rashes, acne, and hives

_____ Flushed face

_____ Cold hands and feet

_____ Dry "cotton" mouth

_____ Nervous stomach; ulcers

_____ Irritable bowel symptoms: abdominal cramps, diarrhea, constipation

_____ Indigestion, heartburn

_____ Nervousness, restlessness

_____ Fatigue, frequently feeling tired and run down

_____ Impotence

_____ Frequent illness

_____ Other (describe)

Psychological Signals

_____ Lack of concentration

_____ Confusion

_____ Forgetfulness

_____ Obsession with details

_____ Concern with excessive "What ifs?"

_____ Being stuck in the past: "If only" and "I should have"

_____ Indecision

_____ Self-criticism

_____ Self-doubt

_____ Racing thoughts

_____ Boredom

_____ Loss of enthusiasm, apathy

_____ Worry

_____ Depression, feeling down

_____ Frustration   *(Continued)*

STRESS AND YOU *(Continued)*

Psychological Signals

_____ Irritability, impatience

_____ Listlessness

_____ Nervousness

_____ Anxiety

_____ Anger

_____ Excessive sensitivity, defensiveness

_____ Decrease in sense of humor

_____ Family problems

_____ Sensation of lack of control

_____ Difficulty setting priorities or saying "no"

_____ Other (describe)

Behavioral Signals

_____ Change in sleep patterns (too much or too little; difficulty sleeping)

_____ Increased cigarette smoking

_____ Increased alcohol consumption

_____ Change in eating behavior: loss of or increase in appetite

_____ Careless driving, other reckless behavior

_____ Increased television viewing

_____ Shaky hands

_____ Nervous activity: foot tapping, finger tapping, nail biting, pacing

_____ Stuttering or quivering voice

_____ Withdrawing, avoiding people

_____ Angry outbursts

_____ Crying

_____ Clumsiness

_____ Making mistakes

_____ Work/school absenteeism, lateness, cutting classes

_____ Decreased productivity, difficulty in classes

_____ Procrastination

_____ Other (describe)

Now answer the following questions:

1. Can you relate any of the symptoms you checked to your stress cycle, especially your stress response? Do you notice any of the symptoms getting worse when you are under excess stress? Do any of your symptoms make stress worse?

2. Does stress seem to play a role in any other health problems not listed here?

3. Which symptoms concern you the most? List two or three that you might like to focus on during this course.

4. Describe any ideas of how you might begin to address these problems. Include things you have already tried that seemed to help.

◼ STUDENT STRESS

JIM'S STRESS SYMPTOMS

Jim enrolled in a stress management course at a nearby community college at his doctor's suggestion when he was diagnosed with borderline hypertension. Jim's father had also developed hypertension, and had died in his 70s after suffering a debilitating stroke, so Jim was very concerned when he received his diagnosis. Jim owned and managed a successful small plumbing business, was 52 years old, and was married with two young children.

"It's too easy to lose sight of what's really important when you're stressed out," he told his stress management instructor after the third class. "Last week I knew I was almost over the edge. I was so wound up about everything I couldn't sleep. We've had two weddings in the family over the last month, and these parties have been a great excuse to drink too much, so of course my blood pressure's back up. The worst part is that I blew up at my 9-year-old for spilling his milk at the table one night, and he burst into tears. My anger was way out of line. That boy is the sweetest kid that ever lived, and he shouldn't have to wear the scars of my stress."

When Jim went through the Stress Symptom Checklist he was surprised at how many symptoms he checked off and how many he had been taking for granted as part of life. He often experienced tight muscles in his neck and chest, and sometimes he felt like he couldn't take a deep breath. The psychological symptoms that concerned him most were irritability and impatience, family problems, and feeling out of control. As he told his instructor, he was especially worried about the effect his stress might have on his family, particularly his children. Of course, his earlier diagnosis of hypertension still weighed heavily on Jim's mind.

Jim considered the questions at the end of the self-assessment. "All these seem to get worse when I'm under stress, and that makes me feel more stressed than ever!" Jim decided to focus on the hypertension and irritability as the two most problematic symptoms. "I've already got a good handle on the hypertension," he told himself. "I'm changing my diet, exercising more, and I've already lost 5 pounds. Come to think of it, on days when I work out I'm more patient with the kids, too. Maybe I can be a true Type A and do two things at once: take the kids out on the weekend and do something active. We'll have fun together, I'll get some exercise, and feel more relaxed."

STRESS AND HEALTH: A FEW MORE THOUGHTS

Research on stress and health appears to justify what many health care workers have observed since the beginning of time: a person's thoughts, feeling, moods, and beliefs influence his or her level of health and the course of disease. Especially harmful appear to be feelings of helplessness, hopelessness, fear, and social isolation—all common to the experience of being sick, and especially to being a patient in a hospital. Preliminary research suggests that psychotherapy and the use of stress management techniques such as positive imagery, relaxation exercises, and humor can help patients feel better and may even have a positive influence on the course of some diseases (Cousins, 1989, 1991; Ornstein & Sobel, 1987). This is not to say that you can live forever by thinking the right thoughts! Also to be avoided is the idea that sick people are somehow "responsible" for their illnesses and would recover if they could only muster up the right attitude. Writer K. B. Alster has noted, "When health is . . . believed to be a state achievable by right acts and sufficient will, illness ceases to be a misfortune and is taken as evidence of moral failing" (Alster, 1989, p. 123). Sickness and death are a part of life, much of which is outside our direct control.

Writer Susan Sontag, who underwent treatment for breast cancer, wrote, "Theories that diseases are caused by mental states and can be cured by will-power are always an index of how much is not understood about the physical terrain of a disease" (Sontag, 1978, p. 55). In the early 1900s, people used to believe strongly in a tuberculosis personality type; now we consider tuberculosis the result of an infectious agent that thrives and spreads in crowded, dark conditions. As our understanding of diseases such as cancer and AIDS grows, the role played by stress, emotional factors, and personality variables will become further illuminated.

Learning to increase your stress resistance will not guarantee you freedom from physical disease and discomfort; it may not give you one more day of life. It will not erase every worry and fear, but it will probably make you healthier in the long run and certainly happier in your daily life. As you learn to see problems more clearly and regulate your stress response more effectively, you will be better able to weather life's storms and see life's changes as challenges to be met rather than obstacles to be overcome.

SUMMARY

1. Prolonged or intense periods of stress contribute to a variety of stress-related disorders.
2. The impact of stress on health is mediated by a number of genetic, environmental, and personality variables.
3. Stressors experienced as uncontrollable and with an outcome that is expected to be negative are more likely to result in stress-related illnesses than stressors that are perceived as controllable and positive.
4. The nature of one's emotional response to stress has a strong effect on how stress affects one's health. Feelings of anger, fear, alienation, isolation, helplessness, and hopelessness are associated with an increased risk of stress-related disorders.
5. Atherosclerosis begins early in life, and its rate of progression is influenced by a number of factors. The four most important factors under our control include sendentary lifestyle, blood pressure, blood cholesterol level, and cigarette smoking.
6. Stress contributes to cardiovascular disease in many ways:
   a. Stress may increase levels of blood cholesterol.
   b. Stress leads to hemoconcentration and faster clotting rates.
   c. Stress contributes to hypertension.
   d. Stress hormones damage the lining of the arteries.
   e. Stress makes unhealthy arteries more prone to spasms that occlude blood flow.
   f. Stress may cause irregular heartbeats.
   g. Stress may lead to maladaptive changes in sleep, eating, and exercise habits as well as increased use of harmful substances such as caffeine, alcohol, tobacco, and other drugs.
   h. Stress may increase artery disease by interacting with personality variables such as hostility, feelings of isolation, and low self-esteem as well as emotions such as anger and depression.

7. The gastrointestinal system is especially vulnerable to chronic stress. While most digestive disorders are not caused solely by stress, stress exacerbates these disorders. Examples are gum disease, esophageal spasms, ulcers, nervous stomach and nausea, irritable bowel syndrome, chronic constipation, chronic diarrhea, and inflammatory bowel disease.

8. When muscles are continually braced for action, painful muscle tension may result and existing musculoskeletal problems may worsen. Areas most vulnerable to such problems include muscles of the jaw, head, neck, shoulders, and back.

9. People are more accident prone during periods of stress.

10. Psychoneuroimmunology is the study of the interrelationships of the nervous, endocrine, and immune systems.

11. Stress may decrease immune response and make people more vulnerable to viral and bacterial infections, such as colds and herpes outbreaks (in people already infected with the virus). Stress may exacerbate allergies and autoimmune disorders.

12. Stress management may enhance the efficacy of medical treatment for some types of cancer.

13. While stress does not cause AIDS, stress management techniques may slow the progression of the disease in its early stages and help people with HIV infection cope with the disease.

14. Mental health is a continuum that runs from optimal mental wellness down to extreme mental illness. Increasing your stress resistance helps you move toward optimal mental wellness.

15. Stress contributes to a number of psychological disorders, including depression, anxiety, phobias, and addictions.

16. While one's stress response contributes to one's state of health, it is only one of many factors. We must avoid the notion that sick people are "responsible" for their illness and would recover if only they could muster up the right attitude and manage their stress more effectively.

17. Type A behavior pattern is characterized by hard-driving competitiveness, hostility, a sense of time urgency, and a concern with achievement and acquisition of objects. Cardiologists Friedman and Rosenman found an association between Type A behavior pattern and artery disease, probably caused by chronic overactivation of the fight-or-flight response. Their research in the 1950s began the scientific investigation of the connections between personality variables, stress response, and health.

REFERENCES

Alamada, SJ, AB Zonderman, RB Shekelle, et al. Neuroticism and cynicism and risk of death in middle-aged men: The Western Electric Study. *Psychosomatic Medicine* 53: 165–175, 1991.

Achterberg, J. *Imagery in Healing: Shamanism and Modern Medicine*. Boston: Shambala, 1985.

Alster, KB. *The Holistic Health Movement*. Tuscaloosa, AL: University of Alabama Press, 1989.

Barrett, DC, MA Chesney, J Burack, et al. Letter to the editor. *Journal of the American Medical Association* 271: 1743, 1994.

Brannon, L and J Feist. *Health Psychology: An Introduction to Behavior and Health*. Belmont, CA: Wadsworth, 1992.

Burack, J, DC Barrett, RD Stall, et al. Depressive symptoms and CD4 lymphocyte decline among HIV-infected men. *Journal of the American Medical Association* 270: 1568–2573, 1993.

Cassileth, BR, EJ Lusk, DS Miller, LL Brown, and C Miller. Psychological correlates of survival in advanced malignant disease? *New England Journal of Medicine* 312: 1551–1555, 1985.

Chesney, MA. Social isolation, depression, and heart disease: Research on women broadens the agenda. *Psychosomatic Medicine* 55: 434–435, 1993.

Cohen, S, DAJ Tyrrell, and AP Smith. Psychological stress and susceptibility to the common cold. *New England Journal of Medicine* 325: 606–612, 1991.

Cooper, CL. Personality, life stress and cancerous disease. S Fisher and J Reason, (eds). *Handbook of Life Stress, Cognition and Health.* New York: John Wiley and Sons, 1988.

Cousins, N. Anatomy of an illness (as perceived by the patient). A Monat and RS Lazarus (eds). *Stress and Coping.* New York: Columbia University Press, 1991.

Cousins, N. *Head First: The Biology of Hope.* New York: EP Dutton, 1989.

Cox, T. Psychobiological factors in stress and health. S Fisher and J Reason (eds). *Handbook of Life Stress, Cognition and Health.* New York: John Wiley and Sons, 1988.

Dantzer, R, and KW Kelley. Stress and immunity: An integrated view of relationships between the brain and the immune system. *Life Sciences* 44: 1995–2008, 1989.

Davis, M, ER Eshelman, and M McKay. *The Relaxation and Stress Reduction Workbook.* Oakland, CA: New Harbinger Press, 1995.

Dembroski, TM, JM MacDougall, PT Costa, et al. Components of hostility as predictors of sudden death and myocardial infarction in the multiple risk factor intervention trial. *Psychosomatic Medicine* 51: 514–522, 1989.

Dimsdale, JE, and JA Herd. Variability of plasma lipids in response to emotional arousal. *Psychosomatic Medicine* 44: 413–430, 1982.

Edlin, G, and E Golanty. *Health and Wellness: A Holistic Approach.* Boston: Jones and Bartlett, 1996.

Eysenck, HJ. Personality and stress as causal factors in cancer and coronary heart disease. MP Janisse (ed). *Individual Differences, Stress, and Health Psychology.* New York: Springer-Verlag, 1988, 129–145.

Fackelmann, KA, and J Raloff. Psychological stress linked to cancer. *Science News* 144(13): 196, Sept 25, 1993.

Farber, EM, and L Nall. Psoriasis: A stress-related disease. *Cutis* 51: 322–326, 1993.

Fawzy, FI, NW Fawzy, CS Hyun, et al. Malignant melanoma: Effects of an early structured psychiatric intervention, coping, and affective state on recurrence and survival 6 years later. *Archives of General Psychiatry* 50: 681–689, 1993.

Fisher, S. Life stress, control strategies and the risk of disease: A psychobiological model. S Fisher and J Reason (eds). *Handbook of Life Stress, Cognition and Health.* New York: John Wiley and Sons, 1988.

Fitzpatrick, R, S Newman, R Lamb, and M Shipley. Helplessness and control in rheumatoid arthritis. *International Journal of Health Sciences* 1: 17–23, 1990.

Frank, JD. *Holistic medicine: A view from the fence.* Johns Hopkins Medical Journal 149(6): 222–227, 1981.

Frasure-Smith, N, and R Prince. Longterm follow-up of the Ischemic Heart Disease Life Stress Monitoring Program. *Psychosomatic Medicine* 51: 485–513, 1989.

Frasure-Smith, N. In-hospital symptoms of psychological stress as predictors of long-term outcome after acute myocardial infarction in men. *American Journal of Cardiology* 67: 121–127, 1991.

Frasure-Smith, N, F Lesperance, and M Talajic. Depression following myocardial infarction: Impact on 6-month survival. *Journal of the American Medical Association* 270: 1819–1825, 1993.

Friedman, M, and RH Rosenman. *Type A Behavior and Your Heart.* Greenwich, CN: Fawcett, 1974.

Futterman, AD, ME Kemeny, D Shapiro, and JL Fahey. Immunological and physiological changes associated with induced positive and negative mood. *Psychosomatic Medicine* 56: 499–511, 1994.

Glaser, R, and JK Kiecolt-Glaser. Stress-associated immune modulation and its implications for reactivation of latent herpesviruses. R Glaser and J Jones (eds). *Human Herpesvirus Infections.* New York: Dekker, 1994.

Goetsch, VL, B VanDorsten, LA Pbert, IH Ullrich, and RA Yeater. Acute effects of laboratory stress on blood glucose in noninsulin-dependent diabetes. *Psychosomatic Medicine* 55: 492–496, 1993.

Green, RG. Stress and accidents. *Aviation, Space, and Environmental Medicine* 56: 638–641, 1985.

Greenberg, JS. *Comprehensive Stress Management.* Dubuque, IA: Wm C Brown, 1996.

Greer, S, T Morris, KW Pettingale, et al. Psychological response to breast cancer and 15-yr outcome. *Lancet* 336: 49–50, 1990.

Grossarth-Maticek, R, DT Kanazir, P Schmidt, et al. Psychosomatic factors in the process of cancerogenesis: Theoretical models and empirical results. *Psychotherapy and Psychosomatics* 38: 284–302, 1982.

Hambrecht, R, J Niebauer, C Marburger, et al. Various intensities of leisure time physical activity in patients with coronary artery disease: Effects on cardiorespiratory fitness and progression of atherosclerotic lesions. *Journal of American College of Cardiology* 22: 468–467, 1993.

Haskell, WL, EL Alderman, JM Fair, et al. Effects of intensive multiple risk factor reduction on coronary atherosclerosis and clinical cardiac events in men and women with coronary artery disease: The Stanford Coronary Risk Intervention Project (SCRIP). *Circulation* 88: 975–990, 1994.

Honzak, R, A Veselkova, and Z Poslusny. Personality traits and neurohumoral stress response in healthy young sportsmen. *Activitas Nervosa Superior* 31: 100–102, 1989.

Ironson, G, A Friedman, N Klimas, et al. Distress, denial, and low adherence to behavioral interventions predict faster disease progression in gay men infected with human immunodeficiency virus. *International Journal of Behavioral Medicine* 1: 90–105, 1994.

Julkunen, J, R Salonen, GA Kaplan, MA Chesney, and JT Salonen. Hostility and the progression of carotid atherosclerosis. *Psychosomatic Medicine* 56: 519–525, 1994.

Kiecolt-Glaser, JK, and R Glaser. Psychoneuroimmunology and health consequences: Data and shared mechanisms. *Psychosomatic Medicine* 57: 269–274, 1995.

Kiyohara, Y, K Ueda, Y Hasuo, et al. Hematocrit as a risk factor of cerebral infarction: Long-term prospective population survey in a Japanese rural community. *Stroke* 17:687–692, 1986.

Kobasa, SC. Stressful life events, personality, and health: An inquiry into hardiness. *Journal of Personality and Social Psychology* 37: 1–11, 1979.

Lahad, A, AD Malter, AO Berg, and RA Deyo. The effectiveness of four interventions for the prevention of low back pain. *Journal of the American Medical Association* 272: 1286–1291, 1994.

Manuck, SB, AL Marsland, JR Kaplan, and JK Williams. The pathogenicity of behavior and its neuroendocrine mediation: An example from coronary artery disease. *Psychosomatic Medicine* 57: 275–283, 1995.

Markovitz, JH, KA Matthews, WB Kannel, JL Cobb, and RB D'Agostino. Psychological predictors of hypertension in the Framingham study: Is there tension in hypertension? *Journal of the American Medical Association* 270: 2439–2443, 1993.

Maseri, A. Coronary vasoconstriction: visible and invisible. *New England Journal of Medicine* 325: 1579–80, 1991 (Nov 28).

Mattiasson, I, F Lindgarde, JA Nilsson, and T Theorell. Threat of unemployment and cardiovascular risk factors: Longitudinal study of quality of sleep and serum cholesterol concentrations in men threatened with redundancy. *British Medical Journal* 301: 461–466, 1990.

Mills, PJ, CC Berry, JE Dimsdale, MG Ziegler, RA Nelesen, and BP Kennedy. Lymphocyte subset redistribution in response to acute experimental stress: Effects of gender, ethnicity, hypertension, and the sympathetic nervous system. *Brain, Behavior, and Immunity* 9: 61–69, 1995.

Monagan, D. Sudden death. *Discover,* January 1986, 64–71.

Muldoon, MF, EA Bachen, SB Manuck, SR Waldstein, PL Bricker, and JA Bennett. Acute cholesterol responses to mental stress and changes in posture. *Archives of Internal Medicine* 152: 775–780, 1992.

Ornish, D. *Dr. Dean Ornish's Program for Reversing Heart Disease.* New York: Bantam, 1990.

Ornish, D, SE Brown, LW Scherwitz, et al. Can lifestyle changes reverse coronary heart disease: The Lifestyle Heart Trail. *Lancet* 336: 129–133, 1990.

Ornstein, R and D Sobel. *The Healing Brain.* New York: Simon and Schuster, 1987.

Patterson, SM, JS Gottdiener, G Hecht, S Vargot, and DS Krantz. Effects of acute mental stress on serum lipids: Mediating effects of plasma volume. *Psychosomatic Medicine* 55: 525–532, 1993.

Powell, LH, LA Shaker, BA Jones, LV Vaccarino, CE Thoresen, and JR Pattillo. Psychosocial predictors of mortality in 83 women with premature acute myocardial infarction. *Psychosomatic Medicine* 55: 426–433, 1993.

Revicki, DA, and HJ May. Occupational stress, social support, and depression. *Health Psychology* 4: 61–77, 1985.

Rosengren, A, G Tibblin, and L Wilhelmsen. Self-perceived psychological stress and incidence of coronary artery disease in middle-aged men. *American Journal of Cardiology* 68: 1171–1175, 1991.

Rosenman, RH, RJ Brand, CD Jenkins, M Friedman, R Straus and M Wurm. Coronary heart disease in the Western Collaborative Group Study: Final follow-up of 8 1/2 years. *Journal of the American Medical Association* 233: 872–877, 1975.

Sargent, JD. Stress and headaches. L Boldberger and S Breznitz (eds). *Handbook of Stress: Theoretical and Clinical Aspects.* New York: Free Press, 1982.

Scheier, MF, and CS Carver. On the power of positive thinking: The benefits of being optimistic. *Current Directions in Psychological Science* 2: 26–30, 1993.

Scheier, MF, and MW Bridges. Person variables and health: Personality predispositions and acute psychological states as shared determinants for disease. *Psychosomatic Medicine* 57: 255–268, 1995.

Schmale, AH, and H Iker. Hopelessness as a predictor of cervical cancer. *Social Science and Medicine* 5: 95–100, 1971.

Schnall, PL, JE Schwartz, PA Landsbergis, K Warren, and TG Pickering. Relation between job strain, alcohol, and ambulatory blood pressure. *Hypertension* 19: 488–494, 1992.

Schuler, G, R Hambrecht, G Schlierf, et al. Regular exercise and low fat diet: Effects on progression of coronary artery disease. *Curculation* 86: 1–11, 1992.

Schultz, R, J Bookwala, J Knapp, et al. Pessimism and mortality in young and old recurrent cancer patients. Presented at the American Psychosomatic Society, Boston, April 15, 1994.

Selye, H. *The Stress of Life.* New York: McGraw-Hill, 1976.

Shekelle, RB, M Gale, AM Ostfeld, et al. Hostility, risk of coronary heart disease, and mortality. *Psychosomatic Medicine* 45: 109–114, 1983.

Silvestrini, B. The paradoxical stress response: A possible common basis for depression and other conditions. *Journal of Clinical Psychiatry* 51: 6–8, 1990.

Simonton, OC, S Simonton, and J Creighton. *Getting Well Again.* Los Angeles: Tarcher, 1978.

Sontag, S. *Illness as Metaphor.* New York: Farrar, Straus and Giroux, 1978.

Sorlie, PD, MR Garcia-Palmieri, R Costas, and RJ Havlik. Hemotocrit and risk of coronary heart disease: The Puerto Rico Heart Health Program. *American Heart Journal* 101:456–461, 1981.

Spiegel, D, JR Bloom, HC Kraemer, et al. Effect of psychosocial treatment on survival of patients with metastatic breast cancer. *Lancet* 335: 888–901, 1989.

Stoney, CM, KA Matthews, RH McDonald, and CA Johnson. Sex differences in lipid, lipoprotein, cardiovascular, and neuroendocrine responses to acute stress. *Psychophysiology* 25: 645–656, 1988.

Stoyva, J, and C Anderson. A coping-rest model of relaxation and stress management. L Boldberger and S Breznitz (eds). *Handbook of Stress: Theoretical and Clinical Aspects.* New York: The Free Press, 1982.

Strickland, BR. Internal-external control expectancies: From contingency to creativity. *American Psychologist* 44: 1–12, 1989.

Tasner, M. TMJ. *Medical Self-Care*, Nov–Dec 1986, 47–50.

Turkkan, JS, JV Brady, and AH Harris. Animal studies of stressful interactions: A behavioral-physiological overview. L Goldberg and S Breznitz (eds). *Handbook of Stress: Theoretical and Clinical Aspects.* New York: Free Press, 1982.

Weiss, JM. Psychological factors in stress and disease. *Scientific American,* June 1972, 104–113.

Williams, JM, TD Hogan, and MB Andersen. Positive states of mind and athletic injury risk. *Psychosomatic Medicine* 55: 468–472, 1993.

Williams, RB. *The Trusting Heart: Great News about Type A Behavior.* New York: Random House, 1989.

Williams, RB. Neurobiology, cellular and molecular biology, and psychosomatic medicine. *Psychosomatic Medicine* 56: 308–315, 1994.

Wright, L. The Type A behavior pattern and coronary artery disease. A Monat and RS Lazarus (eds). *Stress and Coping.* New York: Columbia University Press, 1991.

Yeung, AC, VI Vekshtein, DS Krantz, JA Vita, TJ Ryan, P Ganz, and AP Selwyn. The effect of atherosclerosis on the vasomotor response of coronary arteries to mental stress. *New England Journal of Medicine* 325: 1551–1556, 1991.

chapter 4

Stress and Your Life

Are we there yet? Most readers opening a book about stress management hope they will learn better ways to manage stress in their own lives. Learning about the psychophysiology of stress is a useful starting place, and you may have already seen examples in your own life. At this point, you understand the general nature of stress and the stress cycle. You know that the stress cycle involves sources of stress that can be real or imaginary as well as a stress response—a total body-mind event that includes thoughts, feelings, behavior, and physical preparation for fight or flight. You have seen how the nervous and endocrine systems orchestrate the fight-or-flight response, and you have studied the many physiological effects that occur as you gear up to deal with a potential threat. You have also seen how chronic stress can disrupt the psychophysiological processes that keep you healthy and how such stress can result in a variety of stress-related disorders. You know that stress and its symptoms are not "all in your mind."

Now it is time to look more closely at stress and your life. In this chapter you will examine your stress cycle from several different angles. You will assess the ways in which you are currently dealing well with stress and the ways in which you would like to improve your coping abilities and stress resistance. You will also set some preliminary goals for improving your ability to manage stress.

SOURCES OF STRESS: LIFE EVENTS

Most of us would agree that there is a relationship between feelings of stress and the events in our lives. Selye's concept of the General Adaptation Syndrome, introduced in Chapter 2, explained Selye's theory that any sort of change required adaptation, which required energy (Selye, 1976). For example, if a professor asks you to meet with her after class, you adapt by rearranging your after-class plans and mentally preparing for the meeting. Such adaptation hopefully takes only a little energy (unless are preparing for a hostile encounter), but even small adaptations add up. Larger events such as moving to a new city, starting college, and ending a relationship take quite a bit of energy. In the 1960s, stress researchers Thomas Holmes and Richard Rahe proposed a questionnaire, the Life Events Scale, also known as the Social Readjustment Rating Scale, as a tool for measuring stress (Holmes & Rahe, 1967). This scale measures stress in terms of Life Change Units (LCUs). The original research of Holmes and Rahe tested the hypothesis

STRESS AND YOU

SELF-ASSESSMENT SURVEY

You are the best expert on the role stress plays in your life. You probably have a fairly good idea about what sorts of things bother you most and whether your stress response is sometimes harmful to your health. You may also realize that you have acquired many stress management skills over the course of your life, though you may not have called them that. The following survey is designed to begin your stress management self-assessment.

Begin by closing your eyes and taking a few minutes to be quiet. Become aware of your body, your breathing, sounds reaching your ears. Observe thoughts coming and going without judgment or control. After a few minutes, open your eyes and answer the following questions. Remember: there are no right or wrong answers, only your true feelings.

Stress Management Self-Assessment Survey

1. How do you personally define *stress?*

2. What are the most problematic sources of stress for you?

3. What are some desirable sources of stress (eustress)?

4. How do you know when you are under stress? List signs and symptoms.

that people who reported more stress as measured by this scale would experience more illness. On the average, this was true. Of people reporting 150 to 199 LCUs in one year, 37 percent became ill during the following year. Subjects who scored 200 to 299 LCUs had a 51 percent illness rate, while 79 percent of those scoring over 300 LCUs got sick. So, more change meant more stress, which meant more illness.

Subsequent research has not always found a strong relationship between scores on the Social Readjustment Rating Scale and illness. This is not surprising, since a given source of stress may vary in stress "content" from person to person. For example, starting college may be a welcome event requiring only a minimum amount of adjustment for one person, while another young person, not really wanting to at-

5. How do you cope with problematic sources of stress? How effective are these strategies? Look for both adaptive and maladaptive strategies.

6. How do you impose stress on yourself? Describe.

7. How do health behaviors such as caffeine, alcohol, exercise, and sleep patterns affect your stress level?

8. How would you describe your current stress level?

_____ Interferes substantially with daily activities

_____ Interferes somewhat with daily activities

_____ Bothers me but does not interfere with activities

_____ A high level but not bothersome

_____ A good balance between stimulation and relaxation

_____ Not aware of any stress

tend college, might approach this change full of resentment, loneliness, and fear. Who is to say exactly how many points that event is worth? Nevertheless, calculating your score on such scales can be useful. We are generally well aware of the major stressors in our lives, but we often underestimate how many potentially stressful minor changes occur on a regular basis and require some adjustment. Understanding how much stress you have experienced during the last year can help you understand your current stress level. Two scales are included here. The first is a life events questionnaire adapted from the Social Readjustment Rating Scale; the second is a special version for college students (Anderson, 1972). Use whichever seems more applicable to you.

STRESS AND YOU

SOCIAL READJUSTMENT RATING SCALE

1. Under "Number of Occurrences" indicate how many times in the past year each of the events has occurred.
2. Multiply the number under the "Scale Value" by the number of occurrences of each event and place the answer under "Your Score."
3. Add the figures under "Your Score" to find your total for the past year.

Life Event	Number of Occurrences	Scale Value	Your Score
Death of spouse	_____	100	_____
Divorce	_____	73	_____
Marital separation from mate	_____	65	_____
Detention in jail or other institution	_____	63	_____
Death of a close family member	_____	63	_____
Major personal injury or illness	_____	53	_____
Marriage	_____	50	_____
Being fired at work	_____	47	_____
Marital reconciliation with mate	_____	45	_____
Retirement from work	_____	45	_____
Major change in the health or behavior of a family member	_____	44	_____
Pregnancy	_____	40	_____
Sexual difficulties	_____	39	_____
Gaining a new family member (e.g., through birth, adoption, oldster moving in, etc.)	_____	39	_____
Major business readjustment (e.g., merger, reorganization, bankruptcy, etc.)	_____	39	_____
Major change in financial state (e.g., a lot worse off or a lot better off than usual)	_____	38	_____
Death of a close friend	_____	37	_____
Changing to a different line of work	_____	36	_____
Major change in the number of arguments with spouse (e.g., either a lot more or a lot less than usual regarding child-rearing, personal habits, etc.)	_____	35	_____
Taking on a mortgage greater than $10,000 (e.g., purchasing a home, business, etc.)	_____	31	_____
Foreclosure on a mortgage or loan	_____	30	_____
Major change in responsibilities at work (e.g., promotion, demotion, lateral transfer)	_____	29	_____

Life Event	Number of Occurrences	Scale Value	Your Score
Son or daughter leaving home (e.g., marriage, attending college, etc.)	____	29	____
Trouble with in-laws	____	29	____
Outstanding personal achievement	____	28	____
Wife begining or ceasing work outside the home	____	26	____
Beginning or ceasing formal schooling	____	26	____
Major change in living conditions (e.g., building a new home, remodeling, deterioration of home or neighborhood)	____	25	____
Revision of personal habits (dress, manners, associations, etc.)	____	24	____
Troubles with the boss	____	23	____
Major change in working hours or conditions	____	20	____
Change in residence	____	20	____
Changing to a new school	____	20	____
Major change in usual type and/or amount of recreation	____	19	____
Major change church actitivities (e.g., a lot more or a lot less than ususal)	____	19	____
Major change in social activities (e.g., clubs, dancing, movies, visiting, etc.)	____	18	____
Taking on a mortgate or loan less than $10,000 (e.g., purchasing a car, TV, freezer, etc.)	____	17	____
Major change in sleeping habits (a lot more or lot less sleep, or change in part of day when asleep)	____	16	____
Major change in number of family get-togethers (e.g., a lot more or a lot less than usual)	____	15	____
Major change in eating habits (a lot more or a lot less food intake, or very different meal hours or surroundings)	____	15	____
Vacation	____	13	____
Christmas	____	12	____
Minor violations of the law (e.g., traffic tickets, jaywalking, disturbing the peace, etc.)	____	11	____
This is your total life change score for the past year			____

Source: Reprinted with permission from *Journal of Psychosomatic Research,* Vol 11, TH Holmes and RH Rahe, Social Readjustment Rating Scale, 1967, Elsevier Science Ltd, Pergamon Imprint, Oxford, England.

STRESS AND YOU

COLLEGE SCHEDULE OF RECENT EXPERIENCE

On the followig scale, indicate the number of times during the last 12 months that each of the following life change events has happened to you. Score your questionnaire by adding up the points for each item checked. Predictive value for point totals are similar to the scales for the previous questionnaire.

First, for the number corresponding to each of the life evets . . . , indicate the number of times (1, 2, 3, etc.) that the particular event has occurred in your life during the past 12 months, then multiply each item by the indicated weight and total the scores.

Life Event	Number of Occurrences	Scale Value	Your Score
1. Entered college.	_____	50	_____
2. Married.	_____	77	_____
3. Had either a lot more or a lot less troubles with your boss.	_____	38	_____
4. Held a job while attending school.	_____	43	_____
5. Experienced the death of a spouse.	_____	87	_____
6. Experienced a major change in sleeping habits (sleeping a lot more or a lot less, or a change in part of the day when asleep).	_____	34	_____
7. Experienced the death of a close family member.	_____	77	_____
8. Experienced a major change in eating habits (a lot more or a lot less food intake, or very different meal hours or surroundings).	_____	30	_____
9. Made a change in or choice of a major field or study.	_____	41	_____
10. Had a revision of your personal habits (friends, dress, manners, associations).	_____	45	_____
11. Experienced the death of a close friend.	_____	68	_____
12. Have been found guilty of minor violations of the law (traffic tickets, jay walking, etc.).	_____	22	_____
13. Have had an outstanding personal achievement.	_____	40	_____
14. Experienced pregnancy, or fathered a pregnancy.	_____	68	_____
15. Had a major change in the health or behavior of a family member.	_____	56	_____
16. Had sexual difficulties.	_____	58	_____
17. Had trouble with in-laws.	_____	42	_____
18. Had a major change in the number of family get-togethers (a lot more or a lot less).	_____	26	_____
19. Had a major change in financial state (a lot worse off or a lot better off than usual).	_____	53	_____
20. Gained a new family member (through birth, adoption, older person moving in, etc.)	_____	50	_____

Life Event	Number of Occurrences	Scale Value	Your Score
21. Changed your residence or living conditions.	_____	42	_____
22. Had a major conflict in or change in values.	_____	50	_____
23. Had a major change in church activities (a lot more or a lot less than usual).	_____	36	_____
24. Had a marital reconciliation with your mate.	_____	58	_____
25. Were fired from work.	_____	62	_____
26. Were divorced.	_____	76	_____
27. Changed to a different line of work	_____	50	_____
28. Had a major change in the number of arguments with spouse (either a lot more or a lot less than usual).	_____	50	_____
29. Had a major change in responsibilities at work (promotion, demotion, lateral transfer).	_____	47	_____
30. Had your spouse begin or cease work outside the home.	_____	41	_____
31. Had a marital separation from your mate.	_____	74	_____
32. Had a major change in usual type and/or amount of recreation.	_____	37	_____
33. Had a major change in the use of drugs (a lot more or a lot less).	_____	52	_____
34. Took a mortgage or loan *less* than $10,000 (purchase of a car, TV, school loan, etc.).	_____	52	_____
35. Had a major personal injury or illness.	_____	65	_____
36. Had a major change in the use of alcohol (a lot more or a lot less).	_____	46	_____
37. Had a major change in social activities.	_____	43	_____
38. Had a major change in the amount of participation in school activities.	_____	38	_____
39. Had a major change in the amount of independence and responsibility (for example: for budgeting time)	_____	49	_____
40. Took a trip or a vacation.	_____	33	_____
41. Were engaged to be married.	_____	54	_____
42. Changed to a new school.	_____	56	_____
43. Changed dating habits.	_____	41	_____
44. Had trouble with school administration (instructors, advisors, class scheduling, etc.).	_____	44	_____
45. Broke or had broken a marital engagement or a steady relationship.	_____	60	_____
46. Had a major change in self-concept or self-awareness.	_____	57	_____
Total life change score			_____

Source: From GE Anderson, "College Schedule of Recent Experience." Unpublished Master's Thesis, 1972. Reprinted with permission of the School of Education, North Dakota State University.

A given situation, such as a family gathering, may vary in stress content from person to person.

THINKING ABOUT YOUR LIFE EVENTS

It is important *not* to regard your questionnaire scores as an indication of a future over which you have no control. Remember that college students tend to score high on these questionnaires, but much of the change associated with being in college is positive for most students and thus less likely to lead to stress-related illness. Nevertheless, adaptation does take energy, and that's the main message here. Pace yourself! Recognize all the change that has taken place in your life during the past year, appreciate all the opportunities that are part of this change, and take it from there. Exert what control you do have. Schedule optional events for slower times. When possible, try not to push too much change into a small time frame. Plan ahead and do what you can to make those small changes as nonintrusive as possible. Recognize times when your LCUs are high and remember that you may be more vulnerable to stress-related illness then, so pay special attention to the habits that keep you healthy, like eating well, exercising, and getting enough sleep (Nespor, 1985). Also remember that many people with high scores do *not* get sick any more frequently than people with lower scores. The next section looks at the characteristics of people who tend to be resistant to stress, and helps you assess your stress resistance.

HARDINESS

In the 1970s, a group of researchers looked at the relationship between LCUs and illness from a new angle (Kobasa, 1979; Kobasa et al., 1982). Why, they asked, did some people who score high on the rating scale *not* get sick? As you remember, research had suggested that almost 80 percent of people scoring over 300 LCUs became ill during the following year. What about the other 20 percent? How were they different? Were there some common traits among people who consistently operated under high levels of stress without suffering from stress-related illness? This research group found that several traits discriminated between people who were stress resistant and those who were more vulnerable to the negative effects of stress. People with these traits were described as having "hardy" personalities. According to this research group, hardy people are characterized by high levels of **commitment, control,** and **challenge.** They feel a sense of *commitment* to themselves, their work, families, and other important values. We've already seen that a sense of *control* has come up in many studies as an important stress buffer. Hardy people see the changes in life as *challenges* to master rather than obstacles to be overcome

STRESS AND YOU

HARDINESS SELF-ASSESSMENT

Write down how much you agree or disagree with the statements below, using the following scale:

0 = strongly disagree   1 = mildly disagree
2 = mildly agree   3 = strongly agree

_____ A. Trying my best at work and school makes a difference.

_____ B. Trusting to fate is sometimes all I can do in a relationship.

_____ C. I often wake up eager to start on the day's projects.

_____ D. Thinking of myself as a free person leads to great frustration and difficulty.

_____ E. I would be willing to sacrifice financial security in my work if something really challenging came along.

_____ F. It bothers me when I have to deviate from the routine or schedule I've set for myself.

_____ G. An average citizen can have an impact on politics.

_____ H. Without the right breaks, it is hard to be successful in my field.

_____ I. I know why I am doing what I'm doing at work or school.

_____ J. Getting close to people puts me at risk of being obligated to them.

_____ K. Encountering new situations is an important priority in my life.

_____ L. I really don't mind when I have nothing to do.

To get your scores for control, commitment, and challenge, write the number of your answer, from 0 to 3, above the letter of each question on the questionnaire. Then add and subtract as shown below.

```
____ + ____ = ____        ____ + ____ = ____        ____ + ____ = ____
  A       G                 C       I                 E       K
           _                         _                         _
____ + ____ = ____        ____ + ____ = ____        ____ + ____ = ____
  B       H                 D       J                 F       L

   Control ____          Commitment ____           Challenge ____
```

____   ____   ____   ____
Control + Commitment + Challenge = Total Hardiness Score

Score	Interpretation
10–18	Hardy personality
0–9	Moderate hardiness
Below 0	Low hardiness

Reprinted with permission of American Health. Copyright 1984 by Suzanne Ouellette Kobasa, Ph.D

[W]ith risk comes excitement, and with acceptance of the challenge comes engagement in life. Then, like a surfer, one can actually be held aloft by the waves and currents that sweep others away. It all depends on how they are perceived.

JEAN HARRIGAN

(Kobasa, 1984). We'll talk more about the concept of hardiness in Chapter 14—and indeed throughout this book. The Hardiness Self-Assessment on the previous page will help give you some idea of how hardy you are.

STRESS AND WELLNESS

Don Ardell is one of the original writers who helped shape the wellness concept in the 1970s. He devised the next questionnaire, which offers a wellness approach to stress assessment, and evaluates your stress/wellness level from your perceptions of possible stressors rather than their occurrence in your life. This test is more applicable to older students since it asks about situations that have yet to become a reality for many younger ones, such as career choice and satisfaction with the decision of whether to have children. It is included here to broaden your understanding of stress as a component of wellness and to give you a useful evaluation of how things are going in various arenas of your life so far.

RELAXATION AND ADAPTIVE COPING

Most people already have a coping and relaxation repertoire, things they enjoy doing that help them unwind and feel good. In Chapter 1 we referred to such activities as palliative coping strategies. Take a closer look at yours by completing the Twenty Pleasures exercise on page 78.

USING PLEASURABLE EXPERIENCES TO COPE

It's important to note that the relaxation value of a given activity can vary greatly depending on your mind-set. For example, a hot bath can be very soothing if you focus on relaxing, but it won't be if you spend your time in the tub worrying about how much work you have to do. Watching television can be either relaxing or stressful. Some items on your list, such as having a drink, may be associated with relaxation but actually be causing stress. Evaluate carefully the relaxation activities you wish to promote as adaptive coping measures.

◆ STRESS AND YOU

THE ARDELL WELLNESS STRESS TEST

Rate your satisfaction with each of the following life areas using the following scale: +3 Ecstatic; +2 Very happy; +1 Mildly happy;   0 Noncommital; −1 Mildly disapproving; −2 Very disapproving; −3 Completely dismayed

_____ 1. Choice of career

_____ 2. Present job/business

_____ 3. Marital status

_____ 4. Primary relationships

_____ 5. Capacity to have fun

_____ 6. Amount of fun experienced in the last month

_____ 7. Financial prospects

_____ 8. Current income level

_____ 9. Spirituality

_____ 10. Level of self-esteem

_____ 11. Prospects for having a positive impact on those who know you and possibly others

_____ 12. Sex life

_____ 13. Body—how it looks and performs

_____ 14. Home life

_____ 15. Life skills and knowledge of issues and facts unrelated to your job or profession

_____ 16. Learned stress management capacities

_____ 17. Nutritional knowledge, attitudes and choices

_____ 18. Ability to recover from disappointments, hurts, setbacks and tragedies

_____ 19. Confidence that you are now at or will in the future come reasonably close to your highest potentials

_____ 20. Achievement of a rounded or balanced quality in your life

_____ 21. Sense that life for you is on an upward curve, getting better and fuller all the time

_____ 22. Level of participation in issues and concerns beyond your immediate interests

_____ 23. Choice whether to parent or not and with the consequences or results of that choice

_____ 24. Role in some kind of "network" of friends, relatives and/or others about whom you care deeply, and who reciprocate that commitment to you

_____ 25. Emotional acceptance of the inescapable reality of aging

Score	Interpretation
+51 to +75	This is a self-actualized person, nearly immune from the ravages of stress. There are few if any challenges likely to untrack him or her from a sense of near total well-being.
+25 to +50	This person has mastered the wellness approach to life and has the capacity to deal creatively and efficiently with events and circumstances.
+1 to +24	This is a wellness-oriented person, with an ability to prosper as a whole person, but he or she should give a bit more attention to optimal health concepts and skill building.
0 to −24	This is a candidate for additional training in how to deal with stress. In this case, the Holmes Index does apply, since a sudden increase in potentially negative events and circumstances could cause a severe emotional setback.
−25 to −50	This person is a candidate for counseling. He or she is either too pessimistic or has severe problems in dealing with stress.
−51 to −75	This is a candidate for major psychological care with virtually no capacity for coping with life's problems.

Source: Reprinted with permission from the *Ardell Wellness Report.* For a sample copy, send a stamped self-addressed envelope to the publisher/editor Don B. Ardell at 9901 Lake Georgia Drive, Orlando, FL 32817.

The notion that all stress makes you sick . . . assumes we're all vulnerable and passive in the face of adversity. But what about human resilience, initiative and creativity? Many come through periods of stress with more physical and mental vigor than they had before.

SUZANNE OUELLETTE KOBASA

 STRESS AND YOU

TWENTY PLEASURES

Make a list of twenty things you love to do. They can be big or little things. Ten of them should be things you can do on a daily or weekly basis. Examples: listening to music, talking to a friend, taking a walk.

1. _____

2. _____

3. _____

4. _____

5. _____

6. _____

7. _____

8. _____

9. _____

10. _____

11. _____

12. _____

13. _____

14. _____

15. _____

16. _____

17. _____

18. _____

19. _____

20. _____

When your list is complete, mark with an X those things you already use for relaxation. Mark with an * those things you would like to use more often for relaxation and managing stress.

DEVELOPING A DEEPER UNDERSTANDING OF YOUR PERSONAL STRESS CYCLE WITH A STRESS LOG

Awareness is the first step to improving your stress resistance. Keeping a stress log is one of the best ways to increase your understanding of your personal stress cycle: what types of stressors cause you to overreact, how you respond to various stressors, how your stress response affects your health and stress level, how effective your coping strategies are, and how your health behavior and lifestyle contribute to your current level of stress.

There are many ways to keep a stress log. You may wish to make copies of the sample stress log page in this chapter, or you may wish to devise a notebook of your own. Notice times when you feel stressed, and take notes as soon as possible on what is causing the stress and how you are responding and coping. It is important to include observations on all components of the stress cycle and to record your observations for at least a week—longer if possible. The components of the stress cycle to observe include the following:

1. *Stressors:* Describe the sources of stress.
2. *Physical response:* What did your body feel while you felt stressed? Examples: tense jaw, pounding heart, upset stomach.
3. *Psychological response:* What thoughts and feelings flashed through your mind as you evaluated and responded to the stressor? Examples: I can't do this. Why am I so stupid? She's impossible.
4. *Coping:* Include actions taken, decisions made, palliative strategies used.
5. *Coping evaluation:* You may wish to evaluate coping strategies *after* the stressor and stressful feelings have passed—maybe even a few days later when you can look back on your stress log notes more objectively. Were you satisfied with your coping response? What worked? How could you cope better next time?
6. *Health behaviors that may have influenced the day's stress level:* Examples include not enough sleep, too much coffee, and good feelings and improved coping following exercise.

◆ **STRESS AND YOU**

STRESS LOG

Date: _____

1. Stressors:

2. Physical response:

3. Thoughts and feelings:

4. Coping strategies:

5. Evaluation of coping:

6. Related health behaviors:

ON YOUR MARK, GET SET . . .
DESIGNING A STRESS MANAGEMENT ACTION PLAN

Stress management is about *intervening* in your stress cycle. It is about changing sources of stress and coping with problems more effectively, changing the way you respond to stressors, and improving your stress resistance by building a meaningful, healthful lifestyle. Where do you go from here? Awareness alone often brings change. Over time, simply observing yourself and your stress cycle as objectively as possible will lead to new ways of coping with and evaluating stressors, and to an im-

STRESS AND YOU

EVALUATING YOUR STRESS LOG

We tend to take our stress cycles for granted. When we record our observations in a stress log and then review what we have written, we often see some surprising patterns. Sometimes it's almost like reading about someone else. Having your stress cycle written down in front of you improves your objectivity. After you have kept your log for several days, reread what you have written and answer the following questions.

1. What situations or thoughts commonly trigger a stress response? Do you notice any patterns?

2. Did your *perception* of a stressor sometimes affect your stress response? Did your thoughts and feelings sometimes make stress worse? Did they sometimes improve your coping ability?

3. Do you notice a pattern in your physical stress response? Is there a particular area of your body that seems to be your stress barometer?

4. What kinds of coping strategies did you use? Did you take direct action as often as possible? Did you tend to avoid problems? What palliative strategies did you use? What was good about your coping methods? How can they be improved?

5. What health behaviors seemed to influence your stress patterns?

provement in your physical and psychological stress response. For example, you may observe that you habitually react to minor hassles by holding your breath and tensing your neck and shoulder muscles. Once you become aware of this response you may be able to intervene before you develop major aches and pains.

Observation can also lead to the formulation of stress management goals. Goals help you set your stress management course. Knowing where you want to go makes it more likely that you will get there. It makes you better able to take advantage of opportunities that present themselves. It improves your ability to make decisions, which in turn improves your stress resistance. Now that you have completed the self-assessment exercises and stress log presented in this chapter, it is time to formulate your stress management goals. Goals work best when they have the following characteristics (Gillespie & Bechtel, 1986):

1. Goals must be as clear and specific as possible. It is frustrating to work toward goals that are vague; you feel like you never get there. Instead of writing "I want to be a better student" try something more specific, such as "I want to organize my time and use my study time more effectively."

▲ ACTION PLAN

STRESS MANAGEMENT ACTION PLAN

Step 1: Write your goals. Take a moment to think about what you have read and observed. Review the material and self-assessments from this chapter and the previous chapters, and then write two or three goals that you would like to work toward during your study of stress management. You may wish to use the form on the facing page.

Step 2: Define several action steps for each goal. Action steps are specific activities that will help you accomplish your goal. They should be something you can and will do right away or in the near future. Let's say you wish to write action steps for the goal, "I want to organize my time and use my study time more effectively." Here are some possible action steps:

a. Read and study the chapter on time management in this book.
b. Outline a study schedule for the next seven days.
c. Organize my study environment to limit distractions.

Step 3: Anticipate roadblocks and mobilize your resources. Behavior change is more likely to be successful if you anticipate the future. What things might keep you from sticking to your plan? By thinking about potential problems ahead of time, you will be prepared to deal with them creatively and continue your progress toward your goals. Here are some potential roadblocks for the action steps outlined above:

a. My friends will distract me when I am trying to study.
b. I'll get frustrated when my study time schedule isn't working.
c. I'm not sure how much time to schedule for things like studying for exams and writing lab reports.

Now, think about how you will deal with the roadblocks and get help accomplishing your goals. What kinds of things will help you stick to your plan? Getting support from family and friends is essential. Maybe there are resources on campus or at work that can help you. Some people promise themselves incentives for sticking to their plan. Possible reinforcements for the action steps outlined above might be the following:

a. Get some of my friends to study at the same times I'll be studying. Then we can all go out for ice cream when we're done.
b. The counseling center offers a time management workshop. Maybe I'll sign up for that. Maybe someone there can help me with my study schedule.
c. I'll talk to some of my professors and friends who have taken the courses I'm in and get their advice on the best way to prepare for exams and use my study time in these classes.

2. Goals must feel reasonable to you. You should feel as though you can make significant progress toward your goals over the next few weeks. Goals that are too lofty or focus on areas you are not yet ready to address encourage procrastination.

3. Goals should represent something you really want for yourself, not something someone has told you to change. If your housemates have complained about your slovenly lifestyle, you must first decide that orderliness

Stress Management Action Plan

Stress management goals:

1.

2.

3.

Possible action steps that will help me move toward these goals:

	Action steps	Roadblocks	Reinforcements
Goal 1: 1.			
2.			
3.			
Goal 2: 1.			
2.			
3.			
Goal 3: 1.			
2.			
3.			

is something you want for yourself, something that will bring benefits to you, before making it one of your stress management goals.

4. The process of working toward your goal must seem worthwhile to you. Change takes time and commitment. See this process as educational. Change will occur more readily if you value the learning experience rather than feel frustration at what you perceive as failure to accomplish your goal.

STUDENT STRESS

STEVE'S STRESS MANAGEMENT ACTION PLAN

Steve was trying to write his Stress Management Action Plan. He thought over all he had read, and he reviewed all the questionnaires he had completed. All along, however, he knew what his first goal would be: to do something about his frequent feelings of anger. The section on hostility and artery disease had really hit home for Steve. His father was a perfect example of a Type A person. "They must have used him for a model when they invented Type A behavior pattern," Steve thought when he read the description in the text. His father had suffered a heart attack in his late 50s, five years ago. The cardiac rehabilitation program his father had attended had emphasized stress management along with other lifestyle changes. Steve's father had changed careers and worked hard to develop a more relaxed approach to life. "I don't want to wait until I have a heart attack to manage my stress," Steve decided. "And the stress that's hurting me the worst is these angry feelings."

Steve had observed that his anger tended to rise when he felt frustrated, when things didn't go the way they were supposed to go and people didn't behave the way they were supposed to behave. When he kept his stress log, he noticed that even things that would seem unimportant later could set him off when they happened. He had blown up at the new student worker at the library who had taken a long time to locate the book Steve had asked for in the reserve section. He stewed his way through every class period in his math course because he had difficulty understanding his professor, who spoke English with a foreign accent. The junior varsity soccer coach seemed to change Steve's playing position every week, and Steve had decided the coach was an idiot.

But Steve was beginning to see that even though all this anger felt "normal" because he was so used to feeling this way, it was not good. In fact, it was probably doing him harm. "Some days I can feel my blood pressure stuck on high," he had noted in his stress log. And so Steve wrote Goal 1: Reduce feelings of anger.

The action steps were more of a problem. Steve knew he couldn't simply will his anger away. Since he had a good relationship with his father and he

CREATING A SUCCESSFUL ACTION PLAN

Successful behavior change occurs when you move slowly. Too much change is stressful because you accumulate more LCUs, right? Slow and steady wins the behavior change race. In the Stress Management Action Plan form, you have room to outline action steps for three goals. This is to give you practice with the Action Step process that is used throughout this book. In real life, you might be more comfortable working on one goal at a time, especially if it is a large and complex one, such as the study schedule example given previously.

Most behavior is learned; therefore, it can be unlearned and replaced with more desirable habits. This is the premise of the wellness model for a self-responsible lifestyle. Stress management is a lifelong journey toward self-actualization and optimal well-being. We are continually formulating and reformulating our goals, observing ourselves, dreaming up action plans for change, and then assessing our progress. It's a never-ending cycle of assessment, intervention, and reassessment. If

knew his father had been dealing with his own anger problems, Steve decided to talk to his dad to see what had helped him. That would be action step 1. What else might help? Steve decided to continue the stress logs for another week, paying special attention to one anger-producing incident each day to try to figure out the thoughts that were setting off the anger. Maybe if he could analyze his thinking, he could short-circuit his habitual angry response.

For his third action step, Steve went back to his list of Twenty Pleasures. He had come up with only 12, but he liked the idea of using something fun for relaxation. He had put several sports on his list, but competitive sports sometimes just got him more riled up. "I always feel terrific after I've ridden my bike for 20 miles or so," he noted. He felt himself relax just remembering that happily tired sense of relaxation that seemed to stay with him for several hours after a good ride.

Once he had listed his action steps, Steve had no trouble completing the rest of the action plan. Here's what it looked like:

Goal 1: Reduce feelings of anger.

Possible action steps that will help me move toward these goals:

Action steps	*Roadblocks*	*Reinforcements*
Goal 1:		
1. Talk to dad	Finding a good time Hard to talk about our feelings	Good connection with dad Hear his good advice
2. Continue stress log for 7 more days	It's a bother No time Resistance to this stuff	Get in touch with thoughts that → anger Feel better with less anger
3. Ride bike 3–4 × a week	Weather? No time	Feels great!

We should treat our anxiety, our pain, our hatred, and passion gently, respectfully, not resisting it, but living with it, making peace with it, penetrating into its nature.

THICH NHAT HANH

we look on this as an onerous chore, we are doomed. If we can remember that wellness is not a destination but a way of traveling, we can create a joyful journey.

SUMMARY

1. To some extent, stress is related to life events. The Social Readjustment Rating Scale measures stress in terms of Life Change Units (LCUs). In general, the higher your LCUs, the greater your likelihood of developing stress-related illness.
2. When experiencing a period of time that requires a great deal of adaptation on your part, exert what control you do have to schedule flexible events at less hectic times.
3. Health behaviors such as eating well, exercising, and getting enough sleep are especially important during high-stress times.
4. Research by Suzanne Kobasa and her colleagues found that of people experiencing a great deal of stress (as measured by LCUs), those with hardiness char-

acteristics became ill less frequently than people without these characteristics. These characteristics include a feeling of *commitment,* a sense of *control,* and the ability to perceive a stressor as a *challenge.*

5. Wellness writers such as Don Ardell emphasize that your *perceptions* of potential stressors have as much impact on your sense of feeling stressed as the stressors themselves.

6. Most people already have many effective ways of reducing feelings of stress, including pleasurable experiences such as talking to friends, going for a walk, or spending time on a favorite hobby or recreational activity.

7. Keeping a stress log for a week or more can increase your understanding of your personal stress cycle.

8. Stress management is about intervening in your stress cycle.

9. Effective goals are clear and specific, feel reasonable to you, represent something you really want for yourself, and seem worth working for.

10. An action plan for behavior change includes action steps (concrete activities you can do) that will help you achieve your goals.

11. Anticipating roadblocks helps to ensure the success of a behavior change program.

REFERENCES

Anderson, GE. College schedule of recent life experience. Unpublished Master's thesis, Department of Education, North Dakota State University, 1972.

Ardell, DB. A wellness alternative to managing stress. *Optimal Health,* May/June 1985, 22–25.

Gillespie, PR, and L Bechtel. *Less Stress in 30 Days.* New York: New American Library, 1986.

Holmes, TH, and RH Rahe. The social readjustment rating scale. *Journal of Psychosomatic Research* 11:213–218, 1967.

Kobasa, SC. Hardiness and health: A prospective study. *Journal of Personality and Social Psychology* 337: 1–11, 1979.

Kobasa, SC, SR Maddi, and S Kahn. Hardiness and health: A prospective study. *Journal of Personality and Social Psychology* 42: 168–177, 1982.

Kobasa, SO. How much stress can you survive? *American Health,* Sept 1984, 64–71.

Nespor, K. Stressful life events: A preventive approach. *International Journal of Psychosomatics* 32: 28–32, 1985.

Selye, H. *The Stress of Life.* New York: McGraw-Hill, 1976.

chapter 5

Coping Strategies and Problem Solving

Many people equate stress management with techniques to reduce sympathetic arousal. People often sign up for stress management programs and classes thinking they will learn some of these techniques, such as muscle relaxation, meditation, and breathing exercises. They hope that by learning to relax they will become more easygoing and less stressed. But as you begin to analyze your individual stress patterns and explore the nature of stress, you'll understand that controlling your stress response is only a small part of the stress management picture. Learning to relax is not the most direct or effective way to cope with an inconsiderate neighbor, a difficult employer, homesickness, or trouble starting a project. This chapter begins with an overview of coping strategies, then moves on to the coping strategy of choice: problem solving.

HOW DO YOU COPE WITH STRESS?

Did you notice a pattern in your coping responses when you kept a daily stress log? Although the way we cope with any particular stressor depends to some extent on the type of stressor we are confronting, some general patterns emerge over time. Coping strategies may be categorized in several ways (Amirkhan, 1990; Folkman et al., 1986). Here are a few of the most common strategies.

1. *Problem solving.* Problem solving might be considered the "fight" part of the fight-or-flight response and is probably the most frequently used coping style. It is also the topic of this chapter. When a problem arises, we look for solutions. If your car runs out of gas, you look for a way to get some. If the music is too loud next door, you ask the neighbor to turn it down. If your stress log coping responses tended to include phrases like "tried to solve the problem," "tried to plan a course of action," or "looked for possible solutions," you probably have a problem-solving coping style. (Amirkhan, 1990; Folkman et al., 1986). Problem solving in which an optimal solution is carefully and creatively sought is almost always an adaptive process.

2. *Confrontation.* Some people act first, plan later, and use an aggressive, confrontational style of coping. Such a tack may get them their own way in the short run but create more stress down the road. If your stress log coping responses included phrases like "I refused to give in and fought for what I wanted," "got angry at person causing the problem," or "tried something I didn't think would work but at least that was better than doing nothing," your coping techniques may be confrontive (Amirkhan, 1990; Folkman et al., 1986). Some people mistake confrontive coping for problem solving because both directly address the stressor. The difference is that problem solving involves more planning and negotiation, and it generally has a more satisfactory outcome than confrontive coping. (Note: Carefully and deliberately delivered confrontive coping is appropriate in certain situations. We discuss this further in Chapter 8, Communication Skills.)

3. *Avoidance.* The "flight" option. Avoidance certainly has its time and place. Staying out of the way of a whining friend who dominates conversation might be the best option at times. But avoidance usually works only temporarily. Ignoring that paper due at the end of the week reduces sympathetic arousal, and you may enjoy the time you spend watching television, reading magazines, or sleeping instead of writing it. But what happens when the deadline finally arrives? (Is that why they call it a deadline?) Stress log phrases that indicate an avoidance coping strategy include statements such as the following: "avoided being with people," "tried to make myself feel better by eating, drinking, using drugs," and "ignored the problem" (Amirkhan, 1990; Folkman et al., 1986).

Avoidance behavior often goes along with feelings of helplessness, a sense that one has little control over stress. We've already seen that a sense of control helps to reduce feelings of stress. People who feel that stress is simply bad luck and has little to do with their behavior may just go along with things, trying to escape from problems without really looking for solutions. An avoidance coping style can lead to self-destructive denial. An example is the student who avoids studying and brushes off bad grades as bad luck. She never sees herself as the problem, instead blaming the course, the school, the teachers. A lack of ability to face and solve problems can also lead to the need for a "quick fix" approach and an addiction to drugs, alcohol, food, or anything that will help the person temporarily avoid dealing with problems (Clum & Febbraro, 1994; Elliot et al., 1990; Haaga et al., 1995; Passino et al., 1993).

Avoidance should not be confused with assertively saying "no" to unnecessary requests, such as serving on a committee you don't have the time or interest for. Deciding to say no in certain situations is a very productive problem-solving and time management technique.

4. *Seeking social support.* Most people need human contact in times of stress. We turn to people for help in solving problems, and we turn to them for comfort. We tell friends about our problems and look for sympathy and understanding. We are relieved to talk to others who may have had a similar problem. Seeking social support in a constructive fashion combined with problem-solving strategies is associated with increased stress resistance. Indeed, seeking social support can enhance the effectiveness of problem solving (Winstead et al., 1992; Yang & Clum, 1994). Phrases in your stress log like "asked a friend for advice" and "talked to someone about the situation" indicate seeking social support as a coping strategy (Amirkhan, 1990; Folkman et al., 1986).

Seeking social support is not always an adaptive coping style, however. When our conversations with friends sound more like complaining than constructive problem solving, seeking social support may become counterproductive. Indeed, many people have stories of friends who become a source of stress with their constant complaints and problems. These friends tend to dominate the conversation, keep the focus on themselves and their troubles, and stop by unannounced—eventually becoming unwelcome.

Getting a friend's perspective can help you define a problem and find a solution.

5. *Positive reappraisal.* Sometimes people cope with stress by changing the way they see the stressful situation. Phrases like "tried to see the stressor as a positive challenge," "realized I was blowing the problem out of proportion," and "told myself I could do it" typify positive reappraisal (Amirkhan, 1990; Brack et al., 1992; Folkman et al., 1986; MacNair & Elliot, 1992).

6. *Accepting responsibility.* If the source of stress is something you feel you have caused, such as time pressure due to prior procrastination, you might cope by accepting responsibility. Once you have accepted responsibility for the stressor, you might resolve your feelings of stress by promising yourself you will not procrastinate next time, apologizing to others involved in the project.

7. *Other adaptive palliative techniques.* Palliative techniques help us feel better. They release tension and relieve emotional distress. The avoidance coping strategy mentioned above is a *maladaptive* form of palliative coping. Palliative coping is adaptive when you have done what you can to solve the problem but still need to unwind. It does not interfere with your direct coping efforts. In fact, by reducing feelings of stress, palliative coping can enhance your problem-solving ability.

Coping patterns are influenced by many different factors (Amirkhan, 1994; Blanchard-Fields et al., 1995; Fontana & Palfai, 1994; Lazarus & Folkman, 1984; Nakano, 1991); they have evolved over your lifetime as you received feedback from your attempts to cope with problems. Coping always involves many thoughts and actions, some aimed at solving problems and others used for alleviating emotional distress (Epstein & Meier, 1989; Folkman et al., 1986). You use different coping strategies for different stressors and more than one strategy for a given situation. Self-observation, especially keeping a stress log, can help you identify general coping patterns and give you some sense of your own coping style. Review your stress logs and see which coping strategies you use most frequently. You may find the Coping Strategies Worksheet helpful; it is explained in the Stress and You box.

◆ STRESS AND YOU

COPING STRATEGIES WORKSHEET

Look through your stress logs and categorize your coping strategies. List examples in these categories:

Problem solving: _____

_____

_____

Confrontive: _____

_____

_____

Avoidance: _____

_____

_____

Seeking social support: _____

_____

_____

Positive reappraisal: _____

_____

_____

PROBLEM SOLVING: COPING STRATEGY OF CHOICE

There is no right or wrong coping method, only what works best for you in a given situation. However, problem solving is usually a good way to begin. Research in coping strategies has found that problem solving is the most frequently cited method for coping with stress (Matheny et al., 1986). In one study, 170 adult volunteers were asked how they coped with recent stressful situations (Folkman et al., 1986). These volunteers also evaluated their satisfaction with the situation outcome. Situation outcomes were judged satisfactory if the source of stress was resolved in a manner satisfactory to the volunteer or if his or her subjective feelings of stress were reduced. The two coping strategies consistently associated with satisfactory outcomes were problem solving and positive reappraisal. Other researchers have found similar results (Bhagat et al., 1991 MacNair & Elliott, 1992).

Accepting responsibility: _____

_____

_____

Other adaptive palliative techniques: _____

_____

_____

Other: _____

_____

_____

After you have reviewed the coping strategies you chose during the stress log period, answer the following questions:

1. How often did you chose problem solving over avoidance?

2. Which coping strategies were most effective? Least effective?

3. In which situations would you cope differently now?

The ability to solve problems is a fundamental life skill. Feeling that one has a poor ability to solve problems has been associated with stress and depression (D'Zurrilla & Sheedy 1991; Elliott et al., 1991; Fonagy et al., 1994; Fremouw et al., 1993; Lakey 1988; Mraz & Runco, 1994; Nezu & Ronan, 1988; Quamma & Greenberg, 1994; Rich & Bonner, 1987; Wierzbicki, 1984); training in problem-solving techniques has been found to reduce depression and improve stress resistance, self-esteem, and life satisfaction (Blakemore et al., 1993; Cull, 1991; D'Zurrilla, 1990; Green & Ollendick, 1993; Heaney et al., 1993; Kirkham, 1993; Nezu et al, 1989; Nezu & D'Zurrilla, 1989.). The problem-solving process is especially useful when you have been stuck in a problematic situation for some time and your old habitual solutions are not working.

Life is a series of problems. Do we want to moan about them or solve them?

SCOTT PECK

▶ STRESS RESEARCH

Richard Lazarus: *The Complex Nature of Stress*

Since the 1960s, psychologist Richard Lazarus has led one of the most productive stress research teams. He and his colleagues have developed and tested comprehensive research models of stress and coping that strive to take into account the complexity of the human psyche. Lazarus entered the field of stress research critical of existing definitions of stress, such as that of Selye, which defined stress as a general physical response (see page 28). Lazarus also noted that research such as that of Holmes and Rahe (see page 67), which defined and measured stress in terms of stressors, is able to capture only a small part of the stress picture. He and his colleagues have tried to establish a more comprehensive definition of stress and to develop and refine the measurement of stress and coping skills.

Richard Lazarus and his colleagues have defined psychological stress as a result of a transaction between the person and the environment that is perceived by the person as taxing his or her resources (Lazarus, 1984). In this definition, environment includes all the elements in one's surroundings: other people, organizations, school and job responsibilities, and snarling dogs, to name a few. Lazarus's definition emphasizes the importance of our interpretation or appraisal of the stressor. A given event, such as attending a party, may or may not be perceived as stressful; it depends on your point of view. A person's interpretation of an event has more influence on his or her physiological response than does the actual event itself. The emotional response to a stressor is determined by the nature of the appraisal. The model of the stress cycle presented in this book is adapted from Lazarus's definition.

Lazarus and his collegues have also been interested in the coping process. Lazarus and Folkman have defined coping as "constantly changing cognitive and behavioral efforts to manage specific external and/or internal demands that are appraised as taxing or exceeding the resources of the person" (Folkman et al., 1986, p. 993) Cognition refers to thinking and includes mental processes such as thinking perception, problem solving, memory, and creativity. As we cope, we adjust our thinking and behavior to deal with the situation's stressful demands.

Many psychologists have supported Lazarus's models of stress and coping. The studies that look at physiological response and life events are certainly valuable, and recording blood pressure or total points on a Life Events Scale are generally easier to do than figuring out what people are thinking. However, many stress researchers agree that you can't ignore that difficult-to-describe "black box": the human brain.

PROBLEM SOLVING, STRESS MANAGEMENT, AND STRESS RESISTANCE

Think about the stress cycle from the first chapter. Problem solving has a similar cycle. The problem is the stressor, and we cope by attempting to solve the problem. Thomas J. D'Zurrilla, one of the leading researchers in problem solving training, has defined **problem solving** as the "process by which a person attempts to identify, discover, or invent effective or adaptive coping responses for specific problematic situations encountered in everyday living . . ." (D'Zurrilla, 1990, p. 333). A *problem* is "a life situation that demands a response for effective and adaptive functioning but for which no effective or adaptive response is immediately apparent or available . . ." (D'Zurrilla 1990, p. 333). Sound like stress? Problems may be any size and involve any number of people. They may be personal, interpersonal, family conflicts, or larger community issues. A *solution* is "a coping response . . . that is produced by the problem-solving process and is aimed at altering a problematic situation, and/or one's own emotional reactions to it, so that it is no longer perceived as a problem, while at the same time maximizing other positive consequences and minimizing negative consequences" (D'Zurrilla, 1990, p. 333)

Problem solving is stress management at its best. It encourages us to consider all components of our personal stress cycles as well as our values and goals, and invites us to take advantage of our personal strengths and resources (Feather, 1995). The problem-solving process is adaptable to an endless variety of problems and personalities. In a sense, stress management (and the rest of this book) is information designed to enlarge your problem-solving repertoire.

As we improve our ability to solve problems, our stress resistance increases in several ways. Defining and working through problems gives us a sense of *control*. Although problem solving does not mean we gain absolute control over a problem, it helps us exert what control we do have and choose our best options. Even if a problem is not completely solved, we still feel better for giving it our best shot. An important part of the problem-solving process is learning to evaluate problems in a way that is productive and furthers our search for solutions (Adams, 1986; Estrada et al., 1994; Jacoby, 1993; Kahn & Leon, 1994; Mumford et al., 1993; Tallman et al., 1993). As we improve our ability to evaluate problems, we become better able to view them as *challenges* rather than as obstacles and stressors. Recall the concept of hardiness from Chapter 4. Both a sense of control and the tendency to view stressors as challenges are components of a hardy, or stress-resistant personality (Kobasa et al., 1980).

IMPROVING YOUR PROBLEM-SOLVING ABILITY: PROBLEM ORIENTATION

The problem-solving process is really nothing new or mysterious. We do it every day! Basically, it consists of defining a problem and evaluating your alternatives to come up with the best solution. But perhaps the most important part of problem solving is the way in which you approach a problem. To illustrate this point, consider Jason, whose case study is presented on page 94.

Negative Problem Orientation

Jason's problem-solving ability was compromised because he has a **negative problem orientation.** A negative problem orientation is characterized by several factors (D'Zurrilla, 1990):

1. Having a Tendency to Blame Yourself for the Problem. Blaming tends to block the problem-solving process. Accepting responsibility for stressors can lead to a productive outcome, whereas blaming yourself leads to low self-esteem and doubts about your abilities. This behavior creates stress, which makes it difficult to address problems effectively. The difference between accepting responsibility and blaming yourself is that blaming implies there is something wrong with you while accepting responsibility suggests there is something you can do to improve your ability to cope with a certain situation.

■ STUDENT STRESS

JASON'S PROBLEMS

Jason is beginning his second year in college. Concerned about the cost of education and the size of his college loans, he is trying to complete his degree in three years, a decision that means he must carry a heavy course load. Because he hopes to go to law school, he feels pressured to get good grades and participate in student government and other activities. The only time he really lets go is at parties on the weekend, but his girlfriend complains that lately he drinks too much and is not much fun to talk to or be with. Jason feels like he is always rushing, overextended, and stressed, with no time to relax or even think. He is wondering how he'll make it through the year, let alone through law school. Recently, doubts about his career path have begun to surface, and although he pushes these doubts away, Jason is experiencing a general uneasiness about the way his life is going. He has enrolled in a stress management program that is discussing problem solving this week.

As Jason begins to define his problem, he realizes that he has a lot going on and that he is demanding a lot of himself. He defines his problem as having too much to do in too little time. In his mind's eye he sees himself caught in a whirlpool, and he believes he can stay afloat only by swimming harder. "If I could only get more organized, maybe I would feel more in control," he thinks. When Jason is feeling overloaded, he studies. This makes him feel better temporarily. "At least I am addressing the problem," he thinks. His proposed solutions focus almost entirely on becoming more organized and studying more, since that is what he has always done. He comes up with a few new ideas for streamlining his life and once again feels temporarily more in control. The big questions of his frantic lifestyle and whether his career path is right for him remain unaddressed. They are too overwhelming, and at this point Jason doesn't see them as solvable. He feels that if he were only more organized, the big problem would go away. In Jason's mind, that problem should not be there. He is supposed to be self-assured and goal directed.

Obviously, Jason's "problem solving" will be effective only in the short run. The whirlpool remains, and as Jason continues to struggle in it, stress will take its toll on his physical and mental well-being.

Jason believes that his feeling out of control is somehow his fault. This attitude is counterproductive. When you feel bad about yourself, you approach a problem from a position of weakness and helplessness. When something makes you feel bad, you want to ignore it. Jason's tendency to blame himself for his feelings of stress was one of the reasons he was uncomfortable addressing his uneasiness about the way his life was going.

2. Seeing Problems as Threatening. Perceiving problems as threatening makes you fearful. It's hard to be creative when you are afraid. All problems have some element of threat; that's what makes them problems. But stress-resistant people can also find elements of opportunity and challenge in problems.

One of the most common threats presented by problems is a threat to a person's self-esteem or self-concept. The idea of changing his style or direction was something he could not consider at this point because it threatened his self-concept. Jason's workaholic lifestyle gave him some security and stability.

Calvin and Hobbes   by Bill Watterson

3. Having Little Faith in the Problem-solving Process. Little faith may result from a feeling that a problem is inherently unsolvable or from a belief that one's ability to solve problems is inadequate. Jason was not ready to see that being too busy was a solvable problem. In addition, he may have felt there was nothing he could do to make himself less busy.

4. Needing Instant Answers and Solutions. Most people feel uneasy when the "right" answer is not immediately apparent. Yet it is this very uneasiness that motivates you to solve problems and make changes that over time will help you grow (Peck, 1978). Solving problems takes time: days, weeks, months, and even years. It is an ongoing experiment with no right or wrong answers, only some options that are better than others.

   Jason's strong need for control meant that he had to be "right," and couldn't loosen his grip on his schedule long enough to try something that might help. Getting organized and studying gave him immediate answers and activities that relieved feelings of stress that accompany uncertainty. People who need instant answers and solutions tend to avoid problems or jump on the first solution, which may not be the best solution. Some people try to get someone else to solve problems for them.

Summary. A negative problem orientation leads to negative emotions such as anger, fear, and confusion; these discourage you from dealing effectively with the problem. Avoidance or jumping quickly to a solution, usually the old habitual response that has not been very effective, seem like the only ways to cope.

Positive Problem Orientation

A **positive problem orientation** creates a positive emotional climate for effectively and creatively coping with stress (D'Zurrilla, 1990). To improve your ability to solve problems, try to develop the following characteristics:

1. See Problems as a Fact of Life. Problems are inevitable. They are everywhere, and solving them is something we all do. This understanding allows us to get on with the problem-solving process without getting stuck in the negative emotions generated by self-criticism, or the belief that life is supposed to be problem free. It releases us from thinking that having to cope with problems is somehow not "fair." In *The Road Less Traveled*, M. Scott Peck acknowledges that confronting and solving problems can be a painful process, but "it is in this whole process of meeting and solving problems that life has its meaning. . . . It is only because of problems that we grow mentally and spiritually" (Peck, 1978, p. 16).

2. Develop an Ability to See Problems as Challenges. All problems have both negative and positive elements (Schwartz & Weinberger, 1980). If we focus on the negative, threatening elements, our emotional state will tend to be negative; focusing on potential benefits will decrease distress and enhance our problem-solving ability. With a positive problem orientation you not only see the glass as half full instead of half empty, but you think "Aha! Now there is room for some ice cubes!" People with a positive problem orientation can find opportunities for personal growth or benefit. They believe it is better to try to solve the problem, even if the solution is unsuccessful, than not to try at all.

3. Strengthen Your Belief in Your Ability to Solve Problems. You are more likely to find an answer if you think you can. People with a positive problem orientation will be encouraged to search creatively for solutions. They will also understand that even when solutions cannot be found, the problem-solving process is still valuable because it reduces stress and helps them see the problem in a better light.

4. Understand and Accept the Fact That Solving Problems Takes Time and Effort. Commitment and persistence are vital for increasing your stress resistance and for successful problem solving.

THE PROBLEM-SOLVING PROCESS

It's easier to engage in effective problem solving when you're feeling good; feeling stressed and overwhelmed inhibits your problem-solving ability. Even when there are problems at hand, you can at least approach them at a point in your day when you are apt to be most alert—after some sort of enjoyable break, maybe after your daily workout when you are feeling invigorated and as emotionally distant as possible from the problem you wish to solve, or after you have talked the problem over with a good friend.

There are several ways to approach problem solving (Black, & Frauenknecht, 1990; D'Zurrilla, 1990; McKay et al., 1981; Ostell, 1991) but they all involve four basic steps: (1) define the problem and your response to it, (2) brainstorm possible solutions, (3) evaluate your options and select your solution, and (4) implement and evaluate your solution. It should be no surprise that the best way to improve your ability to solve problems is to practice solving problems. Think about some of the problems you have been having and select one or two to work through as you read this section. (The process that follows has been drawn from the work of D'Zurrilla, 1986, 1990, 1992, and McKay et al., 1981).

1. Define the Problem

Approaching a problem objectively is often difficult because every problem is inherently a mix of the situation and the perceptions we bring to it. When attempting to define and solve a problem, we need to sort out which parts of the problem arise from the situation and which parts involve our perception of the situation and our role in it.

When confronting a problem, we *appraise* it; we decide what it means. Take, for example, an upcoming deadline for a school assignment or project at work. We ex-

Consistency is the hobgoblin of little minds.

RALPH WALDO EMERSON

amine the project to evaluate the demands being placed on us. We look for potential problems. Is there enough information available on this topic? Will there be enough time to do a good job? We also look for possible benefits: can I use some of the research material I collected for a related project? Will it be possible to arrange an interview with a person I would like to work with this summer? Can I study something interesting? Then we evaluate our options for preventing or handling potential difficulties and improving possible benefits. A given project might be appraised in many different ways. To some, it might be just part of the routine. To others, the project might provide attractive opportunities and be perceived as a challenge. But if this project looks daunting, and we are unsure that our abilities can cope with the project's demands, we feel stressed. As an interesting note, some research suggests that the way we view potential problems and our abilities to solve them are more closely related to how stressed we feel than our actual ability to solve problems (D'Zurrilla & Sheedy, 1991).

Sometimes a lack of information is the source of stress. A project becomes less stressful when you ask your teacher or boss to clarify the project's requirements. If you are not sure you are on the right track, run your ideas by the teacher or supervisor and get some help in planning your direction.

Problems must be solvable. In real life, some problems may be very big—divorce, starting college, career change, or the birth of a child. Solving something as big as a major career change can seem overwhelming, but even the biggest problems can be reduced to a series of smaller problems for which we can find solutions. Let's say you feel stressed about starting college. Smaller problems that are a component of this big problem might be difficulty meeting new people, trouble deciding what courses to take, and not knowing how to deal with new financial concerns. As you select problems to practice with, start with the ones that are of a manageable size and that you feel you can find some solutions for.

Defining the problem involves describing the details of the problem situation, defining your response to the problem, defining specific goals, and reappraising the problem. Are you ready?

PROBLEM DESCRIPTION: *Student Worksheet*

Begin by describing the problem. What happens? Where and when does it occur? Who is involved?

Why does it happen?

Now describe your role in the problem situation. What do you do and how do you feel?

(Continued)

What are your problem-solving goals? How do want this situation, or your response to it, to change so that it is no longer a problem?

How is this problem a threat? What are you afraid of?

What are the opportunities?

How much time and effort are you willing to commit to solving this problem?

Now that you have spent some time thinking about and describing the problem, have you learned anything new? Use the information you have written and your new insights to complete the following statements:

The real problem is not _____.

The real problem is _____.

Let's take a look at how Jason might have benefited from the problem-solving process presented in his stress management program.

JASON'S PROBLEM DESCRIPTION

Begin by describing the problem. What happens? Where and when does it occur? Who is involved?
I feel stressed almost all the time. There's too much to do in too little time. I'm always struggling to keep up. I can't relax anymore, and I feel like I'll be this busy forever. Really, the only time I don't feel quite so stressed is when I am doing my work. Otherwise, the feeling is with me all the time and everywhere: in my room, when I'm trying to sleep at night, in my classes, even when I am with friends or at a party. All that work is always nagging at the back of my mind. Who is involved? Mostly me, but I get some pressure from my parents—they've always wanted me to be a lawyer. My girlfriend and I have been arguing a lot lately, and that just makes me feel worse.

Why does it happen?
I've got too much going on. I'm trying to graduate in three years so I can save money. I have to get good grades and get into a good law school so I can get a good job. I've got a lot of pressure on me to do well.

Now describe your role in the problem situation. What do you do and how do you feel?
I study all the time to gain some control over all this work. But sometimes I waste study time worrying about the future or going over the same stuff again because I'm having trouble concentrating. I feel anxious and worried that I'm not doing enough. Sometimes I wonder whether I'm even doing the right thing, wanting to be a lawyer. I worry I'm not cut out for all this hard work. But I've come this far and I hate to think I've wasted all this time. Mostly I'm too busy to stop and think about it. I just worry. I think I've forgotten how to relax.

What are your problem-solving goals? How do want this situation, or your response to it, to change so that it is no longer a problem?

1. Be on top of my work so I feel in control of things.
2. Have more time to relax and enjoy myself.

How is this problem a threat? What are you afraid of?
I'm afraid I'm doing the wrong thing. Sometimes I feel like I don't know who I am or what I want anymore. I used to always feel certain about everything. I also feel like this constant stress is bad for me. My dad had a heart attack when he was 55 and he says that stress did it.

What are the opportunities?
Opportunities? I guess this questioning could be good for me—strengthen my resolve, help me understand myself better. I know my educational experience is an opportunity. I'm learning a lot. I wish I had more time to enjoy my classes. I suppose I'm also learning how to organize my time, although I think I could do better with this.

How much time and effort are you willing to commit to solving this problem?
Part of me says I'm too busy to spend time on this problem, but part of me thinks I'd better do something soon so it doesn't get worse. I can't keep living this way forever.

Now that you have spent some time thinking about and describing the problem, have you learned anything new? Use the information you have written and your new insights to complete the following statements:

The real problem is not _____being busy_____.

The real problem is ___feeling unsure of myself___.

The real problem is not ___having no time to relax___.

The real problem is ___being unable to relax___.

2. Brainstorm Possible Solutions

Here's a chance to be creative. Most of us solve problems by quickly evaluating a few obvious alternatives without stopping to consider a wider range of possibilities. After you have described the problem, your response, and your goals, take some time to write down any and all possible solutions that pop into your mind and might help you achieve your goals for the situation. Suspend judgment. You will evaluate these alternatives later. Brainstorming means giving free rein to the creative part of your brain. Let the images and ideas flow. An idea that seems crazy

Imagination is more important than knowledge, for knowledge is limited whereas imagination embraces the entire world, stimulating progress giving birth to evolution.

ALBERT EINSTEIN

may stimulate a solution that works. Ask yourself how other people would cope with this situation. What would a friend of the opposite gender do? What would your mother do? How would you solve this problem if you were 80 years old? An army general? A millionaire? Could more information be helpful? Include on your list ways you will gather more information. The more ideas you get, the better. Don't stop writing until you have a very long list.

Take a break. Then read your list. Any new ideas? Can you improve on any of the ones already written? The alternatives you have come up with should be general ones. Leave the specific plan until later. Logical thinking interferes with brainstorming.

POSSIBLE SOLUTIONS: *Student Worksheet*

Goal A. _____

1. _____

2. _____

3. _____

4. _____

5. _____

6. _____

7. _____

8. _____

9. _____

10. _____

Goal B. _____

1. _____

2. _____

3. _____

4. _____

5. _____

6. _____

7. _____

8. _____

9. _____

10. _____

Here are some of Jason's ideas.

JASON'S POSSIBLE SOLUTIONS

Goal A. Feel more in control and less worried, feel more sure of myself.

1. Ask a fortune teller what I should do.
2. Study harder.
3. Go to summer school so I don't have to take so many classes next semester.
4. Ask my parents for advice.
5. Ask a career counselor at the career development office for some advice.
6. Drop out of school and become a ski bum.
7. Come to the time management classes in my stress management program to learn how to manage my time better.
8. Take a year off to earn some money; then come back the next year.
9. Take out more loans and go to school an extra year so I don't have to take so many classes at once.
10. Quit student government.

Goal B. Make time to relax, and spend the time relaxing instead of worrying.

1. Attend time management sessions mentioned for first goal.
2. Schedule racquetball twice a week with Bob.
3. Do something besides go to parties on Saturday night. They're getting boring and I always drink too much.
4. Go see a movie with Sara.
5. Take a hot tub.
6. Read something fun for half an hour before I go to bed.
7. Play basketball with the Sunday afternoon group.
8. Join the outing club and get off campus.
9. Ride my bike more.
10. Take at least one weekend day a month to do nothing but have fun.

3. Evaluate Your Options and Select Your Solutions

Now you can be logical while trying to maintain some creativity. Examine the consequences of the various alternatives listed. Consider effectiveness in resolving the problem—how you would feel about the solution. Ask whether each solution would feel right to you. You may wish to begin by crossing out solutions that are clearly unreasonable to you, either because they are impossible or too risky. Mull over the remaining strategies and combine strategies when possible. Then pick three that seem most promising. Evaluate the positive and negative consequences that might result from each solution. Consider the effects each strategy would have on your life, the people in your life, and your relationships with them. Think about both short- and long-term effects.

EVALUATING ALTERNATIVES: *Student Worksheet*

Alternative 1: _____

Pros   **Cons**

_____   _____

_____   _____

_____   _____

_____   _____

Alternative 2: _____

Pros   **Cons**

_____   _____

_____   _____

_____   _____

_____   _____

Alternative 3: _____

Pros   **Cons**

_____   _____

_____   _____

_____   _____

_____   _____

JASON'S EVALUATION OF ALTERNATIVES

Here are some of Jason's alternatives for his first goal, which was "Feel more in control and less worried, feel more sure of myself."

Alternative 1: Ask a career counselor for some advice.

Pros	Cons
It's free.	It will take time.
It might help me feel more sure of myself.	It might make me more confused.
	What if I decide not to be a lawyer?

Alternative 2: Attend time management classes.

Pros	Cons
They're free.	It will take time.
They might help me feel better organized.	I'm afraid they might encourage me to get busier than ever.

Alternative 3: Ask my parents for advice.

Pros	Cons
I am close to my parents and like talking to them.	They'll probably just say what they've always said and encourage me to keep doing what I'm doing.
	We'll get into an argument if I disagree.

Jason decided it was time to face the big questions that appeared to be the true source of his anxiety: Did he really want to be a lawyer? If so, might there be a better and less hectic way to prepare for this career? After completing the problem-solving process, he decided to get some advice from the career counselor and attend the time management classes before speaking to his parents. He was pleased to find that the time management classes helped him to define his lifetime goals and did not simply suggest that he squeeze more work into less time. Jason also added some of his relaxation alternatives to his schedule. Although his alternatives took some time away from his studying and he was still very busy, he began to feel more sure of his direction and less anxious.

4. Implement and Then Evaluate Your Solutions

Without this step, the problem-solving process only creates more stress. One way to put your solutions into action is to list specific, concrete steps you will take to put your solutions into action. For the alternative "Ask a career counselor for some advice," action steps might be these:

1. Ask whether any of my friends have done this and if so, do they recommend a particular counselor.
2. Stop by the career development office and schedule an appointment.

Many alternatives are more difficult than this to implement. Let's say you have decided to try to make some new friends. What would be some specific activities you could do to make friends? Possibilities might include these:

1. Join a cycling club so I will meet other people who like to bicycle.
2. Make a list of people I know but would like to know better. Invite some of them to do something with me:

    Call Karen this evening and invite her to have lunch with me sometime this week.

    Invite Patty and Brock over for dinner this Saturday.

    Ask Michael and Robert if they want to go to the music festival this weekend.

Solution implementation also involves monitoring and evaluating the success of your problem solving. Keeping some sort of journal is often helpful when you are dealing with especially difficult problems. You might use worksheets, such as the ones in this chapter, and then keep notes on the effectiveness of your solutions. If your solutions are not working or you are having too much difficulty implement-

◆ STRESS AND YOU

Problem-Solving Worksheets

Problem Description

Begin by describing the problem. What happens? Where and when does it occur? Who is involved?

Why does it happen?

Now describe your role in the problem situation. What do you do and how do you feel?

What are your problem-solving goals? How do want this situation, or your response to it, to change so that it is no longer a problem?

How is this problem a threat? What are you afraid of?

What are the opportunities?

How much time and effort are you willing to commit to solving this problem?

Now that you have spent some time thinking about and describing the problem, have you learned anything new? Use the information you have written and your new insights to complete the following statements:

The real problem is not _____ .

The real problem is _____.

When you are ready, select two of your problem-solving goals from above and brainstorm possible solutions that will help you reach those goals. Please refer to the more complete directions given earlier in this chapter for more information.

Possible Solutions

Goal A. _____

1. _____

2. _____

3. _____

4. _____

5. _____

6. _____

7. _____

8. _____

9. _____

10. _____

Goal B. _____

1. _____

2. _____

3. _____

4. _____

5. _____

6. _____

7. _____

8. _____

(Continued)

STRESS AND YOU   *(Continued)*

9. _____

10. _____

Evaluating Alternatives

Select the three alternatives you feel would be most helpful and look at the pros and cons to come up with your final plan of action.

Alternative 1: _____

Pros	**Cons**
_____	_____
_____	_____
_____	_____
_____	_____

Alternative 2: _____

Pros	**Cons**
_____	_____
_____	_____
_____	_____
_____	_____

---

ing them, go back to the beginning. Redefine the problem, brainstorm some more, and try some new alternatives.

What if nothing works? Some problems are just too big for an individual to resolve them alone. Professional guidance can be enormously helpful in such situations. A therapist or other counselor may be able to help you generate more solutions to try, or at least give you some direction in reappraising the situation and feeling better about it.

SERENITY, COURAGE, AND WISDOM

God grant me the serenity to accept the things I cannot change, the courage to change the things I can, and the wisdom to know the difference.

Most readers are familiar with the serenity prayer. It embodies some of the best possible stress management and problem-solving advice: "God grant me the serenity to accept the things I cannot change, the courage to change the things I can, and the wisdom to know the difference."

Successful coping with stressful events requires the ability to deal simultaneously with the emotional discomfort induced by stress (find serenity) and effectively with the sources of stress. Attempting change takes courage, because truly

Alternative 3: _____

Pros   **Cons**

_____   _____

_____   _____

_____   _____

_____   _____

Final Action Plan

Now describe your final action plan, and how you will implement and evaluate your solution(s):

_____

_____

_____

_____

_____

_____

_____

_____

effective coping often involves delaying immediate gratification for more meaningful rewards in the future (Peck, 1978; Rosenbaum, 1989). It also requires taking risks, trying out new behaviors, and breaking out of your habitual routines (Adams, 1986). Habits are very comfortable and protective; without them daily life would be a constant chaotic struggle. But your environment is constantly changing, and change requires creative adaptation. Your habitual responses may not work. For example, the way you coped with assignments in high school may not be effective for handling a college workload. A nonassertive coping style might work while you are a student but make you an ineffective manager. Habitual patterns reduce risk and ambiguity; they help you feel secure. You know what to expect, even if the outcome is not what you want. Creativity and change require a leap into the unknown and attitudes that enable you to tolerate a certain amount of risk and ambiguity. When you try a new way of solving a problem, you do not know how well it will work. But such is life. And such is stress management. The answers are not always easy.

Problem-solving practice will help you get to know yourself better as you become more effective at coping directly with sources of stress. Students often find that the greatest change in their problem-solving ability is the way they describe and appraise problems. Before learning problem-solving techniques, many of them tend to jump right into brainstorming solutions, attempting to solve their first impression of the problem. Stress management students grow to understand that time spent defining and understanding the problem and their role in it pay an enormous dividend. It helps them cultivate the wisdom to know the difference.

SUMMARY

1. Common coping strategies include:
   a. problem-solving
   b. confrontation
   c. avoidance
   d. seeking social support
   e. positive reappraisal
   f. accepting responsibility
   g. other adaptive palliative techniques
2. Coping always involves many thoughts and actions, some aimed at solving problems and others used for alleviating emotional distress.
3. Problem-solving is the most frequently used method for coping with stress.
4. Problem-solving increases stress resistance because it gives you a sense of control and encourages you to view problems as challenges rather than obstacles or stressors.
5. The most important part of solving problems is developing a positive problem orientation. A positive problem orientation allows you to take a broad, creative view of the problem, and enables you to take the time to come up with possible solutions.
6. A negative problem orientation is a common cause of poor problem-solving ability, because it generates negative emotions that get in the way of effective coping.
7. People with a positive problem orientation see that problems are a fact of life and don't waste time assigning blame or fretting that life is "unfair" because it is full of problems.
8. People with a positive problem orientation try to see problems as challenges and even opportunities, a mind-set that is more conducive to problem solving than an attitude of worry and fear.
9. People with a positive problem orientation believe in the value of problem solving. Although not all problems can be solved, problem solving is still valuable because it reduces stress and helps you achieve a better understanding of the problem. Belief in the value of problem solving helps you endure periods of uncertainty and delayed gratification.
10. Problem solving has four basic steps:
    a. Define the problem and your response to it
    b. Brainstorm possible solutions
    c. Evaluate your options and select your solution
    d. Implement and evaluate your solution
11. It's important to approach a problem with a holistic perspective, using both your creative and logical abilities. Brainstorming is done most effectively with the creative, intuitive part of your brain whereas evaluating your options requires a more logical approach.
12. Richard Lazarus and his colleagues have developed comprehensive models of stress and coping that emphasize the importance of one's interpretation or appraisal of a stressor.

REFERENCES

Adams, JL. *The Care and Feeding of Ideas: A Guide to Encouraging Creativity.* Reading, MA: Addison-Wesley, 1986.

Amirkhan, JH. A factor analytically derived measure of coping: The coping strategy indicator. *Journal of Personality and Social Psychology* 59: 1066–1074, 1990.

Amirkhan, JH. Seeking person-related predictors of coping: Exploratory analyses. *European Journal of Personality* 8: 13–30, 1994.

Bhagat, RS, SM Allie, and DL Ford, Jr. Organizational stress, personal life stress and symptoms of life strains: An inquiry into the moderating role of styles of coping. PL Perrewe (ed). Handbook of job stress (Special issue). *Journal of Social Behavior and Personality* 6: 163–184, 1991.

Black, DR, and M Frauenknecht. A primary prevention problem-solving model for adolescent stress management. JH Humphrey (ed). *Human Stress: Current Selected Research* (Vol 4, pp 89–110). New York: AMS, 1990.

Blakemore, B, S Shindler, and R. Conte. A problem solving training program for parents of children with attention deficit hyperactivity disorder. *Canadian Journal of School Psychology* 9: 66–85, 1993.

Blanchard-Fields, F, HC Jahnke, and C Camp. Age differences in problem-solving style: The role of emotional salience. *Psychology and Aging* 10: 173–180, 1995.

Brack, G, L LaClave, and AS Wyatt. The relationship of problem solving and reframing to stress and depression in female college students. *Journal of College Student Development* 33: 124–131, 1992.

Clum, GA, and GAR Febbraro. Stress, social support, and problem-solving appraisal/skills: Prediction of suicide severity within a college sample. *Journal of Psychopathology and Behavioral Assessment* 16: 69–83, 1994.

Cull, A. Staff support in medical oncology: A problem-solving approach. *Psychology and Health* 5: 129–136, 1991.

D'Zurrilla, TJ. *Problem-solving therapy: A social competence approach to clinical intervention.* New York: Springer Publishing, 1986.

D'Zurrilla, TJ. Problem-solving training for effective stress management and prevention. *Journal of Cognitive Psychotherapy* 4: 327–354, 1990.

D'Zurrilla, TJ. The Problem-Solving Self-Monitoring Method-Revised (PSSM-R). Unpublished document. Department of Psychology, State University of New York at Stony Brook, 1992.

D'Zurrilla, TJ, and CF Sheedy. Relation between social problem-solving ability and subsequent level of psychological stress in college students. *Journal of Personality and Social Psychology* 61: 841–846, 1991.

Elliott, TR, F Godshall, JR Shrout, and TE Witty. Problem-solving appraisal, self-reported study habits, and performance of academically at-risk college students. *Journal of Counseling Psychology* 37: 203–207, 1990.

Elliott, TR, FJ Godshall, SM Herrick, TE Witty, and M. Spruell. Problem-solving appraisal and psychological adjustment following spinal cord injury. *Cognitive Therapy and Research* 15: 387–398, 1991.

Epstein, S, and P Meier. Constructive thinking: A broad coping variable with specific components. *Journal of Personality and Social Psychology* 57: 332–350, 1989.

Estrada, CA, AM Isen, and MJ Young. Positive affect improves creative problem solving and influences reported source of practice satisfaction in physicians. *Motivation and Emotion* 18: 285–299, 1994.

Feather, NT. Values, valences, and choices: The influence of values on the perceived attractiveness and choice of alternatives. *Journal of Personality and Social Psychology* 68: 1135–1151, 1995.

Fetsch, RJ. The predicament-problem continuum: Dealing with stressors outside our control. *Journal of Counseling and Development* 7: 192–193, 1992.

Folkman, S, RS Lazarus, C Dunkel-Schetter, A DeLongis, and RJ Gruen. Dynamics of a stressful encounter: Cognitive appraisal, coping, and encounter outcomes. *Journal of Personality and Social Psychology* 50: 992–1003, 1986.

Fonagy, P, M Steel, H Steele, A Higgitt, et al. The theory and practice of resilience. *Journal of Child Psychology and Psychiatry and Allied Disciplines* 35: 231–257, 1994.

Fontana, AM, and TG Palfai. Psychosocial factors in premenstrual dysphoria: Stressors, appraisal, and coping processes. *Journal of Psychosomatic Research* 38: 557–567, 1994.

Fremouw, W, T Callahan, and J Kashden. Adolescent suicidal risk: Psychological, problem-solving and environmental factors. *Suicide and Life-Threatening Behavior* 23: 46–54, 1993.

Greene, RW, and TH Ollendick. Evaluation of a multidimensional program for sixth-graders in transition from elementary to middle school. *Journal of Community Psychology* 21: 162–176, 1993.

Haaga, DAF, JA Fine, DR Terrill, BL Steward, and AT Beck. Social problem-solving deficits, dependency, and depressive symptoms. *Cognitive Therapy and Research* 19: 147–158, 1995.

Heaney, CA, BA Israel, SJ Schurman, EA Baker, et al. Industrial relations, worksite stress reduction, and employee well-being: A participatory action research investigation. *Journal of Organizational Behavior* 14: 495–510, 1993.

Jacoby, R. "The miserable hath no other medicine, but only hope": Some conceptual considerations on hope and stress. *Stress Medicine* 9: 61–69, 1993.

Kahn, PM, and GR Leon. Group climate and individual functioning in an all-women Antarctic expedition team. *Environment and Behavior* 26: 669–697, 1994.

Kirkham, MA. Two-year follow-up of skills training with mothers of children with disabilities. *American Journal on Mental Retardation* 97: 509–520, 1993.

Kobasa, SC, SR Maddi, and S Kahn. Hardiness and health: A prospective study. *Journal of Personality and Social Psychology* 42: 168–177, 1980.

Lakey, B. Self-esteem, control beliefs, and cognitive problem-solving skill as risk factors in the development of subsequent dysphoria. *Cognitive Therapy and Research* 12: 409–420, 1988.

Lazarus, RS, and S Folkman. *Stress, Appraisal, and Coping.* New York: Springer, 1984.

MacNair, RR, and TR Elliott. Self-perceived problem-solving ability, stress appraisal and coping over time. *Journal of Research in Personality* 26: 150–164, 1992.

Matheny, K, D Aycock, J Pugh, W Curlette, and K Cannella. Stress coping: A qualitative and quantitative synthesis with implications for treatment. *The Counseling Psychologist* 14: 499–549, 1986.

McKay, M, M Davis, and P Fanning. *Thoughts and Feelings: The Art of Cognitive Stress Intervention.* Richmond, CA: New Harbinger Publications, 1981.

Mraz, W, and MA Runco. Suicide ideation and creative problem solving. *Suicide and Life-Threatening Behavior* 24: 38–47, 1994.

Mumford, MD, WA Baughman, DP Costanza, CE Uhlman, et al. Developing creative capacities: Implications of cognitive processing models. *Roeper Review* 16: 16–21, 1993.

Nakano, K. Coping strategies and psychological symptoms in a Japanese sample. *Journal of Clinical Psychology* 47: 346–350, 1991.

Nezu, AM, CM Nezu, and MG Perri. *Problem-solving Therapy for Depression: Theory, Research, and Clinical Guidelines.* New York: Wiley, 1989.

Nezu, AM, and TJ D'Zurrilla. Social problem solving and negative affective conditions. PC Kendall & D Watson (eds). *Anxiety and Depression: Distinctive and Overlapping Features.* New York: Academic Press, 1989.

Nezu, AM, and GF Ronan. Social problem solving as a moderator of stress-related depressive symptoms: A prospective analysis. *Journal of Counseling Psychology* 35: 134–138, 1988.

Ostell, A. Coping, problem solving and stress: A framework for intervention strategies. *British Journal of Medical Psychology* 64: 11–24, 1991.

Passino, AW, TL Whitman, JG Borkowski, CJ Schellenbach, et al. Personal adjustment during pregnancy and adolescent parenting. *Adolescence* 28: 97–122, 1993.

Peck, MS. *The Road Less Traveled.* New York: Simon and Schuster, 1978.

Quamma, JP, and MT Greenberg. Children's experience of life stress: The role of family social support and social problem-solving skills as protective factors. *Journal of Clinical Child Psychology* 23: 295–305, 1994.

Rich, AR, and RL Bonner. Interpersonal moderators of depression among college students. *Journal of College Student Personnel* 28: 337–342, 1987.

Rosenbaum, M. Self-control under stress: The role of learned resourcefulness. *Advances in Behaviour Research and Therapy* 11: 249–258, 1989.

Schwartz, GE, and DA Weinberger. Patterns of emotional responses to affective situations: Relations among happiness, sadness, anger, fear, depression, and anxiety. *Motivation and Emotion* 4: 175–190, 1980.

Tallman, I, RK Leik, LN Gray, and MC Stafford. A theory of problem-solving behavior. *Social Psychology Quarterly* 56: 157–177, 1993.

Wierzbicki, M. Social skills deficits and subsequent depressed mood in students. *Personality and Social Psychology Bulletin* 10: 605–610, 1984.

Winstead, BA, VJ Derlega, RJ Lewis, J Sanchez-Hucles, and E Clarke. Friendship, social interaction, and coping with stress. *Communication Research* 19: 193–211, 1992.

Yang, B, and GA Clum. Life stress, social support, and problem-solving skills predictive of depressive symptoms, hopelessness, and suicide ideation in an Asian student population: A test of a model. *Suicide and Life-Threatening Behavior* 24: 127–139, 1994.

chapter 6

Time Management Part 1: Clarifying Values, Making Decisions, and Setting Goals

"I feel like I'm always working. I don't think I can remember how to relax."

"I came to college to study social work because helping people makes me feel good. But my course work and my internship don't make me feel like I'm helping anyone, except the system. I wonder what I'm doing here."

"I'm so busy doing what everyone else wants me to do I never get a chance to do what I want to do."

"My life is so hectic I feel totally out of control."

"I work better under pressure, but I also get stressed out from doing everything at the last minute."

"When I have a lot to do I get paralyzed. I waste a lot of time worrying about how it will all get done and trying to decide what to do next."

Many students come to stress management workshops and classes (if they can find the time!) because of the stress they experience from feeling out of control, hurried, and pushed, and from running frantically just to stay in place. These students find that time management is one of the most valuable topics for helping them gain a sense of control of their lives and to feel more confident in their ability to solve problems and make decisions.

This book presents material on time management in two parts. Part 1, this chapter, may be thought of as the larger picture. It includes information on values clarification, decision making, and goal setting, which are the first steps in getting control of your time. The next chapter is Part 2 and focuses on the practical details of organization, study skills, and dealing with procrastination.

TIME MANAGEMENT VERSUS EFFICIENCY

To many people, the term *time management* implies learning to become more efficient at doing what they are already supposed to be doing, to accomplish more work in less time. Visions of workaholics keeping one eye constantly on the clock, making endless lists of lists, compiling minute-by-minute schedules, and busily organizing everything and everyone do not present a very attractive answer to stress. Creating efficient workaholics is *not* the goal of time management (Richards, 1987)! People who are overorganized, always busy, and constantly preoccupied with getting something done are usually neither stress resistant nor personally fulfilled. And they are usually not much fun, either.

Time management is about planning your course in life. This plan is a rough outline of where you want to go and how you plan to travel. It has been said that life is what happens while you are making other plans. How true! Life is full of surprises, but your travel plan allows you to adapt and take advantage of the opportunities and grow from the challenges.

Time management is about living a meaningful and fulfilling life and enjoying each moment as much as possible. Time management teaches you to balance multiple priorities and to use your time well. The information presented in this chapter will help you clarify your values and goals so that you can make better decisions about how to use your time. The next chapter will help you improve your ability to create realistic schedules, eliminate low priority activities, and make room for activities that help you reach your important goals. In these ways, better time management will increase your stress resistance (Britton & Tesser, 1991; King, Winett, & Lovett, 1986; Lang, 1992; Lee, Bobko, Earley, & Locke, 1991; Macan, Shahani, Dipboye, & Phillips, 1990; Schuler, 1979).

> *A wise Man should order his Designs, and set all his interests in their proper Places: This Order is often confounded by a foolish Greediness, which, while it puts us upon pursuing so many several Things at once, that in Eagerness for Matters of less consideration, we grasp at Trifles, and let go Things of greater value.*
>
> R. LA ROCHEFOUCAULD, DUC DE

CHARTING YOUR COURSE: WHY TIME MANAGEMENT IS ABOUT CLARIFYING VALUES, MAKING DECISIONS, AND SETTING GOALS

A life may be seen as a journey, a story, a flow, and a process. Life is time, a series of moments strung together like pearls on a necklace. Time is the medium through which you create your life. And moment by moment you interact with your environment, including the people in your life, and make countless decisions about how to "spend" your time. You decide what to think about, where to go, what to do.

Clarifying your values, making decisions, and setting goals are ways in which you can exert personal control and chart your course in life. Many writers have likened life to a canoe trip down the river. You cannot change the river, but you can navigate its course with greater or lesser skill. Some decisions take you down a smooth, flowing course while others get you hung up in the shallows. Sometimes you run into rapids that require sharp attention. Your values and goals are the tools with which you navigate your course down this river of life. This image is helpful when you are considering the nature of "control" in life, because you actually have little or no control over many things. While this observation may appear discouraging, it also emphasizes the importance of maximizing the control you do have.

VALUES CLARIFICATION

The term **values clarification** is a new one to many students. Values are the rules that guide your life. Values may be classified into two broad categories: moral and

Life is time, a series of moments strung together like dewdrops on a spider's web. These individual moments create the pattern of a person's life.

nonmoral values (McKay, Davis, & Fanning, 1981). Moral values define right and wrong, good and evil. They are the voice of your conscience, the ethical foundation for forming judgments and making decisions. Believing you should tell the truth, keep your promises, and help people who are in trouble are examples of moral values. Nonmoral values describe what you find desirable or undesirable rather than right or wrong (McKay et al., 1981). They reflect personal preferences. You might value hiking in the woods over a walk in town, going to a party over going to a movie, wearing sneakers over wearing dress shoes. Values clarification is the process of defining and evaluating your values and understanding the influence they have on your decisions.

Why values clarification? Don't most people know what they value? Not always. Most people are clear about some of the fundamentals, but they are often unclear about what they value in at least a few areas. In addition, moral values are sometimes in conflict with nonmoral values, and sometimes nonmoral values are in conflict with other nonmoral values: you want different things at the same time and must decide which one you value more highly. For example, you might want a career that is prestigious and pays well, but at the same time you might want to have a lot of free time to travel or write a book. You probably won't find a career that fulfills both values at the same time. (If you do, please drop us a line.) So, to resolve your career path, you must decide which value is more important to you.

Values clarification is a process of self-discovery. It is not so much about having defined your values as it is about the *process* of defining your values and using them to guide your decision making and behavior.

VALUES AND STRESS

Values can both alleviate and cause stress. They alleviate stress when they help you solve problems. They cause stress when they are inappropriate or conflicting. Inappropriate and conflicting values create stress because they block effective decision making and coping.

An inappropriate value is one that does not work because it is unrealistic, confused, or irrational. If you believe being very, very thin is important, you may spend your life trying to lose weight and being obsessed about your body size. In this case, valuing extreme thinness is unrealistic and irrational (not to mention unhealthy!) and creates a great deal of stress. If you value expensive cars and feel that your image and reputation depend on what kind of vehicle you drive, but you must drop out of college to buy and maintain the right car, your unrealistic values interfere with more important long-term goals.

Conflicting values often surface when we are having difficulty making a decision or are trying to choose between alternative solutions to a problem. Choosing a major is a difficult decision for many students. Do you choose (1) the field you have found most interesting? (2) the one that is easiest? (3) the one your parents recommended? (4) the one that will lead to a lucrative career? (5) the one that will give you job security? Here are some of the values represented by these options:

Choice 1: *Choose an interesting major.*
Values:
    You believe college courses should be interesting.
    You believe college should help you find out what you're interested in.

Choice 2: *Choose an easy major.*
Values:
    You should choose a major in which you will get good grades.
    You should study something that won't tie up all your time and energy so you can participate in extracurricular activities.

Choice 3: *Choose a major recommended by your parents.*
Values:
    You value your parents' advice.
    You want to please your parents.
    You must please your parents because you value their financial contribution to your college education.

Choice 4: *Choose a major that will help you find a lucrative career.*
Values:
    You want to make enough money.
    You want to be rich.
    You want to be able to repay your college loans.

Choice 5: *Choose a major that will help you find a job that offers security.*
Values:
    You value security.

How do you make a decision when solution options represent conflicting values? When you examine the values underlying your alternatives, the choice often becomes a little easier. Usually you choose the solution that is congruent with the most important values.

NO VALUES AND STRESS

Children grow up adopting the values of their parents, which they then question and revise as they come into adolescence and adulthood. Indeed, this process occurs throughout life. When some values are rejected as meaningless, others must take their place. But sometimes people reject their old values and are unable to come up with a new set. Social critics have argued that much of today's stress is the result of the devaluing of values. G.W. Morgan (1969) writes that during the 1960s, American popular culture promoted "do your own thing," a path suggesting that values are subjective and merely represent the likes and dislikes of an individual rather than deeper moral beliefs. Without values, argues Morgan, "there is emptiness, boredom, and desperation." Individuals and society suffer when old values are thrown off without appropriate replacements.

Some critics have accused stress management programs of treating stress as somehow separate from the rest of life, solvable with a few deep breathing exercises (Beck, 1986). But as you have seen from our model of the stress cycle and our work so far, the way we cope with stress and solve problems is a reflection of our basic personalities. Each of us is unique, and we each develop our own coping styles. While stress management programs are often offered in a seemingly value-free context to accommodate audience diversity, for each of us, personal values determine how we cope with stress.

VALUES CLARIFICATION INCREASES YOUR STRESS RESISTANCE

Clarification and Control

Control. That word has been coming up a lot. You've seen that a perceived lack of control causes stress while a sense of control increases your resistance to the negative effects of stress. Control is an important component of hardiness. The problem-solving approach to coping with stress presented in the last chapter is designed to increase your sense of control over stressors. Values clarification and goal setting do the same. In fact, they are important components of problem solving. You seek to solve problems in ways that further your goals and are consistent with your personal beliefs and values. A better understanding of your values helps you make decisions more effectively and easily, and this helps you feel more in control and less stressed.

Clarification and Commitment

Getting in touch with your inner self, your feelings and values, is not easy. Although getting in touch relieves stress in the long run, the short-term effect can be an increase in feelings of anxiety as you face unresolved conflicts. Many people want a clear, immediate solution and are uncomfortable waiting for answers to come, an-

Calvin and Hobbes   by Bill Watterson

swers that are rarely cut and dried. Sometimes the right way to deal with a problem is not the easy way.

Recall Kobasa's definition of hardiness: control, challenge, and commitment (Kobasa, 1979). Reaffirming and clarifying your values contributes significantly to the *commitment* component of hardiness. Commitment to your goals and values helps you through demanding times and sustains you as you face difficult issues.

GOAL SETTING AND VALUES CLARIFICATION: WHERE DO YOU WANT TO GO AND HOW DO YOU LIKE TO TRAVEL?

The first question you will need to address in evaluating your time management is this: what are your lifetime goals? To answer it, you will pretend you are very old, near the end of your life, looking back on how you have spent your time. What was meaningful? What would you like to have accomplished? How would you like to have lived? What will you remember most? What will people remember you for?

Many people find this a stimulating question. Embedded in it are other big questions, such as who are you? What is your purpose in life? What is the meaning of life? What is meaningful to you? What gives you satisfaction and pleasure? What do you really like to do? The answers to these questions change throughout your life, as do your goals and lifestyle. Some people spend more time than others answering these basic questions, which themselves can be sources of stress from time to time. Finding the meaning in life when tragedy occurs can be especially difficult. Sometimes the search for answers to life's big questions takes time, and the uncertainty can feel uncomfortable and stressful. Yet the search is an important one, and neglecting the big questions ultimately creates more stress than does trying to find answers.

We are what we pretend to be, so we better be very careful what we pretend to be.

KURT VONNEGUT, JR.

SPIRITUALITY: A SEARCH FOR MEANING

Many times, the search for answers leads into the realm of our spiritual beliefs. Spirituality can be defined as "the process of learning about oneself and one's personal value system and applying this knowledge to the pursuit of one's meaningful purpose in life" (Seaward, 1991, p. 166). Spiritual health has been described as "the ability to live in the wholeness of life" (Bellingham, Cohen, Jones, and Spaniol, 1989). Spirituality may or may not operate in the context of organized religion, although for many people a meaningful relationship with a "divine other" is an important component of their spiritual selves and an important stress buffer (Pollner, 1989).

Spirituality is probably the most neglected wellness dimension, perhaps because it is difficult to talk about or study, or perhaps because it tends to be overlooked by our culture. Religious intolerance is an extremely destructive force and has turned many people away from religion. Spiritual development is often left to the individual, but many individuals receive little help in answering those big life questions.

Many wellness and stress management writers believe that a strong spiritual base increases stress resistance in several ways (Castle, 1983; Chapman, 1987; Hathaway & Pargament, 1991; Kessler in Pollner, 1989; Millison & Dudley, 1992). Don Ardell (1986) writes that personal spirituality can help us do the following:

The external voyages become stressful if the internal spaces are not satisfied.

DAVID CASTLE

1. Transcend difficulties and cope with tragedies and injustices
2. Establish a meaningful purpose in life that guides our actions and decisions
3. Find satisfaction in helping others
4. Learn and grow from what others would call failures
5. Affirm our beliefs in creative work
6. Make choices and decisions

STUDENT STRESS

JOAN'S VALUES CLARIFICATION

Joan's major source of stress these days is trying to decide whether to continue a relationship with David, her boyfriend of two years. They are both graduating this year, and many of their graduating friends are engaged and making wedding plans. David wants to get married and brings up the subject of marriage at least once a week, asking Joan whether and when they should get married. When he brings up the subject, Joan brushes it aside and says she is not ready to talk about marriage at this point. Joan is not sure she and David are meant for a long-term partnership. To cope with this stressor, Joan needs to clarify what she is looking for in a long-term partner and whether she even wants a partner at this time. She needs to evaluate the strengths and weaknesses of her relationship with David and compare her marriage option to other alternatives.

Joan decided to use the problem-solving and values clarification material from her stress management class to help her examine her options. After using the problem-solving exercise from Chapter 5—reframing the problem, clarifying her problem-solving goal, and brainstorming solutions—she came up with several reasonable options. She then listed the values underlying each option to help her evaluate these options and find a possible solution.

Option 1: Talk to David to figure out what the real problem is. Is marriage the issue, or is it something else? Maybe his insecurity?
Values:
- I value honesty and good communication.
- I value personal growth through problem solving.
- The reason I have been avoiding this decision is that I value the security of being in a relationship and am afraid of rejection.

Option 2: Agree to lengthy engagement; this will make David happy, and we can always break off the engagement if the relationship doesn't seem to be working.
Values:
- I value having an immediate solution to the problem.
- I value making David happy.
- I value putting an end to this marriage discussion.
- I want to please my parents; I think they would be happy if David and I got married.

Option 3: Suggest that David and I live together for a while after graduation.
Values:
- I value my independence, keeping my long-term options open.
- I value honesty (this feels more honest to me than a half-hearted engagement to make David happy).
- I value making David happy—maybe this would be second best to marriage.
- I don't like this option because I value marriage over living with someone; I don't want to live with someone without a commitment.

Option 4: Break off relationship now before things get even more complicated.
Values:
- I value my independence, and want to keep my options open now.
- I believe that for someone my age, self-development should come before a committed relationship.
- I believe a committed relationship should feel right.
- I don't like this option because I value our relationship.

While the problem-solving and values clarification exercise helped Joan, she still had trouble making a decision. She decided she valued honesty and personal growth over pleasing others. She also remembered what her mother had once told her: if there's no clear answer, you're probably not ready to make a decision that requires a long-term commitment. Hence, she chose option 1 and dismissed options 2 and 3, which required too much commitment. She also dismissed option 4, since she really did care for David. She decided to quit brushing off David's marriage questions and have a discussion with him about their directions as individuals and as a couple. She also realized she should be honest with David about her ambivalent feelings regarding marriage at this point in her life. Although Joan felt like the problem had not really been "solved" by these exercises, she did think she was moving in the right direction and that eventually a solution would be found.

Other writers have emphasized the importance of feeling connected to oneself, to others, and to a larger meaning or purpose (Bellingham et al., 1989; Adler, 1964; Leak & Williams, 1989; Crandall, 1984). Connectedness means being joined with, as opposed to feeling alienated from and alone. People who are alienated from themselves and from their thoughts and feelings have poorly formulated values and goals; they have difficulty developing a personal direction (Bellingham et al., 1989; Jaffe, 1981). Such lack of connectedness and personal direction is often experienced with feelings of chronic anxiety, apathy, or boredom (Kirkegaard, 1962). Recall Jason, our problem-solving example in Chapter 5, who was suffering from the anxiety of schedule overload, but more deeply from feeling out of touch with his personal direction. Alienation and loneliness increase your risk of stress-related illness. Spiritual health means healthful relatedness, and this connectedness increases your resistance to the negative effects of stress. Spiritual health contributes to life's richness and enhances your ability to know yourself and communicate with others.

Spirituality is based in faith, a sense of the mystery of life, and an awareness of a power or reality that you cannot immediately see but can only sense. Spirituality seems to reside in the heart rather than the head, or perhaps in that part of the head separate from the logical, linear mind-chatter center of decision making. Nurturing your spiritual self can expand your vision and help you solve problems creatively and meaningfully.

NURTURING YOUR SPIRITUALITY AND CLARIFYING YOUR VALUES

There is really no quick and easy short-cut to values clarification. Self-examination is a life-long process. Most people have some idea of what is important to them but may not realize that some value areas are unclear until conflict arises. Something doesn't feel right. You begin asking questions like these: What am I supposed to be doing with my life? What do I really want in a job? What do I want in a relationship? Learning to understand your values requires time alone with yourself to get in touch with your thoughts and feelings. Here are a few suggestions for helping you get more in touch with your spiritual self and your values:

1. *Read and discuss inspirational works.* Reading what others have written about the meaning of life and how to live a meaningful life helps us formulate our own moral values and spirituality. Draw from religious works, psychology, philosophy, and great literature. If possible, take a course that assigns and studies these works. Discuss the books you've enjoyed with your friends. Maybe they can recommend some to you.

2. *Make time for spiritual reflection.* Short on time? Be creative. Focus on a passage from your inspirational readings between classes, before bed, or while doing the laundry or other mindless errands.

3. *Look for examples of spiritual connection in daily life.* An ordinary object can inspire meaningful thoughts. Perhaps an old wire fence reminds you of many people holding hands to create something larger than the sum of its parts. Perhaps you have one of those "Aha!" realizations that draws you out of your everyday routine and gives you a sense of inspiration. Look for that sense of wonder you had as a child when you delighted in learning new things.

4. *Keep a journal.* Write down inspirational passages, spiritual reflections, and examples of spiritual connection that you have observed during the day. Record the most meaningful thoughts and events of the day and what you learned about yourself and your direction in life.

5. *Join a compatible group.* Many campuses and communities have a diverse collection of groups that focus on spiritual concerns—from churches to study groups.

6. *Discuss your problems and value conflicts with a counselor.* When a particular problem has you temporarily stumped, a neutral point of view from a professional can help you clarify what is important and steer you in the right direction.

MAKING DECISIONS

Earlier we said that during the course of each day you make countless decisions about how to spend your time. You decide what to think about, where to go, what to do.

Sometimes you may not experience the act of deciding, since these decisions are often automatic and unconscious. But even when it seems you are just following orders, you decide which orders to follow and how to carry them out. For example, students enrolled in several courses may encounter numerous assignments all due around the same time. They may feel that they are temporarily in the hands of their professors, puppets on strings pulled by "the system." Overwhelmed by multiple demands, they may feel out of control and stressed, believing that someone else is making all the decisions.

Who is deciding what? It is true that individual professors give assignments, and most educational institutions require exams and papers. But students enroll in colleges, select academic programs, and complete assignments by choice, in pursuit of some meaningful goal. Even when you bemoan the necessity of completing a required assignment and attribute your stress to the demanding instructor, realize that you could choose not to complete the project. Instead, you elect to do so because you perceive some future benefit. Underneath exam pressure are individual decisions to complete courses and required assignments and pursue certain career paths.

So, even if you are not aware of it, you are making numerous decisions, moment by moment, about how you spend your time, and thus your life: your lifetime. We make these decisions in many ways (Lakein, 1973) as discussed below:

Habit

Life would be chaos without habits. Routines save time by making decisions easier. But habits can also get you into a rut, block your growth, and cause stress if they cease to be adaptive. Maybe you have gotten into the habit of watching television for two hours every evening without asking yourself whether this is really the very best use of your

time. Similarly, study habits that worked in one environment may not work in another. Perhaps your high school teachers required memorization of details. You developed study skills that let you retain these details (at least until the exam was over). Now in college, with the large volume of required readings, you can't possibly have such detailed retention. You must develop new methods of absorbing and using the material.

Others' Demands

Suppose your current circle of friends always watches two hours of television after dinner. Even though you need to and would rather do other things, your friends always pull you along and tease you mercilessly if you say you must do schoolwork. Of course, the demands of others are important and must be evaluated, but if you're not careful, they can fill up your time and your life.

Impulse

You decide to do something else tonight rather than watch television. You sneak off after dinner and go up to your room. But now what will you do? You decide to go to the gym to work out, but when you get there it's too crowded. You then wander over to the library but don't have the notes you need to start your research project. You putter around digging up some articles, but in the end you can't use most of the material after all. There is certainly a time and place for spontaneity, but it works best in the context of planning.

Taking the First or Easiest Alternative

Tonight your friends have decided to go to a movie instead of watching television and they invite you along. It's a mediocre film you've already seen but you go anyway and don't really enjoy yourself.

Conscious Decision

The problem-solving exercises in the last chapter were an example of using conscious decision. What is the best use of those two hours? The first half hour is a good news show that you really enjoy, so you decide to join your friends for that. But you decide the other hour and a half could be spent doing something more productive or fun. One of your sources of stress is trying to get by on six

STRESS AND YOU

CAREER VALUES CLARIFICATION

Brainstorming exercises can help you clarify your values. Versions of the following exercise are used in career development offices across the country. (This particular version is from the Smith College Career Development Office.) This exercise is designed to help you clarify your values and feelings about your career path and may be helpful as you consider your lifetime goals.

You are going to sort a list of values into three columns, rating each value as "always valued," "sometimes valued," or "never valued." The list includes a wide variety of satisfactions people obtain from their "careers." *Careers* refers to work in the broadest sense—what you do with your time—and includes both paid and unpaid work. Look at the list below and place each value in a column depending on what feels right to you. If a word is vague, feel free to make up your own definition. You may also add other values. There are no right or wrong responses, only what seems right to you.

List of Values

Always valued	*Sometimes valued*	*Never valued*

hours of sleep a night because you stay up late studying. You decide to get an earlier start on homework and go to bed earlier as well or maybe you have always wanted to get involved in the campus theater. You decide to use those 11 hours a week volunteering to work on sets rather than watch television.

All these decision-making methods are valid and helpful at certain times as long as you are happy with the outcome: the way you are spending your time.

Sample Value List

Acquiring	Adventure	Authority
Autonomy	Beauty	Belonging
Challenge	Commitment	Competition
Contributing	Control	Cooperation
Creativity	Curiosity	Duty
Effectiveness	Excellence	Excitement
Exploring	Fairness	Family
Fast Pace	Friendship	Gentleness
Growth	Health	Helping
High Earnings/Profit	Honesty	Humor
Independence	Individuality	Influence
Intimacy	Knowledge	Leading
Location	Making Decisions	Manipulating
Mastery	Moral Fulfillment	Physical Challenge
Potential	Power	Public Contact
Quiet	Recognition	Risk
Security	Sharing	Social Change
Spirituality	Stability	Status
Strength	Structure	Success
Supervising Others	Time Freedom	Tranquility
Trust	Understanding	Uniqueness
Variety	Wealth	Well-Being
Winning	Work Surroundings	Working Alone
Working with Others	Working on Frontiers	
Working under Pressure	of Knowledge	

Once you have placed each value in a column, look at the values in the "always valued" and "never valued" columns. Did you learn anything about yourself? Do you notice any patterns? How many of the "always valued" items are in your current situation, if you have one? A job or activity can be frustrating if it meets few of your values or needs. Use this list to evaluate possibilities and guide you in career decisions. It can help you choose your best options, the opportunities that are the "best fit" for your values and lifestyle.

A similar listing of values can be done for other big issues, such as defining what you want in a relationship or community.

Making conscious decisions does not mean you will turn into some sort of robot, or the super-logical Mr. Spock of Star Trek fame. In fact, improvement in your conscious decision making gives you room for more spontaneity and allows you to respond appropriately to the demands and invitation of others, take advantage of surprise opportunities, and develop constructive habits. Paradoxically, exerting what control you do have over your time and your life allows you more time and freedom to play, relax, and give up control.

TIME MANAGEMENT: SETTING YOUR GOALS

By now you realize that time management is about life expectancy: what you expect from life. Time management begins with goal setting. Once you know where you want to go, you then decide what activities will help you reach those goals.

Goals can be written in many contexts. Most experts recommend lifetime, medium-range, and short-range planning. The goal-setting exercise in this chapter asks you to define lifetime and medium-range goals, since your short-range goals are usually pretty clear: assignments that must be completed and so forth. If you don't already have a list of these, you can include short-range goals, too.

Goals are constantly changing, so don't worry that writing down a goal "commits" you to accomplishing it. Your goals are simply a vignette of how you feel at the moment you're writing them. Keep your goals close at hand; review and revise them from time to time, perhaps monthly. Updating your goals periodically helps keep you on track with your time management and decision making.

Couples often enjoy doing the goal-setting exercises together, since their cooperative lifestyle must be constructed to help both members reach their personal goals.

Because you can't "do" a goal, after you have defined your goals, you will need to think of activities that will help you reach them. This is not always an easy task.

 ## STRESS AND YOU

TIME MANAGEMENT: SETTING YOUR GOALS

This exercise will help you define your lifetime goals. As you do this exercise, remember you are not committing yourself to any particular goal. We are constantly rewriting and revising our lifetime goals. The list you are compiling is simply your best guess from where you are now. Your list is a snapshot of how you are feeling at this moment.

1. Take out a clean sheet of paper and write "My Lifetime Goals." Then imagine you are very old, looking back on your life. What did you want to accomplish? What do you feel best about? Any regrets? Consider all aspects of your life: social, career, personal, family, recreational, spiritual. Return to the mind-set you used when brainstorming solutions in the problem-solving chapter: be creative, suspend judgment, write down anything that pops into your mind, and write as much as you can. You will have time later to go back with your logical mind and evaluate items on your list. Making your list should take you about two or three minutes. When you think your list is complete, go over it for another minute or two and add any more ideas that come to mind.

2. Now take out another sheet of paper for another set of goals. Title this one "Three-Year Goals." On this list, put what you would like to accomplish and describe how you would like to spend the next three years. Three years is a somewhat arbitrary number. If a different time span makes more sense to you, use it. For example, if you graduate from college in two years, make a two-year plan. If you plan to remain in your current job for the next five years,

Many goals, especially lifetime goals, can be very general. How do you reach a goal like "Have a happy family" or "Develop a meaningful career"? Think small, and think of something doable. Here are some steps for the goal "Develop a meaningful career":

1. Complete the Career Values Clarification worksheet in this chapter.
2. Speak with a career counselor about the kinds of jobs that would match my list of "very important" values. Develop a list of possible career opportunities.
3. Prioritize this list, and research my top priorities in the career development library.
4. Interview people working in jobs that might interest me.
5. Develop an internship for next semester in my first choice career area.

The specific steps you list for each goal should include things you can begin working on today: scheduling that appointment with the career counselor, doing some research in the career development library, or planning an interesting internship. Time management means doing something every day toward your top-priority goals. Focus on results rather than "spending time." Instead of saying you'll spend 30 minutes in the library, define what you would like to accomplish there.

At the end of your life, you will never regret not having passed one more test, not winning one more verdict, or not closing one more deal. You will regret time not spent with a husband, a friend, a child, or a parent.

Barbara Bush

make a five-year plan. Take a few minutes to brainstorm your three-year goals and then review the list to stimulate more ideas.

3. Now take out another sheet of paper for your last list: What I Would Do if I Knew I Had only Six Months to Live. Assume good health and unlimited resources and no need to take care of burdensome details such as wills. The point is to list everything you might like to squeeze into those last six months. List your goals for this period, review it, and add some more ideas.

Do not worry if some goals appear to conflict with others. Many people find that their third list is quite different from their three-year goal list. Sometimes this means you are preparing for lifetime goals in a way that requires some delayed gratification, such as by going to college. Your college education may involve some current hardship but will get you into an interesting career. Ideally, some of the goals on your third list can still be incorporated into your three-year plan.

4. Go back over all three lists, and rate each item as *A*, very important; *B*, somewhat important; or *C*, least important. At this point you are still in a creative, brainstorming mode. Don't worry about being realistic.

5. Now evaluate the A items on your three lists and select the two from each list that are the most important to you. List these six goals on a sheet of paper. You will work with them some more in the next exercise.

Source: Adapted from Lakein, 1973; Davis, Eshelman, & McKay, 1995.

EXERCISE

ACHIEVING GOALS WITH AN ACTION PLAN

Goals give you a direction, but they don't tell you how to get there. In this exercise, you will take the six goals you just listed and write down activities that will help you achieve them.

Begin with the first goal you listed. Rewrite the goal, and then define specific tasks that will help you reach that goal. The specific steps you list for each goal should be something you can begin working on today.

Goal 1: _____

Action steps:

1. _____

2. _____

3. _____

4. _____

5. _____

6. _____

Goal 2: _____

Action steps:

1. _____

2. _____

3. _____

4. _____

5. _____

6. _____

Goal 3: _____

Action steps:

1. _____

2. _____

3. _____

4. _____

5. _____

6. _____

Goal 4: _____

Action steps:

1. _____

2. _____

3. _____

4. _____

5. _____

6. _____

Goal 5: _____

Action steps:

1. _____

2. _____

3. _____

4. _____

5. _____

6. _____

Goal 6: _____

Action steps:

1. _____

2. _____

3. _____

4. _____

5. _____

6. _____

Try to schedule an action step that you will do for each important goal over the next few days.

WHO KNOWS WHERE THE TIME GOES?

Some time management experts recommend keeping a log of how you spend your time. An evaluation of how you currently spend your time may highlight ways you could improve your use of time and help you move toward your high-priority goals. Instructions for keeping a time log can be found later in this chapter.

If you find the idea of keeping track of your activities for three days too time-consuming or too overwhelming, do not despair. You may still benefit from a simplified trouble-shooting version. Many people already have some idea of where their time is most wasted: watching television, chatting with friends, running errands, sharpening pencils, rearranging the room. Instead of logging every minute, keep track of time spent on specific low-priority items. Some chatting with friends is fun and important, but is some of it just "passing time" or procrastinating? How much?

WILL TIME MANAGEMENT SOLVE ALL YOUR PROBLEMS?

Time is the most valuable thing a man can spend.

THEOPHRASTUS

Some people will find that time management becomes more of a problem than part of the solution. Some people simply have too much to do and are working at a level that is not compatible with their personal style. Certain jobs, for example, may demand more time than you can give. Parenting takes a lot of energy and provides tremendous stress along with the rewards of family life. But not everyone has the energy or desire to be a parent.

Time management should also not take the place of social justice. Time management tends to throw the burden of a problem, lack of time, onto individuals. But are the time pressures of a single parent working a low-income job and living in a poverty-stricken neighborhood really going to be solved by better time management? Not usually. Better living conditions, access to educational opportunity and

---

▉ STUDENT STRESS

ANDREW'S TIME LOG

Andrew enjoyed college but felt he never had enough time for his school work, or anything else, for that matter. Andrew knew he spent a lot of time talking to his friends. He was very popular, and it seemed that whenever one of his friends was bored, Andrew was the one who was visited and dragged away from his work. Andrew always went willingly and enjoyed his friends, but he was falling behind in his work and felt tired because he wasn't getting enough sleep. He decided to keep track of the time he spent just hanging out with his friends. He discovered that it amounted to several hours each day. Andrew knew he would have to make a change or his grades would be very poor this semester. His friendships were a high priority, but so was school. He decided that since he studied best right after dinner, he would work in the library from 7 P.M. until 10 P.M., knowing that in the library his friends would leave him alone. He would enjoy dinner with them and getting together on the weekend and in the evening when he got back from the library. Andrew felt this was a workable compromise that his friends would support, since many of them studied after dinner, too.

STRESS AND YOU

KEEPING A TIME LOG: HOW DO YOU SPEND YOUR TIME?

To get a better idea of how you spend your time, keep track of what you do for three days. Divide the day into three parts: (1) from waking through lunch, (2) from after lunch through dinner, and (3) from after dinner until going to sleep. Record each activity and how long it took in a small notebook. After you've done this for three days, summarize the time you spend on various activities. Categorize activities in any way that is meaningful to you. For example, you might categorize schoolwork as follows:

Attending classes
Reviewing lecture notes for exams
Other studying for exams
Reading assignments
Research for papers
Writing reports/papers

Nonschool categories might include these:

Telephone calls
Conversations
Sports activities
Eating meals
Preparing meals
Personal hygiene
Night sleep
Naps
Television
Hobbies (list these)
Extracurricular activities (list these)
Reading (for fun)
Errands, chores (like shopping, laundry)

   Invent whatever categories apply to you and summarize the amount of time you spend at each activity. You may wish to differentiate between productive and nonproductive study time. Was the material sinking in or were you daydreaming? Did you gather material you can use for that paper, or did you get sidetracked on peripheral topics?

   Did you find any surprises? Compare the way you currently spend your time to your lifetime goals. How could your use of time be improved? The only way to achieve those long-term goals is to eliminate low-priority items. Do you see any time in your current time budget that could be delegated to long-term goal activities?

job training, and better school systems and social support would all contribute a great deal more to the stress relief of many.

   Life goals and time use vary tremendously from person to person. You will find time management useful only if it means that you are moving more effectively toward your life goals. Remember, less can be more. Doing fewer things with better involvement and concentration may be a more rewarding experience than trying to "do it all." Good time management means finding more time to do the things you enjoy: engaging in pleasurable recreational activities and spending time with family and friends without feeling nagged by deeds left undone.

SUMMARY

1. Time management is not so much about efficiency as it is about setting both short- and long-term goals and learning to structure your use of time so that you make progress toward your goals.
2. Values clarification is the process of defining and evaluating your values and understanding the influence they have on your decisions.
3. Moral values define right and wrong, good and evil; they are the voice of your conscience and the ethical foundation on which you make judgments and decisions.
4. Nonmoral values describe what you find desirable or undesirable, and they reflect your personal preferences.
5. Stress results when values are inappropriate or in conflict with one another.
6. Children grow up adopting the values of their parents, which they then revise as they come into adolescence and adulthood. When old values are rejected, new ones must take their place.
7. Values clarification increases stress resistance because it increases your feelings of control and commitment and helps you make decisions.
8. Spirituality is based in a sense of the mystery of life and an awareness of a power or reality that you cannot immediately see but can only sense. Spirituality is also the process of learning about yourself, what you value, and where you find meaning and connectedness in life.
9. Spiritual wellness increases stress resistance because it helps you clarify your values and make decisions, feel connected to others, and find meaning in life's difficulties.
10. You make decisions on how to spend your time in many ways, including (a) habit, (b) others' demands, (c) impulse, (d) taking the first or easiest alternative, and (e) conscious decision. Improving your conscious decision making can increase your satisfaction with your use of time.
11. The first step to take in improving your time management is to clarify and prioritize your goals, and then to define specific steps that will help you reach your high-priority goals.
12. Keeping a time log can help you learn more about how you spend your time and how you can change your use of time.
13. Time management is a popular and effective method of stress management. However, it throws the burden of the problem—lack of time—back onto individuals, when sometimes institutional or societal change may be called for.

REFERENCES

Adler, A. *Social Interest: A Challenge to Mankind.* New York: Capricorn Books, 1964.

Ardell, D. *High Level Wellness.* Berkeley: Ten Speed Press, 1986.

Beck, JR. Christian reflections on stress management. *Journal of Psychology and Theology* 14: 22–28, 1986.

Bellingham, R, B Cohen, T Jones, and L Spaniol. Connectedness: Some skills for spiritual health. *American Journal of Health Promotion* 4: 18–24, 31, 1989.

Britton, BK, and A Tesser. Effects of time-management practices on college grades. *Journal of Educational Psychology* 83: 405–410, 1991.

Castle, D. You can do something about stress. *Quaker Life,* Dec 1983, pp 15–17.

Chapman, LS. Developing a useful perspective on spiritual health: Love, joy, peace, and fulfillment. *American Journal of Health Promotion* 2: 12–17, 1987.

Crandall, JE. Social interest as a moderator of life stress. *Journal of Personality and Social Psychology* 47: 164–174, 1984.

Davis, M, ER Eshelman, and M McKay. *The Relaxation and Stress Reduction Workbook.* Oakland, CA: New Harbinger Publications, 1995.

Hathaway, WL, and KI Pargament. The religious dimensions of coping: Implications for prevention and promotion. *Prevention in Human Services* 9: 65–92, 1991.

Hemenway, C. Values/style analysis. *New Directions,* Smith College Career Development Office, Northampton, MA, 1987.

Jaffe, D. *Healing from Within.* New York: Alfred A. Knopf, 1981.

Kessler, RC, RH Price, and CB Wortman. Social factors in psychopathology: Stress, social support and coping. *Annual Review of Psychology* 1985, 531–572.

King, AC, RA Winett, and SB Lovett. Enhancing coping behaviors in at-risk populations: The effects of time-management instruction and social support in women from dual-earner families. *Behavior Therapy* 17: 57–66, 1986.

Kirkegaard, S. *Works of Love.* New York: Harper & Row, 1962.

Kobasa, SC. Stressful life events, personality, and health: An inquiry into hardiness. *Journal of Personality and Social Psychology* 37: 1–11, 1979.

Lakein, A. *How to Get Control of Your Time and Your Life.* New York: New American Library, 1973.

Lang, D. Preventing short-term strain through time-management coping. *Work and Stress* 6: 169–176, 1992.

Leak, GK, and DE Williams. Relationship between social interest, alienation, and psychological hardiness. *Journal of Individual Psychology* 45: 369–375, 1989.

Lee, C, P Bobko, PC Earley, and EA Locke. An empirical analysis of a goal setting questionnaire. *Journal of Organizational Behavior* 12: 467–482, 1991.

Macan, TH, C Shahani, RL Dipboye, and AP Phillips. College students' time management: Correlations with academic performance and stress. *Journal of Educational Psychology* 82: 760–768, 1990.

McKay, M, M Davis, and P Fanning. *Thoughts and Feelings: The Art of Cognitive Stress Intervention.* Richmond, CA: New Harbinger Publications, 1981.

Millison, M, and JR Dudley. Providing spiritual support: A job for all hospice professionals. *The Hospice Journal* 8: 49–66, 1992.

Morgan, GW. *The Human Predicament: Dissolution and Wholeness.* Providence, RI: Brown University Press, 1969.

Pollner, M. Divine relations, social relations, and well-being. *Journal of Health and Social Behavior* 30: 92–104, 1989.

Richards, JH. Time management—a review. *Work and Stress* 1: 73–78, 1987.

Schuler, RS. Managing stress means managing time. *Personnel Journal* 58: 851–854, 1979.

Seaward, B. Spiritual well-being: A health education model. *Journal of Health Education* 22: 166–169, 1991.

chapter 7

Time Management Part 2: Organization, Study Skills, and Confronting Procrastination

Daily life. Everything happens here, from progress toward your lifetime goals to laundry, shopping, car repairs, and housekeeping. Good organization in your daily life helps you manage multiple priorities with greater ease. Having routines for the routine frees you to make more creative use of your remaining time and ensures that you have the creative energy required for your high-priority activities. On the other hand, a lack of organization can be a significant source of stress: losing notes for an upcoming exam or project, forgetting an important deadline, misplacing your keys or wallet. Such daily hassles contribute directly to your daily stress levels.

In the previous chapter, you defined and prioritized your goals and listed action steps for the highest priorities. Now you're ready to get organized. How will you fit these steps into real life? This chapter begins with some suggestions on scheduling and organization to help you spend more of your time working toward high-priority goals. A section on study skills should help you get the most out of your study time. The chapter concludes with a discussion of one of the most frequently cited sources of student stress: procrastination.

ORGANIZE YOUR TIME:
MAKING TIME WITH REALISTIC SCHEDULING

Action steps are of little use unless you do them. The best way to be sure you get around to doing them is to put them into your daily schedule.

Why Schedule?

Why have a schedule? A schedule gives you a direction and reaffirms your commitment to completing high-priority tasks. It is a form of conscious decision making—in this case about how you will spend the day. It provides a framework for structuring your day in a way that maximizes progress toward your high-priority goals. Without some sort of schedule, you create stress by wasting time, working inefficiently, and missing opportunities because you didn't plan ahead. But be careful: overschedule yourself and you create stress as well. Learn to create a time management schedule that fits your lifestyle and is flexible and realistic. You will find satisfaction in making progress toward your goals without feeling frustrated or overwhelmed by work overload.

Why Lists Don't Work

Many people operate with some sort of list of things to do. They get satisfaction from crossing items off their "to do" list as these tasks are completed. Unfortunately, most people feel more immediate satisfaction from doing several low-priority items than from getting to the riskier, more difficult high-priority activities. It's easy to do those routine tasks, but frequently they keep you from addressing the important items on your list. For example, you might feel that you've accomplished a lot by cleaning your room, doing the laundry, writing several letters, and organizing the notes you are planning to study for tomorrow's big exam; you get to cross four items off your list! But if you fail to address that one really important item—prepare adequately for tomorrow's big exam—your list method of organization has failed to help you use your time to move toward high-priority goals.

The Art of Creating Realistic Daily Schedules That Highlight Priorities

Creating a realistic plan for activities of each day, week, and month is an art. A schedule needs to be more than a "to do" list. Don't throw that list away, but take out a clean sheet of paper to create a daily schedule for tomorrow. Also take out your time management action plan that lists tasks to help you reach your high-priority goals. Pick one or more of these items that you will do tomorrow. Put a star next to these. Then go ahead and add a few of those other things that must get done tomorrow: school assignments, vacation travel plans, whatever, but try to make it a *realistic* list. Remember, this is not a "wish list" of all you wish you could accomplish. This is a realistic list. Make a game each day of creating a list that actually gets done, in which all items get crossed off. Realistic planning is much more productive than an exhaustive unprioritized list that follows you around from day to day, reminding you of all you have yet to do, and allowing you to spend too much time on low-priority tasks (Lakein, 1973).

Next, from your realistic "to do" list, create a realistic daily schedule. First, write in items already scheduled: classes, practice, rehearsals, meetings, and so forth. Then, block out time for those high-priority activities. Look for time chunks of an hour or more and use these for high-priority projects. The earlier in the day you get to these, the better you will feel. Next check your list for medium-priority items. Schedule these in. What's left? Complete your schedule with other activities that need to get done today.

Be sure you don't pack too much into your day. Build in time for interruptions, problems, and unforeseen snafus. Remember Murphy's Law: if something can go wrong, it will. Leave room in your schedule for recovery from demanding activities, such as exams and presentations. Give yourself an extra ten minutes to get to the bus station. And most of all, give yourself time to relax and have fun. A schedule must not be too rigid. Don't become a prisoner of your plan; change your schedule as you need to, but keep those top priorities in mind and get to them as soon as possible.

Too Much to Do?

What if everything that has to get done doesn't fit into your schedule? That is often the case! Then some things will not get done. Many students are unhappy with this answer at first, but isn't it better for you to decide which items will not get done? If you can't do everything, then don't do items of the lowest priority. Even though you may still feel that you have too much to do, at least you will feel better for having made progress on the items of highest priority—and you will feel more in control of your time, a feeling that increases your stress resistance (Cone & Owens, 1991; Macan, Shahani, Dipboye, & Phillips, 1990).

Make Time to Plan

While this sort of planning may feel time-consuming at first, it will actually create time for you in the long run. Planning means getting to your priorities and reducing time spent on activities you don't really enjoy (Simons & Galotti, 1992). Most people use both daily and longer-range plans. At the beginning of the semester, you will want to compile assignment deadlines from all classes into a semester calendar. Your semester plan will alert you to weeks when you are very busy and those when you are less busy so that you may plan accordingly. Each weekend, you will probably want to look at the upcoming week to plan ahead for assignments due, then you can schedule other activities around these events. Your daily schedule and list can be made either the night before or first thing in the morning, whichever works best for you. Once you are in the habit of assessing your priorities, your daily planning will take less than five minutes.

SCHEDULE AROUND PRIME TIME: GO WITH YOUR FLOW

As you practice creating a realistic daily schedule, consider the concept of *prime time*. Prime time refers to the best time to do certain activities.

Internal Prime Time

Internal prime time refers to your personal energy rhythms. Each of us has a fairly predictable energy flow throughout the day, with periods of high and low energy. Some people have good concentration and are most productive in the morning; others aren't really warmed up until late afternoon and have a great deal of energy in the evening. When possible, schedule more challenging activities for the time you are most alert. Perform routine tasks when you are less energetic. For example, if you are a morning person, getting up an hour earlier to study may be more productive than trying to emulate the study habits of your night owl friends. You will get more accomplished more easily with less stress in less time if you work with your personal energy patterns. As time management experts say, "Work smarter, not harder" (Mackenzie, 1972).

You may also notice that you have high energy days and low energy days. Schedule accordingly. If you are having a great day and feel like moving some mountains, use that energy to tackle the really important tasks. If nothing is going your way today, select items for your schedule that you can really accomplish. If you are coming down with a cold and feel exhausted, slow down and take care of yourself. Maybe you can get to one priority item but not three. This approach saves you time in the long run since you will get well sooner. Taking care of yourself also spares you the stress of banging your head against the proverbial wall of trying to accomplish tasks that take more energy than you have.

External Prime Time

External prime time will also dictate when you can best do certain activities. External prime time refers to accessing resources when they are most convenient to use, or reaching people when they are most available. Know the best times for reaching your professors, supervisor, and co-workers. Ask professors for help during their office hours and they will usually give you all the time and help you need. Try calling them at home at 11 p.m. when you are stuck on a homework problem and the response will not be so pleasant. Need help from a tutor? You will need time to develop a schedule for working together, so don't expect to find someone the week before your final exam. You take advantage of external prime time when you avoid busy hours at the laundromat and rush hour traffic, or when you try to reach someone at a time other than lunch hour. An awareness of external prime time means not trying to print your paper at the computer center an hour before it's due, when everyone else is trying to do the same thing.

The more complicated your life gets, the greater the importance of scheduling around internal and external prime time. Alyssa, a student and mother of two young children, compartmentalizes her activities into three external prime time categories: (1) things that must get done when she is on campus, (2) things that can be done at home while the kids are in school or asleep for the night, and (3) things that can get done with the kids around. Within these parameters, Alyssa takes advantage of her internal prime time, getting important assignments done in the morning when she is most energetic and saving the less demanding assignments for the evening.

MAKE A SEMESTER PLAN

At the beginning of every semester, make a schedule of due dates and prioritize all assignments (Longman & Atkinson, 1988). A notebook is not enough; you'll need a calendar, too. Take note of holidays, school vacations, and extracurricular events: plays, concerts, athletic events, whatever you are involved in. Record exam dates and due dates for all assignments. Which weeks look the busiest? Are there any weeks with two big papers due? Plan ahead. Set your own deadline to get one done early, or ask the professor ahead of time for an extension. Your sister wants to come visit. When is the best time? Not the week that you have three midterms.

ORGANIZE BIG ASSIGNMENTS

Once you have penciled in all events and deadlines, you will want to estimate when to begin various projects. This requires figuring out approximately how long a project will take, a task that is especially difficult if you are in your first year in college. Ask experienced students for help. In general, estimating time needed for a project involves the following steps (adapted from Girdano, Everly, & Dusek, 1993):

1. Define the task, what it's worth, and reasons for doing it.
2. Break the task down into steps.
3. Describe the goal or finished product.
4. List people whose help may be needed and possible problems getting that help.
5. List materials needed, anticipating costs and obstacles.
6. Hypothesize all other possible obstacles and problems that could come up and develop contingency plans for them.

7. Assess the time each step in #2 will take.
8. Add 10% to 15% to this total.
9. Schedule the task on your calendar.

Scheduling Example: Term Paper

This planning method can be applied to any type of project or activity. Since term papers are a common assignment, let's see how this plan might work for writing a term paper.

English Term Paper Plan

1. *Define the task, what it's worth, and reasons for doing it.*
    Fifteen-page term paper due in English worth 25 percent of my grade. I am writing it because it is required, but I also hope it will improve my writing skills.
2. *Break the task down into steps.*
    a. Decide on a few possible topics that sound interesting. Skim the text and readings and get the professor's okay for these.
    b. Go the the library and see how much material is available on these topics. Briefly skim some of the material and choose the topic that would be most interesting and accessible. Copy the articles that look good for my chosen topic.
    c. Gather, read, and take notes on articles for my topic.
    d. Organize notes and write an outline. Get more sources if needed.
    e. Write the paper.
    f. Ask a writing counselor to help me revise the paper, since I have some difficulty writing and this is a new kind of paper for me.
    g. Revise the paper, print it out, hand it in.
3. *Describe the goal, or finished product.*
    A good paper.
4. *List people whose help may be needed, and possible problems getting that help.*
    a. I need the professor to approve my topics. Since it is a small class, I can probably catch her before class. If not, I'll go during office hours.
    b. I want to schedule an appointment with the writing counselor. This has to be done about a week before the appointment, which in turn needs to be at least a week before the paper is due.
5. *List materials needed, anticipating costs and obstacles.*
    I'll need to get to the computer center to type the paper, do the revision, and get it printed.
6. *Hypothesize all other possible obstacles and problems that could come up, and develop contingency plans for them.*
    a. Difficulty getting the articles I need from the library—may need to travel to another library in the next town.
    b. My brother may come visit the weekend before the paper is due so I should plan to have the paper pretty well done before then.
    c. Having to wait to use a computer. Mornings are usually not a busy time, and I have Tuesday and Thursday mornings free before 10 A.M.
7. *Assess the time each step in #2 will take.*
    ½ hr. a. Decide on a few possible topics that sound interesting. Skim the text and readings and get the professor's okay for these.
    1 hr. b. Go to the library and see how much material is available on these topics. Briefly skim some of the material to see what topic would be most interesting and accessible. Copy the articles that look good for my chosen topic.

8 hrs. c. Gather, read, and take notes on articles for my topic.

2 hrs. d. Organize notes and write an outline. Get more sources if needed.

10 hrs. e. Write the paper.

1 hr. f. Ask a writing counselor to help me revise the paper, since I have difficulty writing and this is a new kind of paper for me.

2 hrs. g. Revise the paper, print it out, hand it in.

8. *Add 10% to 15% to this total.*

   This paper may take about 24.5 hr + 10 percent = about 27 hours.

9. *Now schedule the tasks into your calendar.*

SUNDAY	MONDAY	TUESDAY	WEDNESDAY	THURSDAY	FRIDAY	SATURDAY
Skim for topics 5:30–6 p.m.	*Ask prof to approve topics* 1–8 p.m. library *select topic*	1 *3–6 p.m. library research*	2 *make appt. w/ writing counselor* 1–9 p.m. library research	3 *3–6 p.m. library research*	4 *3–5 p.m. organize outline*	5 *trip to another library (if necessary)* 8–12 a.m. *write*
6 *9 a.m.– noon write*	7 *1–10 p.m. write*	8 *9–10 a.m. print 1st draft*	9 *proofread* *see counselor*	10 *3–5 p.m. revise*	11	12 *Brother visits*
13 *Brother visits*	14 *Revise more if needed*	15	16	17 *9–10 a.m. print paper*	18 *10:30 a.m. *paper due*	19
20	21	22	23	24	25	26
27	28	29	30	31		

With time, this sort of planning becomes easier. If you do something similar for all your semester assignments and plan accordingly, the semester should go more smoothly. Spreading the work out over the weeks helps avoid crazy weeks full of deadline stress, but this scheduling takes some discipline at first. Using future "phantom time" to put off doing assignments may give you a carefree day today but a high-stress one tomorrow. One stress management teacher has noted a common occurrence in the stress logs he receives. One day will read, "No stress today. Nothing due. Relaxed with friends, went to a movie in the evening. Perfect day!" only to be followed the next day with this, "Very stressful day. Worked all day on English paper due tomorrow. Major headache. Couldn't get on the computer to type in the paper. Stayed up until 4 A.M. trying to get it printed."

Learning to divide up assignments into their component tasks takes some experience. Students often give each other good advice on how to study for exams, complete lab reports, write papers, and take advantage of campus resources.

▲ *ACTION PLAN*

SCHEDULING AN UPCOMING ASSIGNMENT

Try out the planning method described above for an assignment looming on your horizons, such as a term paper or oral presentation.

1. Define the task, what it's worth, and reasons for doing it.

2. Break the task down into steps.

3. Describe the goal or finished product.

4. List people whose help may be needed and possible problems getting that help.

5. List materials needed, anticipating costs and obstacles.

6. Hypothesize all other possible obstacles and problems that could come up and develop contingency plans for them.

7. Assess the time each step in #2 will take.

8. Add 10% to 15% to this total.

9. Now schedule the task into your calendar.

SUNDAY	MONDAY	TUESDAY	WEDNESDAY	THURSDAY	FRIDAY	SATURDAY

SUNDAY	MONDAY	TUESDAY	WEDNESDAY	THURSDAY	FRIDAY	SATURDAY

ADDITIONAL HELPFUL HINTS FOR REDUCING STRESS WITH BETTER ORGANIZATION OF YOUR TIME

1. *Immerse and enjoy.* Remember that your time management goal is to get the most out of each moment and each day. Get into what you're doing and enjoy yourself as much as possible.

2. *Concentrate on one thing at a time.* The amount of time you spend on a project is meaningless; it's the end result that counts. Uninterrupted, clear concentration produces a better product in less time. People with time management problems often flit from one activity to another, try to do several things at once, and have trouble concentrating because they can't decide which task they should work on next. Decide, then go with your decision. Don't waste time worrying about the other things you "should" get done. Work with your whole brain in gear and focus on one assignment at a time. You will learn more and enjoy your work more as well.

3. *Use the 80/20 rule.* The 80/20 rule can help you establish priorities. This rule has many applications, including the following: 80 percent of the benefit comes from doing 20 percent of the items on your "to do" list. Eighty percent of the exam will cover 20 percent of the material; 80 percent of your paper will come from 20 percent of your sources. Figure out the most beneficial 20 percent and make that your priority.

4. *Learn to say no.* Just say no to low-priority items that beckon you away from what you really want to do and to requests for help with low-priority projects. No one can possibly do everything there is to do; we all set limits by setting priorities. Your schedule says study, but you would rather do the laundry. Is this the best use of your time right now? Say no to the laundry and get to work. Often, setting limits means finding a tactful but firm way of saying no. Friends call to chat while you are cruising on a high-priority task. Ask if you can call them back later in the day or at least limit the conversation to a few minutes. Your friend wants to work on your computer but you were planning to complete an assignment on it tonight. Send him to the computer center. In Chapter 8 we will discuss improving communication skills, including your ability to say no.

Whether you think you can or you think you can't, you're right.

UNKNOWN

5. *Avoid perfectionism.* Striving for excellence means doing your best and learning from the experience. Striving for perfection means failure, for perfection is unattainable. Perfectionists feel that if they can't do a task perfectly, they may as well not do it at all. Striving for perfection leads to fear of failure, procrastination, and then completing projects at the last minute. Since you ran out of time, you now have the perfect excuse for your lack of perfection!

Striving for perfection can also get you stalled on low-priority tasks. Let's say your professor is giving you 2 points toward your final grade for writing a paragraph on a lecture you just attended. How much time should you spend on this? It might take a perfectionist all night for very little return on that investment of time spent writing, rewriting, and worrying about every detail. Instead, do your best, and then move on to more important assignments.

6. *Schedule time for a healthful lifestyle.* A healthful lifestyle increases your stress resistance and keeps you healthy so you minimize the time you spend sick in bed or struggling through the day feeling brain dead. Schedule daily exercise, regular meals, and a good night's sleep. Remember how little gets done when you get sick or feel too stressed and tired to do anything. Activities that contribute to your health are good uses of your time.

7. *Take frequent breaks to relax and refocus.* Get up, stretch, take a walk between activities. Check your schedule and reorganize as necessary to stay on target.

8. *Use small chunks of time to complete routine tasks.* If you have an extra ten minutes, attend to tasks such as household chores or reading the mail. Stuck in line? Use waiting time to brainstorm ideas for an upcoming project, plan tomorrow's schedule, or to simply read and relax.

9. *Develop self-discipline to help you stay focused.* How often do you begin a high-priority task with good intentions and then find yourself drifting away from those riskier, more challenging tasks into the comfortable routine of repetition and distraction? Here you sit, staring at a blank sheet of paper, while your schedule tells you to spend the next hour getting started on an essay due tomorrow. You get up, get something to drink, run into a friend and talk for a while, and then since you have only 15 minutes left before your next class, you decide to write a letter instead of the essay which you tell yourself you will do later.

Later is often phantom time, time that seems to offer more opportunity than it actually holds. The essay will get done *later,* but you may also have left several other projects for *later* as well. School vacations are often phantom time, an excuse to put off as many assignments as possible. When your vacation finally arrives, you cannot possibly complete everything you have planned to do.

Procrastination is discussed in more detail later in this chapter. At this point, let us simply consider the concept of self-discipline, which involves the ability to delay immediate gratification in order to be more fully gratified at a later time. You begin work on the essay today so you will have a better finished product and more free time this weekend. Self-discipline allows you to do something that's a little difficult now (writing that essay) to avoid something that will be more difficult in the future (writing that essay under too much pressure and without enough time or preparation). Self-discipline is cultivated with practice and continual reinforcement. Convince yourself it's easier and more satisfying in the long run to work in an organized, self-disciplined fashion, even though you may have to force yourself to do something you'd rather not do right now.

Make the most of yourself, for that is all there is to you.

RALPH WALDO EMERSON

◆ STRESS AND YOU

HOW ORGANIZED ARE YOU?

Answer yes or no to the following questions. Give yourself one point for every "yes" answer.

_____ 1. Are you almost always late to meetings and appointments?

_____ 2. Do you find yourself always making apologies for being disorganized?

_____ 3. Do you plan only a day at a time—never weeks or months in advance?

_____ 4. Do you find that you "don't have time" for those essential activities that help you take care of yourself—exercise, relaxation, preparing and eating good food, music and arts, quality time with family and friends?

_____ 5. At the end of a day do you often feel that you've been dealing with trivia and haven't done the more important things?

_____ 6. Do you feel you'd like to be more organized, but your life is such a mess you wouldn't know where to begin?

_____ 7. Is your refrigerator badly in need of cleaning?

_____ 8. Do you often forget or misplace your keys, glasses, handbag, briefcase, appointment book, and the like?

_____ 9. Do you find yourself constantly running out of essential supplies at home or at work?

_____ 10. Have you forgotten a scheduled appointment within the past month?

Score   Interpretation

0–1   Congratulations! You have things pretty well under control.

2–4   You are somewhat disorganized.

5–7   You are fairly disorganized. Following the guidelines in this chapter should be helpful.

8–10   You are highly disorganized. Disorganization is probably causing you significant stress. Getting more organized could dramatically change your life.

Source: Adapted from Tom Ferguson, M.D. *Medical Self-Care* Number 16, Spring 1982, p. 26. Used with permission.

OBSTACLES TO ORGANIZATION

If poor organization is such a significant source of stress, why aren't people more organized? Here are three good reasons:

Habit

Sometimes a lack of organization is simply due to old habits: you never learned to be organized when you were young. Setting up a filing system seemed irrelevant and unnatural. Your memory was good enough to remember which pile that letter is in. When you are feeling out of control, you may find yourself organizing and cleaning your room. Many people improve their organization as they move into busier times and the growing number of details must be brought under control.

Resistance to Structure

Some people have a philosophical resistance to structure. They are afraid that setting goals, preparing a schedule, or organizing their workspace will decrease their flexibility. Many stereotypes reinforce the idea that genius and organization are not compatible. The ones that come to mind are images of the absent-minded professor, artist, or composer—people with brilliant creative minds but who have no practical skills in everyday living, people who live entirely in the world of their own minds. Perhaps you have been to a home or office that portrays this lifestyle: absolute clutter and disarray, with a seemingly sane and productive occupant. Is organization merely a preoccupation with the mundane? Is a neat house a sign of a dull mind? As we discussed in the last chapter, a totally spontaneous lifestyle actually tends to limit your options over time since you often do not have the time or resources available to take advantage of opportunities that present themselves. The physical, economic, and social realities of daily life require some daily planning and organization—and long-term goals "happen" in daily life.

People who can function at their best in total chaos are the exception rather than the rule. Sometimes a messy room is fine when you are a child and have a grown-up to keep the rest of the house in order, put meals on the table, and bring you clean clothes. Even a disorderly dormitory room is not too dangerous unless you have a neat roommate. A lack of organization becomes increasingly risky as life becomes filled with more responsibility, when you need to share a living or working space with others, and as you have more "stuff" to keep track of. Despite the stereotype of the absent-minded professor, in real life, successful people (including professors) tend to maintain a fairly high level of organization that supports their personal and professional growth and enhances their enjoyment of life.

If organization is a stranger in your life, try adding suggestions that sound appealing and reasonable to you one at a time. We all have very different styles; the goal of this chapter is not to turn everyone into a superorganized efficiency freak but simply to take some of the stress out of daily life. Time management and organization are associated with academic success (Britton & Tesser, 1991; Macan et al., 1990). In fact, one interesting study found that time management and organization were better predictors of college grade point average than high school! SAT scores (Britton & Tesser, 1991)!

The first step toward improving daily habits that ease the stress of disorganization is awareness. One stress management student had spent his 40-something years developing a total lack of environmental connection—that is, he was a slob. His loving wife accepted him and his slovenly ways, and never nagged. One day, however, she pointed out to him that he had walked *past* the wastebasket with his empty ice cream container and set it on the counter instead. At that point, he realized that simply putting things where they belonged the first time often took rela-

I'm fixing a hole where the rain gets in, and stops my mind from wandering where it will go.

JOHN LENNON AND
PAUL MCCARTNEY

tively little effort and saved time later on. He had to admit that he did enjoy having the house look nice and decided to start trying to pick up after himself.

Procrastination

Procrastination means putting off doing something you have decided to do until a future time. Almost everyone procrastinates about some activities occasionally. But chronic procrastination can develop into a self-defeating habit that prevents you from doing the things you want to do and from reaching goals you have set for yourself (Lay, 1994; Schouwenberg, 1992; Sommer, 1990).

Procrastination can be a major source of stress. Chronic procrastinators often have low self-esteem combined with unrealistically high expectations for their performance (Ferrari, 1991). They berate themselves for procrastinating; but the thought of facing the task at hand is so overwhelming, they procrastinate some more, and thus create a vicious cycle of procrastination, self-denigration, low self-esteem, and further procrastination (Burns, 1980; Ellis & Kraus, 1977; Schafer, 1987).

Procrastination can keep you from addressing many important issues, such as your study schedule, your job search, or your desire to stop smoking. "I'll do it later" gives you the false reassurance it will get done, so you can temporarily put the onerous task out of your mind. But the stress accumulates. That paper still needs to be written, and instead of completing it in a calm and timely fashion, you face enormous time pressure and frustration when things don't go smoothly (and they rarely do). More information on the causes of procrastination and practical advice on confronting procrastination are presented later in this chapter.

ORGANIZE YOUR ENVIRONMENT: REDUCE STRESS BY REDUCING DAILY HASSLES

Many people find that most of their daily stress comes not from those big events that give you lots of life change units (see Chapter 4), like death and divorce, but from the little things that go wrong: the alarm clock that didn't go off, lost keys, trouble getting the materials you need from the library, or difficulty finding a parking space. Minor hassles such as these can cause a major stress response (Kanner, Coyne, Schaefer, & Lazarus, 1981). Organization increases your stress resistance because it reduces the time you waste on trivial activities (Richards, 1987).

Would your feelings of stress be reduced with better organization? Review your stress log noting the stressors that occurred during that period of time. Think also about other stressors that have come up in the past few weeks. Could any of your stressors be eliminated or reduced with better organization? If you frequently become stressed because of losing or misplacing things, or running out of gas, supplies, and so on, a little focused organization and planning may be helpful. If so, make a list of your organizational hassles and brainstorm creative solutions. Here are some examples.

Problem: Trouble finding keys.
Possible solution: At home, always keep keys in top desk drawer. When out, always keep keys in same pocket.

Problem: Needing to shop for food once or twice a day.
Possible solution: Plan menus and shopping list so that one shopping trip gets enough food for several days.

Problem: Cluttered home.
Possible solution: Get rid of items that are not needed. Put things away after using them. Do a quick pickup in the afternoon before dinner. (With a roommate or a family, enlist the help of *everyone.*)

Problem: Difficulty getting out the door on time in the morning.
Possible solution: Get up earlier. Set out things you will need for the morning the night before. Make lunches night before.

Create a Stress-Free Home Environment

Personal needs for an organized environment vary tremendously. For any one person, these needs vary from time to time. You may have no problems with a cluttered work area until you feel stressed, when the first thing you do is clean off the desk. Similarly, you may not mind a messy bedroom but must have an organized kitchen.

Many people find that making their home a sanctuary helps increase their stress resistance. While chaos may rage in the world outside, at least peace and serenity can be found in the home. Creating a peaceful room or corner of one's own can be an effective stress buffer.

Create a Productive Work Environment

Just as you need a place to relax, you need a place to work. You receive messages from your environment at both the conscious and subconscious levels. The television says "Watch me"; the refrigerator says "Have a snack"; the stack of dirty dishes says "Wash me." A work environment should be as free of distractions as possible and should suggest to you that now is the time to get some work done. Part of your response to a work environment is conditioned, or learned. By working at your desk, you learn to associate writing, reading, and studying with that environment. Like any habit, this association builds with time (Longman & Atkinson, 1988).

A consultant who leads study skills workshops for college students once commented on the number of students who do not create a productive work environment. When asked, "Do you study at your desk?" a majority of students in her workshop reply "No." When asked why not, they say "Because it is too cluttered; there's no room to work." "So where do you study?" she then asks. What is the most popular answer? "In bed." "Don't you fall asleep?" she asks. "Yes," reply most students.

A productive work environment means working smarter—getting more good work accomplished in less time so you have more time in your life for other things. Take a look at your work environment and analyze it for comfort, organization, and convenience. Once again, less is more; a cluttered work space is the most common barrier to productivity. When you work in an area with stacks of works-in-progress, you have more difficulty concentrating on the project at hand. The sight of other demands teases your concentration away from the project in front of you: out of sight, out of mind. Clear your desk. Put away everything but that current assignment. At the end of the work day, put away everything but that most important priority you plan to do first thing in the morning.

Get Support

Cultivate support for your organizational efforts, both at home and at work. Housemates and families can have a group meeting to organize efficient ways to deal with household chores. They can set up routines for mealtime and for keeping things neat. In reality, organizational systems never reach a state of perfection, but you will still feel less stress with each improvement, even small ones. Keep an eye on the future as you work for organization. Change always takes effort. In the short run, it is easier to "do it myself" than get your roommate, friends, or children to hang up their coats. But eventually even children (even roommates!) catch on. Decide which changes are most important to you, and begin.

▶ STRESS RESEARCH

Kanner et al.: *Daily Hassles and Uplifts*

> It is not the large things that
>   send a man to the madhouse. . . .
> No, it's the continuing series
>   of small tragedies that send
>   a man to the madhouse
> Not the death of this love
>   but a shoelace that
>   snaps with no time left.
>
>   CHARLES BUKOWSKI

Many readers will agree with the sentiment expressed in this poem. So did researchers Allen Kanner and colleagues, who in 1981 developed a new approach to the measurement of stress. They used two scales that measured daily hassles and uplifts to predict psychological symptoms such as depression and anxiety (Kanner, Coyne, Schaefer, & Lazarus, 1981), and stress-related illness (DeLongis, Folkman, & Lazarus 1988). Their research was partly a response to the pioneering work of Holmes and Rahe on the relationship between life events and health (Holmes & Rahe, 1967) (see page 67). Kanner and colleagues hypothesized that the cumulative effect of daily hassles would have a stronger impact on health than would major life events, and they conducted research that supported this notion.

Both scales continue to be used in stress research today. The hassles scale contains 117 items commonly found to be annoying, and they are rated according to their frequency and sometimes their intensity of occurrence. Hassles are defined as "the irritating, frustrating, distressing demands that to some degree characterize everyday transactions with the environment" (Kanner et al., 1981, p. 3). The uplifts scale contains 135 items. Uplifts are described as "positive experiences such as the joy derived from manifestations of love, relief at hearing good news, the pleasure of a good night's rest, and so on" (Kanner et al., 1981, p. 6). The ten most common hassles and uplifts are identified in the following list. While a score on the hassles scale has shown a fairly strong relationship to psychological and physical health, the

relationship between uplifts and health is less clear (Kanner, Feldman, Weinberger, & Ford, 1991).

Hassles and uplifts may reflect stress and interact with health in several ways. Certainly when our psychological or physical health is low, we perceive more problems and fewer bright spots. These ups and downs may also reflect major life events: rising prices are more likely to be perceived as a real problem if you've just lost your job. In addition, people reporting a high number of irritations may not have very effective coping skills. Poor organization, for example, may lead to several of the difficulties listed below.

Ten Most Frequent Hassles and Uplifts

Hassles
1. Concern about weight
2. Health of a family member
3. Rising prices of common goods
4. Home maintenance
5. Overload of things to do
6. Tendency to misplace or lose things
7. Yard work or outside home maintenance
8. Property, investment, or taxes
9. Crime
10. Physical appearance

Uplifts
11. Relating well with your spouse or lover
12. Relating well with friends
13. Completing a task
14. Feeling healthy
15. Getting enough sleep
16. Eating out
17. Meeting your responsibilities
18. Visiting, phoning, or writing someone
19. Spending time with family
20. Being pleased with your home (inside)

Source: Items are from AD Kanner, JC Coyne, C Schaefer, and RS Lazarus, "Comparison of two modes of stress measurement: Daily hassles and uplifts versus major life events." *Journal of Behavioral Medicine* 4: 14, 1981.

STUDY SKILLS

Most college students get a good start on developing helpful study skills in high school, and these skills become further refined in college, although some research suggests that many students still have room for improvement (Brown, 1991; Turner, 1992). Good study skills evolve into good work skills later in life, so their development is essential to reducing stress throughout your lifetime, not just while you are a student.

Create Productive Work and Study Habits

Study habits are so named for a reason. A study routine becomes second nature. Just as a work environment becomes associated with working, so does a "same time, same place" routine automatically put you in gear for that activity. Set up a realistic schedule for study or project time that takes advantage of your internal and external prime time as much as possible. After sticking to a routine for at least three weeks, your concentration during these times will improve. You will find it easier to get into your work and stick to it. Those around you will also get used to the routine and figure out the best times to catch you. A similar routine every weekday is easiest to follow, although this is not always feasible for students with irregular class schedules. You may at least be able to cultivate a regular Monday–Wednesday schedule and a regular Tuesday–Thursday schedule.

Learn to Concentrate

The amount of time spent studying for an exam or working on a project is almost irrelevant; it's the quality of the work that counts. One productive hour of studying is worth three hours of haphazard review combined with a moderate amount of daydreaming. Concentration improves with practice, and students generally get a lot of practice.

Schedule Uninterrupted Time

Some students have difficulty structuring blocks of uninterrupted time. Concentration is a fragile state, easily broken. Telephones ringing, friends and co-workers dropping by all break that flow of concentration required for working smarter. What sort of interruptions are a problem for you? When you are scheduling time for important projects, block out time periods that are least likely to offer interruptions and then make a plan to minimize interruptions that do occur. Some students find they get more done at a workstation in the library where their friends can't distract them. Another common strategy is for a group of friends to agree to study at the same time so they can get together and do something fun later.

Practice tactful ways of telling people you are busy. When friends stop by to chat, let them know you'll have more time later. Take a look at the clock when the telephone rings and limit calls when you are working on that high-priority project. Return the call later, or let the caller know right away you have just a few minutes to talk. Let the answering machine or voice mail take the call. You don't always have to be this stingy with your time, just during those high-productivity periods when good concentration is a must.

Go with Your Flow

It pays to take advantage of your mood whenever possible. Perhaps you have two or three top priority projects for the day, and you are beginning a three-hour block of time you've reserved for one of these projects. Pick the top priority job that appeals to you most and tackle it. Do you have good ideas in the shower, on the bus, in the middle of the night? Jot them down. It's Saturday afternoon and you had planned to do your shopping, but you feel like working on that paper. Go ahead. Break your schedule whenever doing so makes sense. Inspiration is important for any project, so take advantage of it when it arrives.

Similarly, keep going when you're flowing. If a project is going smoothly, it is easy to be lulled into false security and take a break, assuming the work will always go this well. But often when you return, you've lost the spark. Don't take productive periods for granted. Rearrange your schedule to get the most out of this current flow.

Concentration and productivity are always better when you like the project you are working on. If you dislike a project, completing it will take longer—and seem to take even longer than it does! Besides, life is too short to waste time on things you dislike. Find something to value or enjoy in every project you do. Pick a topic of interest for your research papers, find something in that lab report to enjoy, and remind yourself why you enrolled in a course or program to begin with. And remember: challenges build character and skills.

Student Behavior

There are many things you can do to make your life as a student easier, like staying caught up with your work and scheduling assignments appropriately so that you avoid last minute overload. The next sections offer a few other suggestions.

Attend Class and Take Notes Do we really have to say this? Successful students rarely miss a class. Of course, there are always a few exceptions. Perhaps you know someone who never attends class, studies like crazy for a few days before the exam, and still gets good grades. These examples are rare. The great majority of A students consistently attend class, sit near the front, tune in to what the teacher is discussing, and take good notes.

Why is class attendance so important? The lectures and discussions reinforce the important material—the part most critical for your understanding of the class and, of course, the material most likely to be on the exam. If you have to miss a class, get a copy of the notes. Most students, however, find they learn much more by listening to the lecture and discussion and taking their own notes than by studying someone else's notes.

Students are expected to take notes during a lecture or class discussion to help them remember important material. Notes are also a great exam study guide. Successful note takers develop some sort of shorthand that allows them to write down ideas quickly. Since you can't possibly write down every word the teacher says, you must try to focus on brief phrases that capture the important points. Many students spend some time recopying or filling in their notes after class, when their memory of the class is still fresh. This is an especially good practice for courses in which you are experiencing some difficulty. Going over your notes soon after class reinforces the material and helps you clarify half-completed thoughts and illegible handwriting.

Stay Involved in Class Get the most out of the time you spend in class by staying involved. You are wasting your time if your mind keeps wandering during the lecture and discussion and you miss a lot of what the class was about. Taking good notes is one way to keep your mind on what the teacher is saying. So is talking in class. If the teacher asks a question, volunteer an answer. If something is unclear, ask a question. The adrenaline rush of putting yourself on the spot and speaking up in class keeps you awake and attentive. It helps your mind work better. Talking in class gives you valuable feedback, too. Whether your answer is right or wrong, you will learn something. Maximize your mental involvement in each class to retain more information and understand important concepts.

Do Your Homework Homework such as reading assignments, completing problem sets, or writing essays enhances learning. Even if the homework is not graded, it helps you stay involved in the class and learn important material. You get more out of class if you are prepared. You are probably afraid of asking questions in class when you haven't done all the assigned reading. You're less afraid to talk to the professor when you have a good idea of what he or she is talking about. Since you already know something about the lecture topic, it's easier to take notes.

Talk to Your Professors When you have questions, talk to your professor after class. Visit during office hours. Make an appointment to meet if you are not free during office hours. Send an e-mail message. If you're having trouble with a course, ask for help. Most professors have sympathy for students who show them they are trying. Let your professor know you care and are doing your best, even if your marks don't reflect your hard work.

Professors can be wonderful sources for career counseling. If one of your professors is in a field of interest to you, arrange a time to get information about graduate programs or advice on your job search.

Reading and Studying

Students spend a lot of time reading and studying. You know that some reading and studying time is very productive; other times you may stare at the same page of text for an hour with nothing sinking in. Organize your reading and studying time and approach this period with concentration and involvement. Be sure you get to the high-priority assignments. Outline important readings; make study cards from your notes. Devise memory games to help you remember important concepts. Answer imaginary exam questions you will be likely to encounter on a real exam.

What about study groups? If you study in a group, be sure your group stays on track. Agree on priorities and stick to high-priority topics. Study groups can be very helpful, as members take turns teaching each other important concepts. As with any form of studying, stay involved, concentrate, and participate fully.

Preparing for Exams, Taking Exams, and Scheduling Your Work: The 80/20 Rule Revisited

We've already discussed how to select priorities and design a realistic schedule. The same procedures can be applied to preparing for and taking exams and scheduling your homework. Apply the 80/20 rule to allocate your time: 80 percent of the benefit comes from doing 20 percent of the work. When preparing for an exam, you may not have the time to reread and study every assigned reading, to outline your notes, and redo every homework problem. What is the 20 percent that will at least get you a B on the exam? Memorizing the class notes? Answering the study questions? Whatever it is, begin with that. Do your best with the time you have, then move on to the next priority. The same goes for taking an exam. Spend the most time on the questions with the most points. Don't agonize over a few questions worth only 2 or 3 points each, but keep going. Be sure you have enough time for the essay question worth 25 points at the end. The same goes for allotting time to assignments. Many students make the mistake of spending a great deal of time on a small assignment that may count for only a small proportion of their class grade and not leave enough time for a major term paper that may represent 50 percent of their grade in some other course.

Get Help: Take Advantage of Campus Resources

Most campuses have resources to help students experiencing academic distress (Cone & Owens, 1991). Some offer study skills and time management workshops. Some offer help editing term papers. If you have problems studying for a particular course, you may be able to get help finding (and funding) a tutor. Don't forget to talk to your professors and classmates, residential staff, and counselors. Different study strategies work for different students. Each person has preferred ways of processing and memorizing information (Henry & Swartz, 1992). Gaining an understanding of your particular learning style can be helpful (Griggs, 1990).

CONFRONTING PROCRASTINATION

All this information on setting priorities, designing schedules, and practicing good study skills sounds logical and reasonable. Why is it still so hard to plan ahead and stick to a plan? Procrastination. We've even put off dealing with this topic until the end of the chapter!

Procrastination can stem from deep personal problems, especially fear of failure (Beery, 1975; Schouwenburg, 1972; Williams & Long, 1991) and fear of success (Burka & Yuen, 1983). An aversion to the tasks needing completion and an inability to persevere when faced with difficulty are also problems for many procrastinators (Ferrari, Parker, & Ware, 1992; Lay, 1992; Rothblum, Solomon, & Murakami, 1986; Solomon & Rothblum, 1984). Chronic procrastination has been linked to various types of anxiety, including test anxiety, social anxiety, and self-consciousness (Ferrari, 1991a; Lay, 1994; Milgram, Dangour, & Raviv, 1992; Milgram, Gehrman, & Keinan, 1992) and feelings of dejection (Lay, 1994). Some people use procrastination to protect their self-esteem: they didn't have enough time to do a good job (Ferrari, 1991b; Lay 1990).

When you find yourself procrastinating, the first step is to figure out why. Chronic procrastinators who are really stressed about their procrastination habit will probably need to work with a counselor or therapist on issues underlying their procrastination habit. Mild procrastinators may find success on their own with a little perseverance.

Procrastination Can Be a Good Idea

Sometimes there are very good reasons for procrastinating. The task might be something you don't really need to do: a low-priority item. Cross it off your list! Sometimes you simply need more information before you begin. Getting that information becomes a lead-in to the project. For example, difficulty starting a lab report may be overcome by getting help from the professor or another student in the class.

Sometimes the project doesn't "feel right." You may have doubts about the approach you are considering; you're afraid the project is doomed to failure, that it will be a waste of time. Group projects are especially vulnerable. You may be procrastinating because a project needs more shaping and research before you begin on your part of the task. If your committee has decided to design a campus newletter of some sort and you fear it is a half-baked idea, take your concerns back to the committee. Why waste time writing a column for a newsletter that will never be printed? Your procrastination may have a serious, worthwhile message. Listen to it (Lakein, 1973).

Listen to Your Self-Talk and Question Irrational Beliefs

When you are feeling stressed, listening to the conversations you have with yourself inside your head can provide insight. If you listen carefully, you may catch words or phrases like "I'll never be able to do this," "That teacher is a jerk," or "Writing that paper will be too much work." Sometimes this internal dialogue will reveal your reasons for procrastinating.

Chronic procrastination often stems from **irrational beliefs** that you hold about yourself and the world and the way things ought to be (Ellis & Knaus, 1977; Schafer, 1987). The belief that one must do everything perfectly is an irrational belief, irrational because achieving perfection is not possible. This belief contributes to **perfectionism,** the need to do everything perfectly. Research supports the link between perfectionism and procrastination (Flett, Blankstein, Hewitt, & Koledin, 1992). Perfectionists have several stressful traits. They tend (1) to have unrealistically high personal standards, (2) to perceive their parents to have very high expectations of them and to be very critical of them, and (3) to doubt the quality of their own achievements (Frost, Marten, Lahart, & Rosenblate, 1990; Flett et al., 1992).

Another irrational belief is that one must continually strive to win everyone's love and approval. Obviously this is an impossibility, but it can be a driving force in many of our lives nonetheless. It's easy to see that people can have difficulty studying for an exam if they feel they must do everything perfectly to make everyone like them or life will be horrible! Beliefs like these contribute to low self-esteem and create feelings of anxiety, depression, and hopelessness. How can you possibly be productive when you feel this way?

Two other common causes of procrastination that stem from irrational beliefs are *low-frustration tolerance* and *hostility* (Ellis & Knaus, 1977). Low-frustration tolerance grows out of a belief that one cannot deal with anything boring or difficult. Take studying for example. Studying can be boring and difficult. It takes time and keeps you from doing things you might rather do. Most students, however, have accepted the value of delayed gratification. They believe a little time and effort today will bring future rewards. They would respond, "So studying is not always great, but there are some advantages. Sometimes I learn interesting things, and I really want to pass this course and get my degree. If I don't study I will do poorly on the exam, have to take the course again, and waste the time and money I've already put into the course this semester." The disadvantages of *not* studying outweigh the disadvantages of studying. But the serious procrastinator with a low-frustration tolerance has a different train of thought. "Studying is boring and difficult. I can't deal with boring and difficult tasks. Therefore I can't stand studying. Things I can't stand should not exist. I shouldn't have to study. I just can't bear to sit down and memorize this stuff. Professors are mean and horrible to require studying. I'll show them—I'm not about to waste my time studying for their stupid exams!"

Where does a low-frustration tolerance come from? Some writers have argued that it is supported by our culture and that it goes along with addiction (Ellis & Knaus, 1977; Peele & Brodsky, 1975). The underlying belief is that life should be fair, things should come easily, and there should be a quick fix for any problem that might crop up. Life might be like that in stories, television, and movies. Advertisements advise us to buy a product to solve a problem: the right cigarette will bring you romance, the right soft drink will make you the life of the party. Trouble sleeping? Feeling anxious? Need more energy? Take a pill. A quick solution is more desirable than confronting the issues causing insomnia, anxiety, or lethargy. In real life, difficulties and tragedies arise. Everyone experiences painful emotions from time to time. Stress is a part of life. You must learn to cope effectively with challenges; you must not run away from difficult issues but grow through them—behavior that reduces stress in the long run.

Hostility often goes with low-frustration tolerance (Ellis & Knaus, 1977). Irrational beliefs underlying hostility include the idea that "Other people must treat me nicely and do what I want." People who don't live up to your expectations are evil, horrible, and deserve to be punished. Consider students who procrastinate because they really do not want to be in school. Their thinking might go something like this. "I shouldn't waste my time studying for this stupid exam. I don't even want

We do not see things as they are; we see things as we are.

TALMUD

Calvin and Hobbes   by Bill Watterson

to be in this class, or even this school. I hate this place. Why did my parents make me come here? Good parents don't make their kids do stuff they don't want to do. Why did I end up with such horrible parents? I don't deserve it. Why should they make me study for this exam? I'll show them who's in charge!" Procrastination accompanied by hostility is a form of nonassertive behavior, in which the real issue (in this case, conflict with parents over education) is not addressed, but the procrastinator acts out against the problematic people by procrastinating. This "communication method," if you can call it that, is ineffective and damaging—most of all to the procrastinators themselves. We talk more about effective communication skills in the next chapter, and about irrational beliefs in Chapter 12.

Confront Procrastination

Once you have explored your reasons for procrastinating, you will need to confront your behavior. Sometimes changing your behavior means changing your thoughts and feelings as well. Get to the source of your tendency to procrastinate and cope with the problem. If irrational beliefs and negative self-talk are problems, replace them with realistic self-statements. Instead of perfectionism, tell yourself "I will do my best with the time I have; that's all anyone can do." Instead of "I can't do this," try "Many other people probably find this difficult, too. I'll keep working on it and get help if I need it." Instead of blaming others for your frustration, accept the reality that challenges are a fact of life. It may seem at times that others are to blame, but the blaming process is futile and gets you nothing but anger. Acknowledge the situation and try to solve the problem.

Sometimes you can effectively confront procrastination by analyzing your choices. When you convince yourself that the future difficulties that will result from your procrastination will be worse than completing the job at hand, you may become motivated to stop putting it off (Brown, 1991; Lay & Burns, 1991; Milgram, Gehrman, & Keinan, 1992). Which is easier: taking the car in for routine service or locating and paying for emergency repairs when the car breaks down in a strange town? Looking for an interesting summer internship now or enduring a convenient but boring job you grabbed in June?

Break the Procrastination Habit

People with a mild or occasional procrastination habit have found many behavioral techniques helpful in reinforcing their decisions to not procrastinate. These include the following (Lakein, 1973):

1. *Block off escape routes.* Close your door, turn off the telephone, tell your friends you won't be available for that high-priority time period. Make your workstation work so you don't need to get up to get more paper or the books you need or to spend the first hour clearing a spot to work. Become aware of the distractions you use to avoid working: getting a snack, checking your mail six times a day, or walking down the hall to talk to friends.

ACTION PLAN

GOALS AND ACTION PLAN FOR ORGANIZATION, STUDY SKILLS, AND PROCRASTINATION

Review the topics and suggestions presented in this chapter and select two that would be the most helpful. Write these down, and then break each goal into three or more action steps that you can begin implementing right away, just as we did in the last chapter. Think also about what factors might interfere with the implementation of your action steps and how you will deal with these if they should arise.

Goal 1:

Action steps:

Factors that might interfere:

How I'll deal with these interferences:

Goal 2:

Action steps:

Factors that might interfere:

How I'll deal with these interferences:

■ STUDENT STRESS

ROB'S ACTION PLAN

Rob is a fairly good student and is pretty well organized, but he feels stressed when the work piles up during those weeks when many of his assignments are due at once. Rob decides he likes the idea of planning a whole semester and wants to do more advance planning for assignments so those busy weeks aren't such a surprise. He would also like to improve the study area he uses in his room so he doesn't waste so much time clearing off his desk and getting started when he needs to study.

Goal 1: Semester plan

Action steps:

1. Photocopy pages from my wall calendar. Write in assignment due dates and dates for other events I need to work around.
2. Estimate time needed for assignments. Rough estimates will work for all except my three major projects; I'll break them down like the example in the book.
3. Write in approximate dates for starting all projects.

Factors that might interfere:

1. Procrastination! Writing in the due dates, estimating time needed for assignments will take time, and I already feel short on time!
2. My friends will say I am anal if they see my calendar.

How I'll deal with these interferences:

1. I have a 2-hour block of time this afternoon. I'll do the planning right away so I don't have time to procrastinate.
2. I'll keep my calendar in my desk.

Goal 2: Organize study area

Action steps:

1. Clear off desk.
2. Buy a file box to organize class handouts and other stuff that's lying around in stacks.
3. Ask parents if they have a better light I can borrow.

Factors that might interfere:

1. I don't have time to get organized.
2. I don't have money to buy a file box.
3. My parents might not have a light I can borrow.

How I'll deal with these interferences:

1. I'll break the cleanup project into smaller subprojects so I don't have to do it all at once. I'll start by at least putting everything into piles.
2. Get a box from one of the offices for free.
3. Buy a light at the discount store.

2. *Break projects down into manageable chunks.* Start with a five-minute task. Maybe you can't face writing a paper, but you wouldn't mind skimming the text for topic ideas. Finding a job feels overwhelming, but you can pick up the telephone and make an appointment to speak to a career counselor. Warning: five-minute tasks can help get you started on a difficult project but will rarely be all you need to complete it. Eventually you will need to schedule some high-concentration productive time.

3. *Reward yourself for completing tasks.* Let yourself call a friend once you have selected three possible paper topics. Go out for ice cream after the essay is written.

4. *Get help.* If you are stuck, get help from campus resources: your professor, other students, tutors, advisers, and counselors.

SUMMARY

1. A schedule helps you accomplish the action steps that move you toward your important goals. To relieve rather than create stress, a schedule must be realistic, include activities that move you toward your important goals, and fit your lifestyle.
2. Internal prime time refers to your personal energy rhythms. External prime time refers to the rhythms (and constraints) of the rest of the world. You use your time more effectively when you work with these rhythms and around the constraints.
3. Making a semester plan can help you distribute your work more evenly throughout the semester.
4. You use your time better when you focus completely on what you are doing; concentrate on one thing at a time; address priorities first; say no to unimportant tasks; avoid perfectionism; schedule time for a healthful lifestyle; take breaks to relax and refocus; and use small chunks of time for routine tasks. Developing self-discipline to stay focused on your priorities is essential for sticking to your time management action plans.
5. Common obstacles to organization include habit, resistance to structure, and procrastination.
6. Small changes in your level of organization at home and at school can reduce the daily hassles resulting from misplacing things, forgetting assignments, having no clean socks, and so forth. An organized study environment can help you accomplish more in less time.
7. Study skill improvement helps reduce stress for many students. Creating productive work and study habits helps you concentrate and improve the quality of your work.
8. While almost everyone procrastinates on certain tasks, chronic procrastination can stem from deep personal problems and create a great deal of stress. Chronic procrastinators usually need to work with a professional to uncover their reasons for procrastinating and overcome this behavioral pattern.
9. Chronic procrastination often stems from irrational beliefs that result in perfectionism, a low tolerance for frustration, and frequently expressed hostility.

REFERENCES

Beery, RG. Fear of failure in the student experience. *Personnel and Guidance Journal* 54: 190–203, 1975.

Britton, BK, and A Tesser. Effects of time-management practices on college grades. *Journal of Educational Psychology* 83: 405–410, 1991.

Brown, RT. Helping students confront and deal with stress and procrastination. *Journal of College Student Psychotherapy* 6: 87–102, 1991.

Bukowski, C. The shoelace. *Bukowski Reads His Poetry*, Takoma Records, Santa Monica, CA, 1980.

Burka, JB, and LM Yuen. *Procrastination: Why You Do It, What to Do about It.* Reading, MA: Addison-Wesley, 1983.

Burns, DD. The perfectionist's script for self-defeat. *Psychology Today* 14: 34–52, 1980.

Cone, AL, and SK Owens. Academic and locus of control enhancement in a freshman study skills and college adjustment course. *Psychological Reports* 68: 1211–1217, 1991.

DeLongis, A, S Folkman, and RS Lazarus. The impact of daily stress on health and mood: Psychological and social resources as mediators. *Journal of Personality and Social Psychology* 54: 486–495, 1988.

Ellis, A, and WJ Knaus. *Overcoming Procrastination.* New York: Signet, New American Library, 1977.

Ferrari, JR. Compulsive procrastination: Some self-reported characteristics. *Psychological Reports* 68: 455–458, 1991a.

Ferrari, JR. Self-handicapping by procrastinators: Protecting self-esteem, social-esteem, or both? *Journal of Research in Personality* 25: 245–261, 1991b.

Ferrari, JR, JT Parker, and CB Ware. Academic procrastination: Personality correlates with Myers-Briggs Types, self-efficacy, and academic locus of control. *Journal of Social Behavior and Personality* 7: 495–502, 1992.

Flett, GL, KR Blankstein, PL Hewitt, and S Koledin. Components of perfectionism and procrastination in college students. *Social Behavior and Personality* 20: 85–94, 1992.

Frost, RO, P Marten, C Lahart, and R Rosenblate. The dimensions of perfectionism. *Cognitive Therapy and Research* 14: 449–468, 1990.

Girdano, DA, GS Everly, and DE Dusek. *Controlling Stress and Tension: A Holistic Approach.* Englewood Cliffs, NJ: Prentice Hall, 1993.

Griggs, SA. Counseling students toward effective study skills using their learning style strengths. *Journal of Reading, Writing, and Learning Disabilities, International* 6: 281–296, 1990.

Henry, SA, and RG Swartz. Use of accelerated learning techniques in education. *International Brain Dominance Review* 8: 6–12, 1992.

Holmes, TH, and RH Rahe. The social readjustment rating scale. *Journal of Psychosomatic Research* 4: 189–194, 1967.

Kanner, AD, JC Coyne, C Schaefer, and RS Lazarus. Comparison of two modes of stress measurement: Daily hassles and uplifts versus major life events. *Journal of Behavioral Medicine* 4: 1–39, 1981.

Kanner, AD, SS Feldman, DA Weinberger, and ME Ford. Uplifts, hassles, and adaptational outcomes in early adolescents. A Monat and RS Lazarus (eds). *Stress and Coping: An Anthology.* New York: Columbia University Press, 1991.

Lakein, A. *How to Get Control of Your Time and Your Life.* New York: Signet Books, New American Library, 1973.

Lay, CH. Working to schedule on personal projects. *Journal of Social Behavior and Personality* 5: 91–103, 1990.

Lay, CH. Trait procrastination and the perception of person-task characteristics. *Journal of Social Behavior and Personality* 7: 483–494, 1992.

Lay, CH, and P Burns. Intentions and behavior in studying for an examination: The role of trait procrastination and its interaction with optimism. *Journal of Social Behavior and Personality* 6: 605–617, 1991.

Lay, CH. Trait procrastination and affective experiences: Describing past study behavior and its relation to agitation and dejection. *Motivation and Emotion* 18: 269–284, 1994.

Longman, DG, and RH Atkinson. *College Learning and Study Skills.* St Paul, MN: West Publishing, 1988.

Macan, TH, C Shahani, RL Dipboye, and AP Phillips. College students' time management: Correlationships with academic performance and stress. *Journal of Educational Psychology* 82: 760–768, 1990.

Mackenzie, RA. *The Time Trap.* New York: AMACOM, 1972.

Milgram, NA, W Dangour, and A Raviv. Situational and personal determinants of academic procrastination. *Journal of General Psychology* 119: 123–133, 1992.

Milgram, NA, T Gehrman, and G Keinan. Procrastination and emotional upset: A typological model. *Personality and Individual Differences* 13: 1307–1313, 1992.

Peele, S, with A Brodsky. *Love and Addiction.* New York: Signet, New American Library, 1975.

Richards, JH. Time management—A review. *Work and Stress* 1: 73–78, 1987.

Rothblum, ED, LJ Solomon, and J Murakami. Affective, cognitive, and behavioral differences between high and low procrastinators. *Journal of Counseling Psychology* 33: 387–394, 1986.

Schafer, W. *Stress Management for Wellness.* New York: Holt, Rinehart and Winston, 1987.

Schouwenburg, HC. Procrastinators and fear of failure: An exploration of reasons for procrastination. *European Journal of Personality* 6: 225–236, 1992.

Simons, DJ, and KM Galotti. Everyday planning: An analysis of daily time management. *Bulletin of the Psychonomic Society* 30: 61–64, 1992.

Solomon, LJ, and ED Rothblum. Academic procrastination: Frequency and cognitive-behavioral correlates. *Journal of Counseling Psychology* 31: 503–509, 1984.

Sommer, WG. Procrastination and cramming: How adept students ace the system. *Journal of American College Health* 39: 5–10, 1990.

Turner, GY. College students' self-awareness of study behaviors. *College Student Journal* 26: 129–134, 1992.

Williams, RL, and JD Long. *Manage Your Life.* Boston: Houghton, Mifflin, 1991.

chapter **8**

Communication Skills

Stress often arises from interactions with other people. In fact, other people are involved in most stressors, either as part of the stressor or as a potential solution. Communication, both verbal and nonverbal, is the vehicle of your interaction with others. Every relationship involves communication—from the most casual encounter with a clerk at the grocery store to a meaningful conversation with your best friend. You may say "we don't communicate" about an estranged relative, but your lack of contact is in itself a form of communication that says "stay away."

COMMUNICATION AND STRESS

Good communication skills increase your stress resistance in several ways and influence all components of your stress cycle.

Authentic Relationships and Social Support

Good communication skills help create authentic relationships. Friendships are based on mutual involvement and exchange. How can you be a good friend if you are not sharing yourself with others? If you are always smiling and agreeable while keeping your true feelings to yourself, you will feel lonely since none of your relationships is truly intimate. An important element of friendship will be missing if you never share your real thoughts and feelings with anyone. Other people may "like" you and find you easy to get along with, but they will not know you, and deeper friendships will be unsatisfying and will rarely develop.

Positive social support is an important stress buffer (Cohen, 1988; Cassel, 1974; Elliott & Gramling, 1990). Good communication skills help you create a support network of friends and acquaintances and give you the communication tools you need to access this support. Social support means other people are available to help you when you are in a high-stress period. But this support can be more or less helpful depending on how you communicate. Some people have good intentions but the things they say and do can actually make your stressful situation worse if you do not give them appropriate direction. For example, suppose you are behind in your studies and in danger of failing a course. Your well-meaning mother calls every night to be sure you are studying and to offer support and advice, but these calls just make you more anxious. After you hang up the phone, you have even more trouble concentrating on your work. What do you do? If you politely listen and respond to her calls, you are encouraging her to continue. If instead you say, "Look, Mom, if you really want to help, how about giving me some money to hire a tutor and not calling during my study time? I would love to talk on Saturday mornings when I am not feeling pressured by all my work." In this way, your communication can encourage the positive social support that increases your stress resistance.

Direct Coping

Good communication skills enhance direct coping so that you can effectively change many sources of stress. Effective communication is essential for changing many sources of stress, especially stressors that involve people with whom you find it difficult to work. Effective communication can help you address fairly simple sorts of stressors as well, such as asking for help on projects or changes in your living situation.

Problem Solving and Time Management

Good communication skills are important for implementing other stress management strategies, including problem solving and time management. When disagreements arise, good communication skills can keep you on a problem-solving track and away from personal attack. Time management involves setting limits as well as priorities. Saying no to low-priority requests and following through on your priorities and schedules is easier with good communication skills.

Good Communication Promotes Healthy Emotions

Poor communication often leads to anger, isolation, loneliness, and depression. These emotions are frequently the result of misunderstanding. The way you communicate teaches other people how you expect to be treated. If you say yes to every request for assistance, even when you resent the imposition, you teach others it is all right to ask and that you will do whatever they want. For example, if you always agree to watch the neighbor's children, even when you have to change your plans for the day, you teach the neighbor to keep asking because silence implies consent (Arapakis, 1990). Your resentment grows and you feel angry and stressed. When you feel misunderstood, unappreciated, and offended, you may begin to believe that others do not care about you, a mind-set that leads to isolation, loneliness, and depression.

On the other hand, good communication helps you avoid misunderstandings. If you are not accustomed to direct communication, telling someone you cannot comply with a request or offering a contradictory opinion may make you feel uncomfortable at first, but the long-term emotional consequences will eventually be positive. Once you become more adept at setting reasonable limits and sharing your feelings, you will feel better about yourself and experience less anger. You will also feel better about your relationships with other people.

Communicate to Relate

The best reason to improve your communication skills goes beyond avoiding stress. Deep, meaningful friendships based on true relatedness provide enormous emotional fulfillment. People need more than people. We all need good relationships with people—friendships based on mutual caring and respect. But relationships are demanding, and intimate friendships are often the most demanding of all. Love is not something we "fall" into but a relationship that is sustained through honest, effective communication.

Your health is bound to be affected if day after day you say the opposite of what you feel.

BORIS PASTERNAK

YOUR CHILDHOOD: EARLY LESSONS IN COMMUNICATION

Where do people learn how to communicate effectively? Most people grow up emulating their parents and friends; they imitate the communication styles they see. If your parents were the strong, silent type, rarely letting anyone in on their feelings, you may feel uncomfortable sharing your feelings with others. If your parents dealt with anger by suppressing it, avoiding difficult subjects, and failing to come to mutually satisfying compromises, solving problems when you feel angry may be challenging for you.

Much has been made of the observation that children from dysfunctional families seem to have poor communication and relational skills that they carry with them into adulthood (Gravitz & Bowden, 1987). A dysfunctional family is one in which relationships are not "normal" but are strained by the presence of difficult situations, such as a family member who abuses alcohol or works too much. This strain produces chronic stress that alters family members' relationships and communication patterns with each other and with people outside the family structure. In general, adult children of alcoholics tend to seek approval and affirmation and to be somewhat fearful of expressing their true thoughts and feelings (Edlin & Golanty, 1992; Brown, 1988).

Some observers have argued, however, that up to 96 percent of the U.S. population grows up in a family somewhat dysfunctional in nature and exhibits traits commonly ascribed to adult children of alcoholics, or adult children who grew up in some other form of dysfunctional family (Gravitz & Bowden, 1987; Peele, 1989)! This means that very few people had optimal communication role models growing up, so almost all of us can benefit from improving our communication skills, whether in conjunction with appropriate therapy to deal with the problems that underlie difficulty in communicating or simply beginning with the information outlined in this chapter.

EFFECTIVE COMMUNICATION STARTS WITH LISTENING

When people think about improving their communication skills, most think about talking: delivering a more persuasive argument, giving a more convincing speech, or presenting themselves as more charming and entertaining conversationalists at parties. But improving communication skills really begins with awareness of the audience you are trying to reach.

Receiving Messages: Stop, Look, and Listen

Think about the friends you most enjoy spending time with, the people you have the best time talking to: lengthy conversations on the meaning of life, inspired descriptions of your secret dreams, shared confidences about personal matters—the conversations with real connection. What is it about these people that draws you to them? Probably you will remark on qualities such as feeling understood and appreciated, and sharing interests and experiences. It's not so much that your friends are good storytellers, although that is entertaining, too. More important is that your friends let you share your thoughts and feelings with them. You enjoy talking to friends who are good listeners.

People who don't listen are boring. Have you ever met someone like this at a party—someone who could talk at length on just about any topic but rarely looked you in the eye or asked for your point of view? If cornered by such a conversation hog, you probably looked for a quick way out and more interesting company.

Effective Listening

One of the most important communication skills is *effective listening* (McKay, Davis, & Fanning, 1995). Effective listening is more than listening to another person's words. It means trying to hear the real meaning behind those words and conveying your interest and understanding to the speaker. Learning to be an effective listener offers several advantages. When you practice effective listening, people want to be with you. Effective listening is also the best way to obtain accurate information that can be useful for anything from getting to know someone better to solving difficult problems. When you listen effectively, your own messages will be more likely to connect with your listeners, since you will have a better idea of who your listeners really are. Effective listening is also a more interesting way to spend your time (and your life) than just pretending to listen while your mind is bored and elsewhere, since real relationships with people are based on sending and receiving accurate messages. An important skill known as *active listening* will help you become a more effective listener.

Active Listening

Active listening is usually a part of the effective listening process. When you listen actively, you ask questions that will help you understand what the speaker is saying and respond so the listener can understand what you are hearing. It sounds complicated because communication often is! We all see the world differently and language cannot convey everything we truly think and feel. We can never step completely into each other's shoes.

When conversations get emotional, active listening can provide a lifeboat in dangerous seas. Unfortunately, when we feel angry or threatened, we are more likely to cling to our habitual response patterns. To illustrate, let's use active listening to revise the following conversation between a dating couple, Jill and Kevin:

Jill: I'm really getting tired of going to parties with you every weekend. You disappear the minute we get in the door. If we do get a minute to talk, it's always with a hundred other people around over blaring music with you half-drunk.

Kevin: Well, you'd have more fun if you didn't stand around looking bored. I know you don't like my friends, but you could at least try just once not to act like you're better than everyone else.

Jill: Better than everyone else! Your friends are the ones who act like they're better than everyone else! They never even come over to talk to me unless you're there!

Kevin: So what am I supposed to do? Stay glued to your side like a trained poodle so someone will talk to you?

Can you see what is happening here? Every conversation has a motion, a direction. This conversation has gotten off the track from Jill's original concern that she would prefer not to attend parties every weekend. The direction of this conversation is unproductive. Worse, it is hurting the individuals involved.

Active listeners *paraphrase* what they hear the speaker say. To paraphrase means to put into your own words what you think someone has just said. Let's look at our previous example. This time Kevin practices active listening.

Jill: I'm really getting tired of going to parties with you every weekend. You disappear the minute we get in the door. If we do get a minute to talk, it's always with a hundred other people around over blaring music with you half-drunk.

Kevin: I thought you enjoyed going to parties with me, but it sounds like these parties are not much fun for you anymore.

Jill: What I would really like to do is go out alone with you sometimes, so we would have a chance to talk.

Kevin: It sounds to me like you might enjoy going out to eat or doing something that involves just the two of us once in a while.

Do you see how Kevin was paraphrasing some of Jill's concerns? Paraphrasing has several important effects. It tells people you are really listening and care about what they say. Paraphrasing also allows you to check whether you are interpreting the speaker's words correctly. It can help you clarify what the speaker is saying. Another benefit of active listening is that you become more involved in the conversation and are less likely to listen only partially and miss important information.

At this point, Kevin and Jill may still be harboring some resentment toward each other, but at least they both still have their dignity intact, and they have not reached a communication stalemate where further conversation becomes only more toxic. This active listening conversation can now move in the problem-solving direction. Both Kevin and Jill can talk about what they would like to do most on weekends, and then work out a compromise.

Active Listening Helps Both Speaker and Listener

In the first conversation, both Kevin and Jill seemed to be responding defensively to a personal attack. In the second conversation, Kevin's active listening allowed Jill to lower her guard; and since she felt that Kevin cared about what she was saying, she was then more likely to be receptive to his feelings and concerns as well. Both Kevin and Jill "win" in this situation because they have a better chance to reach a positive solution to the problem and to do so without creating more layers of injury and resentment.

Conversations such as the one above may sound phony and contrived, but you will learn how to paraphrase in your own style. Typical phrases that indicate to a speaker that you are listening include "It sounds like . . . It seems to me that . . . In other words . . . Are you saying . . . ?" The purpose of paraphrasing is to show sympathetic understanding, so avoid statements that might antagonize your speaker: "That must have been difficult because I know you can't take criticism . . ." Simply repeating what the speaker has already said is not active listening, either (and it makes you sound like a jerk). If a friend says, "That professor drives me crazy!" and you respond, "It sounds like that professor drives you crazy," you may drive your friend crazy.

Active Listening for Clarification

Active listening can help you get at underlying events, thoughts, and feelings. You may use it to clarify what your speaker is communicating. To the person who said, "That professor drives me crazy!" you might ask, "What did he do that made you angry?" or simply, "What happened?" Sometimes active listening involves a lot of guessing as you try to get to the real issue behind what the speaker is saying.

Because it can help you clarify misunderstandings, active listening is a potent stress reducer (Steinmetz, Blankenship, Brown, Hall, & Miller, 1980). For example, a student having difficulty with a course once reported visiting a professor during her office hours only to find the professor irritable and distracted. The professor answered the student's questions in a cold, perfunctory manner that made the student quite uncomfortable. The student was insecure in this position, so he at first assumed the professor was annoyed with his boundless ignorance and almost walked out of the office in despair. Fortunately, he decided instead to clear the air and asked the professor, "Have I done something wrong? You seem annoyed with me." The professor immediately apologized: "I'm sorry. My daughter is home sick today and I am worried about her. I didn't mean to be short-tempered with you." Their discussion then became more focused and productive and both felt better about the interaction.

In the example above, the student used active listening to clarify what was going on and to express his own concerns. He was responding to nonverbal messages: the professor's irritable manner, voice tension, body language, and so on. He "paraphrased" the professor's manner: "You seem annoyed with me." By voicing his own discomfort and concern, he was able to clarify the messages being sent by the professor. His words also conveyed what he was thinking and feeling, that the professor might be annoyed *with him*. Active listening allowed him to check the accuracy of his perceptions and to clarify the professor's message.

Listening with an Open Mind

When you listen with an open mind, you suspend judgment and try to understand what speakers are thinking and feeling. You are open to what they are saying. You are also focused on what the speaker is saying and are not thinking about other things. You are aware of the nonverbal messages being sent and are trying to understand the total message (McKay et al., 1995).

Effective listening takes energy and commitment. We often listen to only part of a speaker's message. For example, we may be searching for clues about how the speaker feels toward us, looking for signs of acceptance or rejection. We may be listening for weak points in an argument and planning what we will say next to make our point. Sometimes we pretend to listen to be polite, to make people like us, or because we don't know how to get out of an encounter gracefully. We pretend to listen so someone else will take a turn listening to us (McKay et al., 1995).

Effective listening is blocked in other ways as well. As people speak, we are often unable to hear the entire message because we have already passed judgment on what they are saying. We read their minds, finish sentences for them, and hear only what we are expecting to hear.

Many people are afraid that open listening implies agreement. Not so. Open listening simply allows you to understand the other person better so that your reply will be more effective. It becomes especially difficult to listen with empathy and openness when speakers are angry, criticizing you, or talking about a topic you do not wish to discuss. Some conversations you can get out of. But when the speaker is a close friend, family member, co-worker, or supervisor and the issue involves you, you cannot walk away. In these cases, effective listening is essential for effective communication. Try to maintain some emotional distance—easier said than done. Focus on the behavior the person is concerned about as being separate from you, the person inside. Pretend you are a detective trying to figure out the source of that person's anger. You don't even need to respond or defend yourself at that moment. In fact, waiting for the other person to cool off can be a good move. "I can see you are very upset about my performance this past month. I'll have to think this over. May I get back to you this afternoon with my response and suggestions for improvement?" Letting people know they have been understood helps defuse the anger.

Open listening is really a reflection of the golden rule: listen to others as you would like to be listened to. When you are expressing your feelings, you appreciate listeners who refrain from giving quick solutions and pat replies, like "Don't worry about it" or "You'll feel better tomorrow." You appreciate listeners who appreciate you and take you seriously.

Of course, you will not choose to listen effectively to every sentence spoken to you. You may decide to ignore the chatterbox on the bus or to half-listen to idle dinner conversation. Effective listening is a must, however, when communication content becomes emotional and/or your significant relationships are involved.

Effective Listening Improves Communication with Children

Effective listening can be as powerful with children as with adults (Faber & Mazlish, 1980). It can defuse anger, help children feel better so they behave better, and open up family communication lines. Parents who listen effectively help teach their children how to express themselves better and solve problems more creatively. They also communicate love and understanding, and help their children establish healthy self-esteem. Try to think of a better active listening reply for this example:

> **Young child:** Why do I have to go to school today? I hate going to school.
> **Parent:** Everyone has to go to school today just like you. So quit whining and get your coat on.

How does the child feel? His feelings went unacknowledged. He believes the parent thinks his feelings are unimportant. He still feels as bad as, if not worse than, he did before. There is nowhere for this conversation to go: stalemate.

Did you think of a better way?

> **Young child:** Why do I have to go to school today? I hate going to school.
> **Parent:** Is there something about school you don't like, or is there just something else you'd rather do?
> **Child:** We're always going to work and school. Why can't we stay home?
> **Parent:** I bet it does seem like we are away from home a lot, but the day after tomorrow is Saturday, and we can stay home on Saturday. Is there something special we should do together this Saturday?
> **Child:** Will you play with my modeling clay with me?
> **Parent** (*helping child get his coat on*): That sounds like fun. How about if we also spend some extra time together after dinner tonight?

How does the child feel now? Like the parent cares. Maybe all he was asking for in the first place was more time with Mom or Dad. But unless the parent uses effective listening, he or she won't know whether the real issue is something going on at school or a different problem. Denying feelings, for people of any age, stops the motion of the conversation.

● EXERCISE

PRACTICE EFFECTIVE LISTENING

The only way to learn effective listening is to practice.

1. Select one person with whom you will try out your effective listening skills for a day. Perhaps your two-week stress log indicated a problematic relationship, or maybe you would like to begin with someone less threatening.

   I practiced effective listening with _____.

2. Note how you felt during the exchange:

   _____

   _____

3. Which paraphrasing attempts worked best?

   _____

   _____

4. Which felt most awkward?

   _____

   _____

5. How did the speaker respond?

   _____

   _____

6. Did effective listening seem different from the way you usually listen to this person? If so, how?

   _____

   _____

7. How could you further improve your effective listening skills?

   _____

   _____

Some friends and partners are interested in learning effective listening techniques. Share this information, and then practice with each other. Effective listening will gradually increase your stress resistance and lead to more direct communication and more satisfying relationships.

EXPRESS YOURSELF: SHARING YOUR THOUGHTS AND FEELINGS

We communicate with other people for many reasons. One of the most important is a drive to express ourselves. We want to share our experiences. We communicate our thoughts and feelings so people will understand us and we may connect with others.

Sometimes it is not easy to express ourselves, even about the simple things. We carefully censor the information about ourselves that we give people access to. We work hard to create a certain impression for our professors, supervisors, family members, and friends. This is a normal, healthy response to the complexities of human relationships, but sometimes we overdo it. Sometimes we are so busy giving the "correct" response we lose touch with our real thoughts and feelings. The other extreme is adopting an inappropriately open line of communication with everyone. Casual acquaintances at work may be embarrassed if we start giving them details of our sex life or our medical history. We might feel relieved to "let it all hang out," but others may withdraw and keep their distance from us. Each culture has unwritten rules about the level of openness that is appropriate for each type of relationship. We learn these unwritten rules by experimentation and watching others.

EMOTIONAL INTIMACY: MAKE A CONNECTION

A flow of words doth ever ease the heart of sorrows.

PYLE

When you share your thoughts and feelings with others, it helps them relax and share theirs with you. Sharing draws you into each other's personal space and makes the relationship more interesting. Some sharing works even with strangers, people you've just met at a party or business function. A "right" level of openness varies with your personality, the person you are talking to, the environment, the mood of the conversation, and other factors (McKay et al., 1995).

Each of us must cultivate at least a few relationships that allow us to be ourselves as much as possible. Sharing our thoughts and feelings helps us grow. We learn about ourselves. We enjoy emotional intimacy. Expressing our bottled up emotions, fears, sorrows, and triumphs feels good. Satisfying communication and personal relationships give us energy and increase our stress resistance.

Research has shown that feelings of isolation and loneliness are associated with negative stress effects, including heart disease (Helgeson, 1991; Lynch, 1977; Mumford, Schlesinger, & Glass, 1982; Trelawny-Ross & Russell, 1987). Keeping your feelings bottled up means that you miss out on the stress-buffering effects of social support. Group therapy has a wonderfully healing effect because of the opportunity it offers for honest emotional sharing in a safe environment. Group therapy is a part of many recovery programs. For example, several cardiac rehabilitation programs include group therapy or discussion to encourage patients to "open their hearts" to their own emotions and make a connection to other people (Eliot, 1994; Ornish, 1990).

SEEKING SOCIAL SUPPORT: GENDER DIFFERENCES

Studies show that women are more likely than men to employ social support as a coping strategy when they feel stressed (Friedman & Berger, 1991; Hovanitz & Kozora, 1989). Sharing feelings with friends seems to occur more easily among women than men. Men in our society are more likely to lack intimate relationships and to have a weaker network of social support than women (Helgeson, 1991; Verbrugge, 1985). Some psychologists believe that males in our culture are socialized to avoid intimate communication (Burda & Vaux, 1987) and that this socialization may be associated with significant health risks for them (Harrison, 1978). But just as women receive more support from relationships, they also experience more stress from them. Compared to men, women report more stress when relationships are experiencing difficulty (Wohlgemuth & Betz, 1991).

It is important not to overestimate the implications of these generalized observations for any given individual situation. Many men successfully develop meaningful friendships, intimate relationships, and helpful social support networks.

Improving communication skills increases the strength of all relationships for both men and women.

COPING WITH CONFLICT: ASSERTIVE SELF-EXPRESSION

Interactions in which we have difficulty expressing ourselves appropriately or effectively cause stress. We feel angry if we have agreed to do something we don't think we should have to do, we are frustrated when we feel misunderstood, and we feel guilty for lashing out at a friend when the boss is the person we are angry with. *Assertiveness* is the hallmark of effective communication skills, the epitome of communication problem solving. Assertiveness is the effective communication of personal thoughts and feelings in a way that respects the thoughts and feelings of others (Lange & Jakubowski, 1976; Wolpe, 1958; Wolpe & Lazarus, 1966). Assertiveness means standing up for your legitimate rights without violating the rights of others (Davis, Eshelman, & McKay, 1988). You are behaving assertively when you communicate your true feelings and don't let others take advantage of you while at the same time you are being considerate of others' feelings.

The assertive communication style is more than a superficial behavior. Our words and actions reflect beliefs we hold about ourselves and our place in the world. Research has shown that people who do not assert themselves lack confidence in their feelings, beliefs, and opinions (Jakubowski-Spector, 1973; Alberti & Emmons, 1970). They are less likely to assert themselves in unpleasant social interactions and thus experience more interpersonal stress (Pitcher & Meikle, 1980).

Assertive self-expression is a prerequisite for satisfying relationships. College students who score lower on assertiveness measures report more loneliness than do assertive students (Gambrill, Florian, & Splaver, 1986). Assertiveness reinforces the stress buffering effects of social support. Students who are more assertive derive greater benefits from relationships with others during times of stress and are less likely to suffer from depression (Elliott & Gramling, 1990). Research has shown that people who are assertive develop confidence in their ability to communicate effectively with others and to develop more satisfying relationships (Masters, Burish, Hollon, & Rimm, 1987). Some research suggests that an assertive personality style typifies stress-resistant people and that the health effects of stress may be less severe for them (Honzak, Veselkova, & Poslusny, 1989).

Even though communication style is inextricably interwoven with one's personality, changes do occur with training. Assertiveness training and communication skills training have been found to be effective stress management techniques for a wide variety of populations (Caplan et al., 1992; Hafner & Miller, 1991; Jordan, Cobb, & McCully, 1989; Masters et al., 1987; Matheny, Aycock, Pugh, Curlette, & Cannella, 1986; Rayburn, 1986; Schinke et al., 1986; Woods, 1987).

Communication Styles: Passive, Aggressive, and Assertive

Communication behavior styles may generally be classified into three categories: passive, assertive, and agressive. An understanding of these three styles will help you better evaluate your own communication behavior and increase your assertiveness.

Passive We are passive when we follow along and let others run the show. We are passive when we don't speak up in class because we are afraid of being wrong. We never ask questions because we're afraid our lack of understanding must be our own fault. We let others take control and make the decisions, and we go along with whatever they decide or request. While saying, "I don't care, anything is fine with me," we can feel resentment building, and we blame the decision maker for our bad feelings and any problems that develop. We are passive when we fail to express our thoughts, feelings, opinions, and needs, hoping someone will guess what we are thinking by our lowered eyes, reticent voice and indirect statements: "Well, I don't know, I suppose so . . ." When others fail to be considerate and guess our needs after all we have done for them, we may find that the anger building up inside becomes overwhelming and we blow up over something small and insignificant.

Aggressive We are agressive when we need to control everything and everyone and to have things our way. Holding our feelings inside is not a problem; we are constantly expressing our needs, but we often do so without considering how our behavior is affecting other people. Our lack of sensitivity means others feel hurt, then we feel guilty and regret our lack of restraint. Sometimes, though, we feel angry at other people for getting in our way and not cooperating. We're afraid if we let down our guard, others will take advantage of us. Sometimes our aggressive behavior is a show of bravado to cover up the insecurity we feel inside. We work hard to prove our superiority by dominating meetings, discussions, and other situations, and by putting others down. Since we don't have many friends, we often feel lonely and estranged.

Assertive We act assertively when we are direct, honest, and considerate of others. We can talk about ourselves without being self-conscious, and we can express our likes and interests. We can accept both compliments and criticism. We can negotiate for what we need, disagree with what someone is saying, and ask for clarification when we don't understand something. We can set limits and say no when necessary. Assertiveness is communicating effectively with others and leads to satisfying relationships, less stress, and higher self-esteem (Davis et al., 1988; Lange & Jakubowski, 1976; Steinmetz et al., 1980). Table 8.1 summarizes some of the characteristics of the three communication styles.

> *[People] can alter their lives by altering their attitudes.*
>
> WILLIAM JAMES

All three communication styles have their time and place. In general, the assertive style increases your stress resistance and is the clearest way to communicate, but sometimes, adopting a passive style is easier and less stressful. Suppose you buy a snack at a market where you will probably never shop again; when you open it at home two hours later, you find that it is stale. You have the right to return to the store and get your money back, but the effort may not be worth the time and energy you would spend. On the other hand, if your car mechanic charged you a lot of money but did not fix the problem with your car, you would certainly benefit by adopting an assertive approach for this situation. Choose your battles. Sometimes we are passive with authority figures: a police officer giving us a lecture instead of a citation; an elderly relative we rarely see. Also, assertive behavior and good communication skills are generally lost on people "under the influence." Say what you need to but save complete communication for a later time when they are sober.

Similarly, an aggressive style has its time and place as well. When your health and well-being are being violated, it may be appropriate to use aggressive words and actions to protect yourself. Sexual harassment is a good example of the kind of situation in which aggression can be an appropriate response, especially if your assertiveness is being ignored. Sexual harassment is unwanted and unwelcome sexual behavior (Stein & Sjostrom, 1994); it may manifest as offensive words or behavior. Sometimes sexual harassment continues because of a communication gap. Some harassers may not understand anything except an aggressive NO or threats of punitive action.

TABLE 8.1 *Communication Styles*

	Passive	Assertive	Aggressive
Verbal characteristics	Apologetic words Indirect statements; failing to come to the point Rambling, disconnected speech Failure to say what you really mean	Honest statements of feelings Objective terms Direct statements that say what you mean "I" messages	Threats, accusations Subjective words that label or blame Put-downs "You" messages
Nonverbal characteristics	Actions instead of words; hoping someone will guess what you want Incongruent body language: body language doesn't match words. You look as if you don't mean what you're saying	Effective listening behavior Assured manner, communicating confidence and caring	Exaggerated show of strength Flippant, sarcastic style, air of superiority
	Weak, hesitant, soft voice	Firm, relaxed, warm, even voice	Emotional, tense, shrill, shaky, too loud, or icy cold voice
	Averted, downcast, pleading eyes	Direct eye contact but not staring	Expressionless, staring, cold, squinting eyes
	Fidgety hands	Relaxed motions	Clenched fists, abrupt gestures, finger pointing
	Leaning, stooped posture, head nodding	Posture: well-balanced, erect but relaxed	Hands on hips, stiff, rigid stance
You feel	Ignored Helpless Manipulated Angry	Confident Valued Goal-oriented Effective	Superior Self-righteous Controlling Angry Guilty
Others feel	Frustrated with you, can't understand what you want	Valued, respected	Humiliated, defensive, hurt, resentful
Results	Interpersonal stress Depression Helplessness Poor self-image Lost opportunities Can feel out of control Can dislike self and others May hurt self May develop addiction May be lonely	Solve problems Feel good about others Feel satisfied Have positive self-esteem Create and make the most of opportunities Feel in control of yourself Like yourself and others Are good to yourself	Interpersonal stress Guilt Frustration Poor self-image Lost opportunities Feel out of control Dislike others Hurt self May develop addiction May be lonely

Communication Style and Underlying Beliefs

Our words and actions reflect beliefs we hold about ourselves and our place in the world. We discussed this concept in the section on procrastination in Chapter 7 when we looked at irrational beliefs that reinforce a tendency to procrastinate. We acquire these beliefs from the people around us, especially our families. Some of these beliefs may have been stated aloud; others may have been modeled by parents, teachers, and other important people. Table 8.2 lists some of these irrational beliefs and contrasts them with beliefs that support assertive behavior. Read them carefully and see whether you can understand why the irrational beliefs might encourage indirect, dishonest, and ineffective communication and prevent you from communicating assertively.

TABLE 8.2 *Irrational and Assertive Beliefs*

Irrational Beliefs	Assertive Beliefs
1. It is selfish to put your needs before others' needs.	You have a right to put yourself first sometimes.
2. It is shameful to make mistakes. You should have an appropriate response for every occasion.	You have a right to make mistakes.
3. If you can't convince others that your feelings are reasonable, then they must be wrong, or maybe you are going crazy.	You have a right to be the final judge of your feelings and accept them as legitimate.
4. You should respect the views of others, especially if they are in a position of authority. Keep your differences of opinion to yourself. Listen and learn.	You have a right to have your own opinions and convictions.
5. You should always try to be logical and consistent.	You have a right to change your mind or decide on a different course of action.
6. You should be flexible and adjust. Others have good reasons for their actions and it's not polite to question them.	You have a right to protest unfair treatment or criticism.
7. You should never interrupt people. Asking questions reveals your stupidity to others.	You have a right to interrupt in order to ask for clarification.
8. Things could get even worse, don't rock the boat.	You have a right to negotiate for change.
9. You shouldn't take up others' valuable time with your problems.	You have a right to *ask* for help or emotional support.
10. People don't want to hear that you feel bad, so keep it to yourself.	You have a right to feel and express pain.
11. When someone takes the time to give you advice, you should take it very seriously. They are often right.	You have a right to ignore the advice of others.
12. Knowing that you did something well is its own reward. People don't like show-offs. Successful people are secretly disliked and envied. Be modest when complimented.	You have a right to receive formal recognition for your work and achievements.
13. You should always try to accommodate others. If you don't, they won't be there when you need them.	You have a right to say "no."
14. Don't be anti-social. People are going to think you don't like them if you say you'd rather be alone instead of with them.	You have a right to be alone, even if others would prefer your company.
15. You should always have a good reason for what you feel and do.	You have a right not to have to justify yourself to others.
16. When someone is in trouble, you should help them.	You have a right not to take responsibility for someone else's problem.
17. You should be sensitive to the needs and wishes of others, even when they are unable to tell you what they want.	You have a right not to have to anticipate others' needs and wishes.
18. It's always a good policy to stay on people's good side.	You have a right not to always worry about the goodwill of others.
19. It's not nice to put people off. If questioned, give an answer.	You have a right to choose not to respond to a situation.

Source: From Martha Davis, Elizabeth Robbins Eshelman, and Matthew McKay. *The Relaxation and Stress Reduction Workbook.* Oakland, CA: New Harbinger Publications, 1988. Reprinted with permission by New Harbinger Publications, Oakland, CA, 94609.

◆ STRESS AND YOU

STRESS AND YOUR COMMUNICATION STYLE

Which communication style—passive, aggressive, or assertive—do you tend to use? Review your stress log and think about current stressors in your life. Are any of them due to ineffective communication? Could your coping with some of them be improved with better assertiveness? Take a moment to think about which people and situations cause you stress because you fail to communicate assertively.

People with whom I have difficulty being assertive:

Situations in which I have difficulty being assertive (e.g., when friends ask if they can borrow my car, when classmates ask for help with their homework):

Can you think of two or three stressors that have occurred in your life during the past several weeks for which better communication could have helped to reduce the stress? Use the chart on the facing page to describe problematic situations for which you feel assertiveness could be helpful. Begin by describing the situation. Then describe your preferred resolution. What was your outcome goal? Describe your original response, then describe how you might respond if you could replay the episode.

ASSERTIVENESS TRAINING

Developing a more assertive communication style does not happen overnight. For some people, becoming more assertive is very difficult. Many schools and other organizations offer communication training workshops to teach these skills and let students practice them. In general, assertiveness training helps you develop a method to address problem situations more directly and effectively. The following summary was drawn primarily from *The Relaxation and Stress Reduction Workbook* by Davis and colleagues (Davis et al., 1988).

1. Define Your Rights and Goals

Reread the irrational beliefs in Table 8.2. Are any of these your beliefs? Work to change those that create unnecessary stress in your life. You must really believe you have a right to express your opinion or your assertiveness attempts will not work.

	Revising Communication Stressors		
Situation	My Outcome Goal	Previous Response	Assertive Response
Example: Lab partner always late; I do most of the work.	Lab partner comes on time; we work together.	Say nothing, but look angry.	Tell partner how I feel; ask partner to please come on time.
1.			
2.			
3.			

Have a clear objective in mind as you formulate your assertive response. This will keep the conversation focused. Suppose your roommate frequently comes in late at night after you have gone to sleep. He makes a lot of noise, and when you wake up he wants to talk for a while. Your goal might be to get him to come in quietly and not to talk to you. You'll need to tell him this explicitly rather than asking him to "be more considerate."

Make your request as reasonable as possible. For example, you can't really ask your roommate to spend the night somewhere else if he comes home late. You can't ask him not to go out so often. But coming in quietly is a reasonable expectation that he should be able to accommodate.

2. Set the Scene

Sometimes you plan to try a more assertive approach with a problem that has been building for some time. When you have some advance warning, you can take advantage of your ability to set the scene. Your assertive approach will be easier to deliver and more openly received. When possible, arrange a mutually agreeable time and place to discuss the problem. Beforehand, take time to go over your "speech" and your goals. Use a relaxation or visualization technique to focus yourself for the meeting.

3. Define the Problem and Express Your Request

Begin with an agreement. Open the conversation with some sort of positive statement that will create an open, nonthreatening atmosphere. With your roommate, begin with something you like about him or how much you used to enjoy those 2 A.M. discussions.

Use your problem-solving techniques to define the problem as objectively as possible. As you present the problem, avoid unanswerable questions and ancient history that will get you off track. Keep the conversation focused on your goal. Be specific. Give a description, your thoughts, feelings, and needs. Tell your roommate something like the following: "Several times a week you come back after midnight, make a lot of noise, wake me up, and begin a conversation. I enjoy talking with you and these night sessions were all right last semester. But now I am feeling more pressure from my schoolwork; I have to get up earlier this semester for classes, I'm not getting enough sleep, and I resent being waked up. Could you please come in quietly and try not to wake me?"

Make Your Messages Supportive of Your Listener. If your messages are supportive of the listener and don't use antagonizing words and phrases, they will be better received. When you stated the problem to your roommate, you used "I statements." These avoid labeling your listener and let him know you are "owning" your thoughts and feelings. If you say, "I can't believe how thoughtless you are!" you place him on the defensive, and he is less likely to respond positively to your request. The war escalates. Avoid language that might be interpreted as insulting, especially put-downs disguised as your "real feelings."

Avoid Contaminated Messages. A contaminated message is one that communicates two different and usually incompatible thoughts at the same time (McKay et al., 1995). If you get off track and start adding messages about how lonely you are and how jealous you are that he goes out while you stay home and study, your original message is contaminated. The bottom line gets lost. He won't know what is really bothering you. Effective messages are clear, direct, and focused.

4. Use Assertive Body Language

One of the most common causes of message contamination is incongruent body language in which your voice, facial expression, posture, eyes, and hands say something different from your words. While you are making a request, your body

■ STUDENT STRESS

KARA'S ASSERTIVE RESPONSE

Kara was pleased when at the beginning of the year the students in her dorm elected her to serve as social co-chair. Her job was to work with Melanie, the other co-chair, to organize several social events during the school year. Kara's initial pleasure soon turned into distress as she found herself taking on all the planning and organization of these events with very little help from Melanie. Her stress logs began to revolve around the resentment that seemed to build with each social chair task she completed. Anger at the unfairness of her situation started to build as well. Kara started avoiding Melanie, hoping her anger would motivate Melanie to take some action. But Melanie didn't seem to notice or at least to understand what was indicated by Kara's aloofness. By early November, Kara's anger at the situation and at Melanie was hanging over her like a black cloud.

When Kara read the material on communication skills for her stress management class, her problem with Melanie gained a clearer focus. Kara found that she fit the description of a person with a passive communication style and that she unconsciously lived by almost all the irrational beliefs discussed in the chapter. In particular, she had difficulty asking for help or saying anything that might be construed as criticism or disagreement.

Kara decided she must say something to Melanie. It took her days of planning to get up the nerve finally to ask Melanie for some help with next week's dance. But one night after dinner, she asked Melanie if she had time to discuss the upcoming party. To her surprise, Melanie was more than agreeable. They had a productive meeting and split up the responsibilities. Kara was flabbergasted. All along, Melanie had interpreted Kara's taking over the responsibility as an assertion that she did not need or want any help. Once Kara asked for help, Melanie was more than happy to get involved. Kara was grinning from ear to ear when she told her class about her assertiveness experience.

language may be saying you don't really mean it. If your message is mumbled, rushed, and brushed over and your body language is distracted, you are not connecting with your listener; you are saying the issue is not really important. Assertive body language includes a well-balanced but relaxed posture, direct eye contact, and a confident, firm voice. Assertive body language communicates assurance, confidence, and caring. Table 8.1 describes assertive body language.

5. Use Effective Listening to Reinforce Your Request and Find a Solution

Your listeners will be more likely to listen to you if you listen to them. When you have made your request, give your listeners time to respond and use your effective listening techniques. Try to understand their concerns and what the problems are; paraphrase to let them know you are trying to understand and come to a workable solution. Try to use their responses to reinforce your suggestion as a good solution.

NEGOTIATING A SOLUTION

You've expressed your request and listened to the response. As the discussion continues, try to control your negative emotions as you work toward a solution to the problem. Negotiating a workable compromise can be difficult when the needs of two people are quite different, but it must be done. Negotiating is a fact of life; it occurs whenever people must work or live together. From business and politics to your family's living room, compromise is required for us all to live together in a way that works.

Sometimes a compromise evolves from your discussion. Other times you must use your problem-solving brainstorming to create a list of options, and then work through these to come up with a mutually satisfactory solution. A compromise may be more acceptable to both of you if you agree to follow it for a trial period and then reassess the situation. Some typical negotiating strategies are listed here (Davis et al., 1988):

1. I get part of what I want; you get part of what you want.
2. Try it my way this time; we'll try it your way next time.
3. If my way doesn't work this time, we'll do it your way next time.
4. I'll do X for you if you'll do this for me.

Calvin and Hobbes   by Bill Watterson

COMMUNICATING WITH AGGRESSIVE PEOPLE

Let's face it: sometimes stress is caused by unreasonable people. Sometimes life throws us a loud and obnoxious neighbor or co-worker, or we find ourselves working for a boss who seems like a volcano about to erupt. Family members with whom we must deal may have developed communication problems that no amount of practice on our end can eliminate. When dealing with aggressive people, we commonly feel out of control and become angry and aggressive ourselves. If we must continue to deal with these people, we may feel the lingering effects of such encounters clouding our lives and creating chronic stress. The following suggestions may be helpful for some situations (Davis et al., 1988; Steinmetz et al., 1980), but you may also need to find a way to minimize encounters with problematic people.

Use Active Listening

When an aggressive person unloads on you, first try the familiar active listening paraphrase technique: "You sound very angry about this." Ask questions to get the person to clarify the problem and move toward a solution.

Stay Focused

Aggressive encounters often get sidetracked from the original issue. Do all you can to get back to the main problem. "We've gotten off the subject. You were talking about . . ."

Postpone Discussion

When emotions are hot and active listening is not working, try to postpone the discussion until tempers have cooled. Tell the person, "This conversation is going nowhere and I need some time to think about this problem. Why don't we talk about it again first thing tomorrow morning?"

Try the Broken Record Technique

If you have made a reasonable request in an appropriately assertive manner and the other person blows up and starts ranting and raving, try the broken record technique to reinforce your request. "I know you like to play your music late but quiet hours begin at 11 P.M. I want you to turn it down at 11 or I'll have to go to the head resident." Keep repeating your request even as the other person continues to argue.

This technique is commonly used by parents to reinforce the bottom line message with their children. It keeps them on track without unnecessary explanations. Your broken record message may also be, "I can't discuss this with you when you're screaming at me."

FAMILY COMMUNICATION PROBLEMS

They say you always hurt the ones you love. While difficult neighbors, co-workers, and friends can create a lot of tension, nothing beats family problems when it comes to chronic stress. Communication among members of a household are often built on a long history that cannot be erased with simple communication techniques. If communication problems among family members are especially difficult and have been continuing for a long time, family therapy may be helpful. A family therapist can help partners and family members uncover and correct communication problems and relationship patterns that are creating stress for the whole family.

▲ ACTION PLAN

COMMUNICATION GOAL SETTING AND ACTION PLAN

Review your stress log and think about stressors in your life that might be helped by better communication skills. You may wish to use two of the situations you wrote about in "Revising Communication Stressors." Or you may wish to focus on particular people you have trouble communicating with. Define two areas you would like to change and describe how you will begin to implement these changes over the next few days. Anticipate any problems you might run into when implementing your action plan and think about how you will keep these problems from interfering.

Goal 1:

Action plan:

Roadblocks (possible problems that could get in the way):

How I will prevent these problems from interfering:

Goal 2:

Action plan:

Roadblocks (possible problems that could get in the way):

How I will prevent these problems from interfering:

STUDENT STRESS

ABIGAIL'S COMMUNICATION SKILLS ACTION PLAN

Abigail has a family problem that has been bothering her. Her brother had a dispute with their parents and won't talk to them anymore. For almost a year, Abigail has been the communication liaison between her parents and brother, and she worries about how hurt her parents are with the situation. Acting as a liaison is difficult, however, since she is away at college, 100 miles from her parents' home, and her brother has moved to another town even farther away. The counselor Abigail is seeing at the health center has helped her understand that her powers are limited in this situation and that eventually her brother and parents must work it out themselves. Her parents continue to call her almost every week, however, to relay messages to her brother. She has decided to follow the recommendations on assertiveness training discussed in this chapter.

Goal: To stop acting as the communication pathway between my parents and my brother.

Action steps:

1. Define my rights.
   Remind myself that I have a right to say "no" to my parents' request to call my brother. I don't have to accommodate their needs. I hope they will eventually understand that being placed in this situation is too stressful for me.

   I have a right not to take responsibility for someone else's problem. I've tried to mend the rift between my brother and my parents, but at this point the situation has become too stressful and my actions are not helping. I'll keep working with my therapist to understand that this is not my problem.

   Therefore, I will call my parents and explain to them that I can't continue being the go-between.
2. Set the scene and express my request.
   I will call my parents Saturday morning. I will define the problem and explain why I cannot continue to be the communication conduit. If they keep asking me, I will politely refuse.

Possible roadblocks:
I'll cave. It's easier to give in to my parents than to stand up to them. I feel so sorry for them; my brother's abandonment of them really hurts their feelings.

My response:
Remind myself that while it's easier to give in, in the long run this creates enormous stress for myself. All the stress I am coping with doesn't even help the situation. It helps neither my parents nor my brother, and it certainly is hurting me.

SUMMARY

1. Stress often arises from interactions with other people.
2. Good communication skills increase stress resistance in several ways:
   a. They help you build authentic relationships and social support.
   b. They enhance direct coping strategies, such as asking for change.
   c. They support the implementation of other stress management strategies, such as problem solving and time management.
   d. They promote healthy emotions.
   e. They are essential for building intimate relationships and strong friendships.
3. Because we acquired our communication skills haphazardly by imitating family members and friends during childhood, almost all of us can benefit from improving these skills during adolescence and adulthood.
4. Effective listening means listening carefully to a speaker's words and trying hard to understand the meaning behind the words.
5. Active listening is part of the effective listening process and refers to the practice of asking questions to help clarify the speaker's message and to convey your understanding.
6. Effective listening means listening with an open mind, without judgment or distractions.
7. Effective listening enhances communication with people of all ages, including children.
8. Each culture has unwritten rules about what level of openness is appropriate for each type of relationship.
9. The satisfying communication that occurs in deep friendships and intimate relationships increases our stress resistance, while isolation and loneliness are associated with negative stress effects, including heart disease.
10. In our culture, women are more likely than men to employ social support as a coping strategy when they are feeling stressed.
11. An assertive communication style reinforces the stress-buffering effects of social support and is associated with stress resistance.
12. Communication styles may be simplistically categorized into three different styles: passive, aggressive, and assertive.
13. People's communication styles reflect beliefs they hold about themselves and their place in the world.
14. With practice, a person can develop more effective communication skills, including a more assertive communication style.
15. An assertive communication style is especially important when you are dealing with difficult people.

REFERENCES

Alberti, RE, and M Emmons. *Your Perfect Right.* San Luis Obispo, CA: Act Press, 1970.

Arapakis, M. *Softpower! How to Speak Up, Set Limits, and Say No without Losing Your Lover, Your Job, or Your Friends.* New York: Warner Books, 1990.

Brown, S. *Treating Adult Children of Alcoholics.* New York: Wiley, 1988.

Burda, PC, and AC Vaux. The social support process in men: Overcoming sex-role obstacles. *Human Relations* 40: 31–44, 1987.

Caplan, M, RP Weissberg, JS Grober, PJ Sivo, K Grady, and C Jacoby. Social competence promotion with inner-city and suburban young adolescents: Effects on social adjustment and alcohol use. *Journal of Consulting and Clinical Psychology* 60: 56–63, 1992.

Cassel, J. Social science in epidemiology: Psychosocial processes and "stress," theoretical formulation. *International Journal of Health Services* 4: 537–549, 1974.

Cohen, S. Psychosocial models of the role of social support in the etiology of physical disease. *Health Psychology* 7: 269–297, 1988.

Davis, M, ER Eshelman, and M McKay. *The Relaxation and Stress Reduction Workbook.* Oakland, CA: New Harbinger Publications, 1988.

Edlin, G, and E Golanty. *Health and Wellness: A Holistic Approach.* Boston: Jones & Bartlett, 1992.

Eliot, RS. *From Stress to Strength.* New York: Bantam, 1994.

Elliott, TR, and SE Gramling. Personal assertiveness and the effects of social support among college students. *Journal of Counseling Psychology* 37: 427–436, 1990.

Faber, A, and E Mazlish. *How to Talk So Kids Will Listen & Listen So Kids Will Talk.* New York: Avon Books, 1980.

Friedman, E, and BG Berger. Influence of gender, masculinity, and femininity on the effectiveness of three stress reduction techniques: Jogging, relaxation response, and group interaction. *Journal of Applied Sport Psychology* 3: 61–86, 1991.

Gambrill, E, V Florian, and G Splaver. Assertion, loneliness, and perceived control among students with and without disabilities. *Rehabilitation Counseling Bulletin* 30: 4–12, 1986.

Gravitz, HL, and JD Bowden. *Recovery: A Guide for Adult Children of Alcoholics.* New York: Fireside, 1987.

Hafner, RJ, and RJ Miller. Essential hypertension: Hostility, psychiatric symptoms and marital stress in patients and spouses. *Psychotherapy and Psychosomatics* 56: 204–211, 1991.

Harrison, J. Warning: The male sex role may be dangerous to your health. *Journal of Social Issues* 34: 65–86, 1978.

Helgeson, VS. The effects of masculinity and social support on recovery from myocardial infarction. *Psychosomatic Medicine* 53: 621–633, 1991.

Honzak, R, A Veselkova, and Z Poslusny. Personality traits and neurohumoral stress response in healthy young sportsmen. *Activitas Nervosa Superior* 31: 100–102, 1989.

Hovanitz, CA, and E Kozora. Life stress and clinically elevated MMPI scales: Gender differences in the moderating influence of coping. *Journal of Clinical Psychology* 45: 766–777, 1989.

Jakubowski-Spector, P. Facilitating the growth of women through assertion training. *The Counseling Psychologist* 4: 75–86, 1973.

Jordan, C, N Cobb, and R McCully. Clinical issues of the dual-career couple. *Social Work* 34: 29–32, 1989.

Lange, AJ, and P Jakubowski. *Responsible Assertive Behavior.* Champaign, IL: Research Press, 1976.

Lynch, JJ. *The Broken Heart.* New York: Basic Books, 1977.

Masters, J, T Burish, S Hollon, and D Rimm. *Behavior Therapy.* New York: Harcourt Brace Jovanovich, 1987.

Matheny, K, D Aycock, J Pugh, W Curlette, and KAS Cannella. Stress coping: A qualitative and quantitative synthesis with implications for treatment. *The Counseling Psychologist* 14: 499-549, 1986.

McKay, M, M Davis, and P Fanning. *Messages: The Communication Skills Book.* Oakland, CA: New Harbinger Publications, 1995.

Mumford, E, HJ Schlesinger, and GV Glass. The effects of psychological intervention on recovery from surgery and heart attacks: An analysis of the literature. *American Journal of Public Health* 72: 141–151, 1982.

Ornish, D. *Dr. Dean Ornish's Program for Reversing Heart Disease.* New York: Bantam, 1990.

Peele, S. *Diseasing of America; Addiction Treatment Out of Control.* Boston: Houghton-Mifflin, 1989.

Pitcher, S, and S Meikle. The topography of assertive behavior in positive and negative situations. *Behavior Therapy* 11: 532–547, 1980.

Rayburn, CA. Women and stress: Some implications for therapy. *Women and Therapy* 5: 239–247, 1986.

Schinke, SP, RF Schilling II, MA Kirkham, LD Gilchrist, RP Barth, and BJ Blythe. Stress management skills for parents. *Journal of Child and Adolescent Psychotherapy* 3: 293–298, 1986.

Stein, N, and L Sjostrom. *Flirting or hurting? A teacher's guide on student-to-student sexual harassment in school.* Washington, DC: National Educational Association, 1994.

Steinmetz, J, J Blankenship, L Brown, D Hall, and G Miller. *Managing Stress Before It Manages You.* Palo Alto, CA: Bull, 1980.

Trelawny-Ross, C, and O Russell. Social and psychological responses to myocardial infarction: Multiple determinants of outcome at six months. *Journal of Psychosomatic Research* 31: 125–130, 1987.

Verbrugge, LM. Gender and health: An update on hypotheses and evidence. *Journal of Health and Social Behavior* 26: 156–182, 1985.

Wohlgemuth, E, and NE Betz. Gender as a moderator of the relationships of stress and social support to physical health in college students. *Journal of Counseling Psychology* 38: 367–374, 1991.

Wolpe, J. *Psychotherapy by Reciprocal Inhibition.* Stanford, CA: Stanford University Press, 1958.

Wolpe, J, and A Lazarus. *Behavior Therapy Techniques.* New York: Pergamon Press, 1966.

Woods, PJ. Reductions in Type A behavior, anxiety, anger, and physical illness as related to changes in irrational beliefs: Results of a demonstration project in industry. *Journal of Rational-Emotive Therapy* 5: 213–237, 1987.

chapter 9

Nutrition, Health, and Stress

Your lifestyle can be a source of both stress and strength. The word *lifestyle* refers to those habits and activities that characterize your daily life, such as eating and sleeping habits and recreational pursuits, to name a few. In this section, you will learn how your lifestyle affects your ability to cope effectively with stress.

Lifestyle affects your stress resistance in two important ways. First, your lifestyle can increase your stress resistance by giving you more energy and optimism each day, thus enhancing your productivity, your coping ability, and most of all your enjoyment of life. Second, it can help keep you healthy, or at least minimize the time you lose from your regular routine because of illness. We take our health for granted—until it's not there; then we realize how much we depend on being healthy to be able to do all the things we do. Getting sick can take us out of commission for days, weeks, and even longer: A project that might have taken an hour or two to complete on a good day can remain in fragments after an entire workday when we are frazzled and unable to concentrate. Feeling tired can turn the simplest schedule into an impassable mountain. Of course, no matter how well we take care of ourselves, we all get sick from time to time, and we all have bad days. That makes it even more important to control the things we can to make our days run as smoothly as possible. Optimal health and well-being are not things that just happen. We control many of the factors that affect our good humor and energy level. We emphasized in Chapter 1 that self-responsibility is the cornerstone of the wellness philosophy. We are responsible for developing health habits that not only keep us healthy but also help us maximize our good days. In this section you will see how a little organization and time management applied to your health behavior can significantly increase your stress resistance.

NUTRITION AND STRESS: RUNNING ON EMPTY

Good nutrition and eating habits contribute significantly to good health and stress resistance. They are especially important during high-stress times, but these may be the times when we are least likely to eat well (Stone & Brownell, 1994)! The

cupboard is bare, we have no time to plan a shopping list and no money to go shopping, so we skip meals or grab whatever fast food is closest at hand. Sometimes we depend on a dining hall whose schedule doesn't match our own, or whose ideas of good nutrition and fine cuisine are limited to meat, potatoes, and overcooked vegetables with lots of butter. Dessert is usually the high point of every meal.

Good nutrition improves both short-term and long-term stress resistance. Short-term stress resistance requires a working brain. A poor diet can lead to malnutrition, low blood sugar, and other chemical imbalances. With an inadequate diet, the brain loses power; the symptoms can include anxiety, headache, fatigue, irritability, and dizziness. Our ability to think clearly diminishes; taking exams, completing assignments, and writing papers all become much more difficult. When we are fatigued, molehills turn into mountains. We feel out of control, less able to cope with the demands facing us, and unable to come up with creative ideas.

In the long run, poor nutrition wears us down. We are more likely to get sick with every cold and flu germ that comes along. Poor nutrition also contributes to chronic health problems such as artery disease, obesity, high blood pressure, some types of cancer, and gastrointestinal problems (Katch & McArdle, 1993). Good nutrition promotes high-level wellness and gives us the good health and energy we need to solve problems creatively and to cope with the stressors that come our way (Davis, Esheman, & McKay, 1995).

STRESS, HEALTH, AND THE AMERICAN DIET

North Americans reap many benefits from living in the land of plenty. One of the unfortunate side effects, however, is that we often have problems with food. We eat too much of the wrong things, get too fat or worry about getting fat, go on crazy diets, and have a hard time developing a healthy relationship with food. We are bombarded with nutrition information and misinformation, much of it confusing and

■ STUDENT STRESS

ARTHUR'S EATING HABITS

Arthur has a heavy course load and juggles several extracurricular activities during most of the school year. He has little time for worrying about meals. He rarely manages to get up in time for a sit-down breakfast, so most days he gulps a cup of coffee and wolfs down a doughnut or two on the way to class. Midway through the morning, his eyelids are drooping and his stomach is growling. He has just enough time for a stop at the vending machines for another cup of coffee and a candy bar before his 10:30 class. Lunch is something fast—usually a sandwich, potato chips, and a soda—eaten in ten minutes between errands, and maybe more coffee to keep him awake through his 1:00 class. Late afternoon soccer practice often means he is late to dinner and starving by the time he gets there. He consumes double portions of a main entree and dessert. Late night studying calls for a pizza break and more coffee.

Lately, Arthur has begun wondering whether he should make some changes in his eating habits. He has problems staying awake in his classes and difficulty following the lecture material. His soccer performance is not what it used to be, either. He generally feels hungry and tired when practice starts and just doesn't have the energy and enthusiasm he used to have for the game. His big dinner finally relieves his hunger and gives him energy for his evening studies, but when bedtime finally comes, Arthur often feels nervous and wound up, and recently he has had difficulty sleeping.

contradictory. Eating a healthful diet without getting obsessed with food and weight can be a challenge.

Many authorities believe that the American diet contributes to a number of our health problems. While in many parts of the world a lack of food is associated with poor health, our problem is generally just the opposite: **overnutrition.** We consume too many calories for our sedentary lifestyles, especially the wrong kinds of calories: fat and sugar, which contribute to our high rates of obesity and many of our leading causes of death and chronic illness.

Healthful meals take some organization and planning ahead; when households get busier, fewer meals are prepared and consumed at home. A large part of the overnutrition problem is our penchant for fast food and processed food products, which are convenient, affordable, and readily available. Many fast foods and supermarket convenience foods tend to be high in fat and sugar and low in nutritive value. The next time you visit the supermarket, take note of what you see in the aisles. How much of it is "real food" unchanged from the farm to the store? A small percentage, found mostly in the produce aisle. The rest is products. Corn made into corn syrup made into soft drinks, grains made into flour made into cookies. Of course, some food products are very healthful, but you must read labels to learn what is in food and what has been done to it.

Despite these dismal observations, with a little thought and planning, you can improve your diet. Small changes in your eating habits can make a big difference in your daily energy level and sense of well-being and improve your long-term health. And you can make these changes without increasing the amount of money you spend on food and while you continue to enjoy the pleasure of eating delicious meals.

NUTRITION BASICS

A comprehensive review of nutrition is beyond the scope of this chapter, but a few concepts will help you understand how nutrition affects your stress resistance. The nutrients needed for all life processes are divided into six categories based on their chemical composition: Carbohydrates, proteins, lipids, vitamins, minerals, and water.

Carbohydrate, Protein, and Lipids: Dietary Sources of Energy

Three classes of nutrients provide the energy you need. The primary function of **carbohydrates** is to provide energy. **Complex carbohydrates,** or starches, are found in plant foods such as grains, vegetables, and fruits; they are broken down more slowly than **simple carbohydrates**, or sugars. Sugars are found in fruits and vegetables as well as milk; they are especially concentrated in sweeteners such as table sugar, honey, and molasses. Products made from grains (pasta, bread, and breakfast cereal, for example) contain complex carbohydrates and sometimes sugars as well.

Proteins are found in most foods. Animal products such as eggs, meat, and milk are especially high in protein. Protein is also found in legumes such as soybeans, lentils, and split peas; grains and their products; and nuts and seeds. The body uses protein in many important ways and generally does not break down too much protein for energy except during prolonged exercise.

The **lipid** category includes dietary fats and oils. These provide the body with concentrated sources of energy and are easily converted to body fat, or **adipose tissue,** another concentrated source of energy. This is why a small amount of fat in the diet goes a long way. Lipids provide the body with nine calories per gram while carbohydrates and proteins provide four calories per gram.

Vitamins, Minerals, and Water: Essential for Health and Stress Resistance

People do not obtain energy from the chemical structure of vitamins, minerals, or water, but these nutrients provide important components for the metabolic processes that produce the energy required for growth, development, and all life functions. Vitamins are organic molecules that the body cannot manufacture—at least not in the amounts required for good health. We must therefore obtain vitamins from food or other sources. (We can manufacture vitamin D given enough sunlight, and friendly bacteria that live in the gut manufacture certain B vitamins.) Minerals are classified as inorganic (they contain no carbon). They are required for many metabolic processes and also form various structural components in the body, such as bone. Water is the most essential nutrient. Water makes up about 50 percent to 60 percent of the body's weight and has many essential physiological functions. It is important for proper digestion, transports nutrients and wastes, and helps regulate body temperature.

FOOD AND ENERGY: THE ROLE OF BLOOD SUGAR

Everyone has experienced the fatigue and irritability that can result from being hungry. While many of the body's systems can make energy from fat, the central nervous system, including the brain, relies primarily on blood sugar, or glucose, for fuel. When blood sugar falls, these symptoms of fatigue result. Parents and people who work with children have observed the hungry-cranky connection on many occasions. As adults, we tend to attribute our moods to external events and ignore our internal physiology, but hunger can cause crankiness in us just the same.

Where does blood glucose come from, and what can you do to keep it on an even keel? Blood glucose level is maintained within a fairly narrow physiological range, since either very high or very low blood glucose levels interfere with central nervous system regulation. The result is shakiness, anxiety, disorientation, and in extreme cases, loss of consciousness and even death. The glucose in your bloodstream can come from the digestion of food or from the breakdown of storage molecules. These storage molecules include a carbohydrate called glycogen stored in the muscles and liver, and amino acids (the building blocks of protein) stored in the liver. After you consume a meal, your blood glucose level rises as sugar enters the bloodstream from the digestive tract. A rising blood sugar level signals the pancreas to release **insulin.** Insulin is a hormone that allows sugar to enter the cells and be used for energy. As the glucose gradually leaves the bloodstream, blood glucose levels begin to decrease. When glucose levels fall below a certain point, other hormones, including one called **glucagon,** produced by the pancreas, are called on to encourage the production of glucose from glycogen and other precursors, and the glucose level rises. (See Figure 9.1.)

With all this regulation, why doesn't blood sugar stay at optimal levels? Your body expects to be fed, and eating behavior plays a role in blood sugar regulation. Your body gets used to being fed at certain times, and seems to "learn" to be hungry at mealtimes. If hunger is not satisfied it does eventually subside for some people, but most of us will feel somewhat hungry and out of sorts until we eat something. Some people have more trouble regulating blood sugar than others and are prone to **hypoglycemia,** or low blood sugar, especially if they forget to eat or when they participate in physical activity. Symptoms of hypoglycemia include hunger, shakiness, nervousness, dizziness, nausea, and disorientation. These symptoms are partly due to the effect of the hormone epinephrine, which is released when

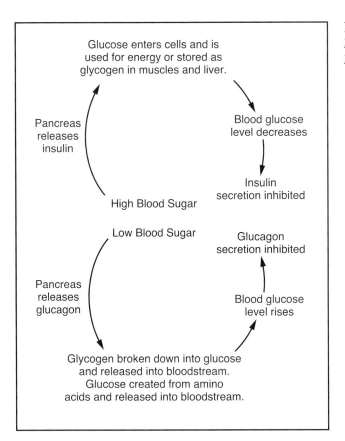

FIGURE 9.1
Blood Glucose Regulation

glucagon fails to do its job of raising blood glucose. As you know, epinephrine is one of the hormones that supports the fight-or-flight response; one of its jobs is to raise the blood glucose level to give you the energy required to fight or flee. That's why the side effects of hypoglycemia feel like stress! Recommendations for keeping your blood sugar at a healthful level without peaks and dips are discussed in the next sections.

Eat Regularly

Your body likes a regular schedule. Skipping meals means guaranteed hypoglycemia in people prone to this condition. Set up times for meals and snacks that are convenient for your schedule and stick to this routine as much as possible. This may mean planning ahead and carrying snacks with you if you are at work or out running errands. Many people, including those with hypoglycemia, find that eating five or six small meals or snacks each day helps them feel more energetic than three large meals.

Include Protein Foods at Every Meal

Carbohydrate foods eaten without foods containing much protein are digested and enter the bloodstream quickly and are thus likely to challenge blood sugar regulatory processes in people prone to hypoglycemia. Protein slows digestion and allows blood sugar to rise more gradually. Protein servings may be small: a slice or two of meat or cheese; a half-cup of cottage cheese, yogurt, or tuna salad; small servings of fish or shellfish; a dish made with lentils or other legumes; or soy products like tofu.

Avoid Sugar Overload

When you eat a large amount of carbohydrates, blood sugar rises quickly. A high blood sugar level calls forth a high insulin response, which in some people causes a sort of rebound effect: glucose enters the cells, and the blood sugar level drops quickly, causing hypoglycemia. While you may feel energized for a short period of time after too much sugar, you may eventually begin to feel tired, irritable, and hungry.

What about Breakfast?

Everyone recommends eating a good breakfast, but some people just can't look food in the face first thing in the morning. If this is true for you, carry a healthful snack to eat later in the morning.

FOOD AND MOOD: THE ROLE OF NEUROTRANSMITTERS

Most people feel relaxed and lazy after a big feast. For this reason many cultures have incorporated a siesta after the large midday meal, and professors who teach a class right after lunch or dinner rarely turn out the lights for a slide show. Why do we feel tired? Certainly our blood sugar should be adequate after eating all that food. Changes in brain biochemistry may be the reason (Wurtman with Danbrot, 1988; Wurtman & Wurtman, 1989). The food we eat supplies the precursor molecules for manufacturing neurotransmitters that inflence our emotions and mood. Some researchers believe that by selecting the right kinds of food we can encourage states of relaxation or alertness.

Big meals, especially those with a lot of fat, take a long time to digest, and with a full stomach we feel like relaxing rather than working. On the other hand, smaller meals low in fat take less time and energy to digest and leave us feeling more energetic and alert.

Meals that are composed primarily of carbohydrates encourage production of the neurotransmitter *serotonin,* which makes us feel drowsy and relaxed. High-carbohydrate meals are a prescription for relaxation and may be the reason some people overeat: it makes them feel good. A small, high-carbohydrate snack before bedtime can encourage sleep. Many people find that eating carbohydrates helps them feel less stressed and more relaxed. Some people find that a meal or snack with carbohydrate but little protein, especially in the middle of the day, leaves them feeling tired.

Meals that include a small serving of protein foods, with or without carbohydrates, encourage alertness by favoring production of neurotransmitters such as *dopamine* and *norepinephrine.* A small lunch that includes protein foods is best for students who need to stay alert for a 1:00 class.

GOOD NUTRITION FOR STRESS RESISTANCE AND HEALTH

So you've got your blood sugar and neurotransmitter levels under control. What else should you be aware of as you select foods during the day? A few suggestions are offered in the next sections (see also Figure 9.2).

Eat More Fruits, Vegetables, and Grains

You get carbohydrates for energy, many important vitamins and minerals, and fiber that helps regulate digestive function from fruits, vegetables, & grains. Some types of fiber found in these foods also help slow the release of glucose from the digestive tract into the blood; they also lower blood cholesterol. Some vegetables, such as soybeans and other legumes (often referred to as dried beans and include pinto,

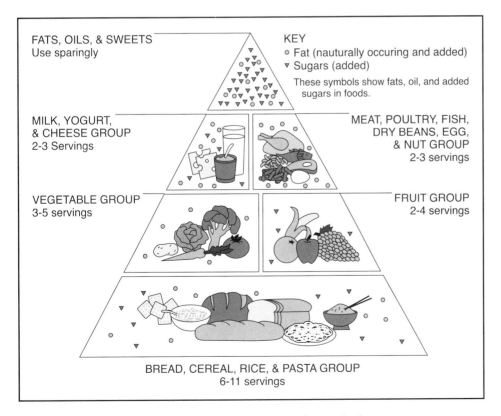

FIGURE 9.2   *Food Guide Pyramid: A Guide to Daily Food Choices*

Source: US Department of Agriculture/U.S. Department of Health and Human Services

navy, and black beans; lentils; and split peas) are good sources of protein; they are especially important for people who consume no foods from animal sources. All these foods contain a wide array of vitamins and minerals and are generally low in fat. We call these foods **nutrient dense,** which means they supply a lot of nutritive value per calorie.

You can add these foods to your diet in several low-fat ways. Eat more salads and steamed or raw vegetables. Root vegetables such as potatoes, yams, and carrots are simple to cook. Try various grain products, such as rice, kasha (buckwheat), and couscous. Add canned beans, such as kidney and garbanzo beans, to salads and casseroles. Soups made from black beans, split peas, and lentils are delicious and easy to prepare. Fruit is a tasty, nutritious, and convenient snack and dessert food.

Keep an Eye on Fat and Sugar

Whoever gives these things [food] no consideration and is ignorant of them, how can he understand the diseases of man?

HIPPOCRATES

You have probably heard by now that fat is the enemy. Too much dietary fat is thought to contribute to artery disease, stroke, obesity, and cancer. The most common dietary recommendation heard today is to replace high-fat foods with those high in starch and fiber: skip the steak and eat more potatoes.

Why is fat such a problem? Fat metabolism raises the blood cholesterol level, which increases risk of artery disease. A high fat intake also leads to obesity and associated risk factors such as type II diabetes and hypertension. Fat is **calorically dense,** which means it offers little nutrition but a lot of energy (calories). A small amount of cheese, cream sauce, or whipped cream goes down easily. You don't feel like you have eaten a lot, but you have. Remember that a gram of fat contains over twice the number of calories provided by a gram of protein and carbohydrate. And while your body uses up some energy converting dietary protein and carbohydrate to body fat, the conversion of dietary fat into body fat is biochemically simple and efficient. Dietary fat tends to go straight into storage.

You can decrease your intake of fat by avoiding food products with added fats and oils: potato chips, roasted nuts, and similar snack foods. Many baked goods are high in fat: doughnuts, cookies, cakes, and pies. Whole milk, cream, and their products, such as yogurt, ice cream, butter, and cheeses are very high in fat. Skim milk and its products, such as nonfat yogurt and cottage cheese are very low in fat.

Calvin and Hobbes   by Bill Watterson

Choose lean cuts of meat rather than meats like bologna, salami, bacon, sausage, and prime rib. Removing the skin from poultry eliminates much of the fat. Avoid fried and especially deep-fat fried anything.

Sugar has gotten a lot of bad press and may not be as terrible as it is often portrayed. A little sugar in a healthful diet is not harmful; indeed, natural sugar is present in many nutrient-dense foods (Clark, 1990). Problems occur when too much sugar in the form of candy, cookies, and other treats replaces healthful meals. Most North Americans need to consume less sugar and limit "empty calories." An exception is people who are physically active and thus can have a higher daily calorie allowance. People with a high energy expenditure can consume more empty calorie foods, assuming their basic diet is fairly nutritious.

Sugar is found in sweeteners and is added to many food products—from ketchup and peanut butter to breakfast cereal and yogurt. Read labels. Anything with "ose" or "syrup" in its name is a sugar: dextrose, maltose, sucrose, lactose, corn syrup, and malt syrup are some examples.

Keep an Eye on Salt Intake

A high-salt diet contributes to high blood pressure in many people. Salt and stress probably interact, since hormones contributing to the stress response regulate salt and water balance ("Stress, salt, and blood pressure," 1993). Even people without high blood pressure should probably approach salt intake with caution, since a diet high in salt appears to be damaging to arteries even in the presence of normal blood pressure. A high-salt diet can exacerbate the water retention many women experience with PMS (premenstrual syndrome). Water retention causes symptoms such as irritability and nervousness.

Like sugar, salt is added to many processed foods, including pickled foods; condiments such as ketchup, soy sauce, mustard, and relish; snack foods like nuts, pretzels, chips, and crackers; canned soups and sauces; and processed meats such as ham and salami. Watch out for Chinese food (sodium is found in monosodium glutamate, soy sauce, and other common ingredients) and pizza (salt in tomato sauce, cheese, and meat toppings).

Drink Plenty of Fluids

Many people fail to maintain optimal levels of hydration. The next time you feel tired, try drinking a glass of water. Dehydration causes fatigue and irritability.

Thirst is not an adequate indicator of dehydration; you become dehydrated before you get thirsty. Nutritionists advise drinking at least four cups of fluid each day, more with physical activity or hot weather. Caffeinated and alcoholic beverages don't count. Not only do they increase your stress but they also dehydrate you and thus increase your fluid needs. Your urine will be pale if you are adequately hydrated; dark-colored urine is a sign of dehydration (Clark, 1990).

Limit Caffeine

Caffeine is a **sympathomimetic** substance, which means its effects mimic those of the sympathetic nervous system and thus cause the fight-or-flight response. If you add caffeine to an already aroused sympathetic nervous system, the results can be stressful and produce high levels of anxiety, irritability, headache, and stress-related illness (Van Dusseldorp et al., 1992; MacDougall, Musante, Castillo, & Acevedo, 1988). Most caffeine drinks, including coffee, tea, and cola soft drinks can also cause stomachaches and nausea, which often get worse under stress ("Caffeine," 1994).

One or two caffeinated beverages consumed judiciously at appropriate times during the day appear to do no harm for most people (Witters, Venturelli & Hanson, 1992). Indeed, a little caffeine can increase alertness. The problem with caffeine is that people are likely to overindulge in it when they are stressed. When summoning the energy necessary to get through the day feels like trying to squeeze water from a rock, they reach for a shot of caffeine. Caffeine cannot substitute for a good night's sleep, however. When you are truly fatigued, caffeine does not help you concentrate; it simply leaves you wired, too jittery to sleep, and too tired to do anything productive.

Caffeine tolerance varies from person to person. Some people who forgo caffeine find they have a more even flow of energy throughout the day without caffeine's energy peaks and valleys. Some people find that any amount of caffeine causes undesirable symptoms such as anxiety and an irregular heartbeat. Others find that one or two cups stimulate them without putting them into overdrive, especially if their eating habits are good (see Table 9.1).

Caffeine is broken down very slowly, so it remains in the bloodstream for many hours. If you have trouble sleeping at night, try to refrain from consuming caffeine in the late afternoon and evening, and see whether your sleep pattern improves.

Limit Alcohol

[Alcohol] stirs up desire, but takes away performance.

SHAKESPEARE

Like they turn to caffeine, people often increase their use of alcohol during periods of stress, and what begins as an attempt to cope emotionally with a problem turns

TABLE 9.1 *Caffeine Content*

Beverage/Food	Amount	Caffeine (mg)
Brewed coffee	5 oz	100–125
Instant coffee	5 oz	15–100
Decaffeinated coffee	5 oz	1–6
Tea	5 oz	30–70
Cocoa	5 oz	5–30
Cola	12 oz	25–50
Chocolate bar	1 oz	20–25

Sources: Adapted from Clark (1990); Witters, Venturelli, and Hanson (1992).

out to compound the problem instead. North Americans reach for coffee to wind them up and alcohol to help them unwind. During periods of stress (and high caffeine consumption), winding down becomes more difficult. Too many people reach for a drink when they feel a need to relax. In Chapter 11 we examine the use and abuse of alcohol. For some people, a drink for the right reasons on the right occasions can be appropriate, but even moderate alcohol use can interfere with the ability to cope with stress. Many people find that even a single drink increases their fatigue and leaves them feeling groggy and less energetic the next morning. Too much alcohol greatly diminishes a person's coping ability and can lead to serious health problems (Brannon & Feist, 1992). If your alcohol use increases when you experience stress, then your drinking behavior may be problematic.

DO YOU NEED MORE VITAMINS AND MINERALS WHEN YOU ARE UNDER STRESS?

Authorities disagree about the effects of stress on a person's nutritional status. Extreme physical stress does require an increased intake of many nutrients, but does mild to moderate emotional stress also have this effect? Nutrition needs probably increase only slightly.

Should you take a vitamin supplement? Nutritionists agree that a nutritious diet should be the primary approach to obtaining an adequate intake of vitamins and minerals. A vitamin supplement may be helpful for people who find that stress takes a toll on their eating habits. Look for a supplement that provides 100 percent of the recommended dietary allowance (RDA) for all the vitamins; a special "stress formula" is a waste of your money. And remember that a supplement can never replace all the goodness provided by food (Gussow & Thomas, 1986; Reynolds, 1994). Fiber and many other beneficial constituents of foods are absent from or present in inadequate quantities in supplements (Adler, 1995; Lipkin, 1995; Napier, 1995; Reynolds, 1994; "Scientists," 1995).

EATING IN RESPONSE TO STRESS: FEEDING THE HUNGRY HEART

Few people look on eating and food only in terms of hunger and nutrition. Every culture in the world has evolved rituals around food and eating. Feasting and fasting carry layers of religious, cultural, and emotional overtones. As children, we learn to associate food with security, comfort, love, reward, punishment, anger, restraint. It's no wonder that we eat for many reasons other than hunger: because we're lonely, angry, sad, happy, nervous, or depressed. Unlike alcohol, which we can give up if we are prone to a drinking problem, we must learn to live with food. If eating is the only way we take the time to nurture ourselves, we eat more than we are really hungry for. In extreme cases, an inability to control eating can develop into an eating disorder known as **compulsive overeating,** that often gets worse under stress. Compulsive overeating refers to an inability to control or stop eating, and often includes binging and rituals that involve food preparation and consumption (APA, 1994).

If overeating is a problem, try to find other palliative coping responses that can substitute for overeating. Get in touch with your feelings of hunger and satiety; eat regular meals and snacks of healthful foods, as recommended in the section on blood sugar regulation. Eat slowly and stop eating when you start to feel full. Enjoy your food, and eat plenty of healthful carbohydrates that help you feel relaxed and less stressed. If compulsive overeating is a big problem for you, consult a qualified professional who specializes in eating problems.

BODY FAT, WEIGHT CONTROL, AND HEALTH

One of the most prevalent sources of nutrition-related stress in North America is concern about body fat and weight control (Serdula et al., 1994). Studies suggest that we should be concerned. According to the National Center for Health Statistics, one-third of the adult population in the United States is obese, judged by standard weight-for-height measures (Kuczmarski, Flegal, Campbell, & Johnson, 1994). Another cause for concern arises from obesity trends in recent years. Americans are much fatter today than they were at the turn of the century. Just 15 years ago, only 25 percent of U.S. adults were considered obese; there has been a 32 percent increase in obesity in 15 years. U.S. adults weigh on average about 8 pounds more than they did 10 years ago. Obesity rates are rising in children as well. The reason appears to be our high fat consumption coupled with our sedentary lifestyle (Pi-Sunyer, 1994). We actually consume slightly *fewer* calories per day than people did in the early 1900s. The problem is that we are getting more of our calories in the form of simple sugars and fats (Liebman, 1995; Ratto, 1986). We're also much less active (McGinnis, 1992).

The weight-control issue is a complicated one for many reasons. For many people, body weight is extremely difficult to control (Brownell & Rodin, 1994). For others, attempts to diet stringently to achieve unrealistically thin physiques lead to eating disorders. Add discrimination against fat people and mountains of media-hype for worthless weight-loss schemes and products and you get, well, stress.

Is Obesity Really a Problem?

You are probably already asking questions about the meaning of the obesity prevalence statistics. An obvious question concerns the validity of obesity measures. Obesity is generally defined as weighing "too much" for a given height. Most researchers use a measure called the **Body Mass Index (BMI)** to define obesity. Body Mass Index is calculated by dividing weight in kilograms by height in meters squared (kg/m^2). Nonmetric readers can calculate BMI by multiplying a person's weight in pounds by 700, then dividing the result by the square of height in inches. Charts are also available (see Table 9.2). BMIs from 20 to 26 are considered safe. For men, a BMI greater than 27.8 is considered obese; a BMI greater than 27.3 is considered obese for women. BMIs can be misleading since they do not take into account the true variable of interest: **body composition,** the proportion of your body that is fat. Many athletes, for example, are "too heavy" according to their BMIs when in reality they are simply large and muscular. Unfortunately, body composition estimates are very hard to get for large groups of people, so we are stuck with height-weight measures such as BMI in most studies. Because people who are muscular and active represent a fairly small proportion of the North American population, statistics showing an increasing weight for U.S. adults probably indicate increasing fatness rather than increasing muscularity.

Another interesting point is that although U.S. adults have become fatter, their health has actually improved somewhat. Our rates of heart disease are declining despite our increase in obesity. Opponents of this argument point out that many studies have found associations between excess body weight and health problems for both men and women, including hypertension, high cholesterol levels, type II diabetes, atherosclerosis, certain cancers, arthritis, gallstones, and lower back problems (Pi-Sunyer, 1993). Risk for these problems increases in a dose-response fashion: the greater the excess weight, the greater is the risk. The typical middle-age weight gain of 20 or 30 pounds experienced by many North Americans appears to increase their health risk. One study found that women who added 22 to 40 pounds after age 18

TABLE 9.2 *Body Mass Index According to Height (in inches) and Weight (in pounds)*

Height (in.)	Body Mass Index														
	20	21	22	23	24	25	26	27	28	29	30	35	40	45	50
						Body weight (lb.)									
58	95	100	105	110	114	119	124	129	133	138	143	167	191	214	238
59	99	104	109	114	119	124	129	134	139	144	149	174	198	223	248
60	102	107	112	117	122	127	132	138	143	148	153	178	204	229	255
61	106	111	117	122	127	132	138	143	148	154	159	185	212	238	265
62	109	114	120	125	130	136	141	147	152	158	163	190	217	245	272
63	113	119	124	130	135	141	147	152	158	164	169	198	226	254	282
64	117	123	129	135	141	146	152	158	164	170	176	205	234	264	293
65	120	126	132	138	144	150	156	162	168	174	180	210	240	270	300
66	124	131	137	143	149	156	162	168	174	180	187	218	249	280	311
67	127	134	140	147	153	159	166	172	178	185	191	223	255	287	319
68	132	139	145	152	158	165	172	178	185	191	198	231	264	297	330
69	135	142	149	155	162	169	176	182	189	196	203	236	270	304	338
70	140	147	154	161	168	175	182	189	196	203	210	244	279	314	349
71	143	150	157	164	171	179	186	193	200	207	214	250	286	321	357
72	148	155	162	170	177	185	192	199	207	214	221	258	295	332	369
73	151	158	166	174	181	189	196	204	211	219	226	264	302	340	377
74	156	164	171	179	187	195	203	210	218	226	234	273	312	351	390
75	159	167	175	183	191	199	207	215	223	231	239	279	318	358	398
76	164	172	181	189	197	205	214	222	230	238	246	287	328	370	411

Source: Table derived from BMI calculations.

had a 70 percent greater risk of death from heart disease and a 20 percent greater risk of cancer than women who had maintained their weight (Manson et al., 1995).

Is obesity the real culprit for these increased risks, or is obesity simply a marker for other lifestyle factors that represent the real risk, such as a sedentary lifestyle and poor eating habits? Some experts believe that excess body fat probably interacts with heredity and lifestyle to affect metabolic processes such as blood sugar regulation that are associated with health risk. Some studies have found that improving diet and starting to exercise improve health even in the absence of any weight loss (Brownell & Rodin, 1994). In other words, obesity with normal blood pressure, cholesterol, and good blood sugar control may not be so harmful to your health if you exercise and eat a nutritious, low-fat diet (Gaesser, 1996).

How Fat Is Too Fat?

Studies of large groups of people can suggest weight guidelines, but it is hard to say how fat is too fat for any given individual. In addition to calculating BMI several factors, discussed next, should be considered.

Body Composition As mentioned above, weight for height may not represent obesity. The scale does not lie, but it does not tell the whole truth, either. If you are big and muscular, you may be too heavy according to the charts but still have a healthy body composition. Body composition can be estimated in several ways, all requiring special equipment. Healthy body fat levels for men range from about 12 percent to 20 percent, with athletes as low as 5 percent. Women should be about 20 percent to 30 percent fat, although female athletes may be 16 percent or less. Like weight, we really do not know exactly what percentage of fat becomes a health risk for any given individual.

Location of Fat Stores Another problem with height-weight tables is that all fat stores are not created equal. Obesity-related health problems are much more likely to occur if extra fat is stored on the torso rather than on the hips and thighs (Campaigne, 1990; Despres et al., 1988). Lower-body obesity is still a health risk, however; people with "pear shapes" are at higher risk for obesity-related disorders than people who are not overweight.

Medical History and Family Medical History Weight control or at least healthful exercise and eating habits are especially beneficial for people who have obesity-related health problems, such as hypertension, high blood cholesterol, type II diabetes, artery disease, or a family history of these disorders.

Age People who are over 70 years old and a bit overweight but apparently healthy probably need not be concerned about losing weight. In the absence of medical indications for weight control, many nutritionists recommend an extra 10 or 15 pounds for people over 70 to help them resist wasting if they should become ill. And if the extra weight is not associated with health risks, losing weight will probably offer them no health benefits.

Focus on Fitness, not Fatness

Too many studies suggest that dieting for many people is not only futile but harmful to their health (Lissner et al., 1991; Rodin, Radke-Sharpe, Rebuffe-Scrive, & Greenwood, 1990; Wadden, 1992). Frequent dieting interspersed with periods of normal or greater-than-normal caloric intake are common in people attempting to lose weight. Those who are eating this way may lose and regain the same 20 or 30 pounds many times, a process known as **weight cycling**. Weight cycling appears to have several harmful side effects, including increased risk of the dieter's developing hypertension, artery disease, and gallbladder disease (Brownell & Rodin, 1994; Lissner et al., 1991). Some of the negative health effects may be explained by the observation that many people who regain weight lost on a diet use progressively less healthful weight control methods (fasting, vomiting, diet pills) on subsequent weight loss attempts (Zimmerman & Hoerr, 1995). Research suggests that moderately obese people who don't try to lose weight are healthier than obese people who have experienced frequent fluctuations in body weight (Gaesser, 1996).

Trying to lose weight can be a frustrating experience that creates more stress, more cravings, and ironically, more obesity (Wooley & Garner, 1991). When attempts to lose weight are unsuccessful, dieters blame themselves rather than the diet. Instead of trying to achieve a specific weight-loss goal, people who are overweight are advised to focus on long-term lifestyle improvement: increasing physical activity, managing stress, and developing healthful eating habits. When lifestyle changes, some weight loss may occur. Slow, steady weight loss is more likely to be permanent and less likely to lead to obsessions with food and weight than is fad dieting. The first 10 to 15 pounds of weight loss can dramatically improve health factors such as blood sugar control and blood lipid profile. In other words, if you are quite a bit overweight, you need not struggle to achieve an unrealistically low weight to improve your health. Best of all, the lifestyle changes that improve your health improve your stress resistance as well!

People who think they are overweight often put their lives on hold: I'll do it after I've lost 20 pounds. "It" may be to end an unhappy relationship, look for a better job, or pursue some other interesting goal. Unfortunately, the 20 pounds remain and long-term goals are put on permanent hold. Recommendations for lifestyle change will work only if you can still love yourself and enjoy life. Change must always come from a desire to be good to yourself because you are worthy of the best treatment.

Compulsive Dieting and Disordered Eating

Our culture has discovered the perfect recipe for the development of eating problems: combine an abundant food supply rich in fat with sedentary occupations, and then establish an unrealistic standard of thinness by which to judge self-worth. Problems with food and body image run the gamut from occasional dieting, eating binges, and some concern about being overweight, to constant worry about food and weight, to the clinical eating disorders **anorexia nervosa, bulimia nervosa** (see Figure 9.3), and **compulsive overeating,** which may become life threatening and involve serious psychological problems. The term **disor-**

Diagnostic criteria for Anorexia Nervosa

1. Refusal to maintain body weight at or above a minimally normal weight for age and height.
2. Intense fear of gaining weight or becoming fat, even though underweight.
3. Disturbance in the way in which one's body weight or shape is experienced, undue influence of body weight or shape on self-evaluation, or denial of the seriousness of the current low-body weight.
4. In postmenarcheal females, amenorrhea (the absence of at least three consecutive menstrual cycles).

Two types of anorexia nervosa specified:

Restricting type: person does not engage in binge eating or purging behavior (self-induced vomiting or misuse of laxatives, diurectics, or enemas).
Binge eating/purging type: person regularly engages in binge eating or purging behavior.

Diagnostic criteria for Bulimia Nervosa

1. Recurrent episodes of binge eating. An episode of binge eating is characterized by both of the following:
   a. eating, in a discrete time (e.g., within any 2-hr period), an amount of food that is definitely larger than most people would eat during a similar period of time and under similar circumstances.
   b. a sense of lack of control over eating during the episode.
2. Recurrent inappropriate compensatory behavior in order to prevent weight gain, such as self-induced vomiting; misuse of laxatives, diuretics, enemas, or other medications; fasting; or excessive exercise.
3. The binge eating and inappropriate compensatory behaviors occur, on average, at least twice a week for 3 months.
4. Self-evaluation is unduly influenced by body shape and weight.
5. The disturbance does not occur exclusively during episodes of Anorexia Nervosa.

Two types of Bulimia Nervosa are specified:

Purging type: person regularly engages in self-induced vomiting or the misuse of laxatives, diuretics, or enemas.
Nonpurging type: person uses other inappropriate compensatory behaviors, such as fasting or excessive exercise, but does not regularly engage in self-induced vomiting or the misuse of laxatives, diuretics, or enemas.

FIGURE 9.3 *Definitions of Anorexia Nervosa and Bulimia Nervosa*

Source: Diagnostic and Statistics Manual for Mental Disorders, 4th ed. DSM IV. American Psychiatric Association.

dered eating refers to this continuum of problems with food and body image (see Figure 9.4).

At an extremely early age, children, especially girls, begin to worry about how they look and they begin to diet ("Body-weight," 1991; Brownell, 1991). The weight-loss industry promotes many misconceptions about food and weight, and vulnerable young girls accept and value these myths. Many adults buy into these myths as well. Advertisements imply, for example, that fatness is shameful, an indication of sloth and gluttony. The attainment of a thin physique, on the other hand, means virtue and self-control. Thinness is equated not only with beauty but with success, love, and happiness. Fat is bad; thin is good. The other myth is that with enough willpower, and perhaps the right products, we can achieve the superslender bodies we see in magazines. We are led to believe that only self-control

▶ STRESS RESEARCH

Jean Kilbourne: *Food, Body Image, and Stress—The Role of the Media*

One of the biggest sources of food-related stress in North America arises from our preoccupation with thinness and physical appearance. Social commentator Jean Kilbourne has spent over 25 years studying the image of women in advertising. She acknowledges that the media are not the only cause of our cultural obsession with thinness, but Kilbourne believes that no influence is more "persuasive and pervasive" (Kilbourne, 1995). Girls and young women appear to be especially vulnerable to the negative effects of the media's relentless presentation of a single standard of feminine physical perfection, a perfection that is absolutely flawless and impossible to achieve. Most of us cannot even get close! Kilbourne proposes that these images are partly to blame for the alarming rise in the occurrence of eating disorders and disordered eating behaviors, an incidence that is especially high among college women.

Kilbourne's video *Slim Hopes* (Kilbourne, 1995) highlights several important issues. The first is that an overwhelming majority of the models and actresses featured in advertisements have a tall, slender, V-shaped body (wide shoulders, narrow hips) that is typical of less than 5 percent of North American women. Most women have rounder, pear-shaped bodies that no amount of dieting will ever transform into a model's figure. In addition to having this special body type, today's models are impossibly thin. Twenty years ago models weighed an average of 8 percent less than the average American woman; today they weigh on average 23 percent less. Yet they set the standards to which girls and women are urged to compare themselves. When the non-model women come up lacking, advertisements suggest some product to remedy the problem. The advertisers' reinforcement of this sense of physical inadequacy drives consumers to spend money, lots of money, on cosmetics, diet products, clothes, cigarettes, and other goods in their search for beauty.

Our culture's glorification of thinness leads us to impart moral judgment on individuals based on their body composition. Thin people are viewed as good and self-disciplined, their appetites under control. Fat represents gluttony and sloth. Fat people are the butt of jokes and are discriminated against

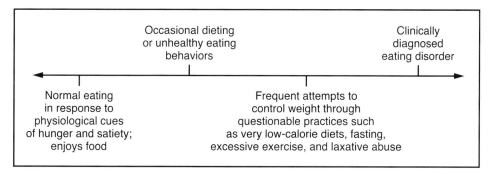

FIGURE **9.4** *Disordered Eating Continuum*

in many ways. Young girls (and boys, too) learn early that fatness is something to be avoided at all costs. Food has acquired similar moral connotations: delicious foods are sinful and decadent. People "cheat" on their diets and feel guilty when they eat dessert. Food is the enemy.

Kilbourne notes the disturbing observation that dieting and body dissatisfaction begin for girls at a very young age. She cites a study reporting 80 percent of girls in the fourth grade are already dieting to lose weight. Research has found that when girls reach adolescence their self-esteem plummets; the same is not true for boys. Why the difference? While several theories have been proposed, Kilbourne believes part of the problem is that girls become dismayed by their rounder figures that no longer fit the media's image of female beauty. If they look to magazines, television, and movies for role models, they will find extreme emphasis on a physical appearance they can probably never achieve. Trying to achieve a super-slender body devoid of hips may begin the cycle of dieting, weight gain, further dieting, and possibly life-threatening eating disorders.

Perhaps the most distressing effect of our obsession with thinness is what Kilbourne calls "the impoverishment of the imagination." Millions of people, both men and women, spend too much of their time and energy worrying about what to eat and how much they weigh when they should be focusing on more important problems like world hunger, the environment, and poverty. Other experts concur (Brownell, 1991). Stand in the supermarket checkout line and you see magazine after magazine urging you to lose weight. In no other domain are we so concerned with achieving perfection. Why the emphasis on physical appearance? Why not urge people to become better students? Better parents? Better workers? Artists? Naturalists? Better people? Why do we keep buying the products that are marketed on the myth that with the right combination of diet and exercise everyone can achieve the ideal body? Shouldn't we be spending our precious time, energy, and money on more important issues?

stands between the bodies we have now and the magnificent specimens we could become.

Many people trying to lose weight focus on some form of **very low-calorie diet (VLCD),** commonly and appropriately known as a crash diet. Such diets are both ineffective and harmful to one's long-term health and stress resistance. They rarely educate the dieter about prudent food choices, so once the diet is over, the dieter usually gains back all the weight lost on the diet, and then some (Bouchard et al., 1990; Brownell et al., 1986; Pavlou, Krey, & Steffee, 1989). Very low-calorie diets often leave the dieter feeling deprived, depressed, and tired. They commonly lead to powerful food cravings, which in turn lead to binges. Binging is followed by guilt, even stricter dieting, greater cravings, and more misery. Sometimes this harmful pattern evolves into a full-fledged eating disorder, especially in people who are psychologically vulnerable to such problems (Brehm & Keller, 1990; Worthington-Roberts, 1990).

Many of us are careful about what we eat and watch our weight because we want to stay healthy and feel good. Unfortunately, this healthy concern can turn

 ## STRESS AND YOU

DISORDERED EATING BEHAVIOR

The following are examples of disordered eating behaviors and attitudes (APA, 1994; Wardlaw, Insel, & Seyler, 1994).

- Frequent worry about body weight
- Rigid dieting, especially frequent adherence to VLCDs
- Unusual eating rituals, especially rituals performed privately
- Fear of weight gain; feeling of panic after a small weight gain
- Secretive binging; controlled eating in front of other people
- Eating in response to feelings of stress, depression, or anxiety.
- Fasting to lose weight
- Fear of not being able to stop eating; inability to stop eating
- Food as primary source of comfort, primary palliative coping method
- Preoccupation with food and body weight, spending several hours a day thinking about body weight and what to eat
- Feelings of purity and superiority with rigid control of food intake
- Excessive exercise
- Purging behaviors: vomiting; laxative or diuretic use
- Smoking to avoid eating
- Use of diet pills and other drugs, legal or illegal, to avoid eating

All these behaviors are cause for concern, although the presence of one or two does not mean you have a clinical eating disorder. If any of these are characteristic for you, perhaps you should address them. Consulting a qualified professional might help if the issues are too large for you to deal with adequately on your own. Prevention is the best defense against the development of eating disorders, which are notoriously difficult to treat. If you can heed early warning signs, you will be more likely to develop appropriate eating behaviors and attitudes, and the positive self-esteem that supports a stress-resistant lifestyle.

into an unhealthy preoccupation with food and weight. Over 50 percent of people who claim they are dieting to lose weight are not overweight (Ornstein & Sobel, 1989). Social commentator Jean Kilbourne notes that one of the greatest problems associated with our society's preoccupation with food and weight is "the impoverishment of the imagination" (Kilbourne, 1995). Many people, especially women, spend their days counting calories or grams of fat, and thinking about what they will have for their next meal. Others are so concerned about ensuring food purity, avoiding carcinogenic additives, or following the perfect eating plan to prevent health problems such as artery disease or cancer that they worry about every morsel they consume. Eating becomes a cognitive act unconnected to appetite and enjoyment, and all food is potential poison.

EAT, DRINK, AND BE MERRY

Food should be enjoyed and eating meals should be a pleasurable experience. Why not? Healthy pleasures increase your stress resistance, as you will see in Chapter 11. Relaxed, enjoyable mealtimes improve the function of your digestive system (which works best when the parasympathetic nervous system is in gear). Try really to taste and enjoy your food. Take a deep breath before you begin your next meal and tune in to the tastes and smells before you. Focus the conversation on pleasant topics. Eating slowly is a treat; the extra ten minutes spent at the table can provide an island of pleasure in a hectic day.

IMPROVING YOUR DIET

Evaluating and changing your eating habits is a lifelong process that requires a realistic, one-step-at-a-time approach (Brownell & Cohen, 1995). Small changes you can live with do more good than dramatic overhauls that drive you crazy and last only a few weeks. Anticipate setbacks and don't despair if your plans don't always work perfectly. Learn from the difficulties and adjust your plans accordingly. Most of all, enjoy your food and appreciate your progress. Use the action plan worksheet on the next page to help increase the stress resistance of your diet.

Assess Your Current Eating Habits

Decide what you are already doing well and what habits could use some improvement. Perhaps you have a nutritious breakfast but the day starts to fall apart by noon, so you grab some high-fat fast food for lunch and a pizza for dinner. Use your problem-solving skills to define your nutrition problem areas and brainstorm some solutions. Some people find it helpful to record their food intake for three or more days. A dietitian or nutritionist can help you assess your diet and suggest appropriate changes. Consulting such a specialist is especially useful if you are pregnant or have health concerns such as food allergies, diabetes, high blood cholesterol, or high blood pressure. Once you have a good idea of the meals that need the most help, you can start to plan ahead.

Make a Plan

Decide how to deal with problems that keep you from eating a more nutritious diet. One stress management student who cooked for her family found that dinner was too often fast food or high-fat snacks rather than a nutritious, low-fat meal. This was because the dinner hour was a difficult time. She would get home

---

▲ ACTION PLAN

NUTRITION PLAN FOR STRESS RESISTANCE AND HEALTH

Take some time to think about your eating habits. Begin by describing what you are already doing well. Then list some areas that could use improvement. Choose two areas you would like to change and describe realistic steps that would help you move toward these goals.

1. Ways in which I am already doing well:

   _____

   _____

   _____

   _____

2. Areas that could use some improvement:

   _____

   _____

   _____

   _____

3. Goals for improvement:

   a. _____

   b. _____

4. Action plan:

   a. Rewrite goal a: _____

---

from work and school with little energy left for preparing dinner and spending time with her family. She solved this problem by beginning dinner preparations in the morning before she left the house. Everything was ready to go when she got home so dinner preparation was minimal, tensions were lower, and the family dinner hour was much less stressful. Meals were better planned and more healthful as well.

If you find you are missing dining hall hours, figure out a way to make a nutritious alternative available. If a twice-a-day dessert habit is getting in the way of weight control, make a plan for occasional desserts and for low-fat dessert replacements. When you go grocery shopping, always have a list and avoid impulse buying. Stick to your list and just say no to junk food.

Specific activities to accomplish this goal:

1. _____

2. _____

3. _____

b. Rewrite goal b: _____

Specific activities to accomplish this goal:

1. _____

2. _____

3. _____

5. Anticipate setbacks: What might keep me from sticking to my plans?

a. _____

b. _____

c. _____

6. How I will prevent these from interfering, or how I will get back on track if they occur?

a. _____

b. _____

c. _____

Make a list of nutritious food you want to have on hand for snacking and meals. We often eat high-fat or empty-calorie foods because we're hungry and reach for the nearest alternative. If you make healthful foods convenient, you'll avoid impulse snacking on high-fat foods and make healthful choices a habit.

If you are in a household that prepares meals, a weekly menu plan saves time and improves meal quality. Plan meals for the upcoming week and shop for the necessary ingredients. Trying to pull a meal together at the end of a busy day can be stressful and fast food every night becomes your coping response. To improve your stress resistance, following a nutritious diet must be as stress free as possible. Organization is the key. The time you spend planning once a week will save the time and stress of last-minute shopping and help you stick to your good intentions.

Planning doesn't mean you will cook every night. Plan meals around your schedule: late classes and evening meetings require simple fare. On busy days, plan to eat healthful take-out meals or leftovers. Decide which nights you'll eat out and adjust the rest of that day's food intake accordingly. A weekly plan can help encourage variety in your diet and give you a sense of control (Clark, 1990).

SUMMARY

1. Good nutrition improves both short-term and long-term stress resistance.
2. Overnutrition, the consumption of too much fat and sugar and too many calories, is the most common nutrition problem in North America.
3. Nutrients are classified into six groups. Carbohydrates supply energy. Protein is used by the body for many structures and metabolic functions; it also supplies some energy. Lipids include dietary fats and oils and are a concentrated source of energy. Vitamins and minerals are required for growth, development, energy production, structural components of the body, and countless metabolic functions. Water is important for many functions, including digestion, transportation of nutrients and wastes, and temperature regulation.
4. Fatigue and irritability result when blood sugar level gets too low. To maintain an even level of blood sugar, eat regularly, consume some protein at every meal, and avoid sugar overload.
5. Blood sugar level is regulated by two important hormones. Insulin is released in response to high blood sugar levels. It allows the sugar (glucose) to leave the blood and enter the cells of the body. Glucagon is released in response to low blood sugar levels. It stimulates the release of glucose from precursors such as glycogen and amino acids.
6. Mood and energy level are partly a function of neurotransmitter activity in the central nervous system. Neurotransmitter activity is partially dependent on diet. High-protein foods consumed with or without carbohydrate are associated with elevated levels of dopamine and norepinephrine, which help you feel alert. Carbohydrate meals are associated with elevated levels of serotonin, which makes you feel sleepy and relaxed.
7. Guidelines for a healthful diet include the following: eat more fruits, vegetables, and grains; limit fat, sugar, and salt intake; drink plenty of fluids; limit caffeine; and limit alcohol.
8. Caffeine is a sympathomimetic substance, which means its effects mimic those of the sympathetic nervous system and thus cause the fight-or-flight response. If you add caffeine to an already aroused sympathetic nervous sytem, the results can be stressful.
9. The need for vitamins and minerals seems to increase only slightly when people are under emotional stress. Supplements may be helpful for people with poor eating habits but can never replace all the benefits derived from a healthful diet.
10. Compulsive overeating is an eating disorder characterized by the inability to control or stop eating; it often includes binging and rituals that involve food preparation and consumption. Compulsive overeating often worsens with an increase in stress.
11. About one-third of adults in the United States are obese. The reasons for our high rates of obesity appear to be our high fat consumption coupled with our sedentary lifestyle.
12. Body composition estimates indicate what percentage of your body is composed of fat.

13. Obesity has been linked to a number of physiological disorders, including diabetes, hypertension, artery disease, gallbladder disease, high cholesterol levels, certain cancers, arthritis, and low-back problems. Some experts believe that the poor diet and inactivity that often accompany obesity may be partly to blame for some of these disorders.

14. A Body Mass Index of 20–26 is generally considered healthy. People deciding whether to try to lose weight should consider other variables as well, including body composition, location of fat stores, medical history, family medical history, and age.

15. Weight cycling refers to repeatedly losing and regaining weight. Weight cycling increases risk for hypertension, artery disease, and gallbladder disease. Slow, steady weight loss is much more healthful, even if only a relatively small amount of weight loss occurs.

16. Frequent attempts to lose weight can result in disordered eating behaviors, such as following very low-calorie diets (VLCDs) and fasting to lose weight. Very low-calorie diets are ineffective and harmful to one's long-term health and stress resistance.

17. Anorexia nervosa is a clinical eating disorder characterized by an extremely low body weight and an intense fear of becoming fat.

18. Bulimia nervosa is a clinical eating disorder characterized by recurrent episodes of binge eating followed by inappropriate compensatory behavior to prevent weight gain, such as self-induced vomiting; misuse of laxatives, diuretics, enemas, or other medications; fasting; or excessive exercise.

19. Food should be enjoyed, and eating meals should be a pleasurable experience.

REFERENCES

Adler, T. Power foods: Looking at how nutrients may fight cancer. *Science News,* Dec 9, 1995, pp 248–249.

American Psychiatric Association (APA). *Diagnostic and Statistical Manual of Mental Disorders (4th ed.)* Washington, DC: American Psychiatric Association, 1994.

Body-weight perceptions and selected weight-management goals and practices of high school students—United States, 1990. *Journal of the American Medical Association* 266: 2811–2812, 1991.

Bouchard, C, A Tremblay, A Nadeau, et al. Long-term exercise training with constant energy intake. 1: Effect on body composition and selected metabolic variables. *International Journal of Obesity* 14: 57–73, 1990.

Brannon, L, and J Feist. *Health Psychology: An Introduction to Behavior and Health.* Belmont, CA: Wadsworth, 1992.

Brehm, BA, and BA Keller. Diet and exercise factors that influence weight and fat loss. *IDEA Today,* Oct 1990, pp 33–38+.

Brownell, KB, GA Marlatt, E Lichtenstein, and GT Wilson. Understanding and preventing relapse. *American Psychologist* 41: 765–782, 1986.

Brownell, KD. Dieting and the search for the perfect body: Where physiology and culture collide. *Behavior Therapy* 22: 1–12, 1991.

Brownell, KD, and J Rodin. The dieting Maelstrom: Is it possible and advisable to lose weight? *American Psychologist* 49: 781–791, 1994.

Brownell, KD, and LR Cohen. Adherence to dietary regimens 2: Components of effective intervention. *Behavioral Medicine* 20: 155–164, 1995.

Caffeine: Grounds for concern? *UC Berkeley Wellness Letter,* March 1994, pp 4–5.

Campaigne, B. Body fat distribution in females: Metabolic consequences and implications for weight loss. *Medicine and Science in Sports and Exercise* 22: 291–297, 1990.

Clark, N. *Nancy Clark's Sports Nutrition Guidebook.* Champaign, IL: Leisure Press, 1990.

Davis, M, ER Eshelman, and M McKay. *The Relaxation and Stress Reduction Workbook.* Oakland, CA: New Harbinger, 1995.

Despres, JP, S Moorjani, A Tremblay, et al. Heredity and changes in plasma lipids and lipoproteins after short-term exercise training in men. *Arteriosclerosis* 8: 402–409, 1988.

Gaesser, GA. *Big Fat Lies; The Truth About Your Weight and Your Health.* New York: Fawcett Columbine, 1996.

Gussow, JD, and PR Thomas. *The Nutrition Debate: Sorting Out Some Answers.* Palo Alto, CA: Bull Publishing, 1986. Chapter 6, Nutritional supplements: To pill or not to pill, is that the question? pp 268–341.

Katch, FI, and WD McArdle. *Introduction to Nutrition, Exercise, and Health.* Philadelphia: Lea & Febiger, 1993.

Kilbourne, J. *Slim Hopes* (video). Northampton, MA: Media Education Foundation, 1995.

Kuczmarski, RJ, KM Flegal, SM Campbell, and CL Johnson. Increasing prevalence of overweight among US adults: The National Health and Nutrition Examination Surveys, 1960–1991. *Journal of the American Medical Association* 272: 205–211, 1994.

Liebman, B. The changing American diet. *Nutrition Action Health Letter,* June 1995, pp 8–9.

Lipkin, R. Vegemania: Scientists tout the health benefits of saponins. *Science News,* Dec 9, 1995, pp 392–393.

Lissner, L, PM Odell, RB D'Agostino, et al. Variability of body weight and health outcomes in the Framingham population. *New England Journal of Medicine* 324: 1839, 1991.

MacDougall, JM, L Musante, S Castillo, and MC Acevedo. Smoking, caffeine, and stress: Effects on blood pressure and heart rate in male and female college students. *Health Psychology* 7: 461–478, 1988.

Manson, JE, WC Willett, MJ Stampfer, et al. Body weight and mortality among women. *New England Journal of Medicine* 333: 677–685, 1995.

McGinnis, JM. The public health burden of a sedentary life style. *Medicine and Science in Sports and Exercise* 24:S196–S200, 1992.

Napier, K. Green revolution. *Harvard Health Letter,* Special Supplement, April 1995, pp 9–12.

Ornstein, R, and D Sobel. *Healthy Pleasures.* Reading, MA: Addison-Wesley, 1989.

Pavlou, KN, S Krey, and WP Steffee. Exercise as an adjunct to weight loss and maintenance in moderately obese subjects. *American Journal of Clinical Nutrition* 49: 1115–1123, 1989.

Pi-Sunyer, FX. Medical hazards of obesity. *Annals of Internal Medicine* 119: 655–660, 1993.

Pi-Sunyer, FX. The fattening of America. *Journal of the American Medical Association* 272: 238–239, 1994.

Ratto, T. Are we really eating healthier? *Medical Self-Care,* Sept–Oct 1986, pp 24–27.

Reynolds, RD. Vitamin supplements: Current controversies. *Journal of American College of Nutrition* 13: 118–126, 1994.

Rodin, J, N Radke-Sharpe, M Rebuffe-Scrive, and MRC Greenwood. Weight cycling and fat distribution. *International Journal of Obesity* 14: 303, 1990.

Scientists spotlight phytoestrogens for better health. *Tufts University Diet and Nutrition Letter,* Feb 1995, pp 3–6.

Serdula, MK, DF Williamson, RF Anda, et al. Weight control practices in adults: Results of a multistate telephone survey. *American Journal of Public Health* 84: 1821–1824, 1994.

Stone, AA, and KD Brownell. The stress-eating paradox: Multiple daily measurements in adult males and females. *Psychology and Health* 9: 425–436, 1994.

Stress, salt, and blood pressure. *University of California at Berkeley Wellness Letter,* April 1993, p 7.

Van Dusseldorp, M, P Smits, JWM Lenders, et al. Effects of coffee on cardiovascular responses to stress: A 14-week controlled trial. *Psychosomatic Medicine* 54: 344–353, 1992.

Wadden, TA. Evidence for success of caloric restriction in weight loss and control: Summary data from clinical research studies. In *Methods for Voluntary Weight Loss and Control. NIH Technology Assessment Conference.* Bethesda, MD: National Institutes of Health, 1992.

Wardlaw, GM, PM Insel, and MF Seyler. *Contemporary Nutrition: Issues and Insights.* St Louis: Mosby, 1994.

Witters, W, P Venturelli, and G Hanson. *Drugs and Society.* Boston: Jones and Bartlett, 1992.

Wooley, SC, and DM Garner. Obesity treatment: The high cost of false hope. *Journal of American Dietic Association* 91: 1248 , 1991.

Worthington-Roberts, B. Directions for research on women and nutrition. *American Journal of Health Promotion* 5: 63–69, 1990.

Wurtman, JJ, with M Danbrot. *Managing Your Mind and Mood through Food.* New York: Harper & Row, 1988.

Wurtman, RJ, and JJ Wurtman. Carbohydrates and depression. *Scientific American* 260: 68–75, 1989.

Zimmerman, D, and SL Hoerr. Use of questionable dieting practices among young women examinined by weight history. *Journal of Women's Health* 4: 189–196, 1995.

chapter 10

Physical Activity and Stress Resistance

Participation in regular physical activity is one of the most effective ways to increase your stress resistance. Countless studies comparing people with high and low levels of stress resistance have found exercise to be one of the most salient discriminators between these two groups (Brown, 1991; Dienstbier, 1991; Kobasa, Maddi, & Puccetti, 1982; Roth & Holmes, 1987; Sheets, Gorenflo, & Forney, 1993). An important note is that the amount and intensity of exercise required to produce stress management benefits need not be overwhelming (Berger & Owen, 1992). While many athletes enjoy extended periods of intense activity, other people find stress relief with a brisk walk, an hour of gardening, or a game of volleyball on the beach.

Physical activity has both short- and long-term effects. Many people report feeling less stress both during and after a single exercise session. Regular exercise, which generally means performing some sort of physical activity at least three times a week, has a cumulative effect as well, and exercisers report feeling less stressed even on days when they don't engage in physical activity (Berger, Friedman, & Eaton, 1988; Helin & Hanninen, 1988; Holmes & Roth, 1988; Morgan, 1985).

The health benefits of exercise read like the promises of a huckster selling snake oil: increased energy, less fatigue, better sleep, weight control, toned muscles, and even a better sex life. Regular exercise reduces your risk of many chronic diseases, including artery disease, type II diabetes, hypertension, obesity, and even some types of cancer (McGinnis, 1992). The mental health benefits of exercise go far beyond stress management. Regular physical activity has been shown to decrease both anxiety and depression and to improve mood and self-esteem (Blumenthal, et al., 1982; Brown & Harrison, 1986; Finkenberg, DiNucci, McCune, & McCune, 1993; Greist et al., 1979; Jasnoski & Holmes, 1981; Klein et al., 1985; Mellion, 1985; Morgan, 1979; Morris & Salmon, 1994; Nicoloff & Schwenk, 1995; Pierce & Pate, 1994; Pronk, Crouse, & Rohack, 1995; Raglin & Morgan, 1987; Stein & Motta, 1992; Taylor, Sallis, & Needle, 1985).

PHYSICAL ACTIVITY, EXERCISE, AND STRESS

Physical activity and exercise both refer to activities requiring movement, usually movement of a repetitive nature. We generally use the term **physical activity** to include all types of movement, from mowing the lawn, gardening, housekeeping, and chasing children to more structured workouts and recreational and sports activities. **Exercise** activities are a subset of physical activity and suggest activity performed intentionally to improve physical fitness. The main difference between the terms *physical activity* and *exercise* is the intention with which the action is performed. Physical activity happens because you need to get something done, or you are doing something you want to do, like dancing or windsurfing; exercise suggests activity performed for the sake of expending energy. The terms are often used interchangeably, however, since all physical activity can be used for exercise.

There are countless forms of physical activity, from bowling to triathlons. Despite the sizable differences among the various types of physical activity, research has found that just about any kind of activity can help reduce stress. This is probably because exercise exerts its stress management benefits in several ways. Exercise can induce biochemical and other physiological changes that help you feel relaxed, help your muscles relax, help you recover faster from emotional stress, and provide health benefits that counterbalance the negative effects of stress. Physical activity can provide a welcome diversion from sources of stress. Some physical activities relieve boredom and provide opportunities for social interaction. By improving people's health and fitness, exercise may help them feel better generally and better about themselves. Mastering a new skill or excelling in a sport improves self-esteem. Some physical activities are even fun, and, to quote Dr. Seuss (1960), "Fun is good."

Physiological Effects: Fight, Flight, or Exercise

On an intuitive level, it certainly makes sense that exercise should help reduce our physical stress response, at least in the short run. After all, the fight-or-flight response gears us up to respond physically to stressors. The physical changes associated with the stress response are practically begging our muscles to move. While it

is certainly not feasible to run right out of a stressful exam and track down your favorite tennis partner for a vigorous game or two, exercise after the fact will allow your body to act out the fight-or-flight response.

Research supports this intuition. Recall from Chapter 2 that stress hormones increase the level of fuel substrates such as sugar and fats in the bloodstream, so you'll have plenty of energy to fight or flee. Exercise allows the stress hormones to exert their effects in a harmless way. Although an increase in energy substrates is harmful at rest, they provide helpful fuel for active muscles. Instead of accumulating in the bloodstream where they can contribute to artery disease, these fuel molecules are used to produce energy.

Exercise High: Endorphins, Hormones, and Neurotransmitters

In addition to canceling the negative effects of stress, exercise may induce some positive biochemical changes. Many exercisers report feelings of euphoria and states of consciousness similar to those described by people using drugs such as heroin. Such accounts have led to use of the term *runner's high,* since these descriptions first came primarily from long-distance runners (Mandell, 1979). These reports have intrigued both exercise scientists and the lay public and have suggested the possibility that certain types of exercise, particularly vigorous exercise of long duration, may cause biochemical changes that mimic drug-induced euphoria (Goldfarb, Hatfield, Armstrong, & Potts, 1990).

As scientists have come to understand something of brain biochemistry, some interesting hypotheses have emerged. The most publicized of these has focused on a group of chemical messengers found in the central nervous system (brain and spinal cord) called opioids, since they are similar in structure and function to the drugs that come from the poppy flower: opium, morphine, and heroin (Carr et al., 1981; Morgan, 1985). **Beta-endorphins** belong to this group. They not only inhibit pain but also seem to have other roles in the brain as well, such as aiding in memory and learning and registering emotions. It is difficult for scientists to measure opioid concentrations in the central nervous system of humans, but animal research has suggested that endogenous (produced by the body) opioid concentrations increase with level of exercise: more exercise, more opioids.

Why are opioids produced? Some will answer, "Because exercise is painful." These chemicals may help the body recover from prolonged exercise, as they seem to enhance mechanisms important during this period: raising pain threshold, slowing heart rate, decreasing blood pressure, and enhancing parasympathetic tone (which leads to the relaxation response) while inhibiting sympathetic activity (the fight-or-flight response) (Thoren, Floras, Hoffman, & Seals, 1990).

Other biochemicals may be involved in the exercise high as well. Some research has suggested that changes in the concentration of certain hormones and neurotransmitters may play a role in causing the positive mood associated with exercise. In particular, norepinephrine and serotonin concentrations have been shown to change with exercise, at least in animals. Since abnormal levels of these chemicals have been associated with depression in humans, some researchers have speculated that the antidepressant effect of exercise may involve improving regulation of these substances in the brain (Dunn & Dishman, 1991; Harte & Eifert, 1995; Harte, Eifert, & Smith, 1995). Another possibility is that the endogenous opioids interact with neurotransmitters in some synergistic fashion to produce euphoria and mood improvement.

Post-Workout Muscle Tone: Relaxation

Muscle tension at rest is called muscle tone. Muscle tone increases during stress, since muscle bracing is part of the physical stress response. Elevated resting muscle tension causes a wide array of stress-related musculoskeletal problems, as well as general feelings of fatigue, and mental and emotional stress. Physical activity, on the other hand, leads to muscle relaxation. A feeling of physical relaxation characterizes a good workout's afterglow. After working hard, muscles relax. One study measuring the electrical activity of muscle found that activities such as walking, jogging, and bicycling decrease muscle tension by over 50 percent for up to 90 minutes after exercise (deVries, Wiswell, Bulbulian, & Moritani, 1981). Physical relaxation translates into mental relaxation as well. This afterglow of relaxation is an important part of the antistress value exercise has for many people.

Rhythmic Exercise: Relaxed Brain Waves

Rhythmic exercises such as walking, running, rowing, and swimming increase **alpha-wave** activity in the brain (Stamford, 1995). The electrical activity of the brain can be monitored in the laboratory using an instrument called an **electroencephalograph (EEG)**. Alpha waves are associated with a calm mental state, such as that produced by meditation or chanting. The rhythmic breathing that occurs during some forms of exercise also contributes to an increase in alpha-wave activity. Rhythmic activity performed to music may be stress relieving in other ways as well (Estivill, 1995).

Decreased Physical Response to Stress

Some research suggests that regular exercise of moderate intensity may provide a sort of dress rehearsal for stress. Several studies have found that people who exercise regularly have an attenuated physical response to laboratory stressors such as difficult mental arithmetic tests (Blumenthal et al., 1990; Steptoe, Kearsley, & Walters, 1993). In other words, when facing laboratory stressors, exercisers had less of a sympathetic response than did nonexercisers. Other studies have found that physically fit subjects recover more quickly than sedentary peers from stressors such as cold exposure or emotional frustration (Crews & Landers, 1987; Dienstbier, 1991; Hollander & Seraganian, 1984). While physical stress responses were similar in both sedentary and fit subjects, variables such as stress hormone levels and heart rate returned to resting levels significantly faster in the fit subjects.

Why? Researchers theorize that exercise itself mimics the physical stress response. Recall the work of Hans Selye, who called the stress response "nonspecific" (see Chapter 2). In other words, he discovered that laboratory animals respond in a physically similar way to all kinds of stressors: noise, cold, heat, electric shock, and exercise. Researchers have since noted that hormonal responses to stressors vary somewhat depending upon whether a person perceives the stressor as a threat or a challenge (Dienstbier, 1991), but Selye's theory may still help explain the stress-resistance effects conferred by physical activity. Your response to a session of moderately vigorous exercise resembles your response to stress: elevated metabolic rate, cardiac output, energy substrate levels, muscle tension, stress hormones, and so forth. Regular exercisers return more quickly to resting metabolic rate than sedentary folks. Regular exercise also "teaches" the body how to recover from the emotional stress response as well. This idea is known as the theory of **cross-reactivity.** Your reactivity to stress becomes conditioned by repeated exposure to the stress imposed by exercise.

Exercise Health Benefits Counterbalance Negative Stress Effects

One of the reasons exercise increases your long-term stress resistance is that even though stressors still arise, your stress response is better managed and does less physical harm (Roth & Holmes, 1987). Regular exercise has all sorts of beneficial health effects that help counteract the long-term wear and tear of chronic stress. While stress raises resting blood pressure, exercise lowers it. Stress increases blood clotting speed; exercise slows it. Stress raises blood sugar; exercise brings it back down. Exercise therefore reduces vulnerability to the negative health effects of excess stress.

Mind Games

The physical part of physical activity may be only part of the stress resistance story. It is likely that the psychosocial aspects of participation in physical activity contribute to the stress resistance effects of exercise as well. Some psychologists have theorized that it is not exercise *per se* that makes people feel better, but the distraction from stressful stimuli that occurs during physical activity (Bahrke & Morgan, 1978; Raglin & Morgan, 1987). Picture this: a day that goes from bad to worse. The alarm doesn't go off so you sleep through your first class, you don't have time to prepare the assignment due for your next class, and you fail a pop quiz in your afternoon lab. Stress overload: you decide to go for a walk off campus, away from the college world. As you walk, your mind begins to wander and pretty soon you are thinking about your upcoming vacation. When you return to campus, life does not look so bad. Tomorrow is another day.

While the distraction provided by physical activity probably makes an important contribution to stress resistance, the distraction value of exercise appears to be only part of the explanation for its stress-reducing effect. Studies comparing other forms of distraction to the distraction provided by exercise suggest that exercise seems to have a longer lasting anxiety-reducing effect (Raglin & Morgan, 1987). In other words, something about exercise over and above distraction helps decrease anxiety. Nevertheless, the distraction hypothesis helps explain why physical activities of very low intensity can reduce feelings of stress and improve mood. Activities such as archery, shooting, and bowling do not call forth the physiological changes associated with vigorous exercise, but they have still been associated with stress reduction. When you are actively engaged in tasks demanding concentration and motor skills, it's hard to keep your mind on your worries.

Several other psychosocial factors may contribute to the stress resistance effects of exercise (Jasnoski & Holmes, 1981). Exercise may relieve boredom or provide opportunities for social interaction. By improving health and fitness, physical activity may help people feel better, and feel better about themselves (Benedict & Freeman, 1993). If exercise improves physical appearance—for example, with weight loss or better muscle definition—self-esteem and self-image may also improve (Brown & Harrison, 1986; DeBenedette, 1988; Howard, Cunningham, & Rechnitzer, 1984; Young, 1985). Physical activity is often enjoyable (Ornstein & Sobel, 1989), and as such confers wonderful health and stress management benefits.

EXERCISE BENEFITS

So far, exercise benefits have been discussed from a stress management perspective, but exercise has a number of other important benefits as well. If you decide to begin (or change) an exercise program to increase your stress resistance, you may wish to maximize health and fitness benefits while you're at it. The health and fitness benefits of exercise depend on what kind of exercise you're performing.

Aerobic Exercise

Aerobic exercise refers to activity that significantly increases metabolic rate for prolonged periods of time (15 minutes or longer). Brisk walking, rowing, cycling, cross-country skiing, and vigorous sports like basketball, squash, and soccer are all examples of aerobic exercise.

Cardiovascular or **aerobic fitness** is a benefit of regular aerobic exercise and refers to improved fitness of the body's cardiovascular and energy production systems. You know your aerobic fitness has improved when you can perform a given amount of work (such as climbing a flight of stairs) with less effort.

Aerobic exercise improves cardiovascular health and decreases risk of artery disease. It does this by strengthening the cardiovascular (heart and blood vessels) system and by helping to control several important artery disease risk factors. Aerobic exercise improves fat metabolism and blood lipid profile. You learned in Chapter 3 that LDL cholesterol is associated with an increased risk of artery disease. Another lipoprotein, **high-density lipoprotein (HDL)** *reduces* risk for artery disease, because HDLs appear to transport cholesterol out of the arteries and back to the liver. Exercise increases HDL-cholesterol levels. It also increases insulin sensitivity, the ability of your body to respond to the presence of insulin in the bloodstream, thus improving blood sugar levels and decreasing risk of type II diabetes. People who exercise regularly are less likely to develop high blood pressure, and regular physical activity may also help lower blood pressure in some people with high blood pressure. With aerobic exercise, blood platelets (responsible for making blood clots) become less likely to clump together, so the danger of obstructive blood clots that could cause a heart attack or stroke is lower for regular exercisers.

All these exercise effects are short-lived; they are apparent for only hours to a few days following the last bout of exercise. What type of aerobic exercise you do is not so important as the fact that you keep doing it (McArdle, Katch, & Katch, 1996). Fortunately, these benefits accrue at all levels of exercise. While higher intensity exercise leads to greater improvements in fitness, even low-intensity exercise such as walking (Duncan, Gordon, & Scott, 1991) appears to be very beneficial in promoting the heart-healthy changes described above. Because it requires increased energy production, regular aerobic exercise is the best way to burn calories and is an essential component of any weight-control program.

Resistance Training

Resistance training occurs when you exert force against something that resists, such as elastic bands or a stack of weights. Resistance training increases **muscular strength** and **muscular endurance.** Muscular strength is a type of force and is measured by the amount of weight you can lift. Muscular endurance is measured by how many times you can perform a given movement.

Your muscles, bones, and joints adapt to the demands of resistance training by becoming stronger. Denser bones are more resistant to **osteoporosis,** a disease in which bones gradually become weaker due to the loss of bone mineral. **Weight-bearing** aerobic exercise, such as walking and tennis, in which the bones must bear the body's weight (as opposed to swimming in which the water bears the body's weight) also helps increase bone density. Stronger muscles and joints are less prone to injury and help you stay active as you get older. Resistance training can also increase muscle size. Metabolic rate is relatively high in muscle tissue, so the more you have, the higher your metabolic rate will be, even at rest. The higher your metabolic rate, the more calories you burn, and the more you can eat without gaining weight. Some studies suggest that resistance exercise can also increase cardiovascular fitness, especially in people with relatively low fitness levels (McArdle et al., 1996).

Stretching

Flexibility refers to the range of motion in a joint. Adequate joint flexibility prevents injury and chronic musculoskeletal problems such as low-back pain. Like strength, flexibility declines as you age. Regular stretching can slow this decline and reduce the stiffness that limits physical activity (McArdle, 1996).

HOW MUCH IS ENOUGH?

The answer to the question of how much exercise you need depends on your goals. The bottom line answer is that something is better than nothing, and a moderately vigorous program that includes some variety in activities is better still. Numerous studies have concluded that a sedentary lifestyle is *as dangerous as smoking* in terms of risk for cardiovascular disease. Many public health organizations have rallied in response to these findings and have concurred on the following recommendation: get at least 30 minutes of moderately vigorous activity almost every day (Pate et al., 1995). This 30 minutes need not be performed at one time. Students may get this 30 minutes simply by climbing several flights of stairs a day and walking briskly around campus to their classes and activities. This bottom line amount provides some health benefits and at least keeps you out of the sedentary category.

What if you don't have 30 minutes to exercise? Then try 20. If you are accustomed to doing no physical activity whatsoever, your goal is simply to introduce activity into your routine. A 15-minute walk may be a good beginning for someone who is currently sedentary. The two most important recommendations are these: start small, and anything is better than nothing!

If you are new to exercise, build your exercise program gradually. Maybe 15 minutes of walking every day is enough for now. Remember that the *worse* your physical fitness is, the *sooner* you will see and feel results. Remind yourself that you are committing for the long haul because a lifetime of physical activity is what counts. Your objective for the first few months is to stay injury free and healthy, have a good time, and set up a routine that's going to become a lifelong habit.

BASIC HEALTH-FITNESS EXERCISE RECOMMENDATIONS

If you were to ask an exercise specialist for recommendations on an ideal exercise program for a healthy young person that would give the greatest amount of health-fitness benefits with the least investment of time, the recommendations would look something like this:

Aerobic activity	3 to 5 times per week 15 to 60 minutes per session
Resistance training	2 times per week 8 to 10 exercises, including all muscle groups 8 to 12 repetitions per exercise
Stretching	3 to 5 times per week, preferably after a workout

Aerobic exercise appears to be beneficial even at fairly low intensities—but the lower the intensity, the longer you should exercise. In other words, 20 minutes per session is long enough if you are working at a relatively vigorous level. If you are walking at a moderate pace, 45 minutes to an hour would be a better length.

EVERY ACTIVITY COUNTS

In addition to these basic recommendations, don't forget that daily activity of every kind contributes to physical fitness, good health, and even to stress management. Take the stairs instead of the elevator, walk on your errands, work in the garden, play with children. All burn calories and contribute to a high-energy lifestyle that reduces risk of artery disease.

PLAY IT SAFE: PREVENT INJURY

Some risk of injury is part of a high-energy lifestyle. Everyone is at some risk, no matter how old, how fit, how experienced, or how careful. Nevertheless, do everything you reasonably can to prevent injuries. Injury is one of the main reasons people quit exercising and can turn an avid fitness enthusiast into an exercise dropout.

The most common injuries for adult recreational exercisers are **overuse injuries,** which usually result from improper training techniques and doing too much too soon. When you exercise, your body adapts to the stress imposed by activity by becoming stronger. The physical changes that occur are called the **training effect:** stronger muscles, a more efficient heart, and a better ability to metabolize fat. However, if there is too much stress, your body does not adapt, but weakens and breaks down. A few simple recommendations will help you understand how to exercise effectively and safely (Peterson & Renstrom, 1986).

Start Slowly

Too often in an enthusiasm to follow recommendations regarding optimal amounts of exercise or to keep up with the athletic model in the video, beginning exercisers may do more than their muscles and joints are ready for. The result? Unnecessary aches, pains, and discouragement. Slow and steady wins exercise success.

Progress Slowly

Physical fitness improves when you ask your body to do more than it is accustomed to doing. You increase the distance, the pace, the intensity, the weight, the number of repetitions, or the duration of exercise. Exercise scientists refer to this increase as **overload.** It is important to increase overload slowly, generally by 10 percent or less per week. If you are walking a mile each session and you are ready to increase your distance, add a tenth of a mile to your walk. Slow, steady progress is the way to go, cutting back at the first sign of injury.

Warm Up and Cool Down

Begin your workout with a **warm-up,** 10 or more minutes of gentle, repetitive movements involving all muscle groups, gradually increasing the intensity. Warm up for jogging by walking briskly and then jogging slowly, swinging your arms. Slow swimming warms you up for a swimming workout. You will know you are warmed up when you feel warm! A warm-up prepares your body for the demands of exercise. It increases circulation and energy production, and improves flexibility, strength, and coordination. Warm joints and muscles are less likely to get injured during your workout. A gradual warm-up is especially important for people unaccustomed to exercise and those with a history of heart disease. An adequate warm-up allows the heart to adjust to exercise and helps prevent an abnormal heart rate response (McArdle et al., 1996).

At the end of your activity, **cool down** by gradually decreasing your exercise intensity. You may use the same activity as in your warm-up: a slower version of what you have been doing or simply walking. A cooldown helps your body adjust back to resting level. After exercise, the blood vessels supplying the skeletal muscles remain dilated, and if activity stops suddenly, blood may pool in the extremeties. This reduces the return of blood to the heart and brain, and may cause dizziness and even fainting (McArdle et al., 1996).

Make Time to Stretch

Stretching exercises are most effective when muscles and joints are warm. Stretching after physical activity (after your cooldown) will help you maintain or improve your flexibility. Joints with adequate flexibility are less likely to reach the limit of their range of motion and suffer injury.

Recognize Warning Signs

Some symptoms indicate possible need for immediate medical attention. These include irregular heartbeats; pain or pressure in the chest, arm, or throat; and dizziness, fainting, or confusion. More common are warning signs that you are simply overtraining and need to reduce training volume. These include soreness in muscles or joints, difficulty sleeping, loss of appetite and weight, and fatigue.

Don't Ignore Pain

Pain is a message that something is wrong. Exercising before an injury has healed or when an overuse injury is in its early stages will only slow the healing process and possibly worsen the injury.

Invest in Good Footwear and Safety Equipment

A good pair of shoes is one of the most important pieces of equipment for almost every activity. If your activities require safety equipment, be sure it meets industry standards and is as comfortable as possible. For example, people who play squash or racquetball should wear safety glasses. Cyclists should wear helmets and be sure bicycles are working correctly. In-line skaters should wear helmets and appropriate guards for wrists, elbows, and knees.

STAYING WITH IT

Starting an exercise program is the easy part. Sticking to an exercise program may take some effort. Here are a few suggestions to help you make physical activity a part of your life—for the rest of your life.

Take the "Work" Out of Your Workouts

Choose activities that are fun and fit best into your lifestyle. If you can't take strenuous exercise, find an activity that requires a more modest effort. Use exercise to accomplish two goals at one time: get some exercise while you meet new friends, spend some time alone, or learn a new skill. And don't forget to have fun!

When it comes to stress reduction, personal exercise preferences are extremely important. While exercise may increase stress resistance under the right conditions, exercise can also increase feelings of stress under the wrong conditions. For example, perfectionists may find the demands of following the perfect exercise program one more thing to worry about. Busy people may find an exercise program yet one more thing to fit into their overloaded days. If your exercise plan includes activities that are not enjoyable, even distasteful, the stress of your upcoming workout may hover over you like a black cloud. The competition imposed by sports such as tennis, volleyball, and basketball can raise blood pressure and stress level. Ready to quit before you start? Don't! The benefits of physical activity will still be yours, but you need the right attitude, and an exercise program that is right for you.

◆ STRESS AND YOU

WHAT PHYSICAL ACTIVITIES ARE RIGHT FOR YOU?

People who stick with their plans to exercise regularly find value and enjoyment in the activities they are performing. Exercise will help you manage stress best if you find the activities enjoyable. At the end of this chapter, you will design an exercise program that's right for you based on your health and fitness goals. But exercise delivers a lot more than health and fitness. A good exercise program fits your heart and soul. What activities do you enjoy the most? Take a moment to consider your personal activity preferences. What are your goals and wishes for your exercise time? Check any that apply:

_____ Spend time with certain friends, family members, co-workers, etc.

_____ Be part of a class

_____ Play a team sport like volleyball or softball

_____ Get away by myself

_____ Use self-discipline; have a structured routine in an activity that is easily measured (walking, swimming, circuit training, etc.)

_____ Spend some time outdoors

Anticipate Setbacks and Plan for Recovery

Everyone experiences setbacks from time to time. Family and school responsibilities get in the way, travel interrupts your routine, the weather won't cooperate, illness keeps you in bed. Think about the sorts of things that are likely to keep you from sticking to your program, and plan ahead. Prevent setbacks when possible, but realize that they will occur. View them as a part of life due to unavoidable situations and not to your personal failure to overcome all obstacles. Forgive yourself, make necessary adjustments, and get back into your program as soon as possible.

Make Your Health a Priority

How easy it is to get bogged down with the demands of the day. When schedules get tight, exercise is often the first thing to go. After all, other things just have to get done today. Long-term goals get put on hold as people scramble to meet short-term demands. Most people would agree that lifelong good health is one of their long-term (and short-term) goals. Neglecting self-care is penny wise and pound foolish. What good is meeting today's deadlines if you develop heart disease at a young age?

Use the 80/20 Rule

Remember the 80/20 rule from Chapter 7, that 80 percent of the good comes, in this case, from doing 20 percent of the exercise recommendations. If there is no way to fit all the recommended activity into your current schedule, give yourself a break. Recognize that you have other things in your life besides your exercise program, and just do your best! Decide which 20 percent of the recommendations will

_____ Learn a new sport

_____ Participate in an activity with a spiritual focus (tai chi, yoga, martial arts)

_____ Other (describe):

What activities would best fill these preferences?

What activities have you enjoyed and benefited most from in the past?

What activities would you like to incorporate into your current exercise program?

help you the most and start with that. For example, an exercise class that meets twice a week and includes some aerobic exercise, some muscular strength and endurance exercises, and some stretching would only take two hours a week and would give you a great deal of fitness benefit.

Keep Expectations Positive but Realistic

We all love instant results. The media abound with advertisements for products that promise unrealistic weight loss, muscle toning, and body sculpting. So we expect great changes from an exercise program. An appropriate exercise program does have many health and fitness benefits, but they don't happen overnight. After six to eight weeks of regular participation you will begin to notice some progress: maybe better muscle definition, a little more energy throughout the day, an easier time climbing the stairs, a period of calm after your workout. As your program continues, you will see more changes. Fitness improvement happens fastest and is most obvious in those most out of shape to begin with. Some exercisers may find that after several months or even years of exercise they maintain a sort of personal in-shape plateau. This may sound discouraging, but there is something to be said for maintaining fitness because fitness tends to decline as we age.

What if this personal in-shape plateau does not lead you to perfection? You don't have to look like an Olympic bodybuilder to be healthy (in fact, bodybuilders often aren't!). Each of us is born with a genetic limit on body shape and muscle development. Most of us also have limited time to exercise and other priorities in life. To improve beyond our personal in-shape plateau may take the kind of time and effort that is simply not available.

▲ ACTION PLAN

DESIGNING A PERSONALIZED EXERCISE PROGRAM

Begin designing an exercise program that is right for you by defining your health and fitness goals and considering your limitations.

Health Concerns

The exercise recommendations listed in Table 10.1 are primarily for healthy people. Many health concerns such as arthritis, diabetes, and high blood pressure impose certain limitations on exercise program design. If you have any questions about your health, speak to your physician about your plans to increase your physical activity. If you are not sure whether you need to consult your physician, you probably should. You definitely should not increase your physical activity level without your physician's consent and guidance if you answer yes to any of the questions in the sample Physical Activity Readiness Questionnaire (Figure 10.1 on p. 224).

Exercise Program Design

1. Do you want to speak with your physician about your exercise program?
   _____ Yes   _____ No

   Date of appointment _____

2. List fitness goals in order of importance, and recommended activities for each. (Table 10.1 on page 224 includes several possible fitness goals, and the exercise recommendations for each.)

Fitness goal	Recommended activities
a.	
b.	
c.	

3. Consider your personal activity preferences listed in the "Stress and You" section earlier in the chapter. List these activities again here. Do any of these help you toward your fitness goals?

4. Which of the activities above are most convenient and feasible? Consider these factors:
   Scheduling
   Cost (equipment, memberships, class fees, court time)
   Convenience (transportation, location)
   Weather (what you will do if it is raining, cold, hot)

5. Describe your current exercise habits.

6. Assess your current program. Is it helping you work toward your health and fitness goals? Is it as enjoyable and convenient as possible?

7. Considering the factors above, design your exercise program, or describe any changes you would like to make in your current program.

Activity   **Time and Days**   **Place**

_____   _____   _____

_____   _____   _____

_____   _____   _____

Anticipating Setbacks

What kinds of things might keep you from sticking to your plans to exercise?

How will you prevent these things from interfering? Or how will you get back into your program if they come up?

How can your friends and family help you stick to your plans?

■ STUDENT STRESS

FIONA'S ACTION PLAN

Fiona exercises sporadically to manage stress and get in shape. She has taken an occasional course in physical conditioning and done aerobics off and on, but once the class ends, exercise ceases to be part of her daily routine. She has noticed that when she is exercising regularly she feels better about herself and is more energetic. Having just read about the stress management benefits of exercise, she has decided to start exercising regularly again. Here is a copy of her action plan:

Exercise Program Design

1. Do you want to speak with your physician about your exercise program?
   _____ Yes   _X_ No

   Date of appointment _____

2. List fitness goals in order of importance, and recommended activities for each.

Fitness goal	Recommended activities
a. Improve muscle tone	Resistance training
b. Increase daily energy level	Aerobic exercise of moderate to vigorous intensity
c. Manage stress	Anything I enjoy

3. Consider your personal activity preferences listed in the "Stress and You" section earlier in the chapter. List these activities again here. Do any of these help you toward your fitness goals?

   In the past, I have really enjoyed being part of an aerobics class. I was really good at attending when some friends and I all went together. I would also like to learn how to use the machines in the weight room.

4. Which of the activities above are most convenient and feasible? Consider these factors:
   Scheduling
   Cost (equipment, memberships, class fees, court time)
   Convenience (transportation, location)
   Weather (what you will do if it is raining, cold, hot)

   Well, I'm lucky to be on a campus that has a great gym and a great activity program! Aerobics is offered every afternoon before dinner; that's a low time for me, so maybe it will get me energized. I could learn more about the weight room by signing up for a weight training class next semester, or asking the monitor for some help. These are both convenient and "free" since I am paying for a full course load.

5. Describe your current exercise habits.

A lot of walking around campus.

6. Assess your current program. Is it helping you work toward your health and fitness goals? Is it as enjoyable and convenient as possible?

What current program?

7. Considering the factors above, design your exercise program, or describe any changes you would like to make in your current program.

Activity	**Time and Days**	**Place**
Aerobics	4:30, Mon and Wed	Gym
Weight training	4:30, Tues and Sat a.m.	Weight room

(and take a class in weight training next semester)

Anticipating Setbacks

What kinds of things might keep you from sticking to your plans to exercise?

1. Too much school work.

2. Getting sick.

How will you prevent these things from interfering? Or how will you get back into your program if they come up?

1. Remind myself I can spare an hour for exercise, and that exercise will give me more energy for doing better work.

Signing up for an exercise class will make me attend even when I am busy.

2. Well, if I am sick I will have to take time off, but I will try to get back into exercising when I am better.

How can your friends and family help you stick to your plans?

I will see if Margot and Alice are still going to aerobics; maybe we can all go over together. I think Ramona uses the weight room a lot; maybe she can help me get started.

TABLE 10.1 *Health and Fitness Goals*

Health and Fitness Goals	Activity Recommendations
Weight control	Aerobic exercise to burn calories; resistance training to increase muscle mass and metabolic rate
Improved muscle tone	Resistance training
Increased muscular strength	Resistance training, using heavy resistance to challenge muscles
Aerobic fitness, endurance, stamina, increase daily energy level	Aerobic exercise of moderate to vigorous intensity; resistance training may work unless fitness level is already high
Heart health	Aerobic exercise
Bone density	Weight-bearing aerobics and resistance training
Flexibility	Regular stretching or activities that include stretching, such as hatha yoga and dance classes
Stress management	Any activity you enjoy or that makes you feel good after you do it. Activities of moderate to vigorous intensity and those requiring concentration are generally most effective

____YES ____NO 1. Has your doctor ever said you have a heart condition **and** that you should only do physical activity recommended by a doctor?

____YES ____NO 2. Do you feel pain in your chest when you do physical activity?

____YES ____NO 3. In the past month, have you had chest pain when you were not doing physical activity?

____YES ____NO 4. Do you lose your balance because of dizziness or do you ever lose consciousness?

____YES ____NO 5. Do you have a bone or joint problem that could be made worse by a change in your physical activity?

____YES ____NO 6. Is your doctor currently prescribing drugs (for example, water pills) for your blood pressure or heart condition?

____YES ____NO 7. Do you know of any other reason why you should not do physical activity?

If you answered "yes" to any of these questions, you must have your physician's consent to exercise.

FIGURE 10.1 *Physical Activity Readiness Questionnaire*

Source: S. Thomas, J. Reading, and R. J. Shephard. Revision of the Physical Activity Readiness Questionnaire (PARQ). *Canadian Journal of Sport Science.* 17: 338–345, 1992.

SUMMARY

1. Participation in regular physical activity is one of the most effective ways to increase your stress resistance.
2. Physical activity has both short- and long-term effects. It relieves stress during and immediately following the exercise session. People who exercise regularly also report feeling less stressed even on days when no exercise occurs.
3. The term *physical activity* refers to all types of movement; *exercise* refers to activities intentionally performed to improve physical fitness.
4. Research has shown that almost every kind of physical activity can deliver stress management benefits, depending on personal activity preferences.
5. Exercise, especially vigorous exercise, may increase levels of beta-endorphin which is associated with relaxation and pain relief.
6. Exercise may change the concentration of other hormones and neurotransmitters, such as norepinephrine and serotonin.
7. After a workout, muscles are relaxed.
8. Rhythmic exercise has a calming effect, as evidenced by alpha-wave brain activity.
9. Some research suggests that regular exercisers have an attenuated response to emotional stressors, at least in the laboratory. People who exercise regularly may also recover from stress more quickly.
10. Health benefits of exercise counterbalance the negative effects of stress.
11. Physical activity may increase stress resistance by providing a temporary distraction from stressors.
12. Physical activity may relieve boredom, provide opportunities for social interaction, and improve self-esteem. Physical activity may reduce feelings of stress because it is often enjoyable.
13. Aerobic exercise refers to activity that significantly increases metabolic rate for prolonged periods of time (15 minutes or longer). Aerobic exercise improves the function of the cardiovascular and energy production systems.
14. Aerobic exercise reduces risk of artery disease. It strengthens the cardiovascular system, improves fat metabolism and blood lipid profile, increases insulin sensitivity, and prevents hypertension. Aerobic activity also slows blood clotting rate and contributes to weight control.
15. Resistance training occurs when you exert force against a resistance. Resistance training increases muscular strength and endurance. It also increases the strength of bones and joints, making them less prone to injury. Resistance training may also increase muscle size, and thus, metabolic rate.
16. Stretching increases flexibility, which refers to the range of motion in a joint. Adequate joint flexibility prevents injury and chronic musculoskeletal problems such as low-back pain.
17. A sedentary lifestyle is as dangerous as smoking in terms of risk for cardiovascular disease.
18. Public health officials recommend at least 30 minutes of moderately vigorous exercise almost every day. This 30 minutes need not be performed at one time.
19. People interested in getting more than the minimum level of physical activity may wish to participate in a variety of activities. The following program will increase aerobic endurance, muscular strength and endurance, and flexibility:

Aerobic activity	3–5 times per week 15–60 minutes per session
Resistance training	2 times per week 8–10 exercises, including all muscle groups 8–12 repetitions per exercise
Stretching	3–5 times per week, preferably after a workout

20. To prevent injury, it is important to start slowly and increase overload gradually; warm up and cool down; make time to stretch; recognize symptoms that may indicate a need for immediate medical attention or a need to reduce training volume; and use good footwear and safety equipment.
21. To increase the likelihood that you will exercise regularly, find activities that are fun and rewarding; anticipate setbacks and plan for recovery; and make your health a priority. Remember that doing even a little bit is better than doing nothing. Keep expectations positive but realistic.

REFERENCES

Bahrke, MS, and WP Morgan. Anxiety reduction following exercise and meditation. *Cognitive Therapy Research* 2: 323–333, 1978.

Benedict, A, and R Freeman. The effect of aquatic exercise on aged persons' bone density, body image, and morale. *Activities, Adaptation, and Aging* 17: 67–85, 1993.

Berger, BG, E Friedmann, and M Eaton. Comparison of jogging, the relaxation response, and group interaction for stress reduction. *Journal of Sport & Exercise Psychology* 10: 431–447, 1988.

Berger, BG, and DR Owen. Mood alterations with yoga and swimming: Aerobic exercise may not be necessary. *Perceptual and Motor Skills* 75: 1331–1343, 1992.

Blumenthal, JA, RS Williams, TL Needels, and AG Wallace. Psychological changes accompany aerobic exercise in healthy middle-aged adults. *Psychosomatic Medicine* 44: 529–536, 1982.

Blumenthal, JA, M Fredrikson, CM Kuhn, RL Ulmer, et al. Aerobic exercise reduces levels of cardiovascular and sympathoadrenal responses to mental stress in subjects without prior evidence of myocardial infarction. *American Journal of Cardiology* 65: 93–98, 1990.

Brehm, BA, and BA Keller. Diet and exercise factors that influence weight and fat loss. *IDEA Today*, October 1990, pp 33–38+.

Brown, JD. Staying fit and staying well: Physical fitness as a moderator of life stress. *Journal of Personality and Social Psychology* 60: 555–561, 1991.

Brown, RD, and JM Harrison. The effects of a strength training program on the strength and self-concept of two female age groups. *Research Quarterly for Exercise and Sport* 57: 315–320, 1986.

Carr, DB, BA Bullen, GS Skrinar, MA Arnold, M Rosenblatt, IZ Beitins, JB Martin, and JW McArthur. Physical conditioning facilitates the exercsie-induced secretion of beta-endorphins and beta-lipotropin in women. *New England Journal of Medicine* 305: 560–562, 1981.

Crews, DJ, and DM Landers. A meta-analytic review of aerobic fitness and reactivity to psychosocial stressors. *Medicine and Science in Sports and Exercise* 19: S114–S120, 1987.

DeBenedette, V. Getting fit for life: Can exercise reduce stress? *The Physician and Sportsmedicine* 16: 185–200, 1988.

deVries, HA, RA Wiswell, R Bulbulian, and T Moritani. Tranquilizer effect of exercise. *American Journal of Physical Medicine* 60: 57–66, 1981.

Dienstbier, RA. Behavioral correlates of sympathoadrenal reactivity: The toughness model. *Medicine and Science in Sports and Exercise* 23: 846–852, 1991.

Duncan, JJ, NF Gordon, and CB Scott. Women walking for health and fitness: How much is enough? *Journal of American Medical Association* 266: 3295–3299, 1991.

Dunn, AL, and RK Dishman. Exercise and the neurobiology of depression. JO Holloszy (ed). *Exercise and Sport Sciences Reviews*, Vol 19. Baltimore: Williams & Wilkins, 1991.

Estivill, M. Therapeutic aspects of aerobic dance participation. *Health Care for Women International* 16: 341–350, 1995.

Farrell, PA, WK Gates, MG Maksud, and WP Morgan. Increases in plasma beta-endorphin/beta-lipotropin immunoreactivity after treadmill running in humans. *Journal of Applied Physiology* 52: 1245–1249, 1982.

Finkenberg, ME, JM DiNucci, SL McCune, and ED McCune. Body esteem and enrollment in classes with different levels of physical activity. *Perceptual and Motor Skills* 76: 783–792, 1993.

Goldfarb, AH, BD Hatfield, D Armstrong, and J Potts. Plasma beta-endorphin concentration: Response to intensity and duration of exercise. *Medicine and Science in Sports and Exercise* 22: 241–244, 1990.

Greist, JH, MH Klein, RR Eischens, J Faris, AS Gurman, and WP Morgan. Running as treatment for depression. *Comparative Psychiatry* 20: 41–53, 1979.

Harte, JL, and GH Eifert. The effects of running, environment, and attentional focus on athletes' catecholamine and cortisol levels and mood. *Psychophysiology* 32: 49–54, 1995.

Harte, JL, GH Eifert, and R Smith. The effects of running and meditation on beta-endorphin, corticotropin-releasing hormone and cortisol in plasma, and on mood. *Biological Psychology* 40: 251–265, 1995.

Helin, P, and O Hanninen. The effects of extended audiocassette-relaxation training and running exercise on physiological responses during a teaching test. *Journal of Psychophysiology* 2: 259–267, 1988.

Hollander, BJ, and P Seraganian. Aerobic fitness and psychophysiological reactivity. *Canadian Journal of Behavioural Science* 16: 257–261, 1984.

Holmes, DS, and DL Roth. Effects of aerobic exercise training and relaxation training on cardiovascular activity during psychological stress. *Journal of Psychosomatic Research* 32: 469–474, 1988.

Howard, JH, DA Cunningham, and PA Rechnitzer. Physical activity as a moderator of life events and somatic complaints: A longitudinal study. *Canadian Journal of Applied Sports Science* 9: 194–200, 1984.

Jasnoski, ML, and DS Holmes. Influence of initial aerobic fitness, aerobic training and changes in aerobic fitness on personality functioning. *Journal of Psychosomatic Research* 25: 553–556, 1981.

Keller, S, and P Seraganian. Physical fitness level and autonomic reactivity to psychosocial stress. *Journal of Psychosomatic Research* 28: 279–287, 1984.

Klein, MH, JH Greist, AS Gurman, RA Neimeyer, DP Lesser, NJ Bushnell, and RE Smith. A comparative outcome study of group psychotherapy vs exercise treatments for depression. *International Journal of Mental Health* 13: 148–177, 1985.

Kobasa, SC, SR Maddi, and MC Puccetti. Personality and exercise as buffers in the stress-illness relationship. *Journal of Behavioral Medicine* 4: 391–404, 1982.

Mandell, AJ. The *second* second wind. *Psychiatric Annals* 9: 153–160, 1979.

McArdle, WD, FI Katch, and VL Katch. *Exercise Physiology: Energy, Nutrition, and Human Performance.* Philadelphia: Lea & Febiger, 1996.

McGinnis, JM. The public health burden of a sedentary lifestyle. *Medicine and Science in Sports and Exercise* 24: S196–S200, 1992.

Mellion, MB. Exercise therapy for anxiety and depression. 1. Does the evidence justify its recommendation? *Postgraduate Medicine* 77: 59–66, 1985.

Morgan, WP. Anxiety reduction following acute physical activity. *Psychiatric Annals* 9: 141–147, 1979.

Morgan, WP. Affective beneficence of vigorous physical activity. *Medicine and Science in Sports and Exercise* 17: 94–100, 1985.

Morris, M, and P Salmon. Qualitative and quantitative effects of running on mood. *Journal of Sports Medicine and Physical Fitness* 34: 284–291, 1994.

Nicoloff, G, and TL Schwenk. Using exercise to ward off depression. *Physician and Sportsmedicine* 23(9): 44–58, 1995.

Ornstein, R, and D Sobel. *Healthy Pleasures.* Reading, MA: Addison-Wesley, 1989.

Pate, RR, M Pratt, SN Blair, WL Haskell, et al. Physical activity and public health: A recommendation from the Centers for Disease Control and Prevention and the American College of Sports Medicine. *Journal of American Medical Association* 273: 402–407, 1995.

Peterson, L, and P Renstrom. *Sports Injuries: Their Prevention and Treatment.* Chicago: Year Book Medical Publishers, 1986.

Pierce, EF, and SW Pate. Mood alterations in older adults following acute exercise. *Perceptual and Motor Skills* 79: 191–194, 1994.

Pronk, NP, SF Crouse, and JJ Rohack. Maximal exercise and acute mood response in women. *Physiology and Behavior* 57: 1–4, 1995.

Raglin, JS, and WP Morgan. Influence of exercise and quiet rest on state anxiety and blood pressure. *Medicine and Science in Sports and Exercise* 19: 456–463, 1987.

Roth, DL, and DS Holmes. Influence of aerobic exercise training and relaxation training on physical and psychologic health following stressful life events. *Psychosomatic Medicine* 49: 355–365, 1987.

Seuss, Dr. *One Fish Two Fish Red Fish Blue Fish.* New York: Random House, 1960.

Sharp, D. The energy dividend. *In Health,* Sept/Oct 1991, pp 94–96.

Sheets, KJ, DW Gorenflo, and MA Forney. Personal and behavioral variables related to perceived stress of second-year medical students. *Teaching and Learning in Medicine* 5: 90–95, 1993.

Sothman, MS, BA Hart, and TS Horn. Plasma catecholamine response to acute psychological stress in humans: Relation to aerobic fitness and exercise training. *Medicine and Science in Sports and Exercise* 23: 846–852, 1991.

Stamford, B. The role of exercise in fighting depression. *Physician and Sportsmedicine* 23: 79–80, 1995.

Stein, PN, and RW Motta. Effects of aerobic and nonaerobic exercise on depression and self-concept. *Perceptual and Motor Skills* 74: 79–89, 1992.

Steptoe, A, N Kearsley, and N Walters. Cardiovascular activity during mental stress following vigorous exercise in sportsmen and inactive men. *Psychophysiology* 30: 245–252, 1993.

Taylor, CB, JF Sallis, and R Needle. The relation of physical activity and exercise to mental health. *Public Health Reports* 100: 195–201, 1985.

Thomas, S, J Reading, and RJ Shephard. Revision of the Physical Activity Readiness Questionnaire (PARQ). *Canadian Journal of Sport Science* 17: 338–345, 1992.

Thoren, P, JS Floras, P Hoffmann, and DR Seals. Endorphins and exercise: Physiological mechanisms and clinical implications. *Medicine and Science in Sports and Exercise* 22: 417–428, 1990.

Young, ML. Estimation of fitness and physical ability, physical performance, and self-concept among adolescent females. *Journal of Sports Medicine* 25: 144–150, 1985.

chapter 11

The Pleasure Principle

Sometimes the source of stress is not having enough sources of pleasure. We live a lifestyle based on shoulds rather than on enjoyment. We work hard and take life too seriously. Or if we are procrastinating and "wasting time," we don't really enjoy ourselves; we simply pass the time or spend it worrying about the work that is not getting done. Even our recreational pursuits have become overly organized and goal oriented. The North American work ethic has taught us to focus on productivity and frown upon "wasted time." Our culture's motto seems to be "No pain, no gain." As we learn to channel our energy into productive directions, we often cut ourselves off from the simple daily pleasures life offers. Instead, we focus on obtaining those things that only *represent,* but do not really deliver happiness: grades, a degree, a good job, the "right" relationship, and money. In the process of becoming more and more productive, we forget how to enjoy a sunset, smell the flowers, play with children. We forget how to relax. When we find ourselves with a few moments and nothing to do, we fill the void with diversion rather than enjoyment. Lacking pleasure, we feel empty inside. Something is missing.

FEELING GOOD: THE PSYCHOPHYSIOLOGY OF PLEASURE

Medical research tends to focus on the negative. We hear about the negative health effects of stress, depression, and anxiety. We study how feelings of stress, loneliness, hostility, and alienation can lead to hypertension, artery disease, drug abuse, and other ills (see Chapter 3). This reflects our culture's medical orientation: find out what's wrong, then try to fix it. Health is often seen merely as the absence of illness rather than a state of well-being. Fortunately, some researchers have stopped to ask a very simple but important question: If negative emotions cause negative health effects, can positive emotions cause positive health effects? Can feeling good help us overcome health problems and promote high-level wellness? Preliminary research suggests that feeling good is in fact good for us.

To begin with, pleasure is often associated with a relaxed contentment and feeling of well-being. Such feelings activate the relaxation response, which is the antithesis of the stress response. You'll remember that the stress response activates the sympathetic branch of the autonomic nervous system while the relaxation response activates the parasympathetic branch. Parasympathetic activation lowers heart rate, breathing rate, and blood pressure; it helps muscles relax, digestion proceed smoothly, and so on. While a chronic stress response leads to an assortment of negative health effects, frequent relaxation helps prevent these ills; it tugs your body in the other direction. Many people mistakenly believe stress reduction is best achieved from esoteric relaxation techniques. In fact, simple activities such as taking a long walk or a soothing hot bath can be as effective for reducing tension as more structured relaxation techniques such as meditation (Druckman & Bjork, 1991).

But the healthy effects of pleasure seem to go beyond a mere cancellation of negative stress. Feeling good is more than not feeling bad. The goodness itself seems to have positive health consequences, although science is just beginning to explore what these might be. We know that emotion is a body-mind biochemical event. Further research will no doubt continue to unravel the biochemical changes associated with pleasure and to elucidate what Norman Cousins (1989) called "the biology of hope." At this point, all we can say is that optimistic, happy people tend to be healthier and live longer than cynical pessimists. Best of all, they enjoy themselves.

FEELING PLEASURE OR KILLING PAIN?

No profit grows where is no pleasure taken . . .

SHAKESPEARE

As you begin to think of ways to make your life more pleasurable, it is important to distinguish between pleasures that increase stress resistance and experiences that more closely resemble maladaptive coping responses, activities that may initially feel good but bring you more stress down the road. Cigarette smoking, binge drinking, and sleeping through morning classes are three examples. These feel good and seem pleasurable at the time but they will likely have negative consequences in the future because they interfere with effective coping and have negative health effects. Sometimes the pleasure people associate with certain negative habits has more to do with killing pain or satisfying addictive cravings than with providing true pleasure.

WHAT IS ADDICTION?

People commonly use the word *addiction* with reference to substance abuse. Heroin addicts, alcoholics, and crack houses spring to mind as well as cigarette and caffeine habits. But people can also become addicted to unproductive relationships, food, gambling, work, taking risks, exercise, and probably even to being a student! To become addicted is to devote or surrender oneself to something habitually or obsessively. It is ironic that the word *addiction* is derived from the Latin verb meaning "to give assent" since we tend to think of addicts as being incapable of giving

STRESS AND YOU

ADDICTION SELF-ASSESSMENT

Think about substances, such as alcohol, drugs, and caffeine, and behaviors, such as exercise and work, that can lead to addiction. Do any qualify as an addiction for you? Answer the following questions. Even a single "yes" answer indicates that the behavior may become a problem, and possibly an addiction (Brehm, 1993).

1. Does the behavior provide the primary source of gratification in my life?

2. Does it provide the primary means of escape or avoidance of problems?

3. Does it decrease my self-esteem?

4. Am I developing a tolerance for the substance, needing more than I did earlier to achieve the desired effect?

5. Do I need it to function?

6. Is it causing (will it cause) the development of health problems?

7. Because of this behavior, have others suggested that I change or stop?

8. Does this behavior occur as a predictable, ritualistic, and compulsive activity?

assent, having lost control of the habit in question. The hallmark of addiction is a reliance on something outside of oneself to cope with life and manage stress. Although people initially become addicted to something because it feels good, after a short while true addictions do not provide pleasure so much as temporary relief, and addicted people do not feel good most of the time.

USE, ABUSE, OR ADDICTION?

As you can see from the Addiction Self-Assessment questions, addiction is not simply a function of frequency or amount of use; rather, it relates to the reasons for and context of use and the effect of the substance or behavior on the user. You might think of addiction as part of a continuum that extends from abstinence, through use and abuse, to addiction.

| Abstinence | Controlled use | Abuse | Addiction |

We can illustrate this continuum concept with alcohol. Alcohol is a powerful depressant drug that slows the nervous system. Alcoholism is the most common drug addiction problem in North America. Alcohol presents an interesting addiction illustration because our culture sends mixed messages about it. On the one hand, its use is sanctioned and it is fairly accessible, even for minors. Yet the effects of alcoholism are tremendously costly and destructive.

At one end of the continuum is **abstinence.** Abstinence refers to no use at all. A desire to avoid the devastating effects of alcoholism is one reason to abstain from imbibing. People may stay away from alcohol for many other reasons as well. Some believe the health risks of alcohol consumption outweigh any benefits. Some do not enjoy drinking or feel that alcohol calories could be better spent on something more interesting.

While some people claim to drink solely because they enjoy the taste, alcoholic beverages are also consumed for their intoxicating effect. Intoxication develops gradually, beginning for most drinkers with a feeling of relaxation. A glass of wine with dinner, a beer with friends while you work on your motorcycle, and a glass of champagne at a wedding are examples of **controlled use** of alcohol. The intoxication is mild (or nonexistent), it causes little harm to the drinker or others, and the drug is consumed in a structured social environment in an appropriate fashion. People who use alcohol in a controlled fashion claim that at its best, a small amount of alcohol can enhance an occasion, helping users to become more sociable and relaxed. In other words, alcohol is consumed in moderation and for positive reasons. It is not used to dull emotional pain, escape from reality, or to help the drinker avoid a situation.

Abuse occurs when the consumption of alcohol hurts or endangers the drinker or those around him or her. Alcohol abuse can occur in a single episode of drinking; driving while intoxicated is always considered alcohol abuse. However, alcohol abuse often consists of frequent heavy drinking that can lead to many health and behavioral problems. Such things as going to class or work while intoxicated, getting into legal trouble as a result of drinking, experiencing blackouts, and getting injured while intoxicated are indicators of a drinking problem. Surveys show that about half of all college students become intoxicated at least occasionally. Although they may restrict drinking to social occasions, once they start drinking they often drink too much because this is considered normal party behavior on many campuses. Although most students will grow out of such use and stop drinking or develop controlled drinking patterns, a significant number of college students do go on to develop an addiction to alcohol. (And for some, alcohol abuse in college reinforces an alcohol addiction developed in high school.)

Controlled users drink to enhance an occasion and enlarge their experience; people with an **addiction** to alcohol drink simply to cope. Addicts feel that they need alcohol to function, that life and its occasions are miserable affairs without it. Controlled users may *enjoy* the feeling of increased sociability that comes with a small amount of alcohol; addicts *rely on* alcohol for permission to socialize. They may feel incapable of social interaction without becoming intoxicated. When drunk, they feel like they are "the life of the party." When sober, they feel like they have nothing to say. Some people become addicted to alcohol because it shields them from difficult issues. Instead of trying to solve problems, they drink. Drinking temporarily eases the hurt of painful emotions and provides a way to put off dealing with conflict (Steele & Josephs, 1988). Eventually, addicts can no longer tolerate any amount of uncertainty or anxiety. New experiences and challenges cease to call forth innovative ideas and creative expression; they become simply an excuse to have another drink.

ADDICTION: AVOIDING LIFE

Addiction is the opposite of stress resistance. The example of alcohol addiction is an obvious illustration. Most of us have some understanding of how substances such as alcohol can be used to avoid confronting reality. Some types of addiction are not so obvious, however. Addictive involvements in work and unhealthy relationships, for example, have received less attention because to a large extent they are sanctioned by our culture. Let's take another look at the meaning of addiction by examining addiction to work.

The word *workaholic* has been coined to refer to someone who works too much and in the process neglects other important parts of life, such as family and recreational pursuits. A hard-driving, Type A business executive springs to mind, or the straight A student who does nothing except study and obsess about grades. As in the alcoholism example above, however, the superficial behavior is only part of the story. The motivation behind the work involvement defines whether it is truly addictive or not.

People with work addictions use work to shield themselves from involvement with others and other parts of life. They enjoy being busy with a task more than involvement in the work itself. Having something concrete to perform helps them deal with the uncertainty of how to deal with problematic children, unpredictable spouses, or lingering questions about the meaning of life. This is in direct contrast to people who work long hours absorbed in a meaningful project. Dedicated students, teachers, artists, scientists, and entrepreneurs, for example, are not concerned with the empty, compulsive, ritual routine of work but are rather personally fulfilled through a stimulating participation that contributes to their growth and satisfaction.

A similar parallel can be drawn for relationships. Devotion to a lover becomes an addiction when that relationship becomes a limitation to involvement in life and personal development (Peele, 1975). An extreme example is **co-dependency.** A co-dependent person typically believes he or she is responsible for the behavior and problems of others, especially a partner (Edlin & Golanty, 1992). Relationships for co-dependent people serve as limitations because the needs and problems of others serve to define and control the co-dependent's life to an extreme, so that the person's own needs go denied and unmet.

At their best, relationships with friends and lovers enlarge your experience; teach you about yourself and the world around you; and stimulate you to meet new people, try new activities, and have more fun. These friends and lovers help you find creative solutions to problems, increase your self-esteem, and serve as a bountiful source of healthy pleasures. On the other hand, addictive relationships get you stuck in a rut. They limit your experience and discourage you from developing your personal potential. If you remain in a relationship simply because it is convenient, you feel needed, or you are afraid of being alone, you should question its value and your motivations for staying.

HEALTHY PLEASURE

Medical researchers Robert Ornstein and David Sobel (Ornstein & Sobel, 1989a) believe that "our health, happiness and future depend upon understanding and reversing [our] deep-rooted cultural denial of sensual pleasure and leisure. . . . Feeling good pays off not only in immediate enjoyment but also in better health" (p. 13). In their book *Healthy Pleasures,* which provides the inspiration for many ideas

STRESS AND YOU

TWENTY PLEASURES

The first step to increasing the pleasure potential of your lifestyle is to recognize things that give you pleasure and make you feel good. List 20 things that you enjoy doing. They can be big or little things. At least 8 to 10 items should be sources of pleasure available to you several times a week. You will come back to this list at the end of this chapter as you design an action plan for adding more pleasure to your lifestyle.

1. _____

2. _____

3. _____

4. _____

5. _____

6. _____

7. _____

8. _____

9. _____

10. _____

in this chapter, they present research to support their notion that Americans should quit worrying and start "living optimistically, with pleasure, zest and commitment." Their advice makes sense. And, best of all, it's fun!

For you to increase the amount of time you spend enjoying yourself, two things must happen. First, you must expose yourself to pleasant experiences; second, you must be open—with your body, mind, and spirit—to the enjoyment and appreciation of these experiences. The first is by far the easier. It begins with exploring your five senses and experiencing pleasurable sensations.

SENSATION-SEEKING REDEFINED

True pleasure often comes from enjoyment of the little things in life. Some people equate feeling excited with feeling good and mistakenly believe that the only way to feel pleasure is to experience an adrenaline rush. Feeling thrilled and excited can be fun, but remember the concept of eustress from Chapter 1: fun and excitement is still a form of stress from which you must eventually unwind. People are so often on sensory overload they forget how to enjoy simple sensory pleasures and find contentment in daily life. Getting back in touch with easily accessible sensory plea-

11. _____

12. _____

13. _____

14. _____

15. _____

16. _____

17. _____

18. _____

19. _____

20. _____

Next to each item, write how often you use that activity for relaxation and enjoyment.

Circle those things you might like to use more often for relaxation and enjoyment.

If other ideas for enjoyable activities come to you as you read this chapter, add them to your list.

sures can help you unwind and experience the pleasure of relaxation. As you consider the five senses, think about pleasurable experiences you may wish to add to your Twenty Pleasures list.

Touch

The sun's warmth on a fresh spring day, a cool breeze on your cheek, a loving caress, a cat's soft fur, a leisurely hot bath, a young child asleep in your arms. Your skin, the largest organ in the body, is constantly transmitting sensory information from the people and environment around you. Tuning in more carefully to the positive messages coming in increases your pleasure. What are these messages? With touch, people communicate comfort and caring. Touch heals the sick (Dreschler, Whitehead, Morrill-Corbin, & Cataldo, 1985; Weiss, 1986) and relieves pain (Fishman, Turkheimer, & DeGood, 1995). Without the minimum daily requirement of touch, babies fail to grow (Reite, 1984) and grownups get grumpy.

North Americans of Northern European descent do not score very high on the international touch scale. Our puritanical upbringing has taught us to be rather conservative about touching each other. Touch is reserved for lovers and young children. The sexual revolution of the 1960s and 1970s has "liberated" us enough

to jump in bed with a total stranger (which usually brings unsatisfying communication along with the risk of disease), but we are hesitant to hug our close friends. In fact, for many people, touch is a four-letter word. Nice people just don't do it, except perhaps in the privacy of their bedrooms. And let's not talk about that. Massage is associated with prostitutes and two men hugging each other are labeled homosexuals. Preschool teachers are afraid to cuddle their young students for fear of sexual abuse charges.

Other cultures, and subcultures in our own country, have a very different view. Hand-holding between friends, a stroke on the arm, a kiss on the cheek are more commonly seen in other cultures. One interesting study (Jourard, 1966) compared the number of times couples in cafes touched each other in several countries. In San Juan, Puerto Rico, couples touched on the average 180 times per hour. In Paris, 110 contacts per hour were recorded. In Gainesville, Florida, the count was down to only twice an hour. And in jolly old England? The couples never touched. A study of young children and their adult caregivers in three countries found a similar result. When caregivers in Greece, the Soviet Union, and the United States were chasing or punishing their charges, touch levels were similar. But in other interactions such as soothing and playing, American children received much less touch (Gibson, Wurst, & Cannonito, 1984).

Touch is enjoyable only if it feels right, if it communicates comfort and caring in a nonthreatening way. You can increase your daily touch enjoyment by learning more about what feels good for you. Trading back rubs with a friend, caressing your child or lover, petting your dog or cat, and learning how to massage the muscles of your own face and neck are enjoyable touch experiences.

One of the most pleasurable sensations our skin brings us is warmth. Most people love hot tubs, saunas, and warm climates. Research has shown that these offer potent stress relief as well. Saunas, on which the most research has been done, seem to decrease muscle tension (deVries, Beckmann, Huber, & Dieckmeir, 1968) and to increase endorphins, chemicals produced by our bodies that relieve pain and produce feelings of relaxation and euphoria (Jezova, Vigas, Tatar, Jurcovicova, & Palat, 1987). Hot baths and showers provide easily accessible sources of pleasure for many people.

Sight

Pleasant sights produce enjoyment and relaxation. Although the concept of "pleasant" varies from person to person, an overwhelming majority of people find natural outdoor scenes to be most pleasing. In one study, when people were asked to view natural and urban photographic slides, they reported more positive feelings for the natural scenes. Natural scenes were also associated with lower physiological arousal (Ornstein & Sobel, 1989b; Ulrich, 1981).

Most people must adapt to an indoor world at certain times in their lives. And many people live in urban areas devoid of waterfalls, prairies, and forests. However, introducing even small tokens of the natural world into your indoor environment can significantly increase your pleasure and your stress resistance. Plants, aquariums, and paintings and photographs of natural scenes can all combat the lifeless atmosphere of many home and office environments (Ornstein & Sobel, 1989a).

Some people experience a great deal of stress when deprived of adequate natural lighting, a condition appropriately known as SAD, for Seasonal Affective Disorder (Jacobson, Wehr, Sack, James, & Rosenthal, 1987). They become depressed in winter when days are short and they must spend more time indoors. People with SAD tend to sleep and eat more in the winter and feel generally depressed from November through March. Some researchers estimate that up to 5 percent of North Americans are affected by SAD ("Boosting winter's light," 1992). Many others suffer from milder symptoms. Treatment for SAD involves lighting up your life: when you are indoors, spend time near windows when possible; exercise outdoors during the daylight hours. Using bright, full-spectrum lighting in your home and work areas is expensive, but it is helpful if SAD is a serious problem.

Sound

The sounds in your environment can provide pleasure or jangle your nerves. Birds singing, crickets chirping, rain falling, ocean waves breaking on the shore—as with sight, nature sounds tend to be more relaxing. On the other hand, horns honking, jackhammers pounding, and engines revving make people nervous. When exposed to such noise for long periods, as when living or working next to a construction site, people become tense and irritable; they can even develop stress-related illnesses. Too much sound, even constant television or radio "background" noise, can be irritating.

Pleasure seekers must do what they can to minimize noise pollution and add pleasant sounds to their environment. Ear plugs are a marvelous invention for soothing nerves as well as protecting your hearing. Covering construction and similar noise with "white noise" such as radio static or recordings of ocean waves, waterfalls, and similar sounds can be helpful. Periods of quiet can be very therapeutic (although hard to come by in some places); enjoy them when you can. Recordings of nature sounds can help you relax.

Music in some form has been important to every human culture. Music awakens a wide array of emotions. It can soothe and calm or stimulate and arouse. It lessens pain, speeds post-operative healing, lowers heart rate and blood pressure, and decreases anxiety and depression (Hatta & Nakamura, 1991; Spintge & Droh, 1983; Standley, 1986). Many readers probably included "listening to music" on

I throw myself to the left.
I turn myself to the right.
I am the fish
Who glides in the water, who glides,
Who twists himself, who leaps.
Everything lives, everything dances, everything sings.

AFRICAN PYGMY

their Twenty Pleasures list earlier in this chapter. Tuning in to how you respond to various types of music helps you learn to use your music collection to adjust your mood. Many people have favorite relaxation music that helps them unwind and recover from stress.

Smell

Smell is probably the most overlooked source of sensual pleasure. Your sense of smell is connected to the areas of the brain that generate emotions, which is why smells have such interesting effects on mood and memory (Gibson et al., 1984). A smell that reminds you of your grandmother's house that you visited as a child does more than awaken a picture of what her house looked like. Instead, it reminds you of the total *feeling* of being there. The smell transports you back to your childhood, back to the you that was visiting your grandmother.

What smells are pleasurable to you—freshly baked bread; roses; peppermint tea; a certain incense, soap, or perfume? Notice your response to various fragrances and try to use them in new ways to enhance your pleasure.

Taste

In our diet- and weight-conscious culture, many people regard the pleasure of good-tasting food as a mixed blessing. We have been conditioned to regard the pleasure of eating with suspicion. We joke that if it tastes good, it can't possibly be good for you.

Our prehistoric ancestors benefited from a taste for sweet, salt, and fat, which led them to consume the nutritious, high-fat foods essential for survival in prehistoric times when getting enough calories was the difference between life and death. We have inherited these tastes, and now, in a land with an abundant food supply and a high availability of processed foods, we cannot rely solely on what tastes good to choose what we eat. But with a little nutrition education, we can still make healthful choices *and* enjoy the pleasure of eating.

Many North Americans worry too much about what they eat. We've heard that eating the wrong way leads to a wide array of ills including obesity, artery disease, diabetes, and hypertension. Most of the advice we get focuses on what not to eat. After years of trying to ignore our appetites and going on and off restrictive diets, food comes to be seen as the enemy. Food and appetite acquire an enormous importance and power the more we curb our appetites and deny ourselves pleasure. In extreme cases, powerful food cravings drive compulsive eaters to wolf down unnatural volumes of food in an effort to satisfy their emotional hunger. The fact that dieting and eating disorders have reached epidemic levels in our culture indicates that something has gone wrong with our relationship to food (Black & Held, 1991).

There is no denying that good nutrition and good health (and stress management) go together, as discussed in Chapter 9. But the way we respond to this connection can be the difference between a healthy desire to take good care of ourselves and an unhealthy obsession with eating. Most dieting and disordered eating evolves not from a desire for good health but from a desire for a certain appearance: a drive to be very thin and a fear of fatness. Statistics show that at least half of all people claiming to be on a weight-loss diet are not overweight by medical standards. They may be five or ten pounds heavier than fashion models and be battling their genetic heritage in an effort to attain an impossible physique. Is it worth the fight? Research has shown that staying somewhat overweight is healthier in the long run than repeatedly gaining and losing weight, a process familiar to chronic dieters known as weight cycling (Van Dale & Saris, 1989). Weight cycling occurs because, as discussed in Chapter 9, restrictive diets don't work. They are an unnatural way of eating, based on monotony and self-denial. They are difficult to live with and do not teach dieters how to develop a healthy relationship with food. People on very low-calorie diets often experience frustration, fatigue, depression, low self-esteem, and uncontrollable food cravings. The stress created by very low-calorie diets is often much worse for your health than being somewhat overweight and enjoying your food. And ironically, restrictive diets may prevent you from losing weight and in the long run, lead to weight gain.

So if diets don't work, what is to be done? Throw caution to the wind and indulge our way to a heart attack? What does work for long-term health and increased stress resistance is moderation combined with enjoyment of our food and getting back in touch with our appetites. We can learn to use our nutrition knowledge and our positive outlook to develop a pleasurable eating plan. We can make healthful eating choices most of the time while enjoying occasional sweets and treats. Healthful weight control and disease prevention develop from eating habits you can live with for a lifetime, based on eating when you are hungry, enjoying your food, and not eating when you are satisfied.

You can get more pleasure from eating if you experiment with your food choices. Cultivate variety, flavor, and texture. Try various spices and other flavorings. Most of all, eat slowly and focus on the pleasure of eating.

ACCEPTING PLEASURE

Cultivating pleasurable experiences and allowing them into your life is a good first step. Small things, like enjoying a cup of coffee, watching the birds at the bird feeder, and listening to a favorite piece of music make a big difference in the way you feel. Much of the pleasure people feel is psychological in origin. If the mental pleasure gates are not open, sensations of pleasure cannot get in. Perhaps you've been there: you are at your favorite vacation spot and it's a beautiful sunset. You can't explain it but although nothing is really wrong, you just don't feel happy.

Where do happiness and pleasure come from? Do they just happen, dropping in unannounced from time to time? Do they depend on our achieving certain goals or being in certain situations? Is there a way to cultivate positive emotions and experiences? Most psychologists believe the latter—that with practice you can develop a more optimistic outlook that helps you become more receptive to pleasurable experiences.

Happiness (like stress) is often equated with major life events: winning the lottery, graduating from college, finding the right partner, landing a well-paying job. But just as research indicates that it's the daily hassles that wear people down, so the small daily moments of pleasure define whether people consider themselves happy (Argyle, 1987; Ornstein & Sobel, 1989a). If we adopt the attitude that we can't be happy until some specific goal is achieved, we are forever waiting in the wings of life's theater. If only this paper were written or I had enough money to buy a car . . . I'll be happy once this week is over, the summer is here, I get my promotion, I lose 20 pounds . . . Something more is always looming on the horizon to serve as an excuse for not trying to be happy now.

Ornstein and Sobel write, "Happiness lies in narrowing the distance between where you see yourself and where you expect to be" (Ornstein & Sobel, 1989a, p. 129). Unhappiness comes from the perception that things should be better than they are. Happiness comes when you perceive that things are going pretty well for you. How do you tell? It's all relative, and it all comes down to your point of view. We will talk more about perception and stress in Section IV. For now, let us introduce the idea that reality is quite subjective. We create for ourselves beliefs and concepts about what's going on out in the world as well as how we are faring in the scheme of things. If you compare yourself to an unfortunate refugee in some wartorn part of the world and count your blessings, you will decide you are really quite well off. If instead you compare yourself only to people who are smarter, richer, and better looking than you, then life is lacking.

The bad news is that reality is the cause of all stress. The good news is that most of us aren't in touch with it.

ESTHER ORIOLI

Let's face it: reality can be depressing. The world is full of suffering, injustice, and pain. But there are also beauty, love, meaningful relationships, and satisfying work. Optimists tend to focus on the latter, to see the glass of life as half full. They are resistant to stress because they view demands as challenges rather than obstacles; they feel hopeful, not helpless. They emphasize the positive and tend to play down the negative. This denial of the negative allows them to move on with their lives in a productive, happy way and not become overwhelmed with stress or stuck in depression. And while we might think that being in touch with "reality" is a sign of mental health, the truth is that mental health is associated with a certain amount of healthy illusion (Bresnitz, 1983; Goleman, 1985; Lazarus, 1979). For example, healthy people tend to overestimate somewhat how much control they have over future events (Dobson & Pusch, 1995; Taylor & Brown, 1988). Remember that a sense of control is an important element of stress resistance. The stress resistance comes not from how much control people actually have but from their *perception* of having control. Obviously, having too many illusions can cause stress (Colvin, Block, & Funder, 1995). If you overestimate your abilities and underestimate the demands of an upcoming exam, you will probably perform poorly. Healthy illusions give you enough optimism to work hard and achieve. Unhealthy illusions impair your ability and create stress.

When presented with the idea that illusions can be healthy, many students are confused: Is this good or bad? Should we ignore the suffering and injustice so that we can be personally happy? Of course not, and optimists don't do this. Ironically, by focusing on the positive, optimists are more likely to effect social change because they are prepared to take on a challenge. Would a realist ever run for government office or go into social services? No, because these jobs take energy, hope, and stress resistance. By focusing on control, commitment, and challenge, stress-resistant optimists can muster the energy to accomplish meaningful work.

What does optimism have to do with healthy pleasures? An optimistic attitude opens the daily pleasure channels. Seeking and expecting pleasure, you are more likely to find it. Stress-resistant people count their blessings many times each day and appreciate the good things in their lives. They realize that happiness comes not from momentary triumphs but from how much of the time each day a person spends feeling good.

CULTIVATE YOUR SENSE OF HUMOR

Laughter is good medicine. Its salubrious effects are both physical and psychological. As physical exercise, it increases breathing rate, raises blood pressure and heart rate, speeds up metabolic rate, stimulates immune function, and gives face and abdominal muscles a workout while relaxing other muscles (Dillon, Minchoff, & Baker, 1985; Fry, 1992). Finding the humor in life increases your stress resistance. People who value humor and actively introduce a humorous perspective during times of difficulty are better able to weather stress (Kuiper, Martin, & Olinger, 1993; Martin, Kuiper, Olinger, & Dance, 1993) and experience fewer negative health effects (Martin & Lefcourt, 1983) than those who look only at the dark side. A sense of humor seems to protect the immune system from negative stress effects (Martin & Dobbin, 1988). Humor seems to be especially helpful for combating stress-related depression (Nezu, Nezu, & Blissett, 1988). People with a good sense of humor report less depression and loneliness and seem to have higher self-esteem (Frecknall, 1994; Kuiper & Martin, 1993; Overholser, 1992). Laughter reduces feelings of stress (White & Winzelbert, 1992). A good sense of humor is associated with optimism and positive feelings (Kuiper, Martin, & Dance, 1992). Humor enhances creativity and helps people get along (Hampes, 1983; Morreall, 1991).

Laughter has positive effects in sickness and in health. Norman Cousins, magazine editor and UCLA professor, was one of the first to promote the positive health effects of laughter, claiming that it enhanced his recovery from serious illness (Cousins, 1991). Some hospitals are introducing humor treatments to help reduce patients' perception of pain and speed the healing process (Cousins, 1989). Some psychotherapists advocate the use of humor with other techniques to help clients cope with stressful situations (Prerost, 1988).

Research suggests that simply appreciating humor that comes your way is not enough; you must actively use humor in stressful situations for it to increase your stress resistance (Martin & Lefcourt, 1983; Nezu et al., 1988). Humor is most helpful when it is used appropriately—not to deny the problems you face but to help you deal with feelings of stress. Humorous remarks must not be destructive to oth-

▶ STRESS RESEARCH

Norman Cousins: *The Biology of Hope*

In 1976, Norman Cousins became one of the most unusual contributors to the field of stress management research with the publication of his article "Anatomy of an Illness (As Perceived by the Patient)" in the prestigious *New England Journal of Medicine*. Cousins's work was unusual in that he wrote from the perspective of a science writer and informed patient rather than as a physician or scientist. As an editor at the *Saturday Review* from 1940 to 1971, Cousins had developed a keen interest in medical science and the healing process, an interest which he applied to himself when he became ill in 1964 with a life-threatening connective tissue disorder known as ankylosing spondylitis.

Medical specialists gave Cousins one in 500 odds of recovering from this extremely painful disorder. Determined to be that one in 500, Cousins conducted his own research on this little-understood disorder, and with his physician's cooperation designed a maverick treatment program. Familiar with the work of stress researchers such as Hans Selye (Chapter 2), Cousins believed that stress had played an important role in the development of his illness. He reasoned, "If negative emotions produce negative chemical changes in the body, wouldn't the positive emotions produce positive chemical changes? Is it possible that love, hope, faith, laughter, confidence and the will to live have therapeutic value?" (Cousins, 1991, p. 52.) Cultivating these positive emotions was a cornerstone of his treatment. Cousins checked himself out of the hospital and into a hotel where he could pursue his treatment program free of the hospital routine and its depressing environment.

Cousins found that he could muster positive emotions, but laughter was difficult to come by as he was in a great deal of pain. His solution was to view "Candid Camera" films and read humor books. He was elated to discover that "ten minutes of genuine belly laughter had an anesthetic effect and would give me at least two hours of pain-free sleep" (p. 55). His health slowly but surely improved over the next several weeks, and he was soon back with his family and at work.

Cousins went on to pursue his interest in positive emotions and health as a faculty member at UCLA, an experience from which he wrote his 1989 book, *Head First: The Biology of Hope*. His work has inspired scientific research on the physiology of laughter and positive emotions.

ers or be used to avoid communication. Have you ever tried to discuss something with a flippant, sarcastic person who turned your serious conversation into a joke? This is not constructive humor because it alienates people. Humor is an effective coping skill when it connects you to others and makes everyone feel good.

How can you cultivate your sense of humor and invite more laughter into your life? Here are a few ideas. Maybe you would like to add some to your Twenty Pleasures list.

1. Look for incongruities, for these are the sources of humor (Hillson & Martin, 1994). We overlook many of these each day. We can also learn to see everyday happenings with a humorous perspective. Make up funny stories about a stranger you see on the street. Give your car a name and a personality. Children are especially adept at finding incongruities and seeing stories in simple events. Take a stressful event you have recently experienced and turn it into a funny story.

2. See yourself as a humor-appreciator, as playful and humorous. Believe that humor cultivation is an important part of your life.

3. Have joke books and other sources of humor available. Collect jokes and funny quotes.

4. Read the comics every day and notice what makes you laugh. Save comics that make you laugh out loud, and look for books with these characters. Post favorite comics in convenient spots: your desk, the refrigerator, bulletin boards. Watch funny movies.

5. Try keeping a humor journal. Write down jokes and include comics that make you laugh and funny things that have happened to you. Use this journal to cheer you up on bad days.

HELPER'S HIGH

One of the most often overlooked sources of pleasure is helping others. When we are in dire straits, sometimes the last thing we think we have energy for is giving, but giving often gives energy back to us—with interest. Several studies have found that people receive a great deal of beneficial pleasure by giving pleasure and helping others. Altruism has even been associated with better health. One study found that men who did no volunteer work were two and a half times as likely to die over the course of the study as men who volunteered at least once a week (House, Robbins, & Metzer, 1982).

One of the reasons pleasure increases stress resistance is that it takes us out of our heads. So does altruism. Research has shown that one of the personality characteristics most related to negative health effects is self-involvement. Self-involved people are overly absorbed in themselves, their feelings, their thoughts, and their activities. They refer to themselves more often in conversation than less self-involved friends: you will hear the words "I," "me," "my," and "mine" more frequently from these folks. Researchers believe such speech reflects how people tend to see the world, and when people feel isolated, they focus more on themselves (Scherwitz, Graham, & Ornish, 1985). Medical researcher Dean Ornish believes that "*anything that promotes isolation leads to chronic stress and, often, to illnesses like heart disease. Conversely, anything that leads to real intimacy and feelings of connection can be healing*" (Ornish 1990, p. 87) (italics are Ornish's). When we help others, the focus shifts away from ourselves. Herbert Benson, a cardiologist who has done a great deal of research on the therapeutic effects of relaxation techniques, believes that altruism may induce the relaxation response that lowers heart rate and blood pressure, increases immune response, and decreases sensitivity to pain (Benson, 1984).

Altruism is most pleasurable when you become involved with other people, even if only for a few hours a week. Donating money doesn't give you the same good feelings. Look for volunteer opportunities near you that match your time availability and interests.

RECREATION

In Chapter 10 you learned about the stress-resistance effects of physical activity and the importance of finding activities that are enjoyable for you. Physical activities, hobbies, and other leisure-time pursuits are forms of *recreation,* activities that refresh you by means of enjoyment and relaxation. Recreation re-creates you; it renews your energy and creativity. Just as preferences vary regarding physical activity, so do they vary regarding recreational activity in general. Studies that have asked people about leisure-time activity preferences have found that such activities provide many types of reward (Tinsley & Eldredge, 1995). They can increase your self-esteem, sense of social support and altruism, sensual enjoyment, mental stimulation, and creativity; they provide opportunities for competition as well as relaxation. It's important to make time for activities you enjoy.

A GOOD NIGHT'S SLEEP

Adequate restful sleep provides an important cornerstone of a stress-resistant lifestyle—and a healthy pleasure as well. But just as stress can wreak havoc on eating habits, it can reduce the quantity and disrupt the quality of one's sleep (Weller & Avinir, 1993). Just when you need a good night's sleep the most, you may be least likely to get it!

Almost everyone has trouble sleeping occasionally, especially when stress levels are high. Fortunately, a few sleepless nights cause no lasting damage, although they may dampen your good humor and interfere with your mental alertness (which is why studying all night before an exam is a self-defeating practice!). Chronic sleep deprivation, on the other hand, can seriously impair your mental and physical health and your ability to manage stress.

Insomnia

Insomnia may include any or all of the following symptoms:

1. Taking a long time to fall asleep
2. Awakening frequently during the night
3. Awakening too early in the morning
4. Feeling tired and dissatisfied with one's sleep on awakening

Insomnia that lasts more than a few weeks requires medical attention since it may be an indication of depression or other serious health problems.

Sleep Therapy

The first step in overcoming insomnia is to figure out the cause of the problem. Examine lifestyle factors that may be responsible. Eliminate or reduce caffeine consumption. Caffeine is a drug that is broken down very slowly in your body, so its effects are very long lasting. Caffeine may keep you awake long after the caffeine buzz is gone. Many people believe alcohol will help them relax and go to sleep, but like sleeping pills, alcohol disrupts the sleep cycle. While alcohol may help you fall asleep, it usually produces a light, restless sleep, and you may awaken suddenly in the night, unable to go back to sleep. Tobacco smoke and smokeless tobacco products contain nicotine, which is a stimulant. Smokers tend to report more sleep problems than nonsmokers (Lexcen & Hicks, 1993).

If psychological stress is the cause of insomnia, develop your stress-management skills. Address sources of stress and practice relaxation training exercises. Professional counseling can be helpful as well.

The Sleep Environment

Create an environment conducive to sleeping. The sleep environment should be comfortable, restful, and associated with relaxation and sleep. A small dormitory room must provide areas for both intense studying and restful sleep. How can this be done? Try not to study in bed; your mind may come to associate the bed with mental activity rather than relaxing sleep. Let your bed be a haven for relaxation and sleep. Try ear plugs or white noise machines to cover disruptive noise. Most people sleep best in a cool room (60°–65°F). Shades that block light can help darken rooms with windows near streetlights or keep out the early morning sun.

Healthy Sleep Habits

College students are prone to sleep problems because they often develop very erratic sleeping habits. They may go to bed at a different time every night, get up early one day but sleep until noon the next, and nap when time for napping is available. Add to this schedule a healthy helping of stress, and insomnia begins. If insomnia is a problem, a regular sleeping schedule may work wonders. Try to get to bed at the same time each night, get up at the same time each morning, and avoid napping.

While a small bedtime snack may help you sleep, a large meal before bed can inhibit sleep. Exercise improves sleep quality, but exercise too close to bedtime can wind you up instead of down. Sleep experts generally recommend exercising in the late afternoon.

Develop a relaxing bedtime routine that helps you go to bed with a peaceful mind. Read something fun, listen to soothing music, write a letter, or knit a sweater. Lie down to sleep only if you are sleepy. If you haven't fallen asleep after 10 minutes, get up and do something relaxing until you get sleepy.

What about Napping?

Many cultures endorse an afternoon siesta. Unfortunately, this practice has gone by the wayside in many industrial countries. If a daily nap is a source of solace and stress relief and does not interfere with your lifestyle, enjoy! Question your napping if you are getting more than 8 or 9 hours of sleep a day; too much sleep may be a symptom of depression or other illness. Consider also whether you are using sleep as a means of procrastination. Sleep is a fairly healthful coping technique, but sources of stress must still be addressed. The biggest problem with napping is that your body wants to sleep at the same time every day. What happens if you have a 1:00 class after you have become accustomed to napping at that hour? Professors generally frown on students who use class time to catch 40 winks!

CREATURES GREAT AND SMALL

Anyone who has ever loved a pet knows the magic of the person-animal relationship. Many readers probably included something about their pets like "playing with Winkie" or "petting Fluffy" on their Twenty Pleasures list. And indeed, pets give a great deal of pleasure. They look nice and do funny things. They force you into the

present moment as you interact with them. Dogs and cats are the most popular pet friends, but people report pleasant relationships with all manner of creatures, from birds to reptiles.

The health benefits of pets seem to go beyond simple daily pleasures (Beck & Katcher, 1983; Vines, 1993). Pets provide companionship and give us something to care for. Like altruism, caring for a pet takes our focus away from ourselves. Furry pets are a pleasure to touch; petting furry friends creates a sense of closeness between owner and pet and causes a relaxation response (Vormbrock & Grossberg, 1988). Pets give us unconditional acceptance. (Dogs give us love and cats may at least deign to bestow upon us an accepting glance now and then.) Although the circumstances of our lives change from day to day, our pets respond to us with constancy. Our partners may leave us, our health may decline, we may lose our jobs, but our pets don't care; we are still the same in their eyes. Pets love you even if you are old, disabled, or depressed (Beck & Katcher, 1983).

ISLANDS OF PEACE

Living with stress is easier if you have "islands of peace" or take "pleasure breaks" throughout the day (Ferguson, 1986). Just because all hell breaks loose in the morning, you need not ruin your afternoon. Many of the items on your "Twenty Pleasures" list probably take five minutes or less and can serve as a way to calm, focus, and regenerate you. In a sense, they provide a sort of mini-vacation that increases your stress resistance and clears your mind. Make the little things count: watching the squirrels in the yard, spending a few minutes petting your dog, watering the plants, enjoying a cup of tea, playing a favorite piece of music, or maybe just thinking about an upcoming vacation. Many of the little things we do without thinking during the day can be cultivated into islands of peace that soothe and refresh. Longer activities are useful, too. Many people find that a walk at the end of the work day helps them unwind. An enjoyable dinner hour can help heal the stress wounds of the day.

Most men pursue pleasure with such breathless haste that they hurry past it.

KIERKEGAARD

MINDFULNESS

Where you focus your attention during pleasurable moments has a lot to do with how much pleasure you experience. Mindfulness simply means being totally aware and in the present moment. Your awareness includes not only sensory information but your thoughts and emotions as well. You are aware as an observer of your thoughts and experiences, which creates a compassionate distance that can bring much learning. Mindfulness is used with meditation, but it can also be used with daily living, to live more fully in the moment, and appreciate life with all your senses (Gillespie & Bechtel, 1986). Try the Mindful Awareness exercise below to increase your sensory awareness.

Don't be surprised if this exercise is more difficult than it sounds. Our inner voices are accustomed to delivering commentary and chattering away every moment of the day. These voices are especially fond of drifting into the future, worrying about what is around the corner, or wandering back into the past to rehash problems and mistakes. This mind chatter often has important messages for us, so our goal here is not to squelch it but to simply acknowledge it without getting involved.

Essential to any kind of relaxation technique is an attitude of "trying not to try." Once we start trying to achieve a goal and do a good job of relaxing, our ability to relax gets worse. Let it go. Stop judgment, and accept whatever happens.

EXPRESSIVE WRITING ENHANCES MINDFULNESS AND RELIEVES STRESS

Many students include writing letters or writing in their journals on their Twenty Pleasures lists. Expressive writing enhances mindfulness and can serve as a productive way to cope with stress (Francis & Pennebaker, 1992; Gelles, 1994; Spera, Buhrfeind, & Pennebaker, 1994). Part of the therapeutic effect of writing in a journal appears to stem from the fact that formulating an explanation of stressful events enhances coping (Burt, 1994). Both letter writing and keeping a journal may help with problem solving and coping with thoughts, feelings, and emotions

▲ RELAXATION EXERCISE

MINDFUL AWARENESS

1. Sit or lie in a comfortable position. Relax for a few minutes, perhaps listening to some soothing music.
2. Close your eyes and focus your awareness on the sensory information reaching you in this present moment. As thoughts come and go, simply observe them without becoming involved, and gently turn your attention back to the present moment. What sounds do you hear? Are they loud? Soft? Harsh? Smooth? What smells are you aware of? Move your hands over nearby surfaces. What do you feel? Be aware of surfaces feeling warm, cool, rough, smooth, hard, or soft.
3. Tune in to the sensations within your body. Your breathing, your heartbeat, muscle tension, pressure, or any other feelings.
4. Tune back in to sensory input: sounds, smells, tactile sensations. Then open your eyes and notice what you see. Pretend you are seeing your surroundings for the first time. Notice shapes, colors, shadows, and composition.

● RELAXATION EXERCISE

EATING AWARENESS

How often do you eat without really tasting your food? Often people down their lunch while reading the mail, watching television, even driving to a meeting. Mindful eating has several advantages. It brings pleasure as you enjoy your food. You eat more slowly and become more aware of feelings of hunger and fullness, so you are less likely to overeat. Eating mindfully encourages relaxation and better digestion. Bringing awareness to eating is simple: tune in to the present moment much as you did in the Mindful Awareness exercise (Davis, Eshelman, & McKay, 1988; Gillespie & Bechtel, 1986; Goleman & Bennett-Goleman, 1985; Hanh, 1990).

1. Select any food you find delicious. Fruit or nuts are easy to start with. Sit down with your food and take a few minutes to relax and focus. You may even wish to begin this exercise by doing a short version of the Mindful Awareness exercise.

2. Look at the food you are about to eat. Examine its shape and color. Now lift it to your nose and smell. Notice how the food feels in your hand, the pressure on your fingers, its weight, and the texture of its surface. If the food needs peeling or other preparation, enjoy the sensory information of that process, too.

3. Now place some of the food in your mouth. Examine the textures and tastes with your tongue. Chew the food very slowly, enjoying the tastes. Feel your teeth and jaw working, your tongue moving the food around in your mouth. Listen to the sound of your chewing.

4. Continue eating the food with this careful awareness. When thoughts occur, simply notice them, and then bring your attention back to the eating. Tune in to feelings of hunger and fullness. Stop eating when the desire for food ceases. When you finish the food in front of you, notice the aftertastes and your thoughts and feelings. Are you full, or still hungry? What are you hungry for?

Most of us would find eating this way much too cumbersome for every meal. Use it simply when you would like the opportunity to slow down. Make eating an orange or drinking a cup of tea an island of pleasure in your busy day. And even if you do not wish to use complete mindfulness at a meal, you will still benefit from relaxing and enjoying your food.

(Seaward, 1994). Both help you get in touch with your feelings. Some research has shown that when people write or talk about stressors, their physical health improves (Pennebaker, 1993). Writing letters contributes to a sense of social support.

One of the pioneers in the use of journal keeping for therapeutic purposes was Jungian psychologist Ira Progoff (Progoff, 1975). Progoff believed that structured journal writing could help individuals get in touch with "the inner resources" of their lives. He promoted journal writing as a means of finding meaning in life. In his book *At a Journal Workshop,* which describes his recommendations for keeping a journal, he describes how this meaning is gradually revealed. "[W]hen a person is shown how to reconnect himself with the contents and the continuity of his life, the inner thread of movement by which his life has been unfolding reveals itself to him by itself. Given the opportunity, a life crystallizes out of its own nature, revealing its meaning and its goal" (Progoff, 1975, p 10). Progoff teaches the journal-keeper to recognize that meaning "lies not in the events of his life in themselves . . . but in his inner relationship to those events" (p. 11). Thus, effective journal entries are not merely a chronicle of external events but also include the writer's thoughts, feelings, associations, memories, and perceptions sparked by events.

Some students are lucky to have had a teacher along the way who encouraged journal writing; they are already comfortable facing a blank page and recording their thoughts and feelings. Beginners who would like to give journal writing a try may begin with paper and pen. Keep in mind the following suggestions for making the most of your journal writing.

1. Take a moment to relax and focus before you begin. Close your eyes and take a few deep breaths, practice the Mindful Awareness exercise, or listen to some soothing music. Journal writing works best when you maintain an inward focus and are in touch with your thoughts and feelings.

2. Keep your journal private. Write only for yourself. Censorship, even when imaginary, can be stifling. Honest self-disclosure is key to a journal's therapeutic effect. Write whatever you wish without fear of repercussions. Keep your journal in a private place safe from prying eyes.

▲ ACTION PLAN

INCREASING HEALTHY PLEASURES AND DAILY ENJOYMENT

You are probably already doing a number of pleasurable things that increase your stress resistance, such as items on your Twenty Pleasures list. Maybe you would like to do some of these more often. Maybe other ideas in this chapter led you to think about simple ways to increase your daily enjoyment of life and decrease your feelings of stress. Write down two changes you might make to take greater advantage of healthy pleasures in your life.

Goal 1:

Action plan:

Goal 2:

Action plan:

3. Suspend judgment and write whatever comes to mind. Don't worry about logic and the other constraints that you must impose on the writing you do for others. If you become famous and someday wish to publish your journal you can always go back and edit!

4. Use your writing to practice creative problem solving, as described in Chapter 5. Avoid turning your journal into a dump for frustration and anger only (although there is plenty of room for all emotion). Journal writing can provide a wonderful stimulus for brainstorming and analysis. Use your writing to bring insight and resolution, not to fan the flames of anger with judgment and justification. Analyze sources of pleasure as well as stressors.

5. Advanced journal keepers who feel that their writing is getting stale may wish to try various techniques to inspire creativity. Try your hand at poetry, write in phrases rather than sentences, draw pictures, or describe books and other writing you have found meaningful. Analyze your dreams, write stories, or create imaginary conversations between yourself and other people or mythical figures.

■ STUDENT STRESS

MEGHAN'S HEALTHY PLEASURES

While Meghan sees herself as a fairly optimistic and cheerful person, she admits that during high-stress periods, like when assignments pile up, she can easily lose her good humor. Here is her action plan:

Goal 1: Try the "Islands of Pleasure" idea. I think these will be especially helpful for breaking the stress cycle during high-stress days.

Action plan: I will cultivate the following "Islands of Pleasure":

1. Breakfast: Slow down and enjoy my food. I really love breakfast. Maybe try a little mindful eating.
2. After morning classes: Slow down and enjoy the walk back to my room. Try to tune in to what I see; watch the people, birds, squirrels. Take deep breaths to relax.
3. Get the mail: Read the mail (if I get any) or a fun magazine and relax for fifteen minutes before lunch.
4. Afternoon workout with Beth and Sara. Use this time to socialize and enjoy working out, trying not to worry or complain about how much work I have while I am with them.
5. Before bed, write in my journal. Open each day's entry with positive outlook, humor, and what has been pleasurable during the day.

Goal 2: More outdoor activity. I really like doing things outside—several outdoor activities are on my Twenty Pleasures list. I would like to use these for relaxation and enjoyment more often.

Action Plan:

1. Get friends to take long walks with me on the weekend.
2. Join the Outing Club and go cross-country skiing with them this winter.
3. Sign up for the canoeing course next semester.

■ STRESS AND YOU

APPRECIATION OF PLEASURES

The relaxing effect of your islands of peace and pleasant moments will be enhanced if you pay more attention to them and make them an important part of your day. One way to do this is to remind yourself of these pleasurable experiences several times throughout the day (Gillespie & Bechtel, 1986). Use this pause for remembering as one of your islands of peace.

1. Sit in a comfortable position and take a few minutes to relax and tune in to the present moment.
2. Remember some of the pleasant moments you have had during the past day or two. These can be little things like eating an orange, taking a walk, thinking about the new flowers coming up in your garden, or having a good talk with a friend. Visualize these experiences and note your thoughts, feelings, and physical sensations.
3. If you are having difficulty fitting healthy pleasures into your day, you may wish to keep some sort of record for a few days. At the end of the day think about your pleasant moments. Ask yourself these questions:

Was I able to appreciate the pleasure while it was happening?

Can I think of ways to increase my feelings of pleasure during these moments?

Which activities brought the most pleasure? The least?

Which were easiest to incorporate into my daily life?

Do I have any ideas to add to my Twenty Pleasures list?

Did practicing and focusing on these pleasures change my day? If so, how?

SUMMARY

1. Positive emotions are associated with positive health effects and increased resistance to the negative effects of stress.
2. It is important to distinguish between pleasurable experiences that increase stress resistance and those that more closely resemble maladaptive coping responses, activities that may initially feel good but bring you more stress in the future.
3. To become addicted is to devote or surrender yourself to something habitually or obsessively. Although people may initially become addicted to something because it feels good, after a short while true addictions do not provide pleasure so much as temporary relief.

4. Addiction is not simply a function of frequency or amount of use, but rather the reasons for and context of use and the effect of the substance or behavior on the user.
5. Experiencing pleasure requires exposing yourself to pleasant experiences and allowing yourself to be in the right frame of mind to experience pleasure. Appreciating the sensory pleasures from touch, sight, sound, smell, and taste can increase your stress resistance.
6. The experience of happiness comes partly from the perception that things are going pretty well for you on a day-to-day basis rather than from major life events.
7. Optimists emphasize the positive in life and are happier than pessimists.
8. Laughter and finding humor in life increase your resistance to the negative effects of stress. Humor helps people combat stress-related depression, improves immune function, enhances self-esteem, stimulates creativity, and helps people get along.
9. Helping others can make you feel good.
10. Pleasurable recreational activities renew your energy and creativity. They can increase your self-esteem; provide a sense of social belonging, sensual enjoyment, and mental stimulation; enhance creativity; and provide opportunities for competition as well as relaxation.
11. Adequate restful sleep is essential for stress-resistance and good health.
12. Pets increase stress resistance by providing companionship and unconditional acceptance.
13. Simple relaxing experiences can provide "islands of peace" throughout the day.
14. Mindfulness means being totally aware and in the present moment. Mindful awareness enhances your enjoyment of healthy pleasures.
15. Expressive writing enhances mindfulness and relieves stress. Both keeping a journal and writing letters can improve problem-solving skills and help you cope with thoughts and feelings.

REFERENCES

Argyle, M. *The Psychology of Happiness*. London: Methuen, 1987.

Beck, A, and A Katcher. *Between Pets and People: The Importance of Animal Companionship*. New York: Putnam, 1983.

Benson, H. *Beyond the Relaxation Response*. New York: Berkeley Books, 1984.

Black, DR, and SE Held. Eating disorders and athletes: Current issues and future research. DR Black (ed). *Eating Disorders Among Athletes: Theory, Issues, and Research*. Reston, VA: American Alliance for Health, Physical Education, Recreation and Dance, 1991.

Boosting winter's light. *University of California Berkeley Wellness Letter*, Jan 1992, p 7.

Brehm, BA. *Essays on Wellness*. New York: HarperCollins, 1993.

Bresnitz, S (ed). *The Denial of Stress*. New York: International Universities Press, 1983.

Burt, CDB. Prospective and retrospective account-making in diary entries: A model of anxiety reduction and avoidance. *Anxiety, Stress, and Coping* 6: 327–340, 1994.

Colvin, CR, J Block, and DC Funder. Overly positive self-evaluations and personality: Negative implications for mental health. *Journal of Personality and Social Psychology* 68: 1152–1162, 1995.

Cousins, N. Anatomy of an illness (as perceived by the patient). A Monat and RS Lazarus (eds). *Stress and Coping*. New York: Columbia University Press, 1991, pp 48–61.

Cousins, N. *Head First: The Biology of Hope*. New York: EP Dutton, 1989.

Davis, M, ER Eshelman, and M McKay. *The Relaxation and Stress Reduction Workbook*. Oakland, CA: New Harbinger, 1988.

DeVries, HA, P Beckmann, H Huber, and L Dieckmeir. Electromyographic evaluation of the effects of sauna on the neuromuscular system. *Journal of Sports Medicine* 8: 61–69, 1968.

Dillon, K, B Minchoff, and K Baker. Positive emotional states and enhancement of the immune system. *International Journal of Psychiatry and Medicine* 15: 13–18, 1985.

Dobson, KS, and D Pusch. A test of the depressive realism hypothesis in clinically depressed subjects. *Cognitive Therapy and Research* 19: 179–194, 1995.

Dreschler, VM, WE Whitehead, ED Morrill-Corbin, and MR Cataldo. Physiological and subjective reactions to being touched. *Psychophysiology* 22: 96–100, 1985.

Druckman, D, and R Bjork. *In the Mind's Eye.* Washington, DC: National Academies Press, 1991.

Edlin, G, and E Golanty. *Health and Wellness: A Holistic Approach.* Boston: Jones and Bartlett, 1992.

Ferguson, T. Dr. Pelletier's guide to do-it-yourself stress management. *Medical Self-Care,* Sept/Oct 1986, pp 46–47+.

Fishman, E, E Turkheimer, and DE DeGood. Touch relieves stress and pain. *Journal of Behavioral Medicine* 18: 69–79, 1995.

Francis, ME, and JW Pennebaker. Putting stress into words: The impact of writing on physiological, absentee, and self-reported emotional well-being measures. *American Journal of Health Promotion* 6: 280–287, 1992.

Frecknall, P. Good humor: A qualitative study of the uses of humor in everyday life. *Psychology* 31: 12–21, 1994.

Fry, WF. The physiologic effects of humor, mirth, and laughter. *Journal of the American Medical Association* 267: 1857–1858, 1992.

Gelles, EB. Letter writing as a coping strategy: The case of Abigail Adams. *The Psychohistory Review* 22: 193–209, 1994.

Gibbons, B. The intimate sense of smell. *National Geographic* 170: 324–360, 1986.

Gibson, J, KK Wurst, and M Cannonito. Observations on contact stimulation provided young children in selected areas of Greece, USA, and USSR. *International Journal of Psychology* 19: 233–243, 1984.

Gillespie, PR, and L Bechtel. *Less Stress in 30 Days.* New York: New American Library, 1986.

Goleman, D. *Vital Lies, Simple Truths: The Psychology of Self-Deception.* New York: Simon & Schuster, 1985.

Goleman, D, and T Bennett-Goleman. Moving toward mindfulness. *American Health,* Mar 1987, pp 80–88.

Gurin, J. Doing better, feeling worse. *American Health,* July/August 1988, pp 105–110.

Hampes, WP. Relation between humor and generativity. *Psychological Reports* 73: 131–136, 1993.

Hanh, TN. *Present Moment, Wonderful Moment; Mindfulness Verses for Daily Living.* Berkeley, CA: Parallax Press, 1990.

Hatta, T, and M Nakamura. Can antistress music tapes reduce mental stress? *Stress Medicine* 7: 181–184, 1991.

Hillson, TR, and RA Martin. What's so funny about that? The domains-interaction approach as a model of incongruity and resolution in humor. *Motivation and Emotion* 18: 1–29, 1994.

House, JS, C Robbins, and HL Metzner. The association of social relationships and activities with mortality: Prospective evidence from the Tecumseh Community Health Study. *American Journal of Epidemiology* 116: 123–140, 1982.

Jacobson, FM, TA Wehr, DA Sack, SP James, and NE Rosenthal. Seasonal Affective Disorder: A review of the syndrome and its public health implications. *American Journal of Public Health* 77: 57–60, 1987.

Jezova, D, M Vigas, P Tatar, J Jurcovicova, and M Palat. Rise in plasma beta-endorphin and ACTH in response to hyperthermia in sauna. *Hormone and Metabolic Research* 17: 693–694, 1985.

Joseph-Vanderpool, JR, and NE Rosenthal. Phototherapy for Seasonal Affective Disorder. *Drug Therapy*, Jan 1988, pp 57–64.

Jourard, SM. An exploratory study of body-accessibility. *British Journal of Social and Clinical Psychology* 5: 221–231, 1966.

Kuiper, NA, RA Martin, and KA Dance. Sense of humour and enhanced quality of life. *Personality and Individual Differences* 13: 1273–1283, 1992.

Kuiper, NA, and RA Martin. Humor and self-concept. *Humor* 6: 251–270, 1993.

Kuiper, NA, RA Martin, and LJ Olinger. Coping humour, stress, and cognitive appraisals. *Canadian Journal of Behavioural Science* 25: 81–96, 1993.

Lazarus, R. Positive denial: The case for not facing reality. *Psychology Today*, Nov 1979, pp 44–60.

Lexcen, FJ, and RA Hicks. Does cigarette smoking increase sleep problems? *Perceptual and Motor Skills* 77: 16–18, 1993.

Martin, RA, and JP Dobbin. Sense of humor, hassles, and immunoglobulin A: Evidence for a stress-moderating effect of humor. *International Journal of Psychiatry in Medicine* 18: 93–105, 1988.

Martin, RA, and HM Lefcourt. Sense of humor as a moderator of the relation between stressors and moods. *Journal of Personality and Social Psychology* 45: 1313–1324, 1983.

Martin, RA, NA Kuiper, LJ Olinger, and KA Dance. Humor, coping with stress, self-concept, and psychological well-being. *Humor* 6: 89–104, 1993.

Morreall, J. Humor and work. *Humor* 4: 359–373, 1991.

Nezu, AM, CM Nezu, and SE Blissett. Sense of humor as a moderator of the relation between stressful events and psychological distress: A prospective analysis. *Journal of Personality and Social Psychology* 54: 520–525, 1988.

Ornish, D. *Dr. Dean Ornish's Program for Reversing Heart Disease.* New York: Ballantine Books, 1990.

Ornstein, R, and D Sobel. *Healthy Pleasures.* Reading, MA: Addison-Wesley, 1989a.

Ornstein, R, and D Sobel. Healthy pleasures. *American Health*, May 1989b, pp 53–58+.

Overholser, JC. Sense of humor when coping with life stress. *Personality and Individual Differences* 13: 799–804, 1992.

Peele, S, with A Brodsky. *Love and Addiction.* New York: Signet, 1975.

Pennebaker, JW. Putting stress into words: Health, linguistic, and therapeutic implications. *Behavioral Research and Therapy* 31: 539–548, 1993.

Prerost, FJ. Use of humor and guided imagery in therapy to alleviate stress. *Journal of Mental Health Counseling* 10: 16–22, 1988.

Progoff, I. *At a Journal Workshop.* New York: Dialogue House Library, 1975.

Reite, M. Touch, attachment, and health: Is there a relationship? CC Brown (ed). *The Many Facets of Touch.* Skillman, NJ: Johnson & Johnson Baby Products, 1984.

Seaward, BL. *Managing Stress.* Boston: Jones & Bartlett, 1994.

Scherwitz, L, LE Graham, and DM Ornish. Self-involvement and the risk factors for coronary heart disease. *Advances* 2: 6–18, 1985.

Spera, SP, ED Buhrfeind, and JW Pennebaker. Expressive writing and coping with job loss. *Academy of Management Journal* 37: 722–733, 1994.

Spintge, R, and R Droh (eds). *Music and Medicine.* New York: Springer-Verlag, 1983.

Standley, JM. Music research in medical/dental treatment: Meta-analysis and clinical applications. *Journal of Music Therapy* 23: 56–122, 1986.

Steele, CM, and RA Josephs. Drinking your troubles away II: An attention-allocation model of alcohol's effect on psychological stress. *Journal of Abnormal Psychology* 97: 196–205, 1988.

Taylor, SE, and JD Brown. Illusion and well-being: A social psychological perspective on mental health. *Psychological Bulletin* 103: 193–210, 1988.

Tinsley, HEA, and BD Eldredge. Psychological benefits of leisure participation: A taxonomy of leisure activities based on their need-gratifying properties. *Journal of Counseling Psychology* 42: 123–132, 1995.

Ulrich, RS. Natural versus urban scenes: Some psychophysiological effects. *Environment and Behavior* 13: 523–556, 1981.

Van Dale, D, and WHM Saris. Repetitive weight loss and weight regain: Effects of weight reduction, resting metabolic rate, and lipolytic activity before and after exercise and/or diet treatment. *American Journal of Clinical Nutrition* 49: 409–416, 1989.

Vines, G. Secret power of pets. *New Scientist* 140: 30–34, 1993.

Vormbrock, JK, and JM Grossberg. Cardiovascular effects of human-pet dog interactions. *Journal of Behavioral Medicine* 11: 509–517, 1988.

Weiss, SJ. Psychophysiological effects of caregiver touch on incidence of cardiac dysrhythmias. *Heart & Lung* 15: 495–506, 1986.

Weller, L, and O Avinir. Hassles, uplifts, and quality of sleep. *Perceptual and Motor Skills* 76: 571–576, 1993.

White, S, and A Winzelbert. Laughter and stress. *Humor* 5: 343–355, 1992.

chapter **12**

Stress? It Depends on Your Point of View

When a given event, thought, or situation is *perceived* by you to be stressful, a stress response occurs; perception is the link between stressors and your stress response. In this section you will take a closer look at the way you perceive yourself and the world, and at how these perceptions influence the nature of your own personal stress cycle. You can reduce feelings of stress by examining the way you appraise potential stressors and your abilities to cope effectively with them. The stress management techniques presented in this chapter are types of *cognitive intervention*—ways to change your stress response by changing the way you think about stress and stressors. Cognitive intervention techniques have been shown to be very effective stress reducers in a variety of population groups (Banken & Mahone, 1991; Castonguay, Goldfried, Wiser, Raue, & Hayes, 1996; Cheung, 1996; Craske, Maidenberg, & Bystritsky, 1995; Deffenbacher, Lynch, Oetting, & Kemper, 1996; Epstein, Baucom, & Rankin, 1993; Forman, 1990; Gidron & Davidson, 1996; Hellman, Budd, Borysenko, McClelland, & Benson, 1990; Hillenberg & Collins, 1986; Maes, 1987; Woods, 1991; Zionts, 1990).

PERCEPTION AND THE NATURE OF REALITY

Perception refers to your awareness and understanding of things. People behave as though their perceptions are reality, but in truth we usually perceive an incomplete and often somewhat inaccurate picture of events around us. The perception of a given event varies from person to person and is influenced by many factors (Chang, 1996; Lee, Hallahan, & Herzog, 1996). Consider the following example: people walking by a professor and student who are having a serious discussion. One student observer cringes and thinks, "Oh, she is really getting nailed by that professor! I wonder what she did wrong." A second student envies the involvement he perceives to be taking place and thinks, "I wish I could get into meaningful discussions with my professors. They never even give me the time of day!"

Children rarely question the veracity of their perceptions. As people get older, they begin to understand that they may misunderstand. It is a sign of maturity to

255

question the accuracy and completeness of your perceptions, to look for more supporting evidence before deciding a perception is indeed true, and to avoid jumping to conclusions.

PERCEPTION AND STRESS

Man is not disturbed by events, but by the view he takes of them.

EPICTETUS

In this section, we enter the domain of the stress response. Your perception of a given stressor is the first step in this response. While some events, such as the death of a loved one, are almost universally perceived to be stressful, most of the stressors that occur in daily life vary in their stress impact depending upon how you perceive them. Can't find the book you need in the library? On a scale of 1 to 10, how stressful is this? On a bad day it may be at least an 8, or even the proverbial straw that breaks the camel's back. On a good day you might give it a 1, shrug it off, and look for a different source. What happened the last time you spilled your drink all over the table? Did you perceive it to be something awful that should never happen, rant and rave, and get bent out of shape? Or did you remember that these things happen in the best of families, sigh, wipe up the mess, and soon forget it ever happened?

Take a look at the stress log you kept for Chapter 4. How did your perceptions affect your stress response? Were any stressors blown out of proportion? Were any created by a misunderstanding? Did you ever consciously adjust your perceptions to feel better and cope more effectively with stress?

We attribute stress to particular situations and events. We say "That made me angry." "It scared me to death." The implication is that our feelings are directly caused by stressors. In the Student Stress example on the next page, Mark might think that the students whispering in the hallway caused his irritation, frustration, and anger. But in truth, Mark's *perception* of that stressor is the important link between the stressor and his stress response. As psychologist Paul Woods puts it, "A flat tire does not upset your stomach" (Woods, 1987). It is the perception that a

■ STUDENT STRESS

CLASSMATES' PERCEPTIONS

Mark is studying in his room when he becomes aware of voices whispering in the hall. It is almost midnight, and he is upset about a problem set he is working on that is due first thing in the morning. His irritation rises as he focuses on the voices. "They should go talk somewhere else, not right outside my door! It's after quiet hours. I should report them to the residential supervisor. Here I am trying to get my work done, but how can I with all the distractions in this place. It's no wonder I am flunking out of school. I can't get any rest and this stupid professor doesn't realize I have three other courses to do assignments for. I'll never get it all done." As Mark's thoughts race out of control, so do his emotions. Irritation turns to frustration and anger, and a full-blown negative stress response ensues.

Adam is Mark's classmate and is also having a midnight encounter with the same problem set. Let's say his room is just across the hall and that he hears the same voices whispering. Momentarily irritated, Adam realizes he has participated in late night hallway conversations from time to time himself. "Well, at least they are whispering and trying not to bother anyone. Their roommates are probably already asleep, so they went into the hall to talk. It's nice to know I am not the only one who is still awake around here!" Adam calmly asks the students if they can talk somewhere else. They head downstairs to the common room, and Adam turns his attention back to his assignment. His rational thinking has calmed his momentary irritation and he is back to his initial focus, free from the distractions of an inappropriate stress response.

flat tire is a problem that upsets your stomach. Adam's perception of the late night conversation did not trigger a full-blown stress response. By perceiving the situation in a less threatening way, he cut the connection. The whispering students became a minor source of irritation, easily dealt with. In fact, as Adam remembered his own whispered conversations in late night hallways, the situation even had some pleasant associations for him.

PERCEPTION AND STRESS RESISTANCE

Your perception of a stressor determines not only whether a stress response will result but also whether that stress response will be harmful to your health. Remember from Chapter 2 that if you perceive a stressor as something over which you have no control and believe it will probably have negative consequences, your stress response is likely to be physiologically more harmful than a stress response that gears you up for a positive challenge (Dienstbier, 1991; Vogel, 1985). As you evaluate, or appraise, a potential stressor, your thoughts, feelings, and even your physical stress response interact with one another. Negative thoughts cause painful emotions that cause tight muscles that cause more negative thoughts, painful emotions, and more physical discomfort. This cycle can lead to a Pandora's box of stress-related physical and psychological symptoms (Davis, Eshelman, & McKay, 1995; Jacobsen & Butler, 1996; Kabat-Zinn, 1990).

The way you appraise potential stressors and perceive reality determine to a large extent how happy you are. Remember from Chapter 11 that objective life circumstances have very little to do with subjective well-being (Diener & Diener, 1996;

Lykken & Tellegen, 1996; Zika & Chamberlain, 1987). Rather, it is largely your point of view, the way in which you perceive the world and your place in it, that creates your degree of satisfaction. If you perceive yourself to be about where you should be, you will tend to feel satisfied. If you long to be somewhere or someone else, you will feel dissatisfied.

Your perception habits are also the basis of the attitude you reflect to people around you. The attitudes you project influence how others respond to you. If you continually find good reasons to feel angry and hostile, you will push others away, except perhaps other angry people. Over time you will find more unfairness and material for more anger and hostility.

REALITY CHECK: AVOID MAKING MOUNTAINS OUT OF MOLEHILLS

An inappropriate stress response often results from inaccurate perceptions regarding the nature of the stressor or your abilities to deal with it. The most common example of the creation of stress by inaccurate perceptions occurs so frequently that there is a cliche for it: making a mountain out of a molehill. Psychologist Albert Ellis has called it "awfulizing" or "catastrophizing" (Ellis, 1975). You awfulize when you tell yourself a situation is overwhelming or too much to bear. Mark's response to the hallway whispers is an example of awfulizing. He perceived that it was awful for the students to be whispering after quiet hours and that it would make him flunk out of school. How much of this was inherent in the stressor itself? Not much. But Mark's awfulizing turned the event into a source of serious stress.

Most of us awfulize from time to time. A low mark on an assignment means we will flunk the class, graduate (if we don't flunk out first) with a low grade point average, never get into the graduate program or career of our choice, alienate our parents, and spend the rest of our life flipping burgers at the fast food restaurant around the corner. Panic ensues. Usually, however, we correct our thinking momentarily and adopt a more pragmatic and rational perspective: the low mark means we don't understand some of the material and need to do some more studying or get some help. We discuss the problem with friends, maybe even the professor; often find out that half the class got low marks; laugh at our silly awfulizing thoughts; and devise a positive way to cope with the problem.

Calvin and Hobbes   by Bill Watterson

SELECTIVE ABSTRACTION: WHAT YOU SEEK YOU SHALL FIND

Danger arises when negative perception develops into a way of life. A negative outlook dramatically decreases stress resistance and often leads to feelings of chronic stress and the development of stress-related illness. Chronic depression, anxiety, and anger develop when a person tends to perceive events in ways that strengthen such feelings (Butterfield & LeClair, 1988; Rich & Bonner, 1987). Aaron Beck, a psychologist who has written extensively about **cognitive therapy** (using cognitive intervention techniques in a clinical psychotherapy setting), has referred to certain types of negative perception as **selective abstraction** (Beck, 1970). Selective abstraction means focusing on certain characteristics in the environment while overlooking others. Some refer to this kind of perception as **tunnel vision** (Davis et al., 1995). People who are chronically angry tend to focus on the unacceptable behavior of others and look for someone to blame when they find situations unfair or not as they "should be." Anxious people have a habit of anticipating problems and worrying that things will not go well. Depression can result from dwelling on what is not going well combined with feelings of hopelessness and helplessness.

A man is as happy as his mind allows him to be.

ABRAHAM LINCOLN

HABITUAL PERCEPTION: YOUR AUTOMATIC PILOT

Cognitive intervention can help people improve their habitual way of viewing life. The first step is to become aware of habits of perception that may be causing stress by tuning in to your **self-talk,** also known as **automatic thoughts.** Both self-talk (Ellis, 1975) and automatic thoughts (Beck, 1970) refer to that commentary that runs in your head throughout the day. Some psychologists have called this commentary "mind chatter" (Gillespie & Bechtel, 1986). Mind chatter includes phrases, pictures, images, snatches of songs, and even complete sentences that you say to yourself. It runs the gamut from "I can't believe it's Thursday already!" and "The chocolate one looks good" to more emotionally laden images such as being buried in work, and phrases like "I can't handle this," "This job is killing me," and "I'll never make it through this day." Most of your self-talk is benign and is simply your interpretation of and reaction to what's going on. Stress-provoking thoughts are the ones to watch out for because they are associated with painful emotions and reduced stress resistance (Nutt-Williams & Hill, 1996). Automatic thoughts can be very destructive when they reinforce an interpretation of reality that fosters chronic anger, anxiety, or depression.

Reality is relative; we each have our own unique way of seeing the world, of interpreting and judging events around us. We may understand this on a rational level, but we still operate on the assumption that our perceptions are an accurate representation of reality and forget that we may not be perceiving the whole picture. Psychologist Aaron Beck coined the term *automatic thoughts* to emphasize that our mind chatter is perceived as automatic, as though it is simply a response to the environment (Davis et al., 1995). In other words, we forget they are even our thoughts and take these perceptions as reality itself.

Automatic thoughts can be hard to hear at first. They often appear as quick glimpses of phrases or images. Automatic thoughts connected with painful emotions often contain the words should, ought, or must, and usually reflect a judgment that something should be other than it is. The result: guilt, anger, disappointment. "I should spend more time studying." "The professor should be more understanding." "I should get paid more for this job." Destructive automatic thoughts tend to awfulize. The Tuning In exercise on the next page helps you see this.

STRESS AND YOU

TUNING IN: CONNECTING EVENTS AND EMOTIONS

Tuning in to your mind chatter gives you a way to examine the accuracy of your perceptions and helps you discover destructive automatic thoughts. While tuning in takes some practice, all it requires is simple self-observation. Try the following exercise the next time you experience an unpleasant emotion, or think back to an incident in the recent past and try to untangle the thoughts and feelings you experienced. First, describe the situation or event that triggered the stress (A). Next, try to describe the thoughts running through your mind in response to the stressor (B). Then describe your feelings and behavior—what you felt and did (C). Sometimes you might find it easier to complete item B, your thoughts, after describing A and C. This exercise is based on Albert Ellis's A-B-C rational-emotive therapy model (Ellis, 1975).

A. Describe the stressor that "caused" the unpleasant emotion:

B. Write down thoughts you had in response to this stressor:

C. Write down your feelings and behavior:

Automatic thoughts reflect your habitual way of viewing the world. You began learning to interpret reality when you were a baby from your family and caregivers, and later from friends, teachers, and other important people in your life. While your early learning to perceive reality may have happened in a rather random fashion, as an adult you have acquired a more rational outlook and you are able to perceive reality more clearly. Since automatic thoughts are learned, the good news is that they can change. You can identify and question harmful thoughts and replace them with more productive ones that improve the accuracy of your perception and increase your stress resistance. You can take your perception off "automatic pilot" and choose a more scenic and interesting route (Braiker, 1989; Mahoney, 1993).

TUNING IN TAKES PLENTY OF PRACTICE

The idea that reality is relative and that one's perceptions can be questioned is new to many students, and untangling the web of perception, reality, and emotion can be very difficult. In other words, don't worry if the Tuning In exercise is difficult for you. Here is an example to help you understand and apply the exercise in your own life.

During study period for final exams, Sandra invited her boyfriend Elliot over for dinner. Theirs was still a fairly new relationship, and Sandra was anxious that the evening be enjoyable. Unfortunately, Elliot was feeling overloaded with school-work, was regretting his acceptance of Sandra's dinner invitation, and felt he should really stay home and study. Sandra was a straight A student and the work seemed to be easy for her. Elliot felt she would never understand his worries. However, he did not want to hurt her feelings, so he came reluctantly to dinner, his mind preoccupied with his work. Sandra had spent the entire afternoon cleaning her apartment, shopping for groceries, and preparing dinner. She couldn't understand why Elliot seemed so distant and self-absorbed. When she asked if everything was OK, he muttered something about all the work he had to do before next Friday; to Sandra, however, it sounded like he was making excuses rather than discussing a real problem. Sandra was disappointed and hurt when Elliot left shortly after dinner to return to his studies. Here is how she filled out the ABC exercise:

A. *Stressor:* Elliot came to dinner. He was extremely distant and cold, and he left early. He said he had schoolwork to do. I put a lot of energy into making a nice evening for us and he had a bad time. I wanted us to feel close and have fun.

C. *Feelings and behavior:* I'm angry, sad, and worried. I feel rejected and unloved. Since Elliot was acting so withdrawn, I didn't want to share my feelings with him, so I withdrew too. I have worried about this all day.

At this point Sandra replayed the scene in her head and tried to capture her thoughts and pin down her perception of events.

B. *Thoughts:* Maybe he is getting tired of me. He doesn't like me. I'm losing him. I wish we felt close again. I must be doing something wrong. I must not be likable and attractive. Why do my relationships always end so quickly?

REWRITING THE SCRIPT

What do you think? How would you feel if you were Sandra? Certainly her disappointment is understandable. But is she getting the whole picture? What would you have done and thought differently? In the second part of this exercise you practice **cognitive restructuring.** What you restructure is your cognition, or thinking; you revise your perception of the stressor, or your abilities and resources, and in doing so alter your feelings and behavior as well (Matheny, Aycock, Pugh, Curlette, & Cannella, 1986). See exercises on page 262.

COGNITIVE RESTRUCTURING FOR STUDENTS: EXAM SELF-TALK

Exams are a common source of stress for most students. A little nervousness before an exam is fine; that's eustress that gets you aroused for a peak performance and opens the doors of your mind so the muse can visit. But some students experience such extreme distress before and during exams that it interferes with their ability to complete the exam. They get flustered, develop blocks, forget material, and generally lose their ability to concentrate. Exam time is a perfect occasion for awfulizing. The pressure is on, and students may overreact if perfect answers are not immediately forthcoming. If you find yourself doing more poorly on exams than you should given the good preparation you have done, listen in on your exam self-talk.

● EXERCISE

REWRITING SANDRA'S SCRIPT

Review the description of Sandra and Elliot's evening together above. Here again is Sandra's description of what happened.

A. *Stressor:* Elliot came to dinner. He was extremely distant and cold, and he left early. He said he had schoolwork to do. I put a lot of energy into making a nice evening for us and he had a bad time. I wanted us to feel close and have fun.

B. *Thoughts:* Maybe he is getting tired of me. He doesn't like me. I'm losing him. I wish we felt close again. I must be doing something wrong. I must not be likable and attractive. Why do my relationships always end so quickly?

C. *Feelings and behavior:* I'm angry, sad, and worried. I feel rejected and unloved. Since Elliot was acting so withdrawn, I didn't want to share my feelings with him, so I withdrew too. I have worried about this all day.

How would you rewrite Sandra's thoughts to make them more rational and positive? How might this change her feelings?

B. *Sandra's revised thoughts:*

C. *Sandra's revised feelings and behavior:*

Here is how one student rewrote Sandra's script:

B. *Sandra's revised thoughts:* Something sure was bothering Elliot. I wonder if it really was his schoolwork. Why couldn't he talk about it? He never discusses his schoolwork with me. I wish I had asked more questions instead of withdrawing and getting offended, but I was so disappointed. I like him a lot and I'm afraid he'll lose interest in me. Maybe he'll feel more relaxed once exams are over.

C. *Revised feelings and behavior:* Although still disappointed, Sandra feels less rejected and depressed. By temporarily letting go of Elliot, she will give him some breathing room. Sandra decides to pursue activities with other friends during exam week and invite Elliot over again when he has finished his exams.

◆ STRESS AND YOU

PART TWO: REVISING YOUR THOUGHTS AND FEELINGS

Someone else's imperfect thinking is much easier to revise than your own "normal" response. But try. Go back to the situation you described on page 260 and try rewriting your script. You may need to rewrite the stressor in even more "realistic" terms as well, trying to remove your irrational perceptions and describe only what really happened (de Moor, 1988).

A. *Stressor:*

B. *Revised thoughts:*

C. *Revised feelings and behavior:*

Some examples of negative self-talk are listed in the exercise on pages 264–265. See whether you can change them to more positive statements, and use these statements yourself the next time you are in an exam stress situation.

THOUGHT STOPPING

Some students find that a simple technique called thought stopping is helpful for stress-provoking, repetitive automatic thoughts. If you have identified certain negative thoughts that recur frequently, you might wish to try thought stopping. When you realize that you are slipping into an old familiar negative thought, simply say to yourself "STOP!" or "Stop this thought." Change the channel to a more positive station. You may be surprised at how much control you have over your thinking.

REACHING DEEPER: IRRATIONAL BELIEFS

You may have wondered, as you revised the fictitious thoughts in the exercises above, whether rewriting the script is just a Band-Aid job. The language sounds stilted and phony. It's textbook writing, not your own voice. Can rewriting the words really change your feelings? Yes. Maybe not right away. But simply replacing the negative words that lead to painful emotions with more positive and realistic words is a start, even if you don't quite yet believe what you are telling yourself (McKay, Davis, & Fanning, 1981; Steinmetz, Blankenship, Brown, Hall, & Miller, 1980). After a while, you start to believe these thoughts. Cognitive restructuring starts to feel more natural. It gets easier to reframe reality, to see events in a more positive way; you feel less threatened by demands. Your stress resistance is increasing.

As you observe your mind chatter, you will uncover patterns of automatic thoughts. Certain themes will emerge. For example, you may discover that you tend to put yourself down when things are not going well. Or perhaps you complain and think it is awful when you have to work hard. Thoughts that cause painful emotions often reflect underlying **irrational beliefs** (Ellis, 1975; Davis et al., 1995). An irrational belief is an unreasonable concept acquired from your upbringing or somewhere along the line. It is something you have assumed to be true but does in fact not really mesh with reality. Not all irrational beliefs cause stress. Those that do generally fall into two categories: (1) beliefs that the world or someone or some-

The real voyage of discovery consists not in seeking new landscapes but in having new eyes.

MARCEL PROUST

● EXERCISE

REWRITING EXAM SELF-TALK

The following are examples of exam awfulizing. The first three statements are thoughts that come while you are waiting to start the exam; the last three occur as you begin to write the answers. Imagine you are well prepared for the exam and revise the thoughts so that they are more realistic and positive.

1. Everyone else is talking about the material before the exam starts. There are so many things I don't know! I probably studied the wrong stuff! Everyone else is much better prepared than I am. I should have studied more for this.

   Revised:

2. I have to get a good grade on this exam. If I don't do well I might not get into graduate school. My whole life will be ruined!

   Revised:

3. Exams are so stupid! Why should I memorize all this stuff? I'm just going to forget it in a few weeks anyway. I hate this school.

   Revised:

4. Oh my God! This test is way too long! I'll never get through in time!

   Revised:

5. Oh no! I don't know the answer to the first question. Oh, what will I do? I know I'm going to fail this exam.

   Revised:

6. Three essay questions! I hate essay questions. I never know what the teacher wants on these.

   Revised:

Of course there are many ways to correct these statements. Your goal is to create self-talk that will encourage the mental sharpness required to do well on exams. That means eliminating awfulizing and focusing on the positive. Here are some of the revisions students have come up with:

Exam Self-Talk

1. Everyone else is talking about the material before the exam starts. There are so many things I don't know! I probably studied the wrong stuff! Everyone else is much better prepared than I am. I should have studied more for this.

   Revised: Everyone else is talking about the material before the exam starts. It makes me nervous that some are mentioning details I didn't memorize. I did my best to study the right stuff. Anyway, I must make the best of it now and focus on how much I do know.

2. I have to get a good grade on this exam. If I don't do well I might not get into graduate school. My whole life will be ruined!

   Revised: I sure would like to do well on this exam since this course is so important for my major and I need to do well to get into graduate school. But there are other things in life besides school. I'll do the best I can and hope I do well.

3. Exams are so stupid! Why should I memorize all this stuff? I'm just going to forget it in a few weeks anyway. I hate this school.

   Revised: I wish I didn't have to take exams; they seem so pointless. Oh well, that's the way school is. I did learn a lot in this course and will give these questions my best shot.

4. Oh my God! This test is way too long! I'll never get through in time!

   Revised: This test has a lot of pages. Just in case I don't have time to complete the whole thing, I'd better start with the questions that get the most points and keep track of the time.

(Continued)

EXERCISE *(Continued)*

5. Oh no! I don't know the answer to the first question. Oh, what will I do? I know I'm going to fail this exam.

   Revised: Hmmm. This first question is difficult. I'll go through the exam and answer the questions I know first and then come back to the others. Maybe more answers will come to me.

6. Three essay questions! I hate essay questions. I never know what the teacher wants on these.

   Revised: Oh joy, oh rapture. Essay questions. (Blech!) I'm not gonna cry, I'm not gonna cry. I'll do these at the end after I'm warmed up. One way or another this exam will be all over in an hour, and by next week I'll be on vacation!

---

thing should be different from the way it, he, or she is, and (2) beliefs that one's perceptions are factual rather than subjective (Rorer, 1991). Irrational beliefs often reflect cultural stereotypes; they may be distortions of these stereotypes. For example, you may have absorbed the teaching that it is wrong to be selfish, that you should always put others first. Maybe your parents always put their needs on hold and kept their resentment bottled up; now you unconsciously do the same.

When your irrational beliefs run up against reality, conflict results and you feel stressed. Consider perfectionists. If you believe everything you do must be perfect, you are sure to be disappointed. It is simply impossible to achieve perfection. If you believe less than perfect is equivalent to failure, you will be afraid to try anything new. Perfectionists often suffer from low self-esteem, since they feel worthless when they fail to achieve their impossible standards (Burns, 1980; Ferrari, Johnson, & McCown, 1995). Remember from Chapter 7 that fear of failure and other irrational beliefs are a common source of procrastination. The following is a list of common irrational beliefs.

Common Irrational Beliefs

1. It is an absolute necessity for an adult to have love and approval from peers, family, and friends.
2. You must be unfailingly competent and almost perfect in all you undertake.
3. Certain people are evil, wicked, and villainous, and should be punished.
4. It is horrible when people and things are not the way you would like them to be.
5. External events cause most human misery—people simply react as events trigger their emotions.
6. You should feel fear or anxiety about anything that is unknown, uncertain, or potentially dangerous.
7. It is easier to avoid than to face difficulties and responsibilities.
8. The past has a lot to do with determining the present.
9. Happiness can be achieved by inaction, passivity, and endless leisure.
10. You are helpless and have no control over what you experience or feel.
11. People are fragile and should never be hurt.
12. Good relationships are based on mutual sacrifice and a focus on giving.
13. If you don't go to great lengths to please others, they will abandon or reject you.

14. When people disapprove of you, it invariably means you are wrong or bad.
15. Happiness, pleasure, and fulfillment can only occur in the presence of others, and being alone is horrible.
16. There is a perfect love, a perfect relationship.
17. You shouldn't have to feel pain; you are entitled to a good life.
18. Your worth as a person depends on how much you achieve and produce.
19. Anger is automatically bad and destructive.
20. It is bad or wrong to be selfish. (Davis, Eshelman, & McKay, 1995. Reprinted with permission by New Harbinger Publications, Oakland, CA 94609)

The mistaken assumptions listed in Chapter 8 are additional examples of irrational beliefs that lead to nonassertive or aggressive behavior, poor communication, and stress.

Do any strike a chord for you? Maybe you have some that are not listed here. Remember, you are concerned here with beliefs that increase feelings of stress and may be associated with automatic thoughts. You may never have verbalized these thoughts before, but some of these irrational beliefs may be subconscious guiding forces. Many studies have documented the link between irrational beliefs and feelings of stress (Bonner & Rich, 1991; Butterfield & LeClair, 1988; Hart, Turner, Hittner, Cardozo, & Paras, 1991; Rich & Bonner, 1987; Zingle & Anderson, 1990). People with more irrational beliefs see the glass as half empty, believing it *should* be full. They are more likely to appraise daily hassles as more stressful than do people with fewer irrational beliefs (Lazarus, 1991; Vestre & Burnis, 1987). People with irrational beliefs experience life in general as more stressful and have more negative emotions. Let's look at an example of how irrational beliefs lead to distorted perception and automatic thoughts that in turn trigger painful emotions and poor coping behavior.

STUDENT STRESS

ANNA'S IRRATIONAL BELIEFS

Anna and Justin have lived together for almost two years. Both attend college, have part-time jobs, and share household duties. It's Friday afternoon, and Anna is tired. She is looking forward to a quiet evening at home, alone with Justin. On her way home, she stops at the grocery store and picks up some food to make one of the easy meals Justin likes best. She imagines the two of them going over events of the day and planning weekend activities, maybe reading for a while in the evening before an early bedtime. When she arrives home, she is very disappointed to find that a friend of Justin's has just stopped by unannounced for a visit. David lives over an hour away so he and Justin do not often have a chance to get together. Although Anna usually enjoys seeing David, she heaves a heavy sigh as she realizes that the evening is going to take a different direction from the one she had planned.

After greeting David and Justin, Anna hurries to the kitchen to unpack the groceries. She starts clenching her teeth as she thinks to herself. "Why tonight? I have absolutely no energy, but now I have to cook dinner and clean up after three of us. I've got to be cheerful and entertaining when all I feel like doing is going to bed. David should know better than to stop by unannounced when we are so busy. He should know I'm tired on Friday night. And now this visit is going to give me a headache."

What's wrong with this picture? Take a look at Anna's self-talk. What are some of the irrational beliefs that seem to be causing stress for her? Anna is first of all distressed that things are not as they should be; it is horrible that things are not as she would like them to be. Instead of switching to a more positive gear, Anna continues to feel distressed as she focuses on how things should be but aren't. She also seems to feel that it is her job to step into the role of perfect hostess—that she must be entertaining and cheerful and shoulder the responsibility for cooking and cleaning up. Perhaps she is playing out some hostess stereotype, grudgingly doing her duty while resenting the burden of it all. And just to prove to herself that she has a right to be annoyed, she gives herself a headache.

Fortunately, Anna is taking a stress management class, and before her jaw tension develops into an uncontrollable pounding tension headache, she takes a deep breath and examines her self-talk. "Wait a minute," she says. "Let's reframe this picture. David's visit is not giving me a headache. I am giving myself this headache by focusing on my disappointment. Let's replay this scene and find a more positive option." Anna takes a problem-solving approach and realizes that her irrational beliefs had dictated an option she would not enjoy: playing cheerful hostess, waiting on Justin and David. Remember from Chapter 5 that the most important part of solving problems is a positive problem orientation and a creative mind. Irrational beliefs limit your ability to see problems and your options clearly. Revise Anna's thinking in the following exercise.

● EXERCISE

REWRITING ANNA'S SCRIPT

Revise Anna's self-talk to reflect more rational thinking and help her find a better way to solve her problem and cope with the stressor.

Anna's new self-talk:

Anna's new feelings and behavior:

One student rewrote Anna's evening like this:

Anna's new self-talk:
Well, there goes my quiet evening with Justin. What should we do now? I'm too tired to cook dinner and clean up. I'll see if they will help me with dinner and clean up, but they probably want to sit around and talk about motorcycles. I know! Let's order a pizza; then nobody has to cook or clean.

Anna's new feelings and behavior:
Without the burden of disappointment, Anna is able to enjoy the evening with Justin and David. They all chip in for a pizza and share the clean-up chores.

CHALLENGING IRRATIONAL BELIEFS

When you are rewriting your self-talk script, it is also a good idea to try to uncover the underlying irrational beliefs that may have led you astray. Anna tries to write the irrational belief that was driving her in the wrong direction:

Irrational belief: It is the girlfriend's job to be the perfect, cheerful hostess when her boyfriend's friends drop in. She must not admit she is tired or ask for help. A good girlfriend will pull together a delicious home-cooked meal on the spur of the moment, set a beautiful table, clean up all the dishes, and make the whole production look easy and effortless.

Once the irrational belief is pulled out of the psychic darkness, turned into a sentence or paragraph, and put down on paper, it may start to look a little silly in the light of day. The next step is to examine the belief with your rational mind. Ask yourself the following questions (Davis et al., 1995):

1. Is there any reason to think this belief is true?
2. What evidence suggests this belief might not be true?
3. What is the worst thing that could happen to me if I reject this belief?
4. What good things might happen if I reject this belief?

After you have examined the validity and consequences of the irrational belief, you can create a new belief to take the place of the irrational belief. Let's see how Anna followed this process.

1. Is there any reason to think this belief is true?
   Well, my mother was always a good hostess and made people feel welcome in our home. I think it is nice to make friends feel welcome.

2. What evidence suggests this belief might not be true?
   But I guess it is not necessarily true that I have to put on the perfect hostess act to make friends feel welcome in our home. I don't think it is really my "job" to magically pull together a meal, do all the cleanup, and make the whole thing look effortless. Anyway, it's not possible, especially on a Friday night after a long week of school and work!

3. What is the worst thing that could happen to me if I reject this belief?
   Justin won't love me as much because I won't be the perfect girlfriend. Oops, this sounds like another irrational belief. What could really happen . . . I think it would be worse to play the martyred girlfriend! If I don't play the perfect hostess, well, I might feel like a failure.

4. What good things might happen if I reject this belief?
   I won't mind having people visit. I'll enjoy Justin and our friends more. Justin won't assume I can always play the perfect hostess—he'll get a better sense of who I really am. He might as well find out now! We will work out ways to have friends over that don't mean I do all the work and then feel resentful or get tension headaches.

Now Anna writes a new belief to take the place of her old irrational one. Compare the two.

Irrational belief: It is the girlfriend's job to be the perfect, cheerful hostess when her boyfriend's friends drop in. She must not admit she is tired or ask for help. A good girlfriend will pull together a delicious home-cooked meal on the spur of the moment, set a beautiful table, clean up all the dishes, and make the whole production look easy and effortless.

New belief: Justin and I want our friends to feel welcome in our home. A good girl-friend takes care of herself and her needs, as well as anticipating what will help everyone have fun together. People can get together and have fun even without a "perfect hostess" present!

Questioning and changing your irrational beliefs can lead to a remarkable increase in your stress resistance (Matheny et al., 1986; Woods, 1991). If you use the Tuning In exercise on page 260 to examine at least one stressful event every day and then question the irrational beliefs behind it, you will probably experience a reduction in stress symptoms in about two or three weeks (Davis et al., 1995).

Students sometimes worry that reframing events in a more positive fashion is artificial and phony. Some agree with Anna that David should call first. A few think Anna should let the men know that she is angry and make David go home. Some students feel that flexibility means compromising your beliefs and principles. We argue here that flexibility and compromise are essential for increasing your stress resistance. We also recommend choosing your battles; some principles should not be compromised. But a friend dropping in unannounced? Anna's initial disappointment is understandable, but she will only make herself miserable if she is unable to adjust her attitude. By all means let David know you would appreciate a call ahead next time. But given that David is going to stay for the evening, Anna needs to make the best of the situation.

Cognitive restructuring should not turn into repression. Cognitive restructuring begins with acknowledging your thoughts and feelings, not denying them, but then examining them for irrational and stress-inducing content. Anna would *not* change her self-talk to say, "Fantastic! I am so happy to spend the evening with Justin and David! I will happily cook them dinner and play the gracious hostess! Aren't we lucky David stopped by!" At its best, cognitive restructuring is really self-observation that questions and subsequently short-circuits stress-producing beliefs and self-talk.

OPTIMISM AND STRESS RESISTANCE: WHAT YOU SEE IS WHAT YOU GET

So far we have discussed revising self-talk and underlying beliefs to bring them more into line with reality. But stress resistance improves even more when you can take the process one step further and use the cognitive restructuring process to create some rose-colored glasses with which to view the world. Studies have shown that stress-resistant people consciously develop the habit of perceiving potential stressors in ways that give life meaning and give them a sense of control (Ornstein, & Sobel, 1989). They look for reasons to be happy and satisfied with life, imperfect as it is.

In some ways, the development of stress resistance is like the quest for happiness. What makes people happy? Money? Many rich people are miserably depressed. Good looks? Plenty of suicidal models. Getting a good job? Look at all the stressed-out "success stories." No, objective life circumstances do not define happiness. Perception does.

Happy people are optimists. They see themselves as doing OK, making the best of what they've got. Although they may have lofty goals, they find their progress toward their goals acceptable. Instead of bemoaning what is wrong with the world, they focus on what is right. They expect good things to happen to them, and this view makes them open to opportunity. When misfortune strikes, as it does in everyone's life, optimists recover more quickly because they find lessons in adversity that contribute to life's meaning. Remember from Chapter 5 that one of the most effec-

● EXERCISE

CHANGING IRRATIONAL BELIEFS

Consider now the irrational beliefs that may be causing stress for you. Can you think of a situation in which your irrational beliefs got you into trouble? Can you find a link between irrational beliefs and negative self-talk in your own life? Try rewriting the irrational beliefs to reflect a more realistic and positive outlook. For example:

Irrational belief:
It is an absolute necessity for an adult to have love and approval from peers, family, and friends.

Revised: I want my peers, family, and friends to love me and approve of the things I do, but I realize that I can't always please everyone all the time. I will do my best, do what I feel in my heart is right, and accept the fact that not everyone will always agree with me.

Irrational belief:
You must be unfailingly competent and almost perfect in all you undertake.

Revised: I will try to do my best, and learn from my mistakes.

Now you try it:

Irrational belief:

Revised:

Irrational belief:

Revised:

tive coping methods for situations that can't be changed is positive reappraisal (Lazarus, 1991). Stress-resistant people are able to see demands as challenges and to gather strength from their ability to see the cloud's silver lining. Just as selective abstraction can reinforce depression, so can it sustain happiness. One student told us she fosters her optimistic attitude by doing the following before going to bed: She asks herself three questions: What did I learn today? What was the nicest thing

Questioning your irrational beliefs improves communication skills and increases stress resistance.

that happened today? What was the funniest thing that happened today? She controls her outlook by controlling her focus.

If you look for injustice and horror, you can certainly find it. Just turn on the evening news. War, famine, disease, and death are all around. Life is not fair. Every person experiences unwanted events such as illness, rejection, loss; things are often not the way "we want them to be." When we respond to stressors,

---

▲ ACTION PLAN

USING COGNITIVE INTERVENTION TO REDUCE STRESS

Take some time to think about the roles your self-talk, irrational beliefs, general attitude, and outlook play in your stress cycle. Begin by describing what you are already doing well; then describe two changes you would like to make to reduce self-created stress. Describe some realistic steps that would help you make these changes.

1. Ways in which my self-talk and outlook are already increasing my stress resistance:

2. Changes that would improve my stress resistance:

   Goal 1. _____

   Goal 2. _____

3. Action steps that will help me achieve Goal 1:

4. Action steps that will help me achieve Goal 2:

STUDENT STRESS

MICHAEL'S ACTION PLAN

Michael was in his fifth year of college, having changed majors midstream and failed two courses. An average student, he worked hard and organized his time well, but he got mostly Cs in his courses. He hoped to graduate at the end of the year. Now he had a job search on top of his course load. "This job search alone is worth three credits," he often thought to himself. His academic struggles over the past few years had had a significant impact on his self-confidence, and he was very worried about finding a good job. He found himself saying, "You can't get a job without experience and you can't get experience without a job. What am I going to do? Who's going to want a C student?" As spring approached, he spent more and more time worrying until he felt like the unemployment cloud was hanging over him most of the time.

Worried about his worrying, Michael enrolled in a stress management course. The material on the roll of perception in the stress cycle really hit home for him. "Mountains out of molehills—that's my specialty. I am creating my own stress by worrying about things too much." As Michael tuned into his self-talk, he found it full of anxiety about the future and statements reinforcing low self-esteem. "I feel like I have no control, and that makes me nervous," Michael concluded. "I think my worrying is an attempt to gain some control, but it doesn't work. It just makes things worse."

Three irrational beliefs stood out as seeming rational to Michael. He had always strived to do things well (trying to be almost perfect), experienced anxiety about the unknown, and felt that his worth de-

pended upon how much he achieved and produced. "No wonder this job search is driving me crazy!" he thought. "I value achievement and production and fear the unknown." Here is how Michael completed his action plan:

1. *Ways in which my self-talk and outlook are already increasing my stress resistance:*
   I have a good sense of humor and can even laugh at myself.
   I think I am good at tuning into my self-talk and can be honestly critical of my thoughts.

2. *Changes that would improve my stress resistance:*
   Goal 1. Change worrying to problem solving. Channel worrying into a more productive direction.
   Goal 2. Change negative thinking with thought stopping and positive self-talk.

3. *Action steps that will help me achieve Goal 1:*
   1. Use material from problem-solving chapter to plan my job search.
   2. Work with a career counselor to get some help with my job search.

4. *Action steps that will help me achieve Goal 2:*
   1. Revise my irrational beliefs and repeat them to myself when I start worrying.
   2. Use thought stopping when I catch myself worrying.
   3. Replace worrying with positive thoughts like "I'm doing my best. Things will work out fine."
   4. Dad always says "Trust the universe."

whether major life events or daily hassles, with the perception "I can't stand it. . . . It shouldn't be. . . . It isn't fair," we are denying reality. Stress resistance (wisdom, too) begins with an acceptance that life has its share of problems. While we will do everything we can to solve the problems and cope effectively with the stressors that come our way, many of these problems cannot be changed. Sometimes the only thing we can change is our attitude, our point of view (Chapman, 1987). We can change ourselves so that we are more compassionate and loving toward ourselves and others. We can emphasize the positive aspects of our lives. We can look for meaning, beauty, love, and peace, and appreciate them when we find them (Barber, 1984). We can use our sense of humor to decrease anxiety. And maybe, with our courage and ability to weather the storms of stress, just maybe, we can even change the world.

SUMMARY

1. Perception is the link between stressors and your stress response. You can reduce feelings of stress by changing the way you appraise potential stressors and evaluate your abilities to cope effectively with them.

2. Cognitive intervention means changing your stress response by changing the way you think about stress and stressors.

3. While some events are almost universally perceived to be stressful, most of the stressors that occur in daily life vary in their stress impact, depending upon how you perceive them.

4. Your perception of a stressor determines not only whether a stress response will result but also whether that stress response will be harmful to your health. For example, if you perceive a stressor as something over which you have no control and believe it will probably have negative consequences, your stress response is likely to be more harmful physiologically than a stress response that gears you up for a positive challenge.

5. The way you appraise potential stressors and perceive reality determine to a large extent how happy you are.

6. "Awfulizing" or "catastrophizing" means perceiving a stressor to be much worse than it really is.

7. A negative outlook dramatically decreases stress resistance and often leads to feelings of chronic stress and the development of stress-related illness.

8. Selective abstraction means focusing on certain characteristics in the environment while overlooking others.

9. The terms *self-talk, automatic thoughts,* and *mind chatter* refer to the commentary that runs in your mind throughout the day. They include phrases, ideas, stories, pictures, images, snatches of songs, and so forth. People perceive their automatic thoughts as an accurate representation of reality.

10. Automatic thoughts that are connected with painful emotions often contain the words *should, ought,* or *must* and usually reflect a judgment that something should be other than it is.

11. Cognitive intervention techniques are based on the notion that you can identify and question harmful thoughts and stop them or replace them with more productive ones.

12. Thought stopping helps interrupt stress-provoking, repetitive automatic thoughts. When you become aware of a negative thought, simply say to yourself "STOP!" or "Stop this thought."

13. Irrational beliefs are unreasonable concepts that you hold to be true but in fact do not mesh with reality. Irrational beliefs that cause stress usually hold that (1) the world or someone or something should be different from the way it, he, or she is, or (2) one's perceptions are factual rather than subjective. They often reflect cultural stereotypes or may be distortions of these stereotypes.

14. Challenging and changing irrational beliefs can reduce negative self-talk and increase stress resistance.

15. Stress-resistant people consciously cultivate the habit of perceiving potential stressors in ways that give life meaning and themselves a sense of control. Cognitive restructuring techniques can be used to cultivate an optimistic outlook.

REFERENCES

Banken, JA, and CH Mahone. Brief cognitive behavior therapy in an undergraduate pilot student: A case report. *Aviation, Space, and Environmental Medicine* 62: 1078–1080, 1991.

Barber, TX. Hypnosis, deep relaxation, and active relaxation: Data, theory, and clinical applications. RL Woolfolk and PM Lehrer (eds). *Principles and Practice of Stress Management,* New York: Guilford Press, 1984.

Beck, AT. Cognitive therapy: Nature and relation to behavior therapy. *Behavior Therapy* 1: 184–200, 1970.

Bonner, RL, and AR Rich. Predicting vulnerability to hopelessness: A longitudinal analysis. *The Journal of Nervous and Mental Disease* 179: 29–32, 1991.

Braiker, HB. The power of self-talk. *Psychology Today,* Dec 1989, pp 23–27.

Burns, DD. The perfectionist's script for self-defeat. *Psychology Today,* Nov 1980, pp 34–46+.

Butterfield, PS, and S LeClair. Cognitive characteristics of bulimic and drug-abusing women. *Addictive Behaviors* 13: 131–138, 1988.

Castonguay, LG, MR Goldfried, S Wiser, PJ Raue, and AM Hayes. Predicting the effect of cognitive therapy for depression: A study of unique and common factors. *Journal of Consulting and Clinical Psychology* 64: 497–504, 1996.

Chang, EC. Cultural differences in optimism, pessimism, and coping: Predictors of subsequent adjustment in Asian American and Caucasian American college students. *Journal of Counseling Psychology* 43: 113–123, 1996.

Chapman, EN. *Attitude: Your Most Priceless Possession.* Los Altos, CA: Crisp Publications, 1987.

Cheung, S-K. Cognitive-behaviour therapy for marital conflict: Refining the concept of attribution. *Journal of Family Therapy* 18: 183–203, 1996.

Craske, MG, E Maidenberg, and A Bystritsky. Brief cognitive-behavioral versus nondirective therapy for panic disorder. *Journal of Behavioral Therapy and Experimental Psychiatry* 26: 113–120, 1995.

Davis, M, ER Eshelman, and M McKay. *The Relaxation and Stress Reduction Workbook.* Oakland, CA: New Harbinger Publications, 1995.

Deffenbacher, JL, RS Lynch, ER Oetting, and CC Kemper. Anger reduction in early adolescents. *Journal of Counseling Psychology* 43: 149–157, 1996.

de Moor, W. A Rational-Emotive "A-B-C" model of emotional disturbances: A stress model. *Psychotherapy in Private Practice* 6: 21–33, 1988.

Diener, E, and C Diener. Most people are happy. *Psychological Science* 7: 181–185, 1996.

Dienstbier, RA. Behavioral correlates of sympathoadrenal reactivity: The toughness model. *Medicine and Science in Sports and Exercise* 23: 846–852, 1991.

Ellis, A. *A New Guide to Rational Living.* North Hollywood, CA: Wilshire Books, 1975.

Epstein, N, DH Baucom, and LA Rankin. Treatment of marital conflict: A cognitive-behavioral approach. *Clinical Psychology Review* 13: 45–57, 1993.

Ferrari, JR, JL Johnson, and WG McCown. *Procrastination and Task Avoidance.* New York: Plenum Press, 1995.

Forman, SG. Rational-Emotive Therapy: Contributions to teacher stress management. *School Psychology Review* 19: 315–321, 1990.

Gidron, Y, and K Davidson. Development and preliminary testing of a brief intervention for modifying CHD-predictive hostility components. *Journal of Behavioral Medicine* 19: 203–220, 1996.

Gillespie, PR, and L Bechtel. *Less Stress in 30 Days.* New York: New American Library, 1986.

Hart, KE, SH Turner, JB Hittner, SR Cardozo, and KC Paras. Life stress and anger: Moderating effects of Type A irrational beliefs. *Personality and Individual Differences* 12: 557–560, 1991.

Hellman, CJC, M Budd, J Borysenko, DC McClelland, and H Benson. A study of the effectiveness of two group behavioral medicine interventions for patients with psychosomatic complaints. *Behavioral Medicine* 16: 165–173, 1990.

Hillenberg, JB, and FL Collins. The contribution of progressive relaxation and cognitive coping training in stress management programs. *The Behavior Therapist* 9: 147–149, 1986.

Jacobsen, PB, and RW Butler. Relation of cognitive coping and catastrophizing to acute pain and analgesic use following breast cancer surgery. *Journal of Behavioral Medicine* 19: 17–29, 1996.

Kabat-Zinn, J. *Full-catastrophe Living.* New York: Dell Publishing, 1990.

Lazarus, RS. Progress on a cognitive-motivational-relational theory of emotion. *American Psychologist* 46: 819–834, 1991.

Lee, F, M Hallahan, and T Herzog. Explaining real-life events: How culture and domain shape attributions. *Personality and Social Psychology Bulletin* 22: 732–741, 1996.

Lykken, D, and A Tellegen. Happiness is a stochastic phenomenon. *Psychological Science* 7: 186–189, 1996.

Maes, S. Reducing emotional distress in chronic patients, a cognitive approach. *Communication and Cognition* 20: 261–276, 1987.

Mahoney, MJ. Theoretical developments in the cognitive psychotherapies. *Journal of Consulting and Clinical Psychology* 61: 187–193, 1993.

Matheny, KB, DW Aycock, JL Pugh, WL Curlette, and KAS Cannella. Stress Coping: A qualitative and quantitative synthesis with implications for treatment. *The Counseling Psychologist* 14: 499–549, 1986.

McKay, M, M Davis, and P Fanning. *Thoughts and Feelings: The Art of Cognitive Stress Intervention.* Oakland, CA: New Harbinger Publications, 1981.

Nutt-Williams, E, and CE Hill. The relationship between self-talk and therapy process variables for novice therapists. *Journal of Counseling Psychology* 43: 170–177, 1996.

Ornstein, R, and D Sobel. *Healthy Pleasures.* Reading, MA: Addison Wesley, 1989.

Rich, AR, and RL Bonner. Interpersonal moderators of depression among college students. *Journal of College Student Personnel* 28: 337–342, 1987.

Rorer, LG. A modern epistemological basis for Rational-Emotive Theory. *Psychotherapy in Private Practice* 8: 153–157, 1991.

Steinmetz, J, J Blankenship, L Brown, D Hall, and G Miller. *Managing Stress Before It Manages You.* Palo Alto, CA: Bull Publishing Co., 1980.

Vestre, ND, and JJ Burnis. Irrational beliefs and the impact of stressful life events. *Journal of Rational-Emotive Therapy* 5: 183–188, 1987.

Vogel, WH. Coping, stress, stressors, and health consequences. *Neuropsychobiology* 13: 129–135, 1985.

Woods, PJ. Reductions in Type A behavior, anxiety, anger, and physical illness as related to changes in irrational beliefs: Results of a demonstration project in industry. *Journal of Rational-Emotive Therapy* 5: 213–237, 1987.

Woods, PJ. Do you really want to maintain that a flat tire can upset your stomach? Using the findings of the psychophysiology of stress to bolster the argument that people are not directly disturbed by events. *Journal of Rational-Emotive Therapy* 5: 149–161, 1991.

Zika, S, and K Chamberlain. Relation of hassles and personality to subjective well-being. *Journal of Personality and Social Psychology* 53: 155–162, 1987.

Zingle, HW, and SC Anderson. Irrational beliefs and teacher stress. *Canadian Journal of Education* 15: 445–449, 1990.

Zionts, P. Coping with self-defeating personal feelings. *Focus on Autistic Behavior* 5: 1–13, 1990.

chapter 13

Self-Esteem

Feeling good about yourself increases your stress resistance in many ways. When you have the self-confidence that results from a healthy self-esteem, you can get into the flow of life. Instead of feeling blocked by self-consciousness, you can focus instead on the challenges at hand and solve problems more effectively. Having faith in yourself enhances your ability to do your best, and this improves your performance and helps you feel successful. Feeling successful in turn reinforces your positive self-esteem. When your self-esteem is strong, mountains become molehills. A positive self-regard attracts others; when you are happier with yourself, you are happier with life and are a pleasure to be with. A healthy self-esteem is essential to clear communication. When you value yourself, you value your thoughts and feelings and can express them more clearly to others. A positive self-esteem allows you to give more of yourself and enjoy other people. Best of all, a positive self-regard gives you freedom, the freedom to try new things, to make the most of opportunities, to be the best you can be, and to get the most out of life.

SELF-CONCEPT AND SELF-ESTEEM

Most of us use the term *self-esteem* to refer to our basic self-regard—how we feel about ourselves. The word *esteem* means a favorable opinion or judgment. In this section, the term *self-esteem* refers to what psychologists call **global self-esteem,** which means a general sense of self-worth. Self-esteem is the evaluative component of **self-concept,** which refers to a broader concept of who we are (Blascovich & Tomaka, 1991; Byrne, 1996; Campbell, 1990). Self-concept is how we might describe ourselves; self-esteem is our evaluation of this description. For example, a person might believe that he is a poor dancer, but this part of his self-concept may have little or no influence on his self-esteem, unless he places a high value on dancing skill. A person who feels socially inept might feel his inability to shine on the dance floor contributes to his social inadequacy. In this example, the concept of being a poor dancer contributes to low self-esteem.

Sometimes people are interested in self-esteem in specific areas. You might consider yourself very competent in certain areas but less able in others. For example, you might have a great deal of confidence in your scholastic ability but feel shy and unsure of yourself in social situations. Or maybe you're not doing so well in

school, but the kids on the basketball team you volunteer to coach are having a terrific experience. Researchers have suggested several important areas of self-esteem, including social confidence, scholastic ability, appearance, and physical ability (Fleming & Courtney, 1984). Self-esteem in the areas of career choice and job performance are also important. All areas contribute to your global self-esteem. The more you value the area, the greater will be its contribution. Most of the information presented in this chapter can be applied to both global and situational self-esteem problems.

SELF-ESTEEM AND YOUR PERCEPTION OF STRESS

Like most of the other topics in this book, self-esteem influences many parts of the stress cycle. It is included in this section on perception because its effects are felt most strongly here. You have learned that your perception of the demands you are facing determines whether you interpret them as stressors or not. Similarly, your perceptions of yourself and your abilities influence your appraisal of your ability to cope effectively with a challenge. Suppose you have a paper to write. You know by now that writing a paper does not inherently cause stress. The stress comes when you *perceive* that you lack the resources and ability to cope effectively with the demands of writing that paper. People with low self-esteem are more likely to underestimate their abilities, which makes the demand seem more stressful.

SELF-ESTEEM, COPING ABILITY, AND STRESS

I'd never join a club that would have me as a member.

GROUCHO MARX

Self-esteem is directly related to your ability to cope effectively with stress. Low self-esteem makes demands seem more stressful, and people with low self-esteem are more likely than others to experience higher levels of fear, which increase their anxiety and inhibit their problem-solving ability. Poor coping skills mean stress. Low self-esteem has been associated with many forms of stress, including loneliness (Peplau & Perlman, 1982), social anxiety (Leary, 1983), depression (Flett, Hewitt, Blankstein, & O'Brien, 1991; Flett, Hewitt, & Mittelstaedt, 1991; McLennan, 1987; Tarlow & Haaga, 1996), substance abuse (Caplan et al., 1992), eating disorders (Frederick & Grow, 1996), job burnout (Golembiewski & Kim, 1989), and alienation (Johnson, 1973). Students with low self-esteem are more likely than others to procrastinate (Beswick, Rothblum, & Mann, 1988). Procrastination then creates stress as students work frantically to meet impending deadlines and find themselves producing poor-quality work. People with inadequate self-esteem sometimes find themselves stuck in destructive relationships with people who put them down, all the while blaming themselves for causing the other person's anger (Johnson, 1986). People with low self-esteem often lack the type of social support that is helpful for solving problems. If they consider themselves unlikable, they may have difficulty seeking meaningful relationships with others. Disappointing relationships, lack of social support, poor problem solving skills, feelings of helplessness and hopelessness, and expectations that things will not go well lead to feelings of distress and a higher susceptibility to stress-related illness.

Of particular concern is the observation that a low level of self-esteem keeps the stress cycle turning in a downward spiral. People who expect to fail often do. When they perceive a stressor to be too challenging for them, they give up too easily. They believe the challenge to be unmanageable and their coping responses to be ineffective (Folkman & Lazarus, 1980; Leventhal & Nerenz, 1982). Their poor attempt then confirms their initial low opinion of themselves, and the cycle is repeated over and over. A low self-esteem turns challenges into stressors; negative thoughts and feelings lead to inadequate coping, failure, and a further decline in self-esteem.

A healthy self-esteem is based on a loving but accurate self-assessment. It should not be confused with egotism, self-centeredness, or snobbishness. People with an artificially inflated self-esteem have fragile egos that are easily bruised; consequently, they experience a great deal of stress and cope in maladaptive ways (Baumeister, Smart, & Boden, 1996).

SELF-ESTEEM AND STRESS RESISTANCE

Several studies have found that people with high levels of self-esteem cope more effectively with stress and are more resistant to its negative health effects (Antonucci, Peggs, & Marquez, 1989; Aspinwall & Taylor, 1992; DeLongis, Folkman, & Lazarus, 1988; Fleishman, 1984; Norris & Murrell, 1984). A healthy self-esteem enhances coping ability by giving people the confidence they need to confront and solve, rather than avoid, difficult problems (Taylor & Brown, 1988). One study of factors associated with successful adjustment of first-year students to college found that positive self-esteem was related to greater use of direct coping strategies, better adjustment to college, and better health (Aspinwall & Taylor, 1992).

A healthy self-esteem is essential for changing problematic behavior patterns. A positive self-regard increases the likelihood that a person can devise or follow recommendations for lifestyle changes that improve stress resistance, such as managing time and exercising (Feuerstein, Labbe, & Kuczmierczyk, 1986). People with high self-esteem feel more powerful; they feel as though they have some control over the course of events. People who score low in self-esteem are more likely to feel relatively powerless and have a fatalistic view of life, believing that chance occurrences or other people are more influential than they themselves. Increasing a person's sense of control may help alleviate stress by increasing that person's self-esteem as well (Phares, 1976).

In order to take control of our lives and accomplish something of lasting value, sooner or later we need to Believe. . . . We simply need to believe in the power that's within us, and use it.

BENJAMIN HOFF
The Tao of Pooh

EXERCISE

SELF-ESTEEM VISUALIZATION

Think about a recent experience that made you feel good about yourself. It can be anything: getting a phone call from a friend who likes you, feeling satisfied with a project you did, getting accepted into college, receiving a special award or compliment, or feeling appreciated by someone you helped. Take a few deep breaths, relax, and spend a moment reliving this experience. Put everything else out of your mind. Try to visualize it as realistically as possible. How did that experience make you feel? Try to recapture that feeling now. Spend a few minutes focusing on that positive experience. Then try another. Make it real in your mind's eye. Enjoy that feeling of success.

Keep a mental collection of these "success experiences" that you can focus on whenever your self-esteem needs a boost. Visualizing past successes is one of the most effective techniques for increasing your stress resistance because it strengthens your self-esteem, and your feelings of stress subside. When you feel good about yourself, you can do anything!

THE BASIS OF SELF-ESTEEM: YOU ARE SPECIAL

Ideally, self-esteem is based on an inherent sense of self-worth, independent of what you achieve (or fail to achieve) from day to day. You are worthy because of your uniqueness and the potential you hold inside. Like every other person, you have special talents and in your own way you are trying to do the best with what you have. You need to believe that the basic spirit inside you is good, kind, loving, and lovable in spite of today's transitory problems. Too often our definitions of ourselves are based on our performance. While your achievements are an important part of who you are and contribute to your self-esteem, you will find yourself in a precarious position if your sense of self is defined solely by your achievements. What happens when you have a bad day? Take a difficult course? Try something new and aren't perfect right away? Get sick and can't work? Take a leave of absence from your job to raise children? Retire? When the external world fails to provide you with positive feedback and you no longer have a yardstick to measure your self-worth, your self-esteem is in jeopardy.

Adolescence is a time when self-esteem changes for many people, as they emerge from the blind securities of childhood into a redefinition of themselves that does not yet have the grounding of long-term experience with life (Bower, 1991). During adolescence, girls are generally more likely to experience a decline in self-esteem than boys (Pipher, 1994). College years, often full of tumultuous change, have a strong effect on self-esteem, ideally increasing self-regard as one acquires new skills, knowledge, and experiences. Sometimes, however, college experiences only challenge further an already shaky foundation. If this is the case for you, it might be some comfort to realize that you have a great deal of company!

Low self-esteem can be a potent stressor at any age. Judging and rejecting yourself is a very painful experience. People who find that they rarely feel good about themselves may begin with the information presented in this chapter, but they will need more help and should seek it from a health professional.

◆ STRESS AND YOU

SELF-ESTEEM SELF-ASSESSMENT

How is your self-esteem? Answer the following questions by assigning each one the appropriate number from the following scale:

1 = strongly agree   2 = agree   3 = disagree   4 = strongly disagree

Self-Esteem Scale

_____ 1. I feel that I am a person of worth, at least on an equal basis with others.

_____ 2. I feel that I have a number of good qualities.

_____ 3. All in all, I am inclined to feel I am a failure.

_____ 4. I am able to do things as well as most other people.

_____ 5. I feel I do not have much to be proud of.

_____ 6. I take a positive attitude toward myself.

_____ 7. On the whole, I am satisfied with myself.

_____ 8. I wish I could have more respect for myself.

_____ 9. I certainly feel useless at times.

_____ 10. At times I think I am no good at all.

Convert answers to numbers 3, 5, 8, 9, and 10 as follows: Change 1 to 4; change 4 to 1; change 2 to 3; change 3 to 2. Then total your responses. The lower your score, the higher is your self-esteem.

Source: Self-Esteem Scale, Rosenberg, 1965.

WHERE DOES SELF-ESTEEM COME FROM?

The development of self-esteem begins in infancy, continues over the years, and constantly changes with your experiences. It initially takes shape out of messages you receive about yourself from others, especially people important to you. In early childhood, important people include family members and others who take care of you. Psychologists believe that infants learn in the first year or two whether their environment is friendly and responsive or hostile and frustrating. Infants and young children learn whether people respond to them with acceptance or disdain, which presumably lays the early groundwork for self-esteem (Pelham & Swann, 1989). Children who receive primarily positive and supportive messages and find the world a predictable and orderly place develop an underlying sense of "I must be OK"; con-

versely, children who encounter negative and confusing messages develop the feeling "Something is wrong; I must not be OK." Later the self-esteem input circle enlarges to include friends, teachers, and the world at large. It includes not only feelings you have from your interactions with others but also ideas you form about the importance of various attributes (Blascovich & Tomaka, 1991; Byrne, 1996). Your self-esteem is influenced by many things: experiences with such things as recreational activities, schoolwork, sports, hobbies, significant others, and later, work-related activities, earning power, relationships with family members, co-workers, and supervisors.

Remember, too, the difference between self-concept and self-esteem. Self-esteem grows not only from a sense of how we are doing in various areas but the *evaluation* of how important these areas are to us (Pelham & Swann, 1989). The discrepancy between where we are and where we should be also affects self-esteem. We all compare ourselves and how we are doing in different areas of our lives to our ideal of how well we think we should be doing. We also compare ourselves and how we think we are doing to other people and how we perceive them to be doing (Buunk, Collins, Taylor, Van Yperen, & Dakof, 1990). Our perception of how others are doing is influenced by many things, including what others tell us and media images. If we believe we are doing about as well as we should be doing, or are at least headed in the right direction, we feel good about ourselves. If we feel we are falling below the standards we have adopted as ideal, we find fault with ourselves.

IMPROVING YOUR SELF-ESTEEM

Self-esteem is gradually acquired from messages you receive, experiences you have, and ideas you form; therefore, you can change your self-esteem by changing these inputs. Anything that is learned can be relearned. Improving self-esteem means taking some control of the messages, experiences, and ideas that shape it. You become the gatekeeper for the information that is allowed to pass into the self-esteem chamber. You can learn to examine your self-talk and interpretation of events, the judgments you pass on yourself, the expectations you have about how you should be doing, and the ways in which you compare yourself to others. Many people have found that the cognitive restructuring techniques introduced in the last chapter are helpful for improving self-esteem. Examining and challenging irrational beliefs that underlie self criticism can help you change the perceptions and negative self-talk that contribute to low self-esteem. If you follow these suggestions, your self-esteem will slowly but surely improve. The rest of this chapter presents ways to help you improve your self-esteem.

1. Challenge Critical Self-Talk

Just as self-esteem affects perception, so too does your perception influence self-esteem. If you monitored your self-talk to uncover automatic thoughts and irrational beliefs as suggested in Chapter 12, you may already have observed perceptions that influence the way you think about yourself and your abilities. Much of the monologue that runs through our heads, interpreting and judging events around us, spews out commentary on our own abilities and performance as well: "I'm no good at math; I'll never understand this stuff." "No one is asking me to dance because I'm overweight." "I'm the only one who hasn't been invited to a party this weekend." Try to figure out what types of situations activate sessions of critical self-talk; these may be the areas that need some work.

■ STUDENT STRESS

EVAN'S SELF-ESTEEM

Evan's self-esteem problems occurred mainly in the area of academic achievement. Ever since he could remember, his parents had always placed a very high value on school performance. Their anxiety regarding his schoolwork was contagious, and by the time Evan was in middle school he was already developing problems taking exams. Now, as a college student, he always felt he was on the verge of failure, even though he was maintaining a B+ average. Evan constantly worried about upcoming assignments and exams.

When he kept his stress log, Evan found that most of his stress came from this habitual worrying. He noted frequent negative thoughts such as "I'll never get this done," "I can't do this," "This work is much too hard for me," and "I shouldn't be in college." These popped into his mind often and were associated with feelings of anxiety and panic.

Evan felt he could benefit from some short-term counseling and made an appointment to see a therapist at the student health center. After working with the therapist and keeping track of his self-talk more closely for a week, he realized that these thoughts served a sort of protective function. By expecting the worst, what really happened was not so bad! The problem was that the negative self-talk almost seemed necessary to ensure an adequate performance. "Without this pressure, I would probably be a complete failure," Evan wrote in his stress log.

Evan tried the initial Self-Esteem Visualization exercise in this chapter, but at first it just made him more nervous. "One more standard I can't live up to," he thought. Evan tended to attribute any successes to luck rather than to his own resources and efforts; as a result, he did not get a good feeling about the success. Over time, however, and with the help of his therapist, Evan worked on changing his negative thinking and accepting himself as special for who he was rather than for what he achieved. He found it somewhat ironic that when his self-esteem became less attached to academic achievement, his schoolwork came more easily and he actually performed better on exams.

Evan's story in the *Student Stress* box provides an important lesson. As you challenge critical self-talk, you must be sure to address the reasons you have fallen into a critical self-talk habit in the first place. For many, such self-talk and the maintenance of low self-esteem are actually ways of coping with stress, albeit somewhat self-defeating ones (Driscoll, 1989; Rich & Dahlheimer, 1989). You may need to correct underlying irrational beliefs and overcome the cognitive distortions that provide fertile ground for the seeds of critical self-talk.

2. Change Irrational Beliefs

Take a look at these irrational beliefs from Chapters 8 and 12. These are often associated with critical self-judgment and low self-esteem:

1. You must be unfailingly competent and almost perfect in all you undertake.
2. You should feel fear or anxiety about anything that is unknown, uncertain, or potentially dangerous (and projects at which you could potentially fail).
3. When people disapprove of you, it invariably means you are wrong or bad.
4. Your worth as a person depends on how much you achieve and produce.
5. It is shameful to make mistakes.

Research has shown that both depression and low self-esteem are related to irrational beliefs, especially those that reinforce high self-expectations and demand for approval, along with feelings of anxiety, helplessness, and a tendency to avoid rather than face problems (McLennan, 1987).

3. Eliminate Cognitive Distortion

Cognitive distortion means you look for evidence to support your low opinion of yourself. Cognitive distortions that reinforce low self-esteem include seeing where you fall short rather than appreciating your achievements (Epstein, 1992). An example is getting back a term paper with the professor's comments all over it and a B+ grade. You may have noticed by now that professors are notorious for pointing out things that could be improved and neglecting to emphasize things done well. They say it is their job to spur students on to try harder and perform better. But to a student with low self-esteem, receiving these papers can be rather intimidating. If you look at the paper and the comments, and think "This is a disaster. I sure blew this one," that is cognitive distortion. You are focusing on what needs improvement, not on how much you accomplished. After all, a B+ is not a bad grade, the paper got written, and hopefully you learned something.

Here are a few more examples: a friend compliments you on your outfit. You decide, "She must be getting ready to ask for a favor," or "I'm such a boring person she can't think of anything else to say." In other words, you perceive events in a way that reinforces the belief that you are inferior.

Cognitive distortion produces the most harm when you are already feeling down, but research suggests that if you have poor self-esteem, this is when cognitive distortion is most likely to occur. People with low self-esteem have a greater tendency to dwell on negative thoughts and memories when feeling low, whereas those with positive self-esteem are better able to generate positive thoughts to combat a negative mood and feelings of stress (Smith & Petty, 1995).

4. Be Wary of Comparison

To thine own self be true.

SHAKESPEARE

It is human nature to compare ourselves to others (Buunk et al., 1990; Taylor & Loebel, 1989). Comparing ourselves to those we perceive to be doing worse than we are makes us feel good. In a perverse sort of way, we enjoy accounts of others' misfortunes because it makes us feel better off. Others' failures are our successes. On the other hand, if we are always comparing ourselves (or being compared to) a successful sibling, friend, colleague, or other figure, we are set up for failure. We may not be able to match that level of achievement in the sphere of concern. Keep in mind that while this person may be doing better in the area of career development (or whatever), you have built a wonderful support system of good friendships, or you are going to nationals with the tennis team. Don't try to be someone else; respect and appreciate yourself for who you are.

5. Polish Up Your Self-Image

Instead of looking for your weaknesses, allow yourself to feel good about your strengths. Complete the Positive Self-Image Worksheet on pages 286–287 and remind yourself of your strengths, successes, and areas of progress from time to time. These reminders can be used to challenge and replace critical self-talk.

6. Cultivate an Optimistic Self-Regard

Optimists look for evidence that life is good and that they are doing all right. They tend to believe that they will generally experience positive outcomes in life. A generous appraisal of your talents enhances self-esteem, increases stress resistance, improves health, and gives you the strength to shoot for the stars (Scheier & Carver, 1993).

Moderate self-overestimation is intrinsically rewarding and produces no unfortunate consequences.

SEYMOUR EPSTEIN

You may not be able to change some aspects of your appearance, personality, or talents, but you can use your cognitive restructuring skills to reframe the importance of these characteristics. If you are a lousy singer but can decide not to base your self-esteem on your singing ability, you will feel better. Increase your regard for your strengths and minimize your evaluation of qualities that are not really important. So you are not tall and thin like the models or muscular like a body builder. You decide that people come in all shapes and sizes and you are doing the best with what you have. You exercise to manage stress and stay healthy, and you realize that having emotional stability is preferable to developing an obsession with body image.

When it comes to a healthy self-esteem, you must learn to believe in your unconditional worth. That kernel of "you-ness" on the inside is special just because you are you, a unique individual, with a unique potential, doing your best with what you've been given. You must regard yourself with compassion and unconditional love, for you are special.

People with a healthy self-esteem understand the importance of lightening up and not taking themselves too seriously. The ability to laugh at yourself is an essential survival skill. A sense of humor is an important stress buffer and is associated with positive self-esteem (Overholser, 1992).

7. Set and Achieve Goals

While self-esteem must not be based solely on achievement, most people find achievement and competence reinforcing (Mull, 1991). Knowing that you can set and achieve personal goals enhances self-esteem. Now that you have taken stock of your strengths, you might try setting some attainable goals in areas of interest to you. Creative writing? An art or craft? A sports activity you enjoy? Maybe you enjoy the theater. Volunteer to help out with the next play on campus, or if you want to perform, try out for a part.

As you think about interests and goals, think also about diversifying your involvements. We have said that putting all your life-satisfaction eggs in one basket is risky. The same goes for self-esteem. If your self-esteem is based solely on your school performance, what happens when things are not going well at school, or you

◆ STRESS AND YOU

POSITIVE SELF-IMAGE WORKSHEET

Take a moment to consider the things you like about yourself. What are your strengths? Imagine the nice things a close friend might say about you. Are you loyal? Creative? Cooperative? Smart? Fun to be with? A good singer? Debater? Write down as many as you can think of.

My strengths:

_____

_____

_____

_____

_____

   Next write down some of your successful experiences, such as those used for the visualization at the beginning of this chapter. They can be big or little things: a project you completed; an important point you made well in class; a good play on your sports team. What were the qualities required to accomplish these successes? For example, if you handed in a term paper, you might write that it took research skills to obtain the necessary information; organization, persistence, and time management to get the job done. It required writing skills to synthesize the information into a readable presentation. Add these to your list of strengths.

My successes, and the qualities represented:

Example: Elected social chair of my dorm. People like me, I'm pretty well organized, and I know how to have fun.

_____

_____

graduate? Self-esteem plummets. So try to think of two or three realistic, attainable goals that will increase your self-regard and help diversify your strengths. By the way, volunteer work is a great self-esteem enhancer!

8. View Mistakes as Lessons That Further Self-Development

A low self-esteem makes you feel especially bad when you make mistakes or when you receive a correction or suggestion for improvement, for you take them as evidence that you are not a good person. In his book *Building Self-Esteem,* Glenn Schiraldi recommends a very effective skill-building activity called Nevertheless (Schiraldi, 1993). The Nevertheless skill helps you acknowledge mistakes while affirming your basic self-worth. People with low self-esteem are likely to use "Because . . . therefore" thinking, such as "Because of (some external condition), therefore I

_____

_____

_____

_____

_____

_____

In this last section, think about goals you have had for yourself over the past several years. Describe progress you have made in any of these areas. Have you improved your assertiveness? Self-confidence in social situations? Auto repair skills? Artistic ability? Writing skills? Ability to manage your finances?

Areas of progress:

_____

_____

_____

_____

_____

_____

_____

am no good." Schiraldi encourages students to replace "because . . . therefore" thinking with "even though . . . nevertheless." Rather than "Because I said the wrong thing in class, therefore I am not a good person," try thinking "Even though I said the wrong thing in class, nevertheless I'm still a good person."

Mistakes are an important part of life. They must be used appropriately and viewed as lessons to further your self development. People who are afraid of making mistakes never try anything new; when you try something new, you will of course not be perfect. Likewise, being overly sensitive about others' opinions of how you are performing is paralyzing. Take responsibility for your mistakes but learn to view them as learning experiences and as part of the package of life. Stress-resistant people realize that everyone makes mistakes, including themselves. Look for the lessons in your mistakes, and then forgive yourself. After all, you were doing the best you could at that moment (McKay & Fanning, 1997).

While people must not rely entirely on others' opinions for their self-concept, everyone needs to feel loved and lovable.

Dance teachers tell a wonderful story of a ballerina participating in a dance class. At one point in the class, trying a movement in a new way, she fell (a terrible mistake for a dancer). But the teacher recognized that she was taking a risk and stretching herself to achieve new heights, and she moved the dancer up to the next class level to reward her trying.

9. Strengthen Your Social Support Network

Just as it is important not to put all your life satisfaction eggs in one basket, so too should you diversify your social connections. Develop friendships with many different people. Friends provide the connectedness that is so essential for healthy self-esteem (Clemes, Bean, & Clark, 1990; Elliott, 1992). While people must not rely entirely on others' opinions for their self-concept, everyone needs to feel loved and lovable. When you feel respected and valued, your self-esteem is strengthened.

10. Develop Inner Peace and Self-Acceptance

Isn't this what stress management is really all about? As you work through the material in this book, self-knowledge and self-acceptance are two of your goals. They are part of your lifelong journey. These will enhance your self-esteem and increase

The Way to Self-Reliance starts with recognizing who we are, what we've got to work with, and what works best for us.

BENJAMIN HOFF
The Tao of Pooh

● EXERCISE

YOUR SOCIAL SUPPORT NETWORK

Take a moment to think about the people you spend time with. Then fill in the following sections:

Close friends. These are the people who buoy you up when you are down, who listen when you need someone to talk to; they are the people (and even pets) who make you feel good.

_____

_____

Special arena friends. Some people are situational friends. You may feel close to someone at work, maybe a supervisor or colleagues who give you positive feedback, but you never see them outside work. Perhaps you enjoy the fellow members of your sports team, even though you see them only at practice. Relationships with these individuals are still very important, even though you might not consider them close friends.

_____

_____

Neutral relationships. Acquaintances that are OK but don't quite connect with you fall into the neutral group. You don't have particularly strong feelings about people in this group, but you may spend time with some of them because they are friends of friends, roommates, colleagues, and so forth.

_____

_____

Harmful relationships. Some people are overly critical, cynical, aggressive, possessive, domineering, and basically unhappy. They tend to drag you into their net of despair. You should avoid these people as much as possible for they can be very damaging to your self-esteem. But what if they are family members? You can still choose to spend as little time with them as possible, or to confront them and communicate your feelings.

_____

_____

Potential friends. Some people seem to take the all-or-nothing approach to social support: they have a few very close friends but hardly talk to anyone else. Best friends are great, but remember that every friend doesn't have to be a best friend. Perhaps you can think of someone you have talked to a little in a class and would like to know better. Maybe you would like to join a group of some sort to meet new people. Maybe some of your special arena friends are material for this category.

_____

_____

Once you have finished listing your social support network, think about whether you would like to make some changes—perhaps spending more time with people who make you feel good about yourself or developing new friendships and acquaintances. If this is the case, you will need to make an action plan to achieve your goals.

your stress resistance. Take time out to get to know yourself better. Make occasions to do things you enjoy doing alone.

11. *Take Good Care of Yourself*

Positive health behaviors help you feel good and feel good about yourself. Regular physical activity improves mood and self-esteem (Sonstroem & Morgan, 1989). Enough sleep and a healthful diet are essential for a positive outlook and the energy you need to maintain a healthy self-esteem during times of stress.

▲ *ACTION PLAN*

ENHANCING SELF-ESTEEM

Review the material from this chapter, and the 11 suggestions for improving self-esteem. Answer the following questions. At the end of this exercise you will choose two self-esteem goals, and list two or three action steps for each.

1. Are you generally happy with your self-esteem?

2. Are there times you feel especially good about yourself?

3. Are there times when you feel bad about yourself? Are there any specific areas of your self-esteem that need attention?

4. How did your family of origin contribute to your self-esteem?

5. What skills have you developed to increase your self-esteem?

SUMMARY

1. Self-esteem is the evaluative component of self-concept, which refers to a broader concept of who you are. Self-esteem refers to how you feel about yourself.
2. Global self-esteem refers to your general sense of self-worth. Self-esteem can also be studied and discussed in regard to a specific area, such as social confidence, scholastic ability, appearance, and physical ability. All areas contribute to global self-esteem. The more you value a given area, the greater is its contribution.
3. Self-esteem affects your perception of stressors and your ability to cope with a given stressor. Poor self-esteem makes stressors seem more challenging than they actually are because you underestimate your coping abilities.

6. Write three positive statements about yourself, using the Positive Self-Image Worksheet earlier in this chapter.

    a. _____

    b. _____

    c. _____

7. Do any of the 11 suggestions for improving self-esteem presented in this chapter sound like they would work for you? Select two of these suggestions as your self-esteem improvement goals, and then devise two action steps (activities you can do) to help you progress toward achieving those goals.

Goal 1: _____

Action steps:

1. _____

2. _____

Goal 2: _____

Action steps:

1. _____

2. _____

4. People with low self-esteem are more likely to experience higher levels of fear under stress, and this increases their anxiety and inhibits their problem-solving ability.
5. Low self-esteem has been associated with many forms of stress, including loneliness, social anxiety, depression, substance abuse, eating disorders, job burnout, and alienation.
6. A healthy self-esteem should not be confused with egotism, self-centeredness, or snobbishness. People with artificially inflated self-esteem actually have fragile egos that are easily bruised; they often cope in maladaptive ways.
7. A healthy self-esteem is associated with effective coping and stress resistance. A healthy self-esteem is associated with a sense of control as opposed to feelings of helplessness and hopelessness.

8. A healthy self-esteem is based on an inherent sense of self-worth.

9. Adolescence is a time when self-esteem changes for many people. College experiences can either enhance or challenge your self-esteem.

10. The development of self-esteem begins in infancy and is based on feedback received from the people who take care of you. Later, the self-esteem circle enlarges to include friends, teachers, and the world at large. Experiences with recreational activities, schoolwork, sports, hobbies, work, and significant others all influence self-esteem.

11. You can improve your self-esteem by learning to view mistakes as lessons that further your self-development, by challenging negative self-talk, by changing irrational beliefs and cognitive distortion, and by learning to respect and appreciate yourself for who you are rather than comparing yourself to others. Reminding yourself of your strengths, cultivating an optimistic self-regard, and achieving goals help improve your self-esteem as well. Self-esteem grows when you strengthen your social support network and improve your stress management skills.

REFERENCES

Antonucci, TC, JF Peggs, and JT Marquez. The relationship between self-esteem and physical health in a family practice population. *Family Practice Research Journal* 9: 65–72, 1989.

Aspinwall, LG, and SE Taylor. Modeling cognitive adaptation: A longitudinal investigation of the impact of individual differences and coping on college adjustment and performance. *Journal of Personality and Social Psychology* 63: 989–1003, 1992.

Baumeister, RF, L Smart, and JM Boden. Relation of threatened egotism to violence and aggression: The dark side of high self-esteem. *Psychological Review* 103: 5–33, 1996.

Beswick, G, ED Rothblum, and L Mann. Psychological antecedents of student procrastination. *Australian Psychologist* 23: 207–217, 1988.

Blascovich, J, and J Tomaka. Measures of self-esteem. JP Robinson, PR Shaver, and LS Wrightsman (eds). *Measures of Personality and Social Psychological Attitudes*. San Diego: Academic Press, 1991, pp 115–160.

Bower, B. Teenage turning point. *Science News* 139: 184–186, 1991.

Buunk, BP, RL Collins, SE Taylor, NW VanYperen, and GA Dakof. The affective consequences of social comparison: Either direction has its ups and downs. *Journal of Personality and Social Psychology* 6: 1238–1249, 1990.

Byrne, BM. *Measuring Self-Concept across the Life Span*. Washington, DC: American Psychological Association, 1996.

Campbell, JD. Self-esteem and clarity of the self-concept. *Journal of Personality and Social Psychology* 59: 538–549, 1990.

Caplan, M, RP Weissberg, JS Grober, PJ Sivo, K Grady, and C Jacoby. Social competence promotion with inner-city and suburban young adolescents: Effects on social adjustment and alcohol use. *Journal of Consulting and Clinical Psychology* 60: 56–63, 1992.

Clemes, H, R Bean, and A Clark. *How to Raise Teenagers' Self-Esteem*. Los Angeles: Price Stern Sloan, 1990.

DeLongis, A, S Folkman, and RS Lazarus. The impact of daily stress on health and mood: Psychological and social resources as mediators. *Journal of Personality and Social Psychology* 54: 486–495, 1988.

Driscoll, R. Self-condemnation: A comprehensive framework for assessment and treatment. *Psychotherapy* 26: 121–129, 1989.

Elliott, JE. Compensatory buffers, depression, and irrational beliefs. *Journal of Cognitive Psychotherapy* 6: 175–184, 1992.

Epstein, S. Coping ability, negative self-evaluation, and overgeneralization: Experiment and theory. *Journal of Personality and Social Psychology* 62: 826–836, 1992.

Feuerstein, M, EE Labbe, and AR Kuczmierczyk. *Health Psychology: A Psychobiological Perspective.* New York: Plenum Press, 1986.

Fleishman, JA. Personality characteristics and coping patterns. *Journal of Health and Social Behavior* 25: 229–244, 1984.

Fleming, JS, and BE Courtney. The dimensionality of self-esteem: II. Hierarchical facet model for revised measurement scales. *Journal of Personality and Social Psychology* 46: 404–421, 1984.

Flett, GL, PL Hewitt, K Blankstein, and S O'Brien. Perfectionism and learned resourcefulness in depression and self-esteem. *Personality and Individual Differences* 12: 61–68, 1991.

Flett, GL, PL Hewitt, and WM Mittelstaedt. Dysphoria and components of self-punitiveness: A re-analysis. *Cognitive Therapy and Research* 15: 201–219, 1991.

Folkman, S, and RS Lazarus. An analysis of coping in a middle-aged community sample. *Journal of Health and Social Behavior* 21: 219–239, 1980.

Frederick, CM, and VM Grow. A mediational model of autonomy, self-esteem, and eating disordered attitudes and behaviors. *Psychology of Women Quarterly* 20: 217–228, 1996.

Golembiewski, RT, and B-S Kim. Self-esteem and phases of burnout. *Organization Development Journal* 7: 51–58, 1989.

Johnson, F. Alienation: Concept, term, and word. F. Johnson (ed). *Alienation: Concept, term and meanings.* New York: Seminar Press, 1973, pp 27–51.

Johnson, HM. *How Do I Love Me?* Salem, WI: Sheffield Publishing Co., 1986.

Leary, MR. *Understanding Social Anxiety: Social, Personality and Clinical Perspectives.* Beverly Hills, CA: Sage, 1983.

Leventhal, H, and DR Nerenz. A model for stress research and some implications for the control of stress disorders. D Meichenbaum and M Jaremko (eds). *Stress Prevention and Management: A Cognitive Behavioral Approach.* New York: Plenum Press, 1982.

McKay, M, and P Fanning. *Self-Esteem.* Oakland, CA: New Harbinger, 1987.

McLennan, JP. Irrational beliefs in relation to self-esteem and depression. *Journal of Clinical Psychology* 43: 89–91, 1987.

Mull, SS. The role of the health educator in development of self-esteem. *Journal of Health Education* 22: 349–351, 1991.

Norris, FH, and SA Murrell. Protective function of resources related to life events, global stress, and depression in older adults. *Journal of Health and Social Behavior* 25: 424–437, 1984.

Overholser, JC. Sense of humor when coping with life stress. *Personality and Individual Differences* 13: 799–804, 1992.

Pelham, BW, and WB Swann, Jr. From self-conceptions to self-worth: On the sources and structure of global self-esteem. *Journal of Personality and Social Psychology* 57: 672–680, 1989.

Peplau, LA, and D Perlman. *Loneliness: A Current Source Book of Theory, Research, and Therapy.* New York: Wiley, 1982.

Phares, EJ. *Locus of Control in Personality.* Morristown NJ: General Learning Press, 1976.

Pipher, M. *Reviving Ophelia: Saving the Selves of Adolescent Girls.* New York: GP Putnam's Sons, 1994.

Rich, AR, and D Dahlheimer. The power of negative thinking: A new perspective on "irrational" cognitions. *Journal of Cognitive Psychotherapy* 3: 15–30, 1989.

Rosenberg, M. *Society and the Adolescent Self-image.* Princeton, NJ: Princeton University Press, 1965.

Scheier, MF, and CS Carver. On the power of positive thinking: The benefits of being optimistic. *Current Directions in Psychological Science* 2: 26–30, 1993.

Schiraldi, GR. *Building Self-Esteem: A 125 Day Program.* Dubuque, IA: Kendall/Hunt, 1993.

Smith, SM, and RE Petty. Personality moderators of mood congruency effects on cognition: The role of self-esteem and negative mood regulation. *Journal of Personality and Social Psychology* 68: 1092–1107, 1995.

Sonstroem, RJ, and WP Morgan. Exercise and self-esteem: Rationale and model. *Medicine and Science in Sports and Exercise* 21: 329–337, 1989.

Tarlow, EM, and DAF Haaga. Negative self-concept: Specificity to depressive symptoms and relation to positive and negative affectivity. *Journal of Research in Personality* 30: 120–127, 1996.

Taylor, SE, and J Brown. Illusion and well-being: A social psychological perspective on mental health. *Psychological Bulletin* 103: 193–210, 1988.

Taylor, SE, and M Loebel. Social comparison activity under threat: Downward evaluation and upward contacts. *Psychological Review* 96: 569–575, 1989.

chapter 14

Hardiness Revisited

Why a chapter on hardiness? After all, hardiness, or stress resistance, is what we have been discussing throughout this book. The purpose of this chapter, however, is to pull together the interventions presented thus far and to put them in the context of your personal stress cycle. Perception, a person's outlook on life and his or her place in it, is really the heart of hardiness, and so we have saved our stress resistance wrap-up for this unit on perception.

PERSONALITY DIFFERENCES AND STRESS RESISTANCE

You encountered the term *hardiness* back in Chapter 4 when we discussed research by Suzanne Kobasa and her colleagues. They found several personality traits that discriminated between people who were stress resistant and those who were more vulnerable to the negative effects of stress. People who coped successfully with stress were described as having "hardy" personalities (Kobasa, 1979). Other researchers have also found evidence that certain qualities are associated with better stress resistance (Funk, 1992; Nowack, 1991).

Perhaps you have thought about the relationship between personality and stress resistance as well. Do you know people who never smile and always complain? No matter what happens, things are never right. In the face of stress, they blame others and feel helpless and hopeless. You have probably met other people who are usually cheerful and try to make the best of life, even when things aren't going their way. Did you ever wonder why some people are stubborn, aggressive, and even angry with life while others seem to be flexible, friendly, and optimistic? In this chapter, we explore further the relationship between personality traits and stress response, and we look at what can be done to develop those traits that increase stress resistance.

PERSONALITY AND ARTERY DISEASE: TYPE A BEHAVIOR

One of the most interesting research areas in the field of personality, stress, and health deals with Type A behavior. Type A behavior was mentioned briefly in Chapter 3 in the context of stress and health. You may remember that the concept grew

STUDENT STRESS

RITA'S STRESS RESISTANCE

After their first semester at college, Rita and Amy were put on academic probation because of their low grade point averages. Although each had been reasonably successful in high school, both young women found the first year away at college to be challenging. A flexible schedule, no parental supervision, and blossoming social lives combined to create a sort of personal and academic chaos. Rita and Amy found themselves disorganized and out of control when exam time rolled around. Panic ensued when they realized how far behind they had gotten, and their low grades reflected their difficult adjustments.

The second semester got off to a better start for both; they vowed to get organized and to keep up with their work. A required English course was especially demanding, however, and both Amy and Rita received failing grades on the midterm and low marks on their papers. So did many others in the class.

The poor grades sent Amy into a tailspin. As the semester progressed, she began to put off working on her assignments for this class. Whenever she thought about the professor she became angry. "He is so unfair! Half the class is failing! They should fire this jerk." She spent hours complaining to her friends and less and less time preparing for the class. She finally stopped attending the class for fear the professor would call on her and discover she had not done the reading. "Why do they require this stupid course anyway? I'm just going to forget all this stuff after it's over! I'm not going to waste my time on it."

In response to her feelings of frustration, Amy began skipping classes for other courses, too, and tried to do just enough work to get by. "If I can just make C's in all these courses I'll be okay. And if I flunk out of this stupid place it's probably all for the best."

Every time her parents called they asked how her work was going, but Amy just said "Fine" and changed the subject. As the end of the semester approached, the stress became intense; Amy started getting headaches whenever she went near her desk. Reading and studying became impossible, and her medical problems enabled her to get extensions on all her assignments. Over the summer, unable to cope with the headaches and the course work hanging over her head, she dropped out of school.

As you have guessed, Rita managed better. "I'm not going to let this course beat me! Others are in the same boat; the professor can't flunk half the class! There must be something I can do. I'll talk to some of the students in my dorm who have taken this course before and figure out how to study better. Maybe I'll get some help with the papers, too. My other courses are going all right, and I am determined to get through this one too!" Rita started to spend a little more time preparing for the English course and made herself attend every class. She found out from others that this professor tended to give low grades during the first part of the course but eased up as the semester went along: this was his method of motivation. Rita got a tutor to review her next paper and was pleased when it got a B. The writing in her other courses began to improve as well. Studying every week night after dinner was becoming a habit, and Rita found she still had some time to party with her friends and do fun things on weekends. Exam time in the spring meant extra pressure but also the beginning of summer. Rita organized her time well, did a reasonably good job preparing for the English final, got a B– in the course, and raised her GPA enough to get off probation.

out of work by two cardiologists, Meyer Friedman and Ray Rosenman. Their work began in the 1950s, when heart disease had reached epidemic proportions in North America and many researchers were attempting to learn why the incidence of atherosclerosis was so high. During this period scientists began exploring the link between artery disease and lifestyle behaviors such as diet, exercise, and smoking. Although common sense dictated a relationship between emotional health and heart disease, Friedman and Rosenman were the first medical researchers to document this relationship and explore it in a scientific manner (Rosenman et al., 1964).

Friedman and Rosenman had observed that their heart disease patients tended to be hard-driving, impatient, competitive, and aggressive overachievers. They usu-

Trying to do two things at the same time is typical of Type A behavior.

ally did everything, including walking, eating, and talking, in a hurry. They seemed more intent on acquiring objects than enjoying them. During a period of several years, Friedman, Rosenman, and their colleagues interviewed over 3,500 people and found evidence that this collection of traits, which they called Type A behavior, predisposed people to greater stress reactivity (larger sympathetic nervous system (SNS) response to stress), higher blood cholesterol levels, increased risk of hypertension, and higher rates of coronary artery disease (Friedman & Rosenman, 1974).

THE TYPE A OUTLOOK: COGNITIVE DISTORTION

Research on Type A behavior and irrational beliefs suggests that irrational beliefs underlie Type A behavior. An interesting study by Westra and Kuiper (1992) highlights three fundamental beliefs that seem to color a Type A person's outlook on life:

1. Self-worth is largely a function of personal achievements and excessive personal standards. The hardcore Type A lives in perpetual fear of being judged worthless.
2. No universal moral principle exists. Type A people fear that justice will not prevail, and they must therefore ensure justice for themselves.
3. Resources are in scarce supply. Type A's fear they will not get their fair share (although their definition of "fair share" is often vague) and therefore they must fight for it.

Type A individuals with these irrational beliefs look for (and perceive) evidence that supports these beliefs. The result is anger and anxiety, a state of mind dominated by fear rather than openness. As we discuss later, this anger is responsible for a majority of the negative health effects associated with Type A behavior.

● EXERCISE

COGNITIVE RESTRUCTURING FOR TYPE A BELIEFS

The irrational beliefs discussed above and their resulting outlook are in direct contrast to those that go with optimism and high self-esteem. People who change their Type A beliefs change their outlook and reduce their feelings of anger. Can you rewrite the following three beliefs to reflect a more optimistic and stress-resistant outlook?

1. Self-worth is largely a function of personal achievements and excessive personal standards. The hardcore Type A lives in perpetual fear of being judged worthless.

   Rewrite:

2. No universal moral principle exists. Type A people fear that justice will not prevail, and they must therefore ensure justice for themselves.

   Rewrite:

3. Resources are in scarce supply. Type A's fear they will not get their fair share (although their definition of "fair share" is often vague) and therefore they must fight for it.

   Rewrite:

Need help? How about the following:

1. I am a loving and lovable person independent of my achievements. I am doing the best I can.
2. While there are certainly exceptions, I believe that most people are basically honest. I expect that most of the time things will work out the way they should.
3. There is enough to go around; another's success does not take away from mine. We can all work together to create a good life for ourselves.

One study (Hart, Turner, Hittner, Cardozo, & Paras, 1991) found that Type A subjects who scored high on a measure of irrational beliefs experienced significantly more anger in the face of stress, as measured by negative life events, than Type A subjects scoring low on irrational beliefs.

ARE WE A TYPE A SOCIETY?

Friedman and Rosenman (1974) felt that Type A traits were part of the American model for success, especially in an urban environment. Type A traits tend to be more prevalent in higher than lower socioeconomic groups and seem to typify "life in the fast lane." Type A behavior is probably engendered by many of our cultural values, including the following (Schafer, 1987; Seaward, 1994; Wright, 1991):

1. *Emphasis on acquiring material wealth.* We value our possessions, sometimes more than we value relationships with others. Our financial worth becomes a measure of how successful or important we are.

2. *Expectation of immediate gratification.* We expect things to come easily and immediately. We want easy answers and quick solutions. We find it difficult to live with ambiguity and shades of gray.

3. *Competition.* We are ranked and compared to others beginning at a very young age. Our schooling tends to encourage competition rather than cooperation.

4. *Secularization.* Spiritual involvement in our public lives is discouraged. Our solution to religious disagreement has been a moratorium on discussion. A decline in spiritual involvement has led to feelings of spiritual emptiness and a lack of connectedness for many. Lack of spiritual values has been replaced with an emphasis on material wealth.

5. *Emphasis on left-brain thinking.* We value logical, linear thought and the scientific method more than creative, emotional, intuitive ways of knowing. We have

overdeveloped certain aspects of our personality and neglected our need for wholeness and holistic development.

6. *Television*. Statistics show that the average American watches between 20 and 40 hours of television each week. Life is becoming a spectator sport. Many of the traits associated with Type A behavior are illustrated by television characters. Television reality is portrayed as intense and often violent. Who wants to watch something boring? We enjoy action, intrigue, and romance. But too much of this, especially for young viewers, colors our perception of reality and shapes too strongly our expectations of life and ourselves: what we should look like, what our relationships should be like, and how we should treat others.

In the section on values clarification in Chapter 6, we encouraged some introspection and evaluation of personal values. How do yours fit with the Type A cultural values presented above? Many people, young and old, are forming values that require cultivation of a more meaningful life. Many are deemphasizing acquisition, turning off their TVs, and living a more creative, spiritual, and holistic lifestyle (Pearce, 1992).

HOSTILITY: THE HEARTBREAK TRAIT

Many researchers have explored the notion that not all Type A characteristics are created equal. Scientists trying to pin down exactly what it is about Type A behavior that leads to illness have found that feelings of hostility, anger, and cynicism are strongly associated with cardiovascular disease, including hypertension (Hafner & Miller, 1991) and heart disease (Barefoot, Dahlstrom, & Williams, 1983; Blumenthal, Barefoot, Burg, & Williams, 1987; Williams, 1989; Williams & Williams, 1993). They also often accompany risk factors for cardiovascular disease, such as a risky blood lipid profile (Knox et al., 1996), cardiovascular reactivity (Powch & Houston, 1996), and platelet reactivity (Markovitz, Matthews, Kiss, & Smitherman, 1996). In one study, researchers looked at the incidence of heart disease in 255 physicians by using a scale designed to measure hostility; those who scored high on the scale experienced five times the number of heart attacks and were six times as likely to die as those with low hostility (Barefoot et al., 1983). These researchers concluded that the components of Type A such as competitiveness, hurrying, and achievement orientation were harmful only to the extent that they cause a person to become hostile and angry.

Several studies have evaluated a variety of interventions for modifying hostility and anger. Treatments that have been most successful so far have been those that focus on cognitive intervention techniques (Deffenbacher et al., 1996; Gidron & Davidson, 1996; Williams & Williams, 1993).

The hostility scale on the facing page will tell you if you have a problem with hostility.

IS TYPE A OKAY?

If you scored fairly low on the hostility scale, does that mean you can ignore your other Type A characteristics? Type A types are inclined to think "Whew! Maybe my rushing, nervous, anxious approach to life is OK." But is it? Maybe you shouldn't let Type A behavior off the hook so easily. If you are fairly hardy and not very hostile, your Type A traits may not send you to an early grave, but let's look at how these qualities contribute to your stress response. Does impatience feel good? Tune in to

◆ STRESS AND YOU

HOSTILITY SCALE

Is hostility a problem for you? Answer the following questions true or false:

_____ I often get annoyed at checkout cashiers or the people in front of me when I'm waiting in line at the supermarket.

_____ I usually keep an eye on the people I work or live with to make sure they're doing what they should.

_____ I often wonder how extremely fat people can have so little respect for themselves.

_____ Most people will take advantage of you if you let them.

_____ The habits of friends or family members often annoy me.

_____ When I'm stuck in traffic, I often start breathing faster and my heart pounds.

_____ When I'm annoyed with people, I always let them know it.

_____ If someone wrongs me, I'll get even.

_____ I usually try to have the last word in an argument.

_____ At least once a week, I feel like yelling at or even hitting someone.

If you answered "true" to five or more of these questions, you may qualify as excessively hostile.

Source: Reprinted with permission of Redford B. Williams, M.D.

your physical and mental sensations next time you are rushing to do too many things in too little time. Researchers Kuiper and Martin (1989) believe that Type A behavior results in a lowered quality of life. Before you accept your Type A traits as harmless, tune in to their effects not only on your health but on your stress response and quality of life as well. You must be the judge of whether Type A traits fit your personality and lifestyle.

HARDINESS: THE ANSWER FOR HIGH-STRESS TIMES?

While you continue to work for a lower-stress lifestyle—accepting the things you can't change, changing the things you can change, and learning to know the difference—periods of stress inevitably arise. Kobasa and her colleagues found that personality traits they defined as control, commitment, and challenge helped protect people undergoing high levels of stress from stress-related illness. Let's take a look at the hardiness concept and what it offers in terms of increasing stress resistance.

Control is the hardiness variable that has received the most research attention and substantiation concerning its relationship to stress response and health. Control is the opposite of helplessness and hopelessness, which greatly increase one's susceptibility to stress-related illness. Hardy people feel that they are in control of their lives. While they certainly cannot control everything, when faced with a stressor they feel as though they have resources and options and can at least influence what is going on around them.

Commitment is another strong card in the hardiness player's hand. Commitment means feeling that what you do is important and valuable. Stressors are viewed as meaningful and interesting in some way. Commitment is the opposite of alienation, isolation, and loneliness. People with commitment are involved in life: in work, family, friendships, community, and their own growth and development (Mansfield & McAdams, 1996; Peterson & Stewart, 1996).

Challenge refers to the stress-resistant person's perception of stressors, to the ability to see demands as opportunities and learning experiences rather than obstacles. Less research has been done on this component of hardiness than on the others, and what has been done is not always supportive of the link between challenge

 STRESS AND YOU

HARDINESS SELF-ASSESSMENT

Here is the hardiness self-assessment you took back in Chapter 4. Take it again and see whether your thinking has changed. Compare your results this time to your earlier scores.

Write down how much you agree or disagree with the statements below, using the following scale:

0 = strongly disagree   1 = mildly disagree
2 = mildly agree   3 = strongly agree

_____ A. Trying my best at work and school makes a difference.

_____ B. Trusting to fate is sometimes all I can do in a relationship.

_____ C. I often wake up eager to start on the day's projects.

_____ D. Thinking of myself as a free person leads to great frustration and difficulty.

_____ E. I would be willing to sacrifice financial security in my work if something really challenging came along.

_____ F. It bothers me when I have to deviate from the routine or schedule I've set for myself.

_____ G. An average citizen can have an impact on politics.

_____ H. Without the right breaks, it is hard to be successful in my field.

_____ I. I know why I am doing what I'm doing at work or school.

_____ J. Getting close to people puts me at risk of being obligated to them.

and health (Hull, Van Treuren, & Virnelli, 1987). But the challenge concept supports the idea that hardy people have an optimistic outlook. Perhaps future research will clarify the role that perception of stressors plays in the stress-illness relationship.

DOES HARDINESS KEEP YOU HEALTHY?

While many researchers have challenged the particulars of the hardiness concept, most agree that hardiness (or a similar construct) does protect against the negative health effects of stress. Several studies have found an association between high hardiness scores and less physical illness not only in white-collar male executives but in women in various occupations (Rhodewalt & Zone, 1989), college students (Roth et al., 1989), adolescents (Shepperd & Kashani, 1991), blue-collar workers (Manning, Williams, & Wolfe, 1988), and other groups (Nowack, 1989, 1991; Westman, 1990).

Hardiness traits also appear to protect you psychologically as well. Hardiness is associated with better job satisfaction, less tension at work, less depression and anxiety, and in general, a better quality of life (Manning et al., 1988). However, while hardiness is protective, it does not confer unconditional immunity to the negative effects of stress. When stress levels are very high, stress can still get under your skin and upset your hardiness homeostasis.

_____ K. Encountering new situations is an important priority in my life.

_____ L. I really don't mind when I have nothing to do.

To get your scores for control, commitment, and challenge, write the number of your answer, from 0 to 3, above the letter of each question on the questionnaire. Then add and subtract as shown below.

$$\underset{A}{\_\_\_} + \underset{G}{\_\_\_} = \_\_\_ \qquad \underset{C}{\_\_\_} + \underset{I}{\_\_\_} = \_\_\_ \qquad \underset{E}{\_\_\_} + \underset{K}{\_\_\_} = \_\_\_$$

$$-\qquad\qquad -\qquad\qquad -$$

$$\underset{B}{\_\_\_} + \underset{H}{\_\_\_} = \_\_\_ \qquad \underset{D}{\_\_\_} + \underset{J}{\_\_\_} = \_\_\_ \qquad \underset{F}{\_\_\_} + \underset{L}{\_\_\_} = \_\_\_$$

Control _____   Commitment _____   Challenge _____

_____   _____   _____   _____
Control + Commitment + Challenge = Total Hardiness Score

Score   **Interpretation**

10–18   Hardy personality

0–9   Moderate hardiness

Below 0 Low hardiness

▶ STRESS RESEARCH

Suzanne Kobasa: *A Focus on the Positive*

The term "hardiness" was coined by Suzanne C. Ouellette Kobasa, Salvatore R. Maddi, and colleagues to refer to a group of personality traits that seem to offer protection from the negative health effects of stress. At the time of their research in the mid-1970s, research on the stress-health association focused primarily on the negative effect of life events and Type A behavior on health.

Kobasa has stated that her research was a reaction to the negative focus of most studies: how people become ill under stress. She wanted to ask the question "What about those people who don't?" (Wood, 1987) Kobasa brought to her psychological research her interests in philosophy and two years of training at the Yale Divinity School. She was interested in acquiring a better understanding of people "facing especially difficult life circumstances and yet doing well" (Wood, 1987).

Rather than simulating stress in a laboratory setting, Kobasa and Maddi found a group of subjects experiencing real-life stress: middle- and upper-level executives at Illinois Bell, a company experiencing considerable disruption, which placed a great deal of stress on its employees. As hoped, some of the subjects were sick less frequently, and the researchers were able to compare them to those who became ill.

This comparison upheld Kobasa's hypothesis that "it is not what happens to you that is important, but how you handle it" (Kobasa, 1984). The "hardy" executives showed higher levels of three traits the researchers called commitment, control, and challenge. Commitment is the opposite of alienation and is typified by involvement. Control is the opposite of helplessness. People scoring high on control believe that they can influence the events in their lives. Challenge refers to the ability to see change as potential opportunity rather than threat.

Many psychologists have challenged Kobasa's hardiness concept. While some have confirmed its relationship to illness (Nowack, 1991; Rhodewalt & Zone, 1989; Roth et al., 1989), others have found only one or two of its subscales (usually commitment and/or control) to be related to psychological or physical health (Lawler & Schmeid, 1987; Shepperd & Kashani, 1991; Williams et al., 1992). Others have argued that the definition of hardiness varies with the population studied—that Kobasa's concept grew from a group of white male executives and may not apply to other groups. However, most but not all subsequent studies have supported its application to women, adolescents, and various occupational groups.

Perhaps the most significant criticism has been that hardiness is not a new concept but is simply measuring degree of mental health and, as such, is the opposite of "neuroticism" or poor mental health (Funk, 1992). Some psychologists have argued that the hardy are not special; they are simply not sick. But wellness enthusiasts continue to embrace Kobasa's emphasis on the positive. We want answers to the question "How can we better manage stress?" And we would rather pursue a quest for the development of hardiness than the avoidance of mental illness.

HOW DOES HARDINESS WORK?

Hardiness probably keeps us healthy in several ways. We examine several of them here.

Hardy People Have an Optimistic Point of View

We have said that perception is the heart of hardiness. Stress resistance is associated with an optimistic point of view. Remember that it is one's perception that turns an event into a stressor and determines the degree and significance of that stress. Hardy people are less likely than others to appraise life experiences as undesirable or requiring a great deal of adjustment (Allred & Smith, 1989; Pagana, 1990; Rhodewalt & Zone, 1989; Wiebe, 1991). They are optimistic and tend to play up the positive and downplay the negative (Hull et al., 1987).

> *I have not failed 10,000 times. I have successfully found 10,000 ways that will not work.*
>
> THOMAS A. EDISON

Hardiness May Decrease the Physical Strain of Stress

The physiological arousal associated with negative stress differs from the arousal associated with eustress. When you feel that you have some control over a stressor and tend to expect positive outcomes, your stress response is not so harmful to your health (Ekman, Levenson, & Friesen, 1983).

Several researchers have found that hardy subjects have a better physical stress tolerance than others. When faced with stressors, hardy subjects have been found to have a lower increase in diastolic blood pressure (Contrada, 1989) and a smaller increase in heart rate (Lawler & Schmied, 1987; Wiebe, 1991).

While stress reactivity gives some information on how individuals respond to stress, it does not tell the whole story. In the right amount, SNS arousal increases your performance and helps you cope with stress. The key is to have the right amount of arousal at the right time. An interesting study of male college students found that subjects scoring low on hardiness experienced high SNS arousal *waiting* for the lab stress simulation test to begin, while those scoring high on hardiness had higher systolic blood pressure during the laboratory stress simulation (Allred & Smith, 1989). The parallel to real life is that hardiness is characterized by active coping, getting aroused at the right time to confront a stressor effectively but not getting aroused (worrying) before the stressor is at hand.

Some researchers believe that as people become accustomed to handling stress in a positive way, they may also get "tough" and physically better able to cope with sympathetic arousal (Dienstbier, 1991). Good coping skills encourage you to seek out greater challenges and get more practice handling stress. As one researcher has written, "As the rich get richer, so the tough should get tougher" (Dienstbier, 1991).

Hardy People Cope More Effectively with Stress

Stress-resistant people are more likely to use problem-focused coping measures, positive thinking, and support-seeking strategies when faced with stress (Cohen & Edwards, 1989; Holt, Fine, & Tollefson, 1987; Nowack, 1989; Williams, 1989). These measures reduce feelings of stress and are associated with positive emotions (Lazarus & Folkman, 1984). People scoring low on hardiness are more likely to deal passively with stress, avoiding the situation and indulging in maladaptive palliative strategies.

Hardy People May Have Better Health Habits

Could it be that hardy people stay healthier in the face of stress because they take better care of themselves? Evidence suggests that this is so (Nagy & Nix, 1989), at least for hardy people concerned about their health (Hannah, 1988). Researchers

Nagy and Nix have hypothesized that hardy people have better health practices partly because they tend to use more effective coping measures. They are less likely to indulge in maladaptive palliative strategies that are harmful to their health, such as abusing alcohol and drugs or acting aggressively, when under stress. In addition, a sense of personal control over one's health behavior has been associated with better health habits, such as exercise, diet, and smoking behaviors. Since hardy people score higher on control, this may help explain why they are healthier than others.

PERSONALITY AND ENVIRONMENT: LOOKING FOR THE RIGHT FIT

Environmental demands vary. We must all find work environments and communities that feel right to us and provide the best match between our abilities and environmental demands. Some people enjoy life in the fast lane. So do not despair, readers with a Type A streak. Some Type A qualities may be adaptive for the American way of life (even the American way that has strong spiritual values and limits television viewing). In fact, Kobasa and her colleagues found that Type A types who scored high on measures of hardiness were the healthiest group of subjects in their study of stressed executives (Kobasa 1983)!

But Kobasa's study also found that the Type A's *without* hardiness were the *most* prone to illness in the face of stress. Like hardiness, Type A is a conglomeration of traits, and some, especially anger and hostility, seem to have a stronger relationship than others with stress-related illness. In other words, there are many manifestations of Type A behavior; some of these are dangerous to your health and well-being but some may be relatively benign.

The components of hardiness, commitment, control, and challenge are quite compatible with Type A behavior and appear to buffer Type A people from the negative effects of stress. Take commitment, for example. Type A's with a strong job involvement value their work, perform well, and often reap personal and financial rewards without falling prey to stress-related illness. Job commitment *fits* the cultural and personal expectations for many people, and the Type A focus on striving for high achievement works in this environment.

We have said that Type A behavior is generally more typical of city dwellers than their country cousins. One New Yorker told us of weekend ski trips to a backwoods location. Impatient at the grocery checkout counter, one of his friends said to the clerk, "Can't you hurry?" The clerk looked the young city slicker in the eye

Calvin and Hobbes   by Bill Watterson

and said, "Son, one thing we never do is hurry." Type A qualities that help us thrive in a fast-paced, urban environment may not translate into success in a culture that does not value speed and getting everything done in a hurry.

OTHER VARIABLES THAT INCREASE STRESS RESISTANCE

Exercise

As discussed in Chapter 10, many studies have found that regular physical activity makes a strong contribution to stress resistance. The body-mind effects of exercise are wonderfully therapeutic (Wilcox & Storandt, 1996).

Self-Esteem

Without adequate self-regard, stress resistance is impossible. Self-esteem is the cornerstone of control, commitment, and challenge. When self-esteem is low, people feel out of control, alienated, and overwhelmed (DeLongis, Folkman, & Lazarus, 1988).

Optimism

The health benefits of optimism were presented in the previous chapter. Optimism enhances perception of personal control, deepens your involvement in life, and helps you see change as a challenge. It also helps you stay healthy and recover quickly from illness and injury when they occur (Everson et al., 1996; Jenkins, 1996; Seligman, 1991).

Social Support

The perception that you have emotional support from friends and family helps protect you from the negative effects of stress (Coyne & DeLongis, 1986) and improves your quality of life (Newsom & Schulz, 1996). Social support may signify coping re-

sources as well as healthy communication and intimacy. Many researchers believe that "a trusting heart" (Williams, 1989) and "opening our heart" to others (Ornish, 1990) are essential for stress resistance. Involvement with others is the opposite of hostility, which closes the channels of communication and forces us into isolation.

Spiritual Health

A step beyond commitment and social support, spiritual health emphasizes your larger connection to others and to your own spiritual growth. Spiritual health gives life meaning and value in the deepest sense; it is a potent stress buffer (Bellingham, et al., 1989; Kabat-Zinn, 1994; Zika & Chamberlain, 1987).

Tolerance for Ambiguity

Be patient towards all that is unsolved in your heart and try to love the questions themselves.

RAINER MARIA RILKE

Some researchers have emphasized the importance of this variable for healthful adaptation to stress (Witmer et al., 1983). After all, every stressor implies some form of change. Change means a new way of doing things. Newness usually means uncertainty. If you expect always to have the right answer, to be able to feel certain that your response or performance will be perfect, you will often be disappointed. Modern times demand flexibility that allows people to live with an exploding rate of change and uncertainty.

STRESS RESISTANCE: VARIATION ON THE SELF-ACTUALIZATION THEME

A classics teacher was frequently heard to remark, "There's nothing new under the sun." Redford Williams has noted that his advice on decreasing hostility is a repackaging of the tenets of the major world religions. This discussion of hardiness characteristics is truly an echo of work by many other thinkers and writers about the qualities that make for a well-adjusted, mentally healthy person. Readers who have studied psychology may be familiar with Abraham Maslow's concept of self-actualization (1970). Maslow developed his definition of self-actualization in the 1960s from his observations of people he felt represented true fulfillment of their personal potentials (Maslow, 1970). The following description of the self-actualized (SA) person is taken from Maslow's work (de Vries, 1979; Maslow, 1970). Can you relate this description to the hardiness characteristics discussed in this chapter?

1. SA people perceive reality, including other people, more efficiently. They are more comfortable with reality and are not threatened or frightened by the unknown.
2. SA people have an acceptance of self, others, and the world.
3. SA people are relatively spontaneous in their behavior and even more spontaneous in their thoughts and inner life. They do not allow convention to keep them from doing something they consider important.
4. SA people are problem-centered rather than self-absorbed. They often have a mission in life, usually one that is concerned with larger philosophical or ethical issues.
5. SA people have a quality of detachment that gives them a healthy objectivity for effective problem solving. They enjoy periods of solitude and are often protective of their privacy.
6. SA people appreciate with wonder the good things about life. They enjoy healthy pleasures.
7. SA people commonly have mystic or "peak" experiences: times of strong, intense emotions in which there is a temporary transcendence of normal reality.

8. SA people have deep feelings of identification, sympathy, and affection for other people and humankind in general in spite of occasional anger or impatience with particular individuals.
9. SA people have satisfying interpersonal relationships.
10. SA people are extremely ethical and have high moral principles.
11. SA people have a philosophical, nonhostile sense of humor.
12. SA people are especially creative and inventive.

WHERE DOES STRESS RESISTANCE COME FROM?

Throughout time, people have observed personal differences in temperament and behavior and wondered where they come from. During Shakespeare's time, in the 1600s, people believed that temperament was governed by the four "humors": blood, phlegm, black bile, and yellow bile. A predominance of one humor was thought to predispose an individual to the trait associated with that humor. People dominated by blood developed a sanguine, or cheerful, disposition. A phlegmatic individual has a slow and stolid temperament. A predominance of black bile was thought to make one atrabilious (from the Latin for black bile), or melancholy. Yellow bile made one choleric, or hot tempered. Hence, one's outlook was believed to be colored by one's biochemistry, a belief we hold today, albeit on a different level.

Likewise, the quest for an understanding of how to develop personality traits that allow one to live in harmony with others (the ultimate form of stress resistance) is certainly not new. Folk wisdom is full of advice on the effects of various personality traits on happiness, success, and so forth.

Personality and stress resistance characteristics probably arise from some mixture of nature and nurture. Children are certainly born with a personality all their own, which is further developed and refined as they interact with others and their environment. Meyer Friedman believes that Type A behavior is primarily learned and results from inadequate love and support in infancy and childhood (Friedman & Rosenman, 1974). Cardiologist Redford Williams believes that traits such as hostility are learned and that certain child-rearing practices can help people raise emotionally healthy children (Williams, 1989).

Children are expert imitators, so probably the most important influence on them is their parents' behavior. If a parent models patience, love, and happiness, this is what the child absorbs. Children need plenty of love and touch: holding, hugs, and positive reinforcement when they are doing the right thing. They need safety, security, and consistency that help them feel the world is a predictable and friendly place. Williams and other writers believe that our beliefs about our children are extremely important (Williams, 1989). We must believe they are basically good and free from evil intentions. We must believe they are capable of good behavior and reward it when it appears; this is the true spirit of the child coming forth.

Children have never been very good at listening to their elders, but they have never failed to imitate them.

PAM LEO

If your family fit this loving ideal, and your parents raised you in the manner described above, congratulations! You are in the extreme minority. Most of us bear at least a few battle wounds from childhood. Parents are people, after all—not perfect, just doing the best they can. If you dwell upon the injustices of your upbringing, your forward progress is halted. Blaming others for your situation is detrimental to your health and wellness. Instead, move on. Get help if you need it, and do your best to increase your own wellness and stress resistance.

HOW CAN YOU INCREASE YOUR STRESS RESISTANCE?

The previous chapters should have already reinforced the many ways in which you are coping effectively with stress and have given you some ideas on further increasing your stress resistance. Here are a few more.

Changing Type A Behavior

Friedman and Rosenman (1984) followed over 500 post–heart attack patients who participated in a program designed to help them modify their Type A behavior. These patients were able to achieve a 44 percent decrease in Type A behaviors and reduced their incidence of recurring heart attacks.

Friedman's program focused on behavior change. Participants practiced patience and slowing down: choosing the longest line at the supermarket, driving in the slowest lane of traffic. They learned to walk, talk, and eat more slowly. They practiced listening to others and taking life a little less seriously (Friedman & Rosenman, 1974).

Reducing Hostility: The Trusting Heart

In his book *The Trusting Heart,* Redford Williams (1989) recommends cognitive restructuring and behavior modification to reduce anger and hostility. He encourages an examination of the thought and behavior patterns that create the hostility and anger in the first place. He suggests a 12-step program:

1. *Monitor your cynical thoughts.* Williams suggests keeping a hostility log, similar to the stress log you kept in Chapter 4. The goal is to assess how often and in what situations you experience feelings of hostility.

2. *Confess your hostility problem to a close other.* Sharing your problem with a spouse or close friend opens your heart and increases your ability to trust.

3. *Stop hostile thoughts.* Williams recommends thought stopping when you find hostile thoughts intruding. As soon as you realize you are having a hostile thought, yell silently but loudly into your mind's ear STOP!

4. *Reason with yourself.* Question those irrational thoughts and beliefs. Williams suggests that when you feel anger coming, you ask yourself three questions:

> Is my anger justified?
> Does the situation deserve continued attention?
> Do I have a constructive response?

So, for example, if someone cuts in front of you in heavy traffic, is your anger justified? Sure! Does it deserve continued attention? Well, there is nothing you can do now. Shouting obscenities, blasting your horn, or tailgating the other car is not constructive. It will only make that anger snowball and encourage negative health effects.

5. *Put yourself in the other person's shoes.* Try to understand others, especially those causing you irritation. Williams also encourages altruistic activities, since helping others encourages empathy and trust and makes you feel good.

6. *Learn to laugh at yourself.* Humor is great at deflecting anger. Laugh at your hostile thoughts and they will become smaller and less significant.

7. *Learn to relax.* Williams recommends meditation, which will be described in the next chapter.

8. *Practice trust.* Look for opportunities to trust others. Share your feelings; expect things to work out the way they should.

9. *Learn to listen.* Practice the active listening techniques described in Chapter 8.

10. *Learn to be assertive.* Assertiveness means clear communication and a win-win attitude toward negotiation.

11. *Pretend today is your last.* This enhances your ability to discern what is really important.

12. *Practice forgiving.* Instead of feeling hostile, forgive those who have mistreated you. Blame leads to anger; forgiveness heals. (See also Kaplan, 1992, 1993.)

Hardiness Training

Kobasa's colleague, Salvatore Maddi, has designed short-term courses in hardiness training. In as little as 15 weeks, participants have improved their hardiness scores and job satisfaction, and they have reduced their resting blood pressure (Fischman, 1987). Maddi's hardiness training emphasizes three techniques:

1. *Situational reconstruction.* Maddi encourages people to take a broader perspective on stressful events and to use cognitive restructuring techniques to get a clearer vision of the larger picture. Positive appraisal then leads to better use of problem-solving techniques, a hallmark of the hardy personality.

2. *Focusing.* Maddi believes that people often cannot put their finger on what is wrong; they go around feeling down but are unable to define the cause of their unhappiness. He teaches participants to concentrate on the physical sensations of anxiety, or whatever the problem is, and to try to figure out what starts these sensations and emotions. Once they know what the problem is, they can begin looking for a solution.

Let's say you have been feeling anxious about a term paper that is due, and you just can't seem to get started on it. You might sit quietly and imagine the steps you must take to complete this project. Maybe as you imagine trying to find resources in the library, your stomach tightens and feels tense. Focusing on your thoughts

Luke Skywalker: I don't believe it!
Yoda: That is why you fail.

GEORGE LUCAS
The Empire Strikes Back

▲ ACTION PLAN

STRESS RESISTANCE GOAL SETTING AND ACTION PLAN

Formulate two goals that you think will increase your stress resistance, and then write an action plan that lists concrete activities to help you reach your goals.

Goal 1: _____

Action plan:

1. _____
2. _____
3. _____

Goal 2: _____

Action plan:

1. _____
2. _____
3. _____

STUDENT STRESS

AMY'S STRESS RESISTANCE ACTION PLAN

Let's not leave Amy hopeless and helpless after her difficult first year at college. Instead, let's enroll her in a stress management class offered at her local junior college. Her physician has prescribed medication for her headaches but has suggested that learning to manage her stress more effectively would also be useful.

After studying this chapter on hardiness and taking the self-assessments, Amy formulates the following goals and action plans:

Goal 1: Increase my commitment to what I am doing. To do this, I will review my lifetime and short-term goals so that I have a better sense of direction.

Action plan:

1. Review the chapter on time management and redo my goals.
2. Plan action steps for my most important goals.
3. Talk to a career counselor here about completing my college education and examining possible fields of study.

Amy's long-term goals included a career in the helping professions, and she began investigating social work careers and education programs. Once she had a clearer direction for her education, she felt more commitment to her studies.

Goal 2: Increase my self-esteem through compensatory self-improvement along with better academic achievement.

Action plan:

1. Take seminar on study skills and time management to help me improve my academic performance.
2. Take the international cooking class offered Tuesday nights. I love to cook, and the instructor is supposed to be great.
3. Practice positive self-statements to increase self-esteem, and stick to my self-improvement plans.

The study skills and time management seminar greatly improved Amy's commitment and school performance. The cooking class gave her great pleasure and led to a part-time job with a catering business. Her positive self-statements helped her feel better and kept her on track.

and physical sensations, you might realize that you just don't know how to start finding your resources. There. You have the problem. Instead of avoiding the problem and just feeling bad, you decide to get some help with a computer search and schedule some library time in the near future. Defining your roadblock means that now you can engage in active problem solving. You feel better already!

3. *Compensatory self-improvement.* When a situation truly cannot be changed, people often benefit from making progress in a different area altogether. Let's say Rita, from our case study, is doing what she can for her difficult English class but is stuck with this difficult situation. Perhaps she starts working out in the weight room regularly. As she improves her strength and muscle tone, she feels better about herself and her hardiness increases, even though she must still tolerate her English class until the end of the semester.

SUMMARY

1. Several personality traits discriminate between people who are resistant to the negative health effects of stress and those who are not.

2. Friedman and Rosenman coined the term *Type A behavior* to describe people who are hard-driving, impatient, competitive, and aggressive overachievers. They found that Type A behavior was associated with greater stress reactivity, higher blood cholesterol levels, increased risk of hypertension, and higher rates of coronary artery disease.

3. Several irrational beliefs seem to underlie Type A behavior: (1) Self-worth is largely a function of personal achievements and excessive personal standards. (2) No universal moral principle exists. (3) Resources are in scarce supply.

4. Type A behavior is at least partly learned. Many Type A traits are part of the American model for success, especially in higher socioeconomic groups and urban environments.

5. Not all Type A traits are necessarily associated with negative health effects. Hostility, cynicism, and anger are most strongly linked to stress-related illness, especially cardiovascular disease and several risk factors for cardiovascular disease, including hypertension, poor blood lipid profile, and platelet reactivity.

6. Kobasa, Maddi, and colleagues found that a cluster of variables contributed to a "hardy" personality that was relatively resistant to the negative health effects of stress. They described control, commitment, and challenge as components of the hardy personality.

7. Hardiness may have protective effects for several reasons: (1) Hardy people are optimists, and optimism itself is protective. (2) Hardy people may have a more "healthful" stress response and not experience as much physical strain when stressed. (3) Hardy people may cope more effectively with stress. (4) Hardy people may have better health habits.

8. Other variables that increase stress resistance include exercise, self-esteem, optimism, social support, spiritual health, and a tolerance for ambiguity.

9. Abraham Maslow's description of the self-actualized person illustrates many characteristics of stress resistance.

10. Personality and stress resistance characteristics probably arise from some mixture of nature (genetic or biological predisposition) and nurture (environmental influences).

11. Several interventions have been created to help people develop the personality traits associated with stress resistance. Most of these are based on cognitive intervention techniques that help people change their perceptions of stressors, themselves, and the world around them.

REFERENCES

Allred, KD, and TW Smith. The hardy personality: Cognitive and physiological responses to evaluative threat. *Journal of Personality and Social Psychology* 56: 257–266, 1989.

Barefoot, JC, G Dahlstrom, and RB Williams. Hostility, CHD incidence, and total mortality: A 25-year follow-up study of 255 physicians. *Psychosomatic Medicine* 45: 59–63, 1983.

Bellingham, R, B Cohen, T Jones, and L Spaniol. Connectedness: Some skills for spiritual health. *American Journal of Health Promotion* 4: 18–24, 1989.

Blumenthal, JA, J Barefoot, MM Burg, and RB Williams, Jr. Psychological correlates of hostility among patients undergoing coronary angiography. *British Journal of Medical Psychology* 60: 349–355, 1987.

Cohen, S, and JR Edwards. Personality characteristics as moderators of the relationship between stress and disorder. R Neufeld (ed). *Advances in the Investigation of Psychological Stress.* New York: Wiley, 1989.

Contrada, R. Type A behavior, personality hardiness, and cardiovascular responses to stress. *Journal of Personality and Social Psychology* 57: 895–903, 1989.

Coyne, JC, and A DeLongis. Going beyond social support: The role of social relationships in adaptation. *Journal of Consulting and Clinical Psychology* 54: 454–460, 1986.

Deffenbacher, JL, RS Lynch, ER Oetting, and CC Kemper. Anger reduction in early adolescents. *Journal of Counseling Psychology* 43: 149–157, 1996.

Delongis, A, S Folkman, and RS Lazarus. The impact of daily stress on health and mood: Psychological and social resources as mediators. *Journal of Personality and Social Psychology* 54: 486–495, 1988.

De Vries, HA. *Health Science: A Positive Approach.* Santa Monica, CA: Goodyear Publishing Co, 1979.

Dienstbier, RA. Behavioral correlates of sympathoadrenal reactivity: The toughness model. *Medicine and Science in Sports and Exercise* 23: 846–852, 1991.

Ekman, P, RW Levenson, and WV Friesen. Autonomic nervous system activity distinguishes among emotions. *Science* 221: 1208–1210, 1983.

Everson, SA, DE Goldberg, GA Kaplan, RD Cohen, E Pukkocla, J Tuomilehto, and JT Salonen. Hopelessness and risk of mortality and incidence of myocardial infarction and cancer. *Psychosomatic Medicine* 58: 113–121, 1996.

Fischman, J. Getting tough. *Psychology Today* 21: 26–28, December 1987.

Friedman, M, and RH Rosenman. *Type A Behavior and Your Heart.* New York: Knopf, 1974.

Funk, SC. Hardiness: A review of theory and research. *Health Psychology* 11: 335–345, 1992.

Gidron, Y, and K Davidson. Development and preliminary testing of a brief intervention for modifying CHD-predictive hostility components. *Journal of Behavioral Medicine* 19: 203–220, 1996.

Hannah, ET. Hardiness and health behavior: The role of health concern as a moderator variable. *Behavioral Medicine* 14: 59–63, 1988.

Hafner, RJ, and RJ Miller. Essential hypertension: Hostility, psychiatric symptoms and marital stress in patients and spouses. *Psychotherapy and Psychosomatics* 56: 204–211, 1991.

Hart, KE, SH Turner, JB Hittner, SR Cardozo, and KC Paras. Life stress and anger: Moderating effects of Type A irrational beliefs. *Personality and Individual Differences* 12: 557–560, 1991.

Holt, P, MJ Fine, and N Tollefson. Mediating stress: Survival of the hardy. *Psychology in the Schools* 24: 51–58, 1987.

Hull, JG, RR Van Treuren, and S Virnelli. Hardiness and health: A critique and alternative approach. *Journal of Personality and Social Psychology* 53: 518–530, 1987.

Jenkins, CD. Editorial comments: ". . . While there's hope, there's life." *Psychosomatic Medicine* 58: 122–124, 1996.

Kabat-Zinn, J. *Wherever You Go, There You Are*. New York: Hyperion, 1994.

Kaplan, BH. Social health and the forgiving heart. *Journal of Behavior Medicine* 15: 3–14, 1992.

Kaplan, BH. Letter to the editor. *Psychosomatic Medicine* 55: 473–474, 1993.

Knox, SS, DR Jacobs, Jr., MA Chesney, J Raczynski, and H McCreath. Psychosocial factors and plasma lipids in black and white young adults: The coronary artery risk development in young adults study data. *Psychosomatic Medicine* 58: 365–373, 1996.

Kobasa, SC. Stressful life events, personality, and health: An inquiry into hardiness. *Journal of Personality and Social Psychology* 37: 1–11, 1979.

Kobasa, SC, SR Maddi, and S Kahn. Hardiness and health: A prospective study. *Journal of Personality and Social Psychology* 42: 168–177, 1982.

Kobasa, SC, SR Maddi, and MA Zola. Type A and hardiness. *Journal of Behavioral Medicine* 6: 41–51, 1983.

Kobasa, SO. How much stress can you survive? *American Health*, Sept. 1984, 64–71.

Kuiper, NA, and RA Martin. Type A behavior: A social cognition motivational perspective. GH Bower (ed). *The Psychology of Learning and Motivation: Advances in Research and Theory* (Vol 24). New York: Academic Press, 1989.

Lawler, KA, and LA Schmeid. The relationship of stress, Type A behavior and powerlessness to physiological responses in female clerical workers. *Journal of Psychosomatic Research* 31: 555–563, 1987.

Lazarus, RS, and S Folkman. *Stress, Appraisal, and Coping*. New York: Springer, 1984.

Manning, MR, RF Williams, and DM Wolfe. Hardiness and the relationship between stressors and outcomes. *Work and Stress* 2: 205–216, 1988.

Mansfield, ED, and DP McAdams. Generativity and themes of agency and communion in adult autobiography. *Personality and Social Psychology Bulletin* 22: 721–731, 1996.

Markovitz, JH, KA Matthews, J Kiss, and TC Smitherman. Effects of hostility on platelet reactivity to psychological stress in coronary heart disease patients and in healthy controls. *Psychosomatic Medicine* 58: 143–149, 1996.

Maslow, A. *Motivation and Personality*, 2nd ed. New York: Harper & Row, 1970.

Nagy, S, and CL Nix. Relations between preventive health behavior and hardiness. *Psychological Reports* 65: 339–345, 1989.

Newsom, JT, and R Schulz. Social support as a mediator in the relation between functional status and quality of life in older adults. *Psychology and Aging* 11: 34–44, 1996.

Nowack, KM. Coping style, cognitive hardiness, and health status. *Journal of Behavioral Medicine* 12: 145–158, 1989.

Nowack, KM. Psychosocial predictors of health status. *Work and Stress* 5: 117–131, 1991.

Ornish, D. *Dr. Dean Ornish's Program for Reversing Heart Disease*. New York: Ballantine Books, 1990.

Pagana, KD. The relationship of hardiness and social support to student appraisal of stress in an initial clinical nursing situation. *Nursing Education* 29: 255–261, 1990.

Pearce, JC. *Evolution's End*. New York: HarperCollins, 1992.

Peterson, BE, and AJ Stewart. Antecedents and contexts of generativity motivation at midlife. *Psychology and Aging* 11: 21–33, 1996.

Powch, IG, and BK Houston. Hostility, anger-in, and cardiovascular reactivity in white women. *Health Psychology* 15: 200–208, 1996.

Rhodewalt, F, and JB Zone. Appraisal of life change, depression, and illness in hardy and nonhardy women. *Journal of Personality and Social Psychology* 56: 81–88, 1989.

Rosenman, RH, M Friedman, R Strauss, M Wurm, R Kositchek, W Hahn, and NT Werthessen. A predictive study of coronary heart disease. *Journal of the American Medical Association* 189: 15–22, 1964.

Roth, DL, DJ Wiebe, RB Fillingim, and KA Shay. Life events, fitness, hardiness, and health: A simultaneous analysis of proposed stress-resistance effects. *Journal of Personality and Social Psychology* 57: 136–142, 1989.

Schafer, W. *Stress Management for Wellness.* New York: Holt, Rinehart, and Winston, 1987.

Seaward, BL. *Managing Stress.* Boston: Jones and Bartlett, 1994.

Seligman, MEP. *Learned Optimism.* New York: Knopf, 1991.

Shapiro, D, IB Goldstein, and LD Jamner. Effects of cynical hostility, anger out, anxiety, and defensiveness on ambulatory blood pressure in black and white college students. *Psychosomatic Medicine* 58: 354–364, 1996.

Shepperd, JA, and JH Kashani. The relationship of hardiness, gender, and stress to health outcomes in adolescents. *Journal of Personality* 59: 747–768, 1991.

Westman, M. The relationship between stress and performance: The moderating effect of hardiness. *Human Performance* 3: 141–155, 1990.

Westra, HA, and NA Kuiper. Type A, irrational cognitions, and situational factors relating to stress. *Journal of Research in Personality* 26: 1–20, 1992.

Wiebe, DJ. Hardiness and stress moderation: A test of proposed mechanisms. *Journal of Personality and Social Psychology* 60: 89–99, 1991.

Wilcox, S, and M Storandt. Relations among age, exercise, and psychological variables in a community sample of women. *Health Psychology* 15: 110–113, 1996.

Williams, PG, DJ Wiebe, and TW Smith. Coping processes as mediators of the relationship between hardiness and health. *Journal of Behavioral Medicine* 15: 237–255, 1992.

Williams, RB. *The Trusting Heart.* New York: Times Books (Random House), 1989.

Williams, RB, and V Williams. *Anger Kills.* New York: HarperCollins, 1993.

Witmer, JM, C Rich, RS Barcikowski, and JC Magine. Psychosocial characteristics mediating the stress response: An exploratory study. *Personnel Guidance Journal* 62: 73–77, 1983.

Wood, C. Buffer of hardiness: An interview with Suzanne C. Ouellete Kobasa. *Advances: Journal of the Institute for the Advancement of Health* 4: 37–45, 1987.

Wright, L. The Type A behavior pattern and coronary artery disease: Quest for the active ingredients and the elusive mechanism. A Monat and RS Lazarus (eds). *Stress and Coping.* New York: Columbia University Press, 1991.

Zika, S, and K Chamberlain. Relation of hassles and personality to subjective well-being. *Journal of Personality and Social Psychology* 53: 155–162, 1987.

Relaxation Techniques: Decreasing Your Physical Stress Reactivity and Increasing Self-Awareness

So far you have attempted to cope with stress directly by eliminating or changing the sources of stress in your life. You've solved problems, communicated more effectively, and managed your time. You've clarified your goals and values, and you have organized your life. You've also tried to increase your stress resistance by improving your health behaviors and increasing your enjoyment of daily life. You have seen how your perception of stressors and outlook on life influence your stress cycle; you have worked to reduce irrational beliefs and cognitive distortion, raise your self-esteem, and increase personality characteristics that are associated with hardiness.

But despite your best efforts to reframe problems and cope directly with stress, sometimes you may still *feel* stressed—and in many cases there is not a lot you can do about a problematic situation. You may simply have to accept it and live with it as well as you can, at least for a while. Even positive stress can get you overly wound up. Have you ever fallen madly in love or been so excited about an upcoming event that you've been unable to eat or sleep? In this chapter you will learn several simple relaxation techniques that you can call on when you need to reduce sympathetic arousal.

Learning to relax has many benefits beyond increasing your ability to reduce sympathetic arousal. Relaxation techniques can also help you get in touch with your thoughts and feelings, and get better acquainted with your inner self. Relaxation techniques can help you listen to your body and prevent mild stress-related disorders from becoming chronic health problems. These techniques are especially powerful when used in combination with the other material discussed in this book.

Relaxation techniques enhance your ability to discern irrational beliefs, challenge negative thinking, and develop hardiness traits. They can help you stick to your plans for improving your health behavior. The relaxation engendered by experiencing pleasure allows you to experience that pleasure more fully and to reap more health benefits from it. Relaxation helps you communicate more effectively, set clearer goals and values, evaluate problems, and dream up creative solutions. Relaxation is essential for maintaining optimal health and well-being and for preventing stress-related disorders.

THE RELAXATION RESPONSE

The relaxation response is the opposite of the stress response. It occurs naturally and is not something you have to learn; your body knows how to relax already. Just as you geared up to fight or flee from the vicious dog at the beginning of this book, so too will you eventually unwind once you reach safety.

The physiology of the relaxation response is simply the opposite of the stress response, and is governed by the activation of the parasympathetic nervous system (PNS). The parasympathetic division of the autonomic nervous system is primarily responsible for conserving and restoring energy during times of rest and recovery (Tortora & Grabowski, 1993). So, for example, while sympathetic stimulation puts gastrointestinal activity on hold, parasympathetic stimulation encourages digestion and absorption of food. Heart rate slows, and the force of the heart's contraction decreases. Blood pressure returns to resting level. Breathing becomes slower and deeper. Skeletal muscles relax. The production of stress hormones stops, and your body recovers its homeostasis.

Too often we get out of balance and seem to be stuck in a chronic stress response. Chronic sympathetic nervous system (SNS) arousal leads to a myriad of health problems, as described in Chapter 3 (Sapolsky, 1994). Many people have found that spending more time each day in relaxation mode is an effective antidote for stress-related illness (Matheny et al., 1986). As medical researchers have come to understand the harmful effects of too much stress, they have also come to appreciate the therapeutic benefits of relaxation (Woolfolk & Lehrer, 1984; Sachs, 1991; Schneider, 1987). And research supports the practice of many physicians who are now prescribing relaxation techniques for the treatment of stress-related disorders such as headaches (Holmes & Burish, 1983; Sorbi & Tellegen, 1986), gastrointestinal problems (Hellman et al., 1990), pain due to muscle tension (Kabat-Zinn, 1990), hypertension (Benson, 1975; Patel & Marmot, 1988), heart disease (Bohachick, 1984; Ornish, 1990), insomnia (Hellman et al., 1990; Kirmil-Gray et al., 1985), academic stress (Rajendran & Kaliappan, 1990), job-related stress (Stanton, 1991), and anxiety (Borkovec et al., 1987; Sachs, 1991). Relaxation techniques have become popular for easing the pain associated with childbirth (Kitzinger, 1991; Worthington, Martin, & Shumati, 1982), for treating addiction (Rohsenow, Smith, & Johnson, 1985), and for helping people cope with chronic pain (Hellman et al., 1990; Kabat-Zinn, 1982). Relaxation techniques have been used successfully with all kinds of subjects: healthy people, hospital patients (Bohachick, 1984), children and adolescents (McDonnell & Bowden, 1989; Parrott, 1990; Smith & Womack, 1987), and college students (Archer, 1986; Rajendran & Kaliappan, 1990; Thomas & Scott, 1987).

While Western medicine has given many relaxation techniques some new packaging, most of these techniques have been around in some form for thousands of years. Religious and medical practices in many cultures have used various forms of prayer, meditation, breathing, and movement to clear the mind and heal the body, to understand the meaning of life and talk to the gods.

■ STUDENT STRESS

STEPHEN'S INSOMNIA

Stephen had a summer job working at a camp for children with disabilities. He found the work tremendously rewarding but also emotionally exhausting. He had great respect for the camp directors and other members of the staff, who all worked hard and enthusiastically. His days were busy and full, with hardly a moment of down time. Although he had breaks scheduled into his day, he rarely took them because there was always something he could do to help one of the kids. He loved working with the children and became quite close to many of them.

After the first two weeks of this new job, Stephen started having problems sleeping. He just couldn't stop thinking about the kids, and as he lay in bed he felt as though he was on a mental merry-go-round, with his thoughts whirling and spinning around in his head. He would toss and turn, look at the clock, get upset, then toss and turn some more. Morning would find him exhausted. At first, his energy returned once he began the day, but after a few weeks of insomnia, he was starting to feel tired all the time.

The camp nurse gave him some suggestions for dealing with his sleep problems. She encouraged him to find some islands of relaxation during the day, to take a few short breaks and use them to relax. At the end of the day, after all the children were in bed, Stephen developed an unwinding routine to prepare himself for a good night's sleep. Instead of going straight from work to bed, he took a warm shower, then went to the main lodge and sat quietly for an hour. First he would write in his journal, and then he would read an entertaining book. He found that the journal writing gave his busy thoughts the air time they needed and that the book helped him change his mental channel and let go of the day. He convinced himself that he could give more to his work by withdrawing his involvement for the night, so that he could get a good night's sleep and bring plenty of energy to the kids the next day. As he lay in bed, he practiced breathing deeply and slowly and imagined the physical sensations of deep sleep. After a week of his new routine, sleep began coming more easily, and Stephen could start his day rested and refreshed.

WHO NEEDS RELAXATION TECHNIQUES?

Relaxation techniques are especially helpful for people who are "hot reactors." Hot reactors are people who startle easily, who feel stressed easily, and who tend to overreact physically to stress. Relaxation techniques are essential for people with stress-related illnesses. They are often used in conjunction with other medical treatment modalities. But almost everyone can benefit from learning something about relaxation, even if it is just a few simple breathing exercises that will help him or her fall asleep more easily during times of stress.

GETTING STARTED: WHICH TECHNIQUES ARE BEST?

Most people try several different relaxation techniques before settling into one or two that seem to work best for them. Trial and error seems to be the only reliable method for finding what will work best for you. Give each of the techniques presented in this chapter and the next a try. You will soon discover which are appealing and effective for you.

GUIDELINES FOR PRACTICE

While specific instructions for each technique are given below, here are a few general suggestions for successful practice.

1. *Schedule a convenient time and place, and practice regularly.* People are often tempted to call on relaxation techniques only as a last resort, once stress has hit full force. But in order for these techniques to be used effectively, they must first be practiced and learned. If you cannot control your thoughts during stress-free times, controlling them during high-stress times will be almost impossible.

Successful practice is most readily achieved with a regular practice schedule. Many people prefer to use relaxation practice as a wind-down at the end of the day. Some find the practice energizes them, so they prefer first thing in the morning. Others find a break in the middle of the day helpful. Whatever works for you is fine.

2. *Be as comfortable as possible.* Loosen tight clothing, remove eyeglasses, use a comfortable chair that supports your back. If you are lying down, use a mat or thick carpet and be in a comfortable position. Some people find that rolled towels or blankets placed under the knees and lower back help maintain spinal alignment in a comfortable position, as shown in Figure 15.1.

3. *Try not to try.* Maintain a passive attitude. Simply observe with a nonjudging awareness what is occurring. With relaxation techniques, the harder you try, the tenser you get. It can be difficult to let go of your expectations and judgments, but with practice this becomes easier. Many techniques give your mind an assignment: for example, focus on your breathing, tune in to muscle tension, or imagine a pleasant place. But the mind tends to wander. When this happens, gently bring your attention back to the technique, without judgment, scolding, or frustration. Simply let go of extraneous thoughts and regain your focus.

4. *Keep a relaxation log.* Keeping track of your progress is rewarding and reinforces your commitment to relaxation practice. Beginners find a log especially helpful. Once a relaxation technique is a part of your routine, a log may not be necessary. Some people like to write a paragraph or two after every session, including ideas and feelings that came to them during practice. Others may simply note the day and time with a brief comment or two.

5. *Maintain medical treatment protocols if you are being treated for a medical disorder.* Relaxation works slowly. Inform your physician you are practicing, but continue to follow any medical treatment as prescribed.

6. *Avoid falling asleep.* Relaxation techniques require concentration and active awareness. Relaxation is not the same thing as lethargy. If you start to feel sleepy, open your eyes, practice in a well-lighted room, and use a sitting posture. Of course, you may ignore this advice if you are using relaxation at bedtime for the express purpose of falling asleep!

7. *Finish relaxation sessions by coming back slowly.* At the end of your practice session, slowly bring your focus back to the here and now, gently stretch your muscles,

FIGURE 15.1
Relaxation Position

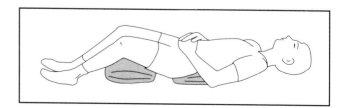

and open your eyes if they were closed. If you are lying down, roll over onto your side and then up to a sitting position. When your muscles are deeply relaxed, it is stressful to ask them to contract suddenly. You may strain your back muscles if you suddenly perform a sit-up after deep relaxation. It also feels better (and is less likely to elicit a fight-or-flight response) to ease back into the daily routine rather than shock yourself back into demanding thoughts and stress-producing pressures. Let yourself come back slowly. Try to hold on to that feeling of alert, focused relaxation as you resume your day.

A Word about Relaxation Anxiety

In some cases, people experience *increased* anxiety when they practice relaxation techniques (Borkovec et al., 1987). This may involve a discomfort with "letting go" and a fear that one is losing control (Rice, 1992). If you notice that these techniques increase your anxiety, discuss this problem with your therapist or teacher. You may wish to use healthy pleasures or exercise instead of relaxation techniques to help you relax at this time.

Some people occasionally experience a panic attack during practice. A panic attack is like an acute stress response and typically includes a fast, pounding heartbeat, rapid shallow breathing, and feelings of panic and anxiety. If this happens to you, try to breathe deeply, interrupt your practice, and calm yourself down by talking to a friend, going for a walk, or doing some chores. If possible, try to remember the thoughts and feelings that triggered the attack and examine them when you feel ready.

Tuning In: Increasing Your Awareness of the Physical Signs of Stress

The techniques in this chapter have as their theme tuning in to physical stress symptoms and using your awareness, breathing, and movement to reduce these symptoms. The first exercise presented here is the body scan. The Body Scan exercise on page 322 is designed to help increase awareness of physical sensations—the messages your body is continuously sending to your brain but that are often ignored because you are too busy doing something else. Learning to tune in to these messages can help you become aware of physical stress symptoms at an early stage, sometimes before you are conscious of feeling stressed. Ideally, early awareness will improve body-mind communication so that your body won't need to shout so loudly to get your attention.

What lies behind us and what lies before us are tiny matters compared to what lies within us.

OLIVER WENDELL HOLMES

Practice the body scan several times in a quiet, comfortable place. Then try to perform a quick body scan periodically throughout your normal daily life. Briefly close your eyes and scan your body for sensations. Once you are familiar with the technique, this may take as little as one minute.

Progressive Relaxation

Progressive relaxation, or progressive muscular relaxation as it is sometimes called, is a relaxation technique developed by Edmund Jacobson in the early part of this century (Jacobson, 1929, 1976). Jacobson's groundbreaking work was some of the first to convince Western scientists that people can achieve control over what were once considered involuntary physiological functions, such as heart rate, metabolic rate, and level of resting muscle contraction. His progressive relaxation technique remains one of the most popular for the treatment of physical stress disorders such as insomnia, hypertension, and pain due to muscle tension, including headaches, low back pain, and temporomandibular joint (TMJ) syndrome (Seaward, 1997).

 EXERCISE

BODY SCAN

The body scan exercise is a good way to begin any relaxation session (Davis, Eshelman, & McKay, 1995; Gillespie & Bechtel, 1986). Begin by sitting or lying in a comfortable position. Eyes may be open or closed. Turn your attention to the sensations in your body.

1. Begin at your toes and note any sensations, such as
     tension
     relaxation
     pain
     warmth
     coolness
     heaviness
     floating
     no sensation
2. Work your way up your body, beginning first with one leg, then the other. Scan ankles, calves, shins, knees, thighs, and buttocks. Compare legs. Does one side feel tighter? Heavier? Warmer? Note any differences. Do the same for your arms, starting first on one side with fingers, hand, wrist, forearm, elbow, and upper arm, then compare sides.
3. Continue scanning your pelvis, abdomen, chest, lower back, upper back, shoulders, and neck.
4. Gently roll your head from side to side. Notice where your neck feels loose and where any tightness occurs.
5. Now become aware of your face muscles, including the muscles of your forehead, the area between your eyebrows, the muscles around your eyes, your jaw, and tongue. Tune in to the muscles of your scalp.
6. Now repeat your scan. Have any sensations changed? Do any areas feel more relaxed? Less relaxed?
7. Make a mental note of the areas where you feel tension. Common areas of tension include legs, hands, pelvis, abdomen, chest, back, shoulders, neck, and face.
8. Take a big stretch and open your eyes if they were closed.

Variation: The body scan can also be performed with suggestions to each body part to relax. After scanning your body with awareness, repeat the scan while imagining each part is letting go and becoming more relaxed.

Jacobson noticed that many of his patients exhibited a great deal of excess muscle tension. He theorized that physical tension leads to mental tension, which increases physical tension, and so forth. He suggested that by breaking this cycle, a person could instead start a cycle the other way. By physically relaxing, one could possibly achieve mental relaxation as well. Progressive relaxation teaches people how to relax and how to become aware of unnecessary muscle tension both during relaxation and throughout the day. Jacobson felt that by reducing chronically over-tense muscles, people could better cope with stress.

Progressive relaxation asks you to alternately contract, then relax specific muscle groups. The goal is for you to become aware of the difference between feelings of muscle contraction and muscle relaxation. Each muscle group is contracted for

5 to 7 seconds, and then relaxed for 20 to 30 seconds. Initially, you contract designated muscle groups 100 percent, then let go quickly to achieve as deep a relaxation as possible in that group. Over time, you progressively (hence the name) contract groups with less and less force until you are barely contracting each muscle group. In this way you become able to discriminate between true deep relaxation and unnecessary levels of muscle tension, and you gain voluntary control over tense muscles.

One of the goals of progressive relaxation training is to help you achieve **differential relaxation** throughout the day. Here you are contracting only those muscles necessary to accomplish the task at hand while all others are relaxed (McGuigan, 1984). So, for example, if you are driving a car, you will need some muscular contraction to depress the accelerator, brake, and clutch, and some to steer. Posture muscles remain activated to maintain good sitting alignment. Unnecessary muscle contraction would include hunching your shoulders, gripping the steering wheel, and clenching your jaw (McGuigan, 1984).

Progressive relaxation can be implemented in several ways. Jacobson's original training procedure required a great deal of practice time in its initial stages. People practicing the technique would focus on one muscle group for an entire 45-minute session. Today, many therapists recommend going through all 16 groups in one session and then progressing to shorter versions after three or four sessions if you wish (Bernstein & Given, 1984). See pages 324 and 325 for exercises.

TUNING IN AND MINDFULNESS

The body scan and relaxation exercises can enhance your experience of mindfulness, as presented in Chapter 11. Increasing your awareness of muscle tension and other physical sensations during relaxation helps increase your awareness during simple activities such as eating and walking. You may wish to give the mindful exercises in Chapter 11 another try and to enjoy being in the present moment more often and more fully during your daily life.

TAKE A DEEP BREATH

When stress management teachers run into former students, the teachers are sometimes inclined to ask, "So, has the course been helpful?" Of course the students are obliged to say yes. The teacher may then ask, "And are you still using any of the relaxation techniques?" The former students usually break eye contact at this point, give a weak smile, trying to remember what those techniques were anyway, and confess, "Well, I do use the breathing."

Deep breathing is the easiest and most accessible relaxation technique (Loehr & Migdow, 1986). It can be used any time and any place. Breathing has often been called the bridge between body and mind. It can occur as either an automatic or conscious act. Most of the time, we give little thought to our breathing; we are occupied with other matters. If we had to consciously remember to breathe, we would have little time to think about anything else! But we can easily switch from automatic to conscious control whenever we wish, and we can use this bridge to help calm both body and mind.

The next time you feel stressed, notice what happens to your breathing. It tends to become shallow and irregular, and your chest feels constricted. It is natural to hold your breath when you are stressed. In fact, simply breathing in this fashion

Using the breath to bring us back to the present moment takes no time at all, only a shift in attention. But great adventures await you if you give yourself a little time to string moments of awareness together, breath by breath, moment to moment.

JON KABAT-ZINN
Wherever You Go There You Are

● *EXERCISE*

PROGRESSIVE RELAXATION

(When learning this technique, many people find it helpful to tape the instructions or have a friend read them aloud.)

Instructions: Relax in a comfortable position. You may wish to begin by taking a couple of minutes to scan your body for tension and focus your attention on physical sensations.

Listed below are the major muscle groups and how to contract them to achieve muscle tension. Tense each group for 5 to 7 seconds, and then relax for 20 to 30 seconds. You can use any words that help you focus on the instructions. For example:

> *Clench your right hand into a fist. Make your fist tighter and tighter, studying the tension as you do this. Become aware of the tension in your hand and forearm. Now relax, let go of the tension, and tune in to the feeling of relaxation. Feel the difference. Let go more and more, letting those muscles become more and more deeply relaxed.*

Caution: If you are prone to muscle spasms in certain muscle groups, such as the jaw, feet, or neck, do not contract those groups too hard.

Muscle Group	How to Contract
Hands and forearms	Clench dominant hand into a fist, then other hand, then both
Biceps	Bend elbows, so hands come up to shoulders
Triceps	Straighten arms and press down against chair or floor
Forehead	Wrinkle forehead and frown
Eyes	Squeeze tightly shut
Jaw	Press teeth together
Tongue	Press against roof of mouth
Lips	Press together
Neck	Isometric contraction; try to raise and lower chin at same time OR if lying on floor, press head back against the floor and down toward your chest at the same time
Shoulders, upper back	Hunch shoulders up to ears
Chest	Inhale deeply, hold breath, then exhale
Abdomen	Tighten stomach muscles and press lower back into chair or floor
Lower back	Arch lower back
Buttocks and thighs	Tighten buttocks and press heels into the floor
Calves	Point toes downward
Ankles and shins	Bend feet up toward head

● EXERCISE

PROGRESSIVE RELAXATION—SHORT VERSION

The format of this exercise is similar to that of the standard method but asks you to contract several muscle groups at the same time (Davis et al, 1995; Bernstein & Given, 1984). As before, tense each group from 5 to 7 seconds, and then relax for 20 to 30 seconds, focusing your attention on the sensations of tension and relaxation.

1. *Arms and hands:* Contract both arms and hands by making fists and tightening biceps and triceps, like a body builder flexing arm muscles.
2. *Face and neck:* Contract face muscles by wrinkling forehead, squeezing eyes shut, pressing lips together, clenching your teeth, and pressing your tongue against the roof of your mouth. At the same time contract your neck muscles.
3. *Torso:* Take a deep breath and hold as you arch your back. Release. Then take a deep breath and hold as you tighten your stomach muscles and press your lower back into the chair or floor.
4. *Legs and feet:* Pull feet and toes up toward knees to tighten shins. Release. Then point toes down while tightening muscles of legs and buttocks.

● EXERCISE

COUNTING DOWN—VERY SHORT VERSION

If you are able to achieve deep relaxation using the short version of progressive relaxation, you might find the following technique effective (Bernstein & Given, 1984). In this procedure, you omit the tension stage and simply relax all muscle groups by recalling the sensations associated with relaxation. Count slowly from 1 to 10, letting each count coincide with an exhalation. You may simply imagine the four sets of muscle groups, or you might use simple relaxation suggestions such as the following:

> *Relax deeply, letting go more and more with each count. 1 . . . 2, let your arms and hands become more deeply relaxed. 3 . . . 4, relax the muscles of your face and neck. 5 . . . 6, allow the muscles of your shoulders, back, chest, and abdomen to relax more deeply. 7 . . . 8, feel the muscles in your legs and feet relax more and more. 9 . . . 10, enjoy deeper and deeper relaxation throughout your entire body.*

will cause you to feel stressed—it works in both directions. Similarly, forcing yourself to breathe more deeply automatically begins to make you feel more relaxed.

The breath has been regarded as a pathway to the soul in many cultures. The word *inspiration* is used for both breathing and thoughts that seem to well up from a deeper source; it evolved from the same Latin root as *spirit.* Many traditions have recognized the link between breathing and life energy. In yoga practice, deep breathing is called *pranayama* and refers to the control of one's energy or life force

---

● EXERCISE

BREATHING AWARENESS

This exercise is easier to do lying down than sitting up; if possible, lie down in a comfortable position. Breathe through your nose if you can, but if you have nasal congestion this exercise may be done breathing through your mouth.

1. Become aware of your breathing and the movement that occurs as you inhale and exhale. Place your hand where you feel the most movement, the place that seems to rise and fall the most as you breathe. If this spot is in your chest, your breathing could be more relaxed.
2. Now bring the breath deeper into your abdomen. Place both hands on your abdomen. Feel your belly gently rise and fall with each breath. This is where the most movement will occur when you are relaxed.
3. Now keep one hand on your abdomen and place one hand on your chest. Can you feel your chest moving in harmony with your abdomen, or is it tight and rigid? Try not to try, but relax and allow this breathing to develop naturally.
4. Finish by scanning your body for tension. Pay special attention to your abdomen, chest, throat, jaw, and other face muscles.

● EXERCISE

ALTERNATE NOSTRIL BREATHING

This technique may feel a little cumbersome at first, but after one or two tries it will feel quite natural. It is a potent stress reducer and energizer.

1. This technique is more easily performed in a comfortable sitting position with good posture.
2. Rest your index and middle finger on your forehead.
3. Close your right nostril with your thumb. Inhale slowly through your left nostril.
4. Now close your left nostril with your ring finger and open your right nostril. Exhale through your right nostril.
5. Inhale through your right nostril.
6. Close your right nostril with your thumb and open your left nostril. Exhale through your left nostril.
7. Begin the cycle again by inhaling through your left nostril.

Once you get used to this technique, try to make exhalations twice as long as inhalations.

(Ornish, 1990). Deep breathing can help you control your energy level. It can help you recover from that scattered, fragmented feeling that occurs with stress, and to feel more calm, directed, and focused.

ABDOMINAL BREATHING

When you are relaxed, abdominal breathing comes naturally. Watch a baby, young child, or even your pet cat or dog, and you will see abdominal breathing. Abdominal breathing is also called diaphragmatic breathing because the diaphragm mus-

● EXERCISE

DEEP BREATHING

Deep breathing can be practiced in either a sitting or lying position. If you start to feel dizzy or short of breath, you may be hyperventilating or breathing too quickly. Resume normal breathing if this occurs. Let your breathing be slow and smooth.

1. Place one hand on your abdomen and one hand on your chest, as you did before. As you inhale, feel your abdomen rise.
2. After filling the lower portion of your lungs with air, keep inhaling, filling the middle portion of your lungs in your lower chest. You will feel the hand on your chest rise and your ribs expand.
3. Continue to inhale and feel the air filling your upper lungs. You will feel your collarbone rise as your lungs fill completely. After practicing this exercise a few times, these first three steps will be performed in a smooth, continuous motion and will take only a few seconds.
4. Exhale slowly, from the top of your lungs to the bottom. Near the end of your exhalation, allow your abdominal muscles to contract slightly, pushing out that last bit of air.
5. The exhalation phase of the breath is when relaxation occurs. To increase relaxation, lengthen the exhalation. Once the deep breathing feels somewhat natural, try letting the exhalation phase take twice as long as your inhalation. So for example, let your inhalation take 3 slow counts, and your exhalation 6. There will also be short pauses between inhalation and exhalation phases.

Variation: Add some mental imagery to the deep breathing (Davis et al, 1995). Place one hand on your solar plexus (the spot in the center of your torso, right under your ribs). As you inhale, imagine energy gathering in your solar plexus. You might visualize this energy as a ball of light, growing larger and brighter as you inhale. As you exhale, imagine this energy flowing out to all parts of your body. If one part of your body is injured or in pain, place one hand here and send the light to that part as you exhale.

cle rather than the chest muscles accomplishes the breathing. If you felt your abdomen rising and falling as you practiced the Breathing Awareness exercise, you were performing abdominal breathing.

The diaphragm is a big, strong muscle that stretches across your chest from side to side and from front to back. It separates your chest from your abdomen. When this muscle contracts, it pulls down toward your abdomen, creating a vacuum as your lungs expand. Air is drawn in; inhalation occurs. When the diaphragm relaxes, the lungs contract, and you exhale.

When you inhale deeply, your rib cage opens and rises to allow your lungs to expand fully. This action involves the deep muscles of your chest and shoulders as well as your diaphragm. When you breathe tensely and shallowly, these muscles are activated as well, but without the full assistance of your diaphragm.

PHYSICAL ACTIVITY AND THE RELAXATION RESPONSE

Tense, relax. Deep breathing. Become aware of your body. All these relaxation techniques remind us once again of the benefits of exercise, so perhaps this is a

◼ STUDENT STRESS

CARLA'S RELAXATION PRACTICE

Students often respond quickly to the breathing exercises in a stress management program. Carla found them very effective for collecting her thoughts when she felt scattered and stressed.

Carla decided to take a stress management class to improve her time management, study skills, and ability to concentrate. She said that one of her greatest stressors was difficulty organizing her study time. Sometimes she felt as though she had so much work to do she didn't know where to begin. And to top it off, this semester she had to declare her major. How could she think about choosing a major when there was so much else on her mind?

Every weeknight after dinner Carla would sit down at her desk and prepare to do her work. She would start to think about a major, then start working on a paper that was due soon, then switch to reading for another class, and then ten minutes later start looking for her notes for yet another class. As she flitted quickly from project to project, nothing much got accomplished, and she would end up more pressured and frustrated than when she began. She began to dread sitting down at her desk, and she would feel anxiety rising as she tried to decide what to work on first.

After covering the material on goal setting and time management and learning the breathing techniques, Carla tried approaching her evening study session in a new way. First, she practiced the Deep Breathing exercise a few times, and then she did ten cycles of the Alternate Nostril Breathing. This took only about 10 minutes, and Carla figured that in the end, getting calm and centered probably saved her hours of ineffective studying.

Once she was through with the breathing exercises, Carla could more easily decide how best to use her three hours of study time. She would select one or two of her most important assignments, taking into account what was due during the upcoming weeks and months. Once she had decided what to work on, she stuck to it without wavering about her decision. Carla found her ability to concentrate improving daily, so she could accomplish tasks more quickly.

Carla also found the breathing helpful for deciding what major to choose. Her adviser had recommended that she look back over the classes she had taken thus far in her college career to see what she had enjoyed most and performed well in. She had also gone to a career counselor and taken some tests that highlighted the types of work that fit her personality. This helped her narrow her choices down to three or four possibilities.

One evening she did the breathing exercises for ten minutes, as she usually did before studying. Then she just let images flow through her mind, without really thinking about her major at all. Suddenly she just knew which major to choose. She had great memories of her work in that field thus far; she felt the department was supportive and had good faculty. Students she had spoken to gave the major a good recommendation. All at once it just felt right, and her decision was made.

good place to mention again that physical activity can help reduce physiological arousal and increase the relaxation response (Folkins & Sime, 1981; Holmes & Roth, 1988; Long & Haney, 1988). Exercise can help not only to increase your all-around stress resistance but serves well as an intervention for acute stress. Angry with someone? Hit a tennis ball. Frustrated with a difficult problem set? Go for a run. Exercise is a great way to get stress out of your system.

A stress management student we'll call David once experienced a great deal of frustration serving on a campus committee. One man in particular, a senior faculty member, drove him crazy. This man would argue, whine, bully, and generally behave in a very unprofessional manner. The other committee members tried to mollify him and move the committee's work forward as well as they could. Fortunately, the work of this committee was almost complete, so David only had a few more weeks of meetings.

David usually worked out in the late afternoon, but one day, he happened to do his workout in the morning, before the noon meeting. His workout was quite vigorous and consisted of a run followed by 30 minutes of weight lifting. After his workout, he felt great. He arrived at the committee meeting feeling happy and relaxed. Nothing bothered him that day, not even the senior professor's ranting and raving. It just didn't seem important. David couldn't believe what a difference that workout had made in his ability to tolerate the stress of the committee meeting.

BODY AWARENESS MAY INCREASE YOUR NEED FOR FITNESS

Some people find that tuning in to their bodies does not feel good. Body awareness reminds them that their muscles are tense and out of shape, and that sitting at a desk all day is leading to a decline in their physical condition. When this occurs three options are available: (1) stop being aware of your body, (2) keep feeling bad about your deconditioned body, or (3) start exercising to improve your physical condition.

If certain areas of your body always feel tight, try some strengthening and stretching exercises. These often help decrease tension and pain, especially if these exercises are performed regularly for several weeks. Stretching and strengthening tight muscles is an important part of physical therapy. If you have ever been to a physical therapist or athletic trainer for an injury, you probably received an exercise prescription to help stretch and strengthen injured muscles.

Strengthening exercises are often performed using some form of resistance training, such as weight lifting or calisthenics. Good sources on how to lift weights are the books by Fahey (1994) and Westcott (1994), listed in the references at the end of this chapter. One of the best sources on stretching is the book *Stretching* by Bob Anderson (1980).

RELAXATION THROUGH BODY WORK: HATHA YOGA

Some types of activity incorporate relaxation and meditation techniques into their practice. Examples are many of the martial arts, Tai chi ch'uan (Jin, 1992; Seaward, 1997), and yoga (Ornish, 1990; Seaward, 1997).

It is with the heart that one sees rightly; what is essential is invisible to the eye.

ANTOINE DE SAINT-EXUPERY
The Little Prince

The ancient tradition of yoga offers many stress management benefits (Patel, 1984). Indeed, most relaxation techniques are connected in some way to a form of yoga. The word *yoga* comes from the Sanskrit word for *yoke*, and means to bring together, to unite and make whole. It refers to the union of body, mind, and spirit. While stress management is one benefit of yoga practice, its true purpose is to help the practicer attain spiritual enlightenment. Yoga is not based in any particular religious tradition and its practices can complement those of any religion.

▲ *ACTION PLAN*

RELAXATION PRACTICE

Use the following questions to help you make a plan for relaxation practice.

1. How might regular relaxation practice be beneficial for you?

   _____

   _____

2. Choose the best time for daily relaxation practice:

   _____

3. Where will you practice? How will you avoid interruptions (e.g., find a time when roommate is not home, unplug the telephone, etc.)?

   _____

   _____

4. What problems (real or perceived) might encourage you to skip your relaxation practice? Describe how you might deal with each problem.

   _____

   _____

   _____

Some students find that recording their relaxation practice helps them follow through with their plans to find a technique that works. Simply record the date and time of practice, and any observations or thoughts that come to you.

Date	Time	Relaxation Technique	Notes
____	____	_____	_____
____	____	_____	_____
____	____	_____	_____
____	____	_____	_____
____	____	_____	_____
____	____	_____	_____

Tai chi ch'uan is an activity that combines a meditative focus with physical movement.

Hatha yoga is the branch of yoga that emphasizes physical postures that incorporate breath control and mental concentration. Within hatha yoga, there is a wide variety of approaches that range from very strenuous to quite gentle and relaxing. All forms increase strength and flexibility. If you are new to yoga and would like to give it a try, a yoga class is preferable to trying postures from a book, especially if you have any kind of physical limitations or have not exercised in a long time. Effective technique often requires expert coaching. Hatha yoga has become quite popular over the last 20 years, so finding a class has become easier.

SUMMARY

1. Practicing relaxation skills allows you to voluntarily reduce sympathetic arousal and thus counteract the fight-or-flight response.
2. Relaxation techniques can help increase self-awareness. They enhance your ability to discern irrational beliefs, challenge negative thinking, and develop hardiness traits.
3. Relaxation practice helps you communicate more effectively, set clearer goals and values, evaluate problems, dream up creative solutions, and improve health behavior.
4. Regular relaxation is essential for maintaining optimal health and well-being.
5. The relaxation response is governed by the parasympathetic branch of the autonomic nervous system. The relaxation response is associated with a slow, calm heartbeat; low resting blood pressure levels; slow, deep breathing; and relaxed muscles. While the fight-or-flight response inhibits digestion, parasympathetic stimulation encourages the digestion and absorption of food.
6. Regular relaxation practice can help prevent and treat stress-related illness such as headaches, gastrointestinal problems, pain due to muscle tension, hypertension, heart disease, insomnia, and anxiety.
7. Guidelines for successful relaxation practice include the following: (1) schedule a convenient time and place; (2) be as comfortable as possible; (3) try not to try; (4) keep a relaxation log; (5) avoid falling asleep; (6) finish relaxation sessions by coming back slowly.

8. Maintain medical treatment protocols if you are being treated for a medical disorder, and do not rely on relaxation for an immediate cure.

9. Occasionally people experience anxiety or even panic attacks during relaxation practice. If this happens, breathe deeply, interrupt your practice, and calm yourself down by talking to a friend, going for a walk, or involving yourself in familiar tasks.

10. The Body Scan exercise is designed to help increase your awareness of physical sensations that are normally ignored when you are busy.

11. Progressive muscular relaxation is a relaxation technique designed by Edmund Jacobson in the 1920s. Jacobson was one of the first researchers to convince Western scientists of the value of relaxation practice. Progressive muscular relaxation asks you to alternately contract then relax specific muscle groups, and it increases your awareness of muscle tension levels.

12. Mindfulness exercises are powerful relaxation techniques.

13. Deep breathing may be the easiest and most accessible relaxation technique. Despite its simplicity, its relaxation effects can be very powerful.

14. Abdominal breathing, or diaphragmatic breathing, results from contraction of the diaphragm muscle rather than the chest muscles. Abdominal breathing is associated with relaxation.

15. Physical activity can help reduce physiological arousal and increase the relaxation response during the period of time following exercise.

16. Certain forms of physical activity such as hatha yoga, Tai chi ch'uan, and many of the martial arts incorporate relaxation and meditation techniques into their practice.

REFERENCES

Anderson, B. *Stretching.* Bolinas, CA: Shelter Publications, 1980.

Archer, J. Stress management: Evaluating a preventive approach for college students. *Journal of American College Health* 34: 157–160, 1986.

Benson, H. *The Relaxation Response.* New York: Morrow Press, 1975.

Bernstein, DA, and BA Given. Progressive Relaxation: Abbreviated methods. RL Woolfolk and PM Lehrer (eds). *Principles and Practice of Stress Management.* New York: Guilford Press, 1984.

Bohachick, P. Progressive relaxation training in cardiac rehabilitation: Effect on psychologic variables. *Nursing Research* 33: 283–287, 1984.

Borkovec, TD, AM Mathews, A Chambers, S Ebrahimi, R Lytle, and R Nelson. The effects of relaxation training with cognitive and nondirective therapy and the role of relaxation-induced anxiety in the treatment of generalized anxiety. *Journal of Consulting and Clinical Psychology* 55: 883–888, 1987.

Davis, M, ER Eshelman, and M McKay. *The Relaxation and Stress Reduction Workbook.* Oakland, CA: New Harbinger Publications, 1995.

Fahey, TD. *Basic Weight Training for Men & Women.* Mountain View, CA: Mayfield, 1994.

Folkins, CH, and WE Sime. Physical fitness training and mental health. *American Psychologist* 55: 373–389, 1981.

Gillespie, PR, and L Bechtel. *Less Stress in 30 Days.* New York: Signet Books, 1986.

Hellman, CJ, M Budd, J Borysenko, DC McClelland, and H Benson. A study of the effectiveness of two group behavior medicine interventions for patients with psychosomatic complaints. *Behavioral Medicine* 16: 165–173, 1990.

Holmes, DS, and TG Burish. Effectiveness of biofeedback for treating migraine and tension headaches: A review of the evidence. *Journal of Psychosomatic Research* 27: 515–532, 1983.

Holmes, DS, and DL Roth. Effects of aerobic exercise training and relaxation training on cardiovascular activity during psychological stress. *Journal of Psychosomatic Research* 32: 469–474, 1988.

Jacobson, E. *Progressive Relaxation.* Chicago: University of Chicago Press, 1929.

Jacobson, E. *You Must Relax!* New York: McGraw-Hill, 1976.

Jin, P. Efficacy of Tai Chi, brisk walking, meditation, and reading in reducing mental and emotional stress. *Journal of Psychosomatic Research* 36: 361–370, 1992.

Kabat-Zinn, J. An outpatient program in behavioral medicine for chronic pain based on the practice of mindfulness meditation: Theoretical considerations and preliminary results. *General Hospital Psychiatry* 4: 33–48, 1982.

Kabat-Zinn, J. *Full Catastrophe Living: Using the Wisdom of Your Body and Mind to Face Stress, Pain, and Illness.* New York: Delta, 1990.

Kirmil-Gray, K, JR Eagleston, CE Thoresen, and VP Zarcone, Jr. Brief consultation and stress management treatments for drug-dependent insomnia: Effects on sleep quality, self-efficacy, and daytime stress. *Journal of Behavioral Medicine* 8: 79–99, 1985.

Kitzinger, S. *The Complete Book of Pregnancy and Childbirth.* New York: Alfred A. Knopf, 1991.

Loehr, JE, and JA Migdow. *Take a Deep Breath.* New York: Villard Books, 1986.

Long, BC, and CJ Haney. Coping strategies for working women: Aerobic exercise and relaxation interventions. *Behavior Therapy* 19: 75–83, 1988.

Matheny, KB, DW Aycock, JL Pugh, WL Curlette, and KAS Cannella. Stress coping: A qualitative and quantitative synthesis with implications for treatment. *The Counseling Psychologist* 14: 499–549, 1986.

McDonnell, L, and ML Bowden. Breathing management: A simple stress and pain reduction strategy for use on a pediatric service. *Issues in Comprehensive Pediatric Nursing* 12: 339–344, 1989.

McGuigan, FL. Progressive Relaxation: Origins, principles, and clinical applications. RL Woolfolk and PM Lehrer (eds). *Principles and Practice of Stress Management.* New York: Guilford Press, 1984.

Ornish, D. *Dr. Dean Ornish's Program for Reversing Heart Disease.* New York: Ballantine Books, 1990.

Parrott, L. Helping children manage stress: Some preliminary observations. *Child and Family Behavior Therapy* 12: 69–73, 1990.

Patel, C. Yogic therapy. RL Woolfolk and PM Lehrer (eds). *Principles and Practice of Stress Management.* New York: Guilford Press, 1984.

Patel, C, and MG Marmot. Efficacy versus effectiveness of relaxation therapy in hypertension. *Stress Medicine* 4: 282–289, 1988.

Rajendran, R, and KV Kaliappan. Efficacy of behavioural programme in managing the academic stress and improving academic performance. *Journal of Personality and Clinical Studies* 6: 193–196, 1990.

Rice, PL. *Stress and Health.* Pacific Grove, CA: Brooks/Cole, 1992.

Rohsenow, DJ, RE Smith, and S Johnson. Stress management training as a prevention program for heavy social drinkers: Cognitions, affect, drinking and individual differences. *Addictive Behaviors* 10: 45–54, 1985.

Sachs, BC. Coping with stress. *Stress Medicine* 7: 61–63, 1991.

Sapolsky, RM. *Why Zebras Don't Get Ulcers.* New York: WH Freeman & Co., 1994.

Schneider, CJ. Cost effectiveness of biofeedback and behavioral medicine treatments: A review of the literature. *Biofeedback and Self-Regulation* 12: 71–92, 1987.

Seaward, BL. *Managing Stress.* Boston: Jones and Bartlett, 1997.

Sorbi, M, and B Tellegen. Differential effects of training in relaxation and stress-coping in patients with migraine. *Headache* 26: 473–481, 1986.

Smith, MS, and WM Womack. Stress management techniques in childhood and adolescence. *Clinical Pediatrics* 26: 581–585, 1987.

Stanton, HE. The reduction of secretarial stress. *Contemporary Hypnosis* 8: 45–50, 1991.

Thomas, BJ, and A Scott. A student stress management and referral system. *Journal of American College Health* 3: 232–233, 1987.

Tortora, GJ, and SR Grabowski. *Principles of Anatomy and Physiology.* New York: Harper-Collins, 1993.

Westcott, WL. *Strength Fitness: Physiological Principles & Training Techniques.* Dubuque, IA: Brown & Benchmark, 1994.

Woolfolk, RL, and PM Lehrer (eds). *Principles and Practice of Stress Management.* New York: Guilford Press, 1984.

Worthington, EL, Jr, GA Martin, and M Shumate. Which prepared childbirth coping strategies are effective? *Journal of Obstetric, Gynecologic, and Neonatal Nursing* 11: 45–51, 1982.

chapter 16

Meditation and Visualization: It's the Thought That Counts

Once viewed as the domain of cave-dwelling hermits, meditation has shaken off much of its mystery and has joined the ranks of respected relaxation techniques. Because of its effectiveness, meditation practice is included in many disease treatment and stress-reduction programs. Meditation has been used successfully to relieve the pain of headaches, backaches, and other musculoskeletal disorders (Kabat-Zinn, 1990; Sharma, Kumaraiah, Mishra, & Balodhi, 1990). Many people have used meditation to help control blood pressure and prevent the progression of atherosclerosis (Benson, 1984; Ornish, 1992; Sothers & Anchor, 1989). Meditation has helped people to cope with cancer therapies and chronic pain (Kaplan et al., 1993) and to lessen the severity of many other disorders (Deepak, Manchanda, & Maheshwari, 1994; Gaston et al., 1991; Kabat-Zinn et al., 1992). Meditation instruction is found in hospitals (Benson, 1984; Kabat-Zinn, 1990), prisons (Kabat-Zinn, 1994), athletics programs (Cox, 1991), workplaces (Alexander et al., 1993; Collings, 1989; Smith, 1993), and schools and colleges (Fergusson, Bonshek, & Boudigues, 1994; Greene & Hiebert, 1988; Laselle & Russell, 1993).

Meditation is not complicated; that may explain why many Westerners warm up to the practice of meditation slowly. We are accustomed to complicated instructions, activity, stimulation, and busy-ness. To sit quietly and observe our thoughts goes against our nature. A first attempt at meditation can feel strange and uncomfortable, but many students have found that learning to meditate is worth the effort. College students especially are likely to have a hectic pace and little quiet time. Those with roommates or families may rarely have a chance to be alone with their thoughts. The practice of meditation can provide a much-needed antidote to jam-packed days. Listening to the voices inside can help us sort out our values and priorities and can guide us as we make decisions and plan our lives.

Meditation has as its goal a change in a person's mental state. There are many types of meditation, and all include some sort of directed focus. So, when you practiced the Body Scan exercise in the previous chapter and focused on the various physical sensations in your body, you were meditating. Some forms of meditation train you to focus on one thing at a time to achieve control over your thoughts. That one thing might be a word or phrase, a visual image, or your breathing. Other forms ask you simply to observe your thoughts and feelings and to be open to insights that happen. Since body and mind are connected, meditation can be used to achieve physiological changes as well as changes in mental state. Meditation practice can result in heightened awareness, euphoria, and/or deep relaxation (Alexander et al., 1993; Delmonte 1986, 1990; Ikemi et al., 1986; Kabat-Zinn, 1994; Soskis, Orne, Orne, & Dingis, 1989; Wallace & Benson, 1972).

MEDITATION MEETS SCIENCE

Peace comes from within; do not seek it without.

BUDDHA

Meditation practices are as old as recorded history. They are found in almost every religion, where they are often used to quiet thoughts and to make the mind receptive to divine inspiration. Meditation practices are especially important in the Eastern religions, such as Hinduism and Buddhism, and in many Asian cultures (Seaward, 1997). They have also been used in Western traditions, often combined with forms of prayer.

The potential of meditation as a treatment to reduce stress and physiological arousal began to receive popular notice in North America in the 1960s when interest in Eastern spiritual practices surged. Stories of the mysterious physical and mental control achieved by practitioners of yoga piqued the curiosity of scientists and seekers alike. Researchers verified accounts of yogi masters who could decrease their heart rate to ten or fewer beats per minute, change the temperature of their bodies, alter their brain wave patterns, and dramatically lower their systolic blood pressure (Brown, 1974, 1984; Green & Green, 1977; Green, Green, & Walters, 1972; Rice, 1972; Wenger & Bagchi, 1961). Native American medicine men and Sufi mystics showed similar abilities (Green & Green, 1977).

Scientific verification of this control was exciting for two reasons. First, it required scientists to revise their theories of animal physiology. Researchers had previously believed that autonomic functions, such as regulation of heart rate, blood pressure, and body temperature, were outside voluntary control. Demonstration of the physical changes that could be induced by meditation meant that the textbooks had to be rewritten. Second, medical researchers began to wonder whether such control could be achieved by ordinary people and whether the power of meditation could be harnessed to produce therapeutic results, such as blood pressure control.

Meditation became popular among many groups in the 1960s with the advent of transcendental meditation (TM), a technique popularized by the Maharishi Mahesh Yogi. The Maharishi simplified mantra yoga practice to make it more palatable to a secular Western lifestyle. A mantra is a phrase from a prayer or other spiritual text that is repeated during meditation. It is used for its sound quality. Early interest in TM grew out of a desire to achieve an altered state of consciousness without drugs, but meditators also benefited from the relaxation they experienced when performing the meditation. People desiring to learn TM enroll in a short series of training sessions. At the last session, a guide aids the student in selecting a secret mantra or word. During meditation, TM practitioners continuously repeat their mantra (Rice, 1992).

Because of its timing and popularity, TM attracted quite a bit of attention from both the lay and scientific communities. Practitioners of transcendental meditation have provided a convenient subject pool for researchers interested in the effects of meditation. One group of researchers included Harvard cardiologist Herbert Benson. Observing the physiological relaxation that occurred during transcendental

meditation, Benson wondered whether the seemingly simple procedure of meditation would still be effective without the secret ceremonies and expensive price tag. Benson further simplified the TM meditation technique and taught it to his patients to learn whether meditation could help them control their hypertension. It could (Benson, 1984).

Benson called his meditation technique the Relaxation Response, as it evoked the physiological relaxation of resting homeostasis. It contained the elements found in most meditation techniques: sitting in a comfortable position in a quiet environment combined with a mental focus. When Benson first began teaching his meditation technique, he advised people to pick any word or phrase to repeat silently with each exhalation. For people who couldn't think of a word, he suggested the word "one," which is relatively value-free and could fit into any belief system. Benson later discovered that patients who had chosen a prayer or other deeply meaningful phrase to meditate with had better results both in terms of adherence to their meditation practice and their clinical improvement (Benson, 1984). Benson concluded that drawing upon one's spiritual beliefs during meditation created a more potent meditation experience.

THE PSYCHOPHYSIOLOGY OF MEDITATION

Like all relaxation practice, meditation affects both body and mind. Meditation is therapeutic because the relaxation response can reduce pain and allow natural healing processes to work at their maximal level. By calming thoughts and reducing anxiety, meditation can short-circuit the escalating cycle of pain causing panic causing further pain and panic. By relieving stress, meditation may reduce cortisol levels. You may remember from Chapter 3 that cortisol works to increase energy availability for short-term emergencies. This is an adaptive response in the short run, but when levels remain elevated, cortisol causes long-term havoc by inhibiting immune function and tissue repair.

Meditation affects brain function by changing normal thought patterns. The brain emits electrical charges, just as the heart and muscles do. These tiny currents can be amplified and displayed by a machine known as an electroencephalograph (EEG). Different brain waves indicate different states of consciousness. Alpha waves reflect a relaxed, meditative state and can be produced at will by people experienced in meditation (Rice, 1992). People who regularly practice some form of meditation report fewer stressors and illness symptoms; lower levels of anxiety, depression, and hostility; and higher levels of subjective well-being than people who rarely or never meditate (Alexander et al., 1993; Beauchamp-Turner & Levinson, 1992; Gelderloos, Hermans, Ahlscrom, & Jacoby, 1989; Pearl & Carlozzi, 1994; Shapiro, 1992; Zika, 1987). Many people find that meditation practice increases their stress resistance (Collings, 1989; Delmonte, 1990; Seaward, 1997).

MEDITATION BASICS

Although there are many varieties of meditation, most include the following elements.

1. Quiet Environment

Reduce the distraction potential of your meditation environment as much as possible. Choose a time when you will not be interrupted, turn off the telephone, and put a sign on the door. If you have a roommate or family, find a time when they will respect your need to practice and not need to disturb you. Many meditators find that first thing in the morning before the household (and the rest of the world) awakens is best.

A truly silent environment is often impossible. Perhaps you hear voices out in the hall, traffic noise outdoors, dogs barking, or children playing. No problem. These noises are part of real life, and meditation must take place despite real life. Learning to meditate with some background noise is valuable practice.

2. A Comfortable Position

Although lying down is permitted for some of the relaxation exercises, meditators find the position too suggestive of sleep. A sitting posture produces a more alert mental state. Your sitting position should be as comfortable as possible—one you can maintain for at least ten minutes to begin with. You might think a slouch in your chair is best, but you'll find it uncomfortable after a while. Sitting with a straight back presents the best musculoskeletal balance, with no one muscle group taking all the antigravity stress. A straight back is also conducive to an alert mental state. During meditation, you may either close your eyes, or keep them focused on a point in front of you. Examples of sitting positions are shown in Figure 16.1.

3. A Mental Focus

Pick one. If you wish, try the word *one* to begin with. Or choose a suggestive word or phrase like *relax, peace,* or *let go.* A short line or phrase from a favorite prayer works well. The word or phrase should help you feel safe, secure, and relaxed. For many meditators, relaxation is enough. But remember Benson's observation that faith and meaning conferred superior clinical advantages. Many meditators will use a word or phrase that helps them feel connected to a deeper reality than daily life, a

FIGURE 16.1 *Sitting Positions for Meditation*

word that will help them achieve transcendence. Transcendence is a grand word for a reachable experience. When you transcend your daily "normal" state of mind, you step outside the daily grind. You may sense a connection to a larger spiritual reality. But whether you believe in a god or spiritual power, you might at least feel as though you are part of the continuum of history, the family of humanity, and life on earth. And if the idea of transcendence is not relevant to your present experience, read on! The relaxation benefits are still yours to enjoy.

4. Physical Relaxation and Calm Breathing

Meditation practice often begins with a minute or two of physical relaxation and breathing awareness. With a quick body scan and a few deep breaths, you can lower your physiological arousal and bring your awareness into the present moment. The mental focus is often coordinated with the breath. For example, try repeating your word or phrase with each exhalation.

5. Passive Attitude

A passive attitude prevents your judgmental mind from interfering with your meditation practice. The harder you try and the more harshly you criticize your wandering mind, the farther you stray from the relaxation response. The first minute or two might seem easy. Then your mind might begin to wander, until your thoughts sound something like this: "Relax . . . relax . . . relax . . . I'm doing it! Relax . . . relax . . . what happens next? Is ten minutes up yet? Oh, 9 more to go . . . relax . . . relax . . . I hope I do OK on that exam this afternoon. OOPS, I'm not doing it any more, RELAX . . . Relax . . . relax." When your mind starts to wander, simply bring your attention back to your focus, without judgment, scolding, or frustration.

6. Regular Practice

Like everything, meditation gets easier with practice. Practice is essential for the realization of meditation's benefits. If you are new to meditation, start with one 10-minute session per day, gradually increasing the time to 15 or 20 minutes when you are ready. How will you know when the time is up? Setting an alarm ruins your relaxation. Keep a clock within reach of your peripheral vision and sneak a glance at it periodically.

JUST SITTING: MINDFULNESS MEDITATION

We discussed mindfulness in Chapter 11 in the context of allowing yourself to experience pleasure, to bring your awareness to the present moment. Mindfulness meditation is the meditation version of mindfulness and grows out of Buddhist

---

● EXERCISE

THE RELAXATION RESPONSE

1. Pick a focus word or phrase.
2. Sit quietly in a comfortable position.
3. Close your eyes or focus them on a point in front of you.
4. Relax your muscles.
5. Become aware of your breathing, letting the breath come slowly and naturally. Repeat your word or phrase as you exhale.
6. Maintain a passive attitude. If other thoughts come along, disregard them and turn your attention back to your focus word.
7. Continue for 10 to 20 minutes.

Source: This exercise is drawn from Benson (1984), *Beyond the Relaxation Response.*

Many people enjoy combining meditation and journal writing, using insights that arise during meditation to explore meaningful themes.

meditation practice. It is similar in practice to the Relaxation Response except that you do not repeat a word or phrase. Instead, you try to keep your awareness in the present moment, using your breath as a focus.

Like other forms of meditation and relaxation, the goal of mindfulness meditation is to step outside your habitual thought patterns and automatic thoughts. Mindfulness meditation gives your linear, judgmental left brain a time out and allows your creative, intuitive brain some room to stretch its wings and to help you soar above the daily ruts that are so easy to get stuck in.

Remember from Chapter 12 how we interpret and unquestioningly accept our perceptions as "reality." Our habitual thought patterns tend to keep us mainly in the past, ruminating over what we did or failed to do, or in the future, worrying about what is yet to come. Mindfulness meditation helps us let go of un-

● EXERCISE

SITTING

Mindfulness meditation begins with a balanced sitting posture and observation of your breathing. Your breathing serves to anchor your awareness in the present moment. As your mind wanders, simply observe your thoughts with that trying-not-to-try detachment, that nonjudgmental attitude that you have been cultivating in all the relaxation exercises. Bring your attention back to the present moment, back to your breathing. Keep your awareness on what is happening in the present moment.

Source: This exercise is drawn from Kabat-Zinn (1994), *Wherever You Go There You Are.*

necessary attachment to prior judgment and automatic thoughts that limit our perception.

One of the goals of mindfulness meditation is to break the spell of the automatic thoughts that keep you from experiencing the present moment, and thus to bring more present-moment awareness into your daily life. Such awareness can help you see more clearly and to accomplish more effectively the action plans you have set in previous chapters. With this awareness you become more in touch with your values and life goals, so you make better decisions and you make them more easily. You become a better problem solver because you see a broader picture and think creatively to come up with more effective solutions. You become a better listener and communicate more directly and clearly. You will have less trouble deciphering troubling emotions, such as anger and hostility, and you will achieve a greater understanding of their sources. You will find strength in yourself so you need not look to outside addictive agents, such as food, alcohol, or drugs, for relief. Mindfulness is about waking up from ignorance and responding more appropriately to potential sources of stress.

■ STUDENT STRESS

NINA'S MEDITATION PRACTICE

Nina came back to finish college after spending four years as an administrative assistant in a fast-paced corporation. Although her English was very good, it was her second language. She did well in her courses by working very hard. During her second semester back at school, she began having severe headaches that interfered with her studying, not to mention her good humor. As there was no underlying physiological disease causing the headaches, Nina's doctor gave her a prescription for painkillers and pronounced her "healthy," but Nina knew she wasn't. She enrolled in a stress management class, hoping to learn some relaxation techniques that would help eliminate her headaches.

At first, Nina wasn't too sure the class would be helpful. During the first part of the semester, the class topics—organization and time management skills—did not address Nina's problem. Indeed, she had each moment of her day organized weeks in advance. She worked part-time while carrying a full course load and seemed to have put her own needs on hold until some point in the future. Her direction was clear: she wanted a business career that would bring her more money and prestige than her previous position. Nina loved deadline pressure and life in the fast lane. Why the headaches? She was beginning to feel that they would jeopardize all she was working so hard to achieve.

One of the assignments in Nina's stress management class was to attend some sort of stress management-related workshop or seminar in the area. She noticed a poster announcing a meditation workshop when she was at church one Sunday morning and decided to go. The workshop was led by the priest at her church, a man Nina respected and admired. He presented information about the health and spiritual benefits of meditation and the simple technique of mindfulness meditation. Nina's stress management class also required the students to select one relaxation technique for two weeks of daily practice, so Nina decided to give meditation a try.

At first, just sitting for ten minutes was hard. Nina felt she should be doing something productive. She must have looked at the clock at least forty times.

An excellent description of meditation comes from Jon Kabat-Zinn's book on mindfulness meditation, *Wherever You Go There You Are* (1994):

> *Meditation does not involve trying to change your thinking by thinking some more. It involves watching thought itself. . . . By watching your thoughts without being drawn into them, you can learn something profoundly liberating about thinking itself, which may help you to be less of a prisoner of those thought patterns—often so strong in us—which are narrow, inaccurate, self-involved, habitual to the point of being imprisoning, and also just plain wrong. (p. 94)*

VISUALIZATION: DIRECTING THE POWER OF MEDITATION

To visualize is to make real in your mind's eye. When you combine your imagination with a meditationlike focus, you are using visualization techniques. Most of us have already had experience visualizing things we want to come true or things we are afraid of. We imagine opening that acceptance letter or job offer that comes in

"I never thought time could go so slowly!" she thought to herself. "Is this all that happens? How am I supposed to feel? What's the big deal?" But being a good student, she would return her awareness to her breathing and the present moment. "I'll just have to have faith that something will happen." As the days passed, her ability to let go of her thoughts improved. She would imagine each thought wrapped in a bubble, the way thoughts are written in comics, and that the bubble was floating up and away. She had occasional glimpses of herself as separate from her thoughts. It felt good.

At first disappointed that there was no miraculous change in her headaches, Nina found the meditation sessions so refreshing that she continued them. She joined a group that met to meditate on Sunday night at her church. She made several friends in the group over the following months and enjoyed the hour that was "just for myself" and not "productive" in the usual sense of the word. She realized the headaches had given her the opportunity to put her needs first for a change.

Nina began to become more mindful in her busy, daily life. Her ability to concentrate on one thing at a time made it easier for her to complete assignments more efficiently. Her increased awareness helped her pinpoint the triggers that started the headaches: tightening in her neck and shoulder muscles and a feeling of rushing to accomplish what she perceived to be "an overwhelming volume of work." As she learned to tune in to these cues before a full-blown headache developed, she became better able to intervene in her stress response. Instead of viewing the work volume as "overwhelming," she would focus exclusively on her top priority assignment. She would take a moment to breathe deeply, massage her neck and shoulders, do a few stretches, and think some pleasant thoughts: vacation in two more weeks! This would often short-circuit the headache completely, so Nina was able to use less and less of the pain medication.

▶ STRESS RESEARCH

Jon Kabat-Zinn: *Behavioral Medicine*

As medical researchers have discovered the important connection between stress overload and illness and have learned that each plays into the other, a natural response has been the development of treatment modalities that address the patient's need for improved stress management skills. Many of these treatment modalities fall under the rubric of behavioral medicine.

Behavioral medicine incorporates stress management and relaxation training along with other types of lifestyle change into programs designed to help patients improve their health by modifying their behavior. Behavioral medicine is based on the observation that "mental and emotional factors, the ways in which we think and behave, can have a significant effect, for better or worse, on our physical health and on our capacity to recover from illness and injury" (Kabat-Zinn, 1990, p. 1).

Behavioral medicine is not a substitute for but rather complements more traditional treatment programs. People usually participate in a behavioral medicine program while they are undergoing standard medical treatment for a stress- or lifestyle-related disorder. People with chronic neck and shoulder pain, for example, may still fill their prescriptions for muscle relaxants and use them as necessary. But they also attend sessions at the behavioral medicine clinic that teach them how to better manage their stress and short-circuit muscle tension so that problems do not become such a "pain in the neck."

One of the most successful behavioral medicine programs was founded by medical researcher Jon Kabat-Zinn. Inspired by Herbert Benson's pioneering work incorporating the Relaxation Response into hypertension treatment programs, Kabat-Zinn has applied relaxation training to the treatment of many other disorders and has created a training program to make mindfulness meditation more accessible to people suffering from stress-related disorders. Kabat-Zinn's clinic in turn later became the "inspiration and model" (Borysenko, 1990) for Benson's Mind/Body Medical Institute and many other well-respected behavioral medicine clinics as well.

Kabat-Zinn's clinic at the University of Massachusetts Medical Center has guided over 4,000 people through an eight week program called the Stress Reduction and Relaxation Program (SR&RP). According to Kabat-Zinn (1990), SR&RP consists of systematic training in mindfulness, which he defines as "moment-to-moment awareness. . . . It is a systematic approach to developing new kinds of control and wisdom in our lives, based on our inner capacities for relaxation, paying attention, awareness, and insight" (p. 2).

Behavioral medicine gives the responsibility for healing back to the patient. Kabat-Zinn writes that his program "is not a rescue service in which people are passive recipients of support and therapeutic advice. Rather it is a vehicle for active learning, in which people can build on the strengths that they already have and come to do something for themselves to improve their own health and well-being" (p. 2). Behavioral medicine exemplifies the wellness approach to health promotion and disease prevention because it treats disease not as an event belonging to a single organ but to the whole person and his or her environment.

the mail. The phone rings and we imagine it is that special someone, or we imagine having a nice vacation on the beach. We are also experts at imagining disasters. Your friend is late for lunch with you. An accident? Heart attack? Standing you up because of something you said yesterday?

When you use visualization for stress management or healing, you purposefully direct your imagination and sharpen the focus. Visualization is often used in stress management programs to counteract the fight-or-flight response and achieve deep relaxation. It is used medically to induce relaxation and stimulate the healing process (Achterberg, 1985; Achterberg & Lawlis, 1980; Brown 1974, 1984; Ornish, 1992; Simonton, Matthews-Simonton, & Creighton, 1978). Visualization is also used to reprogram destructive thoughts and behaviors and to replace self-defeating beliefs with more realistic and positive ones (Gawain, 1978).

ANY SUGGESTIONS? HYPNOSIS AND VISUALIZATION

One of the earliest forms of visualization to be used by Western medicine is hypnosis (Ulett & Peterson, 1965). While hypnosis has been around for a long time, it is probably the least understood of all stress management techniques, and scientists disagree on what actually occurs during hypnosis. Some believe that the person undergoing hypnosis enters an altered state of consciousness or hypnotic trance (Barber, Spanos, & Chaves, 1974). Studies suggest, however, that only about 16 percent of people who undergo hypnosis actually achieve a deep trance (Edmonston, 1981). Therefore, many researchers believe that subjects are willing to carry out suggestions given during hypnosis simply because they have positive expectations that make them willing to do what is requested by the hypnotist (Barber et al., 1974).

Hypnotism helps people achieve a state of cortical inhibition. Like other visualization and meditation techniques, hypnosis may inhibit the processes associated with the dominant cortical hemisphere (linear thinking, logic, language) and allow more input from the nondominant hemisphere (ideas, pictures) (Cox, 1991).

Hypnosis should be performed only by a trained professional, since hypnotized people are vulnerable to suggestions made during hypnosis. Hypnosis begins with a clarification of goals and procedures between the therapist and the client. The therapist then begins the induction process during which the client is guided into a deep relaxation and possibly a hypnotic trance. During the relaxation or trance, the therapist makes therapeutic suggestions. For instance, a student dealing with test anxiety might receive suggestions that "when waiting for the teacher to pass out the exams, you will feel calm and confident." At the end of the session, the therapist brings the client out of the trance and reinforces the suggestions.

Hypnosis has been used effectively to treat a variety of stress-related complaints. It is often used in combination with other forms of psychotherapy (Sachs, 1986; Stanton, 1989). Its usefulness is limited in that it requires the involvement of a hypnotherapist. However, many hypnotherapists work with a client for only a few sessions, then turn the responsibility over to the client to continue with self-hypnosis procedures.

AUTOGENIC TRAINING: DO-IT-YOURSELF RELAXATION

Autogenic training is a very popular form of self-hypnosis, which grew out of research on hypnosis by physiologist Oskar Vogt at the end of the nineteenth century. Vogt noticed that many patients reported an improvement in medical symptoms such as fatigue, headaches, and muscle tension following hypnosis. He taught his experienced patients to put themselves in a trance to obtain these benefits (Davis, Eshelman, & McKay, 1995).

Vogt's work piqued the interest of Johannes Schultz, a Berlin psychiatrist. He noted that Vogt's patients had reported physical feelings of warmth and heaviness in their arms and legs when coming out of their trances. Schultz found that by simply imagining heaviness and warmth in your arms and legs you can create a state of relaxation similar to a hypnotic trance. Schultz combined autosuggestion with some yoga techniques to create his system called autogenic training, which he published in a book by the same name in 1932 (Schultz & Luthe, 1959).

Like other relaxation methods, autogenic training is designed to counter the fight-or-flight response and induce relaxation. Autogenic training has been found helpful for many stress-related disorders (Davis et al., 1995). Its simplicity makes it an ideal relaxation technique for beginners. Autogenics uses visualization of certain physical sensations as its focus. During relaxation, you repeat phrases silently to yourself or listen to them on a tape. Each phrase is repeated three to six times.

● EXERCISE

AUTOGENIC TRAINING

Autogenic training is most effectively practiced in a quiet environment. A relaxed posture is recommended. Try one of these:

1. Lying down with your legs about eight inches apart, arms resting comfortably at your sides.
2. Sitting in a comfortable chair with head, back, arms, and, if possible, legs supported.

Close your eyes to better visualize physical sensations. As you repeat the phrase, try to visualize the sensation being described. For instance, as you repeat "My right arm is heavy," you might imagine your right arm to be made of lead, so heavy you are unable to lift it. And above all, try not to try. Imagine, but don't force. The harder you try to make your hand heavy, the less successful you will be. Observe your visualization with the same passive, nonjudging awareness you have been using in the other relaxation exercises.

The sensations induced by autogenic training may be placed into six categories. Therapists who teach autogenic training recommend taking from four to ten months to master all six areas (Davis et al., 1995; Rice, 1992). So for the first two weeks, you might practice only the heaviness theme. Add the warmth theme for weeks three and four, and so forth. Some students jump right in and do fairly well practicing all six areas right away, even though this is not what is clinically recommended.

Here are the categories and the phrases used for each:

1. *Arm and leg heaviness:* Begin with your dominant arm; then focus on the other arm.

   "My right arm is heavy."
   "My left arm is heavy."
   "Both my arms are heavy."
   "My right leg is heavy."
   "My left leg is heavy."
   "Both my legs are heavy."
   "My arms and legs are heavy."

2. *Arm and leg warmth:*

   "My right arm is warm."
   "My left arm is warm."
   "Both my arms are warm."

FINE TUNING: BIOFEEDBACK FOR RELAXATION AND HEALING

With autogenics, you are attempting to change the way your body feels. Autogenic training and other relaxation training methods can be combined with biofeedback training to help you monitor your response. Biofeedback instruments give you information about what is happening in your body and enable you to use this information to gain control of the variables being monitored. For example, people who suffer from tension headaches can use biofeedback to learn how to relax tense muscles in the head and neck. Electrodes are attached

"My right leg is warm."
"My left leg is warm."
"Both my legs are warm."
"My arms and legs are warm."

"My arms and legs are heavy and warm."

3. *Regular and calm heartbeat:* Tuning into one's heartbeat makes some people uncomfortable. If this is the case for you, skip this one and come back to it in the future. Otherwise repeat this phrase:

"My heartbeat is regular and calm."

4. *Breathing calm and relaxed:*

"My breathing is calm and relaxed."
"It breathes me."

5. *Solar plexus warmth:* The solar plexus is located in the upper abdomen above the stomach but below the heart, near the base of the sternum (breastbone).

"My solar plexus is warm."

6. *Cool forehead:*

"My forehead is cool."

Begin your practice by relaxing, then start repeating the phrases silently to yourself. You may wish to add some general suggestions such as the following:

"My whole body feels quiet, heavy, comfortable, and relaxed."
"My mind is calm and quiet."
"I feel serene and still."

When you have achieved deep relaxation, you may also wish to suggest what Schultz called "Intentional Formulae" to help with changes you wish to make. These are similar to affirmations, which are discussed shortly. They should be believable and brief: "I am exercising and getting stronger every day," to encourage adherence to your exercise program, "My lungs are healing as I breathe fresh, clean air," to reinforce your plans to quit smoking.

Finish your session by repeating this phrase, "When I open my eyes, I will feel refreshed and alert." Give your muscles a stretch and bring your awareness back to your regular activities.

to the skin over one of the offending muscles, typically the frontalis muscle of the forehead. The electrodes detect muscle electrical activity: the more activity, the more contraction. The electrodes send this information to the biofeedback instrument, which converts it into a signal such as a beep or flashing light that can be received by the user. As you relax your forehead muscle, the beeps or lights slow down; if the muscle gets more tense, they speed up. Biofeedback instruments respond instantaneously to any change in muscle electrical activity, so users receive immediate feedback on how they are doing in their relaxation training.

Can't you just become aware of muscle tension levels without a machine? You can, but biofeedback machines have more sensitivity than most people do, so they can speed the relaxation training process. Their ultimate goal, however, is to help you increase your own awareness. As you may have noticed when you tried progressive relaxation (Chapter 15), some muscle groups are harder to tune in to. Muscles that are chronically contracted are especially difficult to feel. Biofeedback can help you learn to sense contraction in and relax these important muscle groups.

If a body response can be monitored, biofeedback training can be applied. Responses most commonly measured are those that are most accessible. Electromyography (EMG) senses the electrical activity of muscles, as described in the example above. Electroencephalography (EEG) gives information about brain wave activity. The electroencephalograph is the instrumentation that allowed scientists to describe the alpha wave production seen in meditation discussed above. Using EEG, people can learn to produce the types of brain waves associated with relaxed or creative mental states. The galvanic skin response (GSR), also known as electrodermal response (EDR), is what lie detector tests use. Changes in the electrical conductivity of the skin reflect minute changes in sweat gland activity and skin cell membrane permeability, which occur in response to stress.

Biofeedback instruments can also sense changes in skin temperature, which reflect vasodilation (opening) of peripheral blood vessels. The more relaxed a person is, the greater will be the peripheral vasodilation. Blood pressure, heart rate and rhythm, and even stomach acid secretion can also be controlled with biofeedback training.

HOW DOES BIOFEEDBACK WORK?

Where the mind goes, the body follows.

CHINESE PROVERB

No one knows exactly how autonomic functions are brought under voluntary control. Learning to elicit the relaxation response results in the physiological changes associated with activation of the parasympathetic nervous system and hormone levels associated with resting homeostasis; this is probably at least part of the answer. If you ask people who have used biofeedback to induce relaxation how they make their headaches go away, they'll say they make their arms heavy, or they imagine they're on the beach, or they focus their eyes in a certain way.

People learning to use biofeedback usually work with a therapist who adjusts the instruments and gives suggestions. When biofeedback is used to decrease sympathetic arousal, people usually practice a relaxation technique, such as meditation, autogenic training, or some other form of visualization. If you are trying to increase blood flow to your cold hands, you might focus on the autogenic phrase "My hands are warm." You might imagine putting your hands into a hot bath, making this image the focus of meditation. Once the therapist has set up the instrumentation, the success of the biofeedback program is in the hands of the person seeking treatment. The machines can't make you relax; they can only tell you about your progress. If the beeps slow down, you know whatever you're visualizing is helping; whatever you are doing (or not doing) is working. What works varies from person to person. With practice, you learn to associate certain images, thoughts, and sensations with relaxation. As with any relaxation technique, the practitioner must maintain an attitude of passive attention, a "trying not to try." Willing the arteries in the hand to open only leads to more tension and less opening. Instead, you must simply be aware, tune in, relax, and notice what seems to work.

An important part of biofeedback training is learning to transfer the skills learned during practice sessions to real-life situations. A person must be able to regulate blood pressure while driving in traffic, talking to friends, and performing a job, not just when meditating in a quiet room or hooked up to the biofeedback machine.

CLINICAL APPLICATIONS OF BIOFEEDBACK

Biofeedback treatment can be expensive and difficult to find, so most people seek it only when driven by some sort of health problem that appears to be stress related. It has been effective for treating ulcers, colitis, irritable bowel syndrome, hypertension, tension and migraine headaches, and muscle tension problems such as back pain and TMJ syndrome (Albright, Andreassi, & Brockwell, 1991; Greenspoon & Olson, 1986; Jones, 1989; King, 1992; Shellenberger, Turner, & Green, 1986; Thackwray-Emmerson, 1988, 1989). Biofeedback has also been helpful for a disorder called Raynaud's disease whose symptoms are cold extremities due to peripheral vasoconstriction (Green & Green, 1977). Depression, insomnia, and psychological anxiety disorders, such as phobias, often respond to biofeedback training (Hudesman, Beck, & Smith, 1982). Biofeedback has also been helpful in the treatment of addiction (Denney & Baugh, 1992).

CREATIVE VISUALIZATION

Have you ever talked yourself into doing something you once believed you couldn't do? Or did you ever convince yourself that you would fail at something that you could really have succeeded at? Your beliefs are enormously important in shaping your reality. Self-talk has been discussed in this regard. Daydreams and memories continually shape one's present reality as well. All are forms of visualization.

So far we have presented visualization techniques that take more focus than imagination. In the rest of this chapter you will explore visualization techniques that call more deeply on the creative power of your imagination. You are already familiar with the idea that reality is at least partly what you perceive it to be. Creative visualization is based on the premise that your perception is not only a reflection of the reality that is "out there" but that your perception and imagination also help to create that reality. You are probably familiar with the phrase "a self-fulfilling prophecy." And perhaps you have heard people say, "Be careful what you wish, for it might come true." These may come from observations that predictions and wishes, even those that appear far-fetched, can subconsciously guide your actions and create opportunities for them to be realized.

Visualization exercises may be classified into two categories:

1. *Programmed visualization.* With programmed visualization, you focus on an image decided on beforehand. Programmed visualization is similar to self-hypnosis. You might focus on an image that makes you feel relaxed, or you might visualize a goal you hope to attain, a new behavior pattern, or an improvement in your health. Athletes might visualize competitive success, and heart patients might visualize arteries healing and adequate cardiac blood flow.

2. *Receptive visualization.* Psychologist Carl Jung used receptive visualization with many of his patients. He asked them to meditate in a fashion similar to the mindfulness meditation described earlier in this chapter, with no goal or focus. He told his patients simply to observe the images that came into their awareness during the meditation session. These images were later explored in therapy (Davis et al., 1995). In receptive visualization exercises, you might also ask your deeper mind questions. You might ask, "Why am I not comfortable with this relationship?" or "Why can't I get going on this project?" Sometimes you get no answer, but sometimes the answers that come from your deeper wisdom are surprisingly helpful. Receptive visualization often begins with a programmed visualization that is somewhat open-ended. You might begin with a pleasant place visualization (described on page 351), then visualize some sort of inner guide entering the scene to whom you direct your questions and from whom you receive advice.

GUIDELINES FOR VISUALIZATION PRACTICE

1. Begin visualization practice by lying down in a comfortable, quiet place. Let your eyes close.

2. Practice a relaxation technique, such as the body scan or diaphragmatic breathing, to relax your body and mind.

3. Focus on the visualization you have decided to practice, using all your senses to make the images as real as possible in your mind's eye. For example, if you are imagining walking through a beautiful garden, visualize the lovely surroundings. Hear the sound of the wind rustling the leaves and feel the wind against your skin. Imagine touching the soft flower petals and smelling the fragrances. Perhaps you can even taste the sweet nectar of the honeysuckle or chew on a blade of grass. The more real you can make your image, the more successful your visualization will be.

4. Practice regularly.

EFFECTIVE IMAGES

It may take time and practice to create effective images for your visualization practice. For example, designing your "special place" (see exercise on the opposite page) might take several visits. One stress management student initially thought a garden would make a nice special place, but once she imagined relaxing there she found too many bees buzzing around, and thoughts of the hours of weeding that needed to be done in her garden at home kept intruding on her ability to relax. The next time she went to an imaginary cottage at the beach! Images are entirely personal and must feel right and work for you.

Behavior change visualizations must be believable. You must be able to visualize them as though they are already a reality. If the images are too phony, your subconscious mind will reject them. One stress management student, who was on the verge of failing two of his courses, was trying to manage his time better and reduce his tendency to procrastinate. During his visualization practice in class, he tried to imagine himself looking at his straight-A report card, but having never received straight-A's in his life, he couldn't believe his image. Instead, he came up with an image of himself going to the library at a set time each afternoon to do his homework. This image was more constructive and reinforced the behavior he needed to strengthen.

VISUALIZATION FOR STRESS MANAGEMENT

You can use both programmed and receptive visualization for stress management. Visualizing a relaxing scene elicits the relaxation response. Reinforcing behavior change for stressful behaviors, such as procrastination, is also helpful. You can imagine yourself beginning research for the paper you have put off, or visualize yourself getting to that aerobics class you've been meaning to attend. Receptive visualization can help you explore questions that need answering: What do I want to be when I grow up? Where does this relationship want to go? What do I want to major in?

BEYOND RELAXATION: VISUALIZATION FOR SUCCESS

Observe the faces of athletes right before competition. What are they thinking about? They are visualizing probably the upcoming event and focusing on peak performance. Successful athletes train their minds as well as their bodies. They

● EXERCISE

PLEASANT PLACE VISUALIZATION

Here is the relaxation visualization voted most popular by college students. You design an imaginary place that becomes your retreat and serves as an introduction to further visualization and relaxation practice. Performers visualize their special places before rehearsals and performances, athletes before competition, students before exams. Once you have practiced visualizing your special place for a few weeks, you can "go there" whenever you need to pull yourself together.

As you begin to create your special place, be sure that it feels comfortable and safe. You might imagine a place you actually know and enjoy, or a place you knew as a child. It might be a place you have read about, seen in a movie, or dreamed of. Most students find that creating their special place takes some time; they prefer to design their special place before they begin the visualization exercise. Once you have your special place, you might wish to tape record the instructions below, or have a friend read them to you slowly. Each time you perform this exercise, you may make any changes that create a more secure and relaxing image. Add details to your special place that increase your feelings of well-being and relaxation: a breeze blowing through white lace curtains, a gurgling stream, the smell of freshly baked bread. Surround your place with a magic rainbow. Pretend you are at the end of the fairy tale where everyone lives happily ever after. As you go along with your visualization, if something doesn't feel right, change it.

Relaxing in Your Special Place

Begin to visualize your special place by lying down in a comfortable position and taking a few deep breaths. Scan your body for tension; feel yourself becoming more relaxed with each exhalation.

Now begin to imagine yourself exploring your special place. What do you see? Look all around and make the images as real as possible in your mind's eye. Notice what is in the distance and what is nearby. Take in as much detail as you can. . . . What can you hear in your special place? Make the sounds as vivid as you can. . . . Now imagine the smells in your special place. . . . Reach out and touch something nearby. What textures and temperatures do you feel?

Now sit or lie down in your special place; feel yourself becoming more and more relaxed. Focus on the wonderful way you feel in your special place: peaceful, relaxed, secure, content, and comfortable. Spend a few minutes enjoying these good feelings.

Now slowly bring your awareness back to your surroundings. Open your eyes, stretch your muscles, and enjoy the feeling of relaxation.

practice visualization exercises to keep distracting thoughts from interfering with their performance and to allow the parts of their brain responsible for peak performance to be uninhibited by anxiety or fear.

Visualization exercises improve your ability to concentrate on one thing at a time and can thus enhance the quality of your work or performance in any area. Visualization practice turns down the volume of that constant "mind chatter" that can get in the way of problem solving, clear thinking, and performance. It's difficult to deliver a powerful tennis serve if you are thinking, "I'll never be able to do this."

You probably can't deliver an oral presentation with confidence if you keep saying to yourself, "I'm not prepared for this. I hate talking in front of people."

Sport psychologists have long known that the learning and execution of motor skills is inhibited by distracting mental monologues. Players learn to visualize the successful performance of a motor skill before playing and to put all their attention on the activity at hand, without the distraction of mental verbiage. This is what some sport psychologists have termed *playing out of your mind*. Such practice results in better progress and performance.

Visualization can also help you make a commitment to positive behavior change, such as exercising regularly, choosing healthful foods, or quitting smoking. When you set behavior change goals and visualize yourself achieving these goals, your motivation and chances of success improve.

One of the most important benefits of visualization is the formation of a more positive outlook and self-concept. Visualization can change the way you talk to yourself, see yourself, and perceive events around you. This in turn affects your behavior; it helps you take better care of yourself and communicate more effectively with others.

Since visualization techniques calm busy minds, they decrease feelings of stress and promote good health. Some people take advantage of these relaxation effects and use visualization to assist the body's natural healing processes. They focus on images of healing, like immune cells engulfing foreign invaders. People with chronic pain use visualization to induce relaxation and reduce pain severity.

AFFIRMATIONS: POSITIVE SELF-TALK TO REINFORCE YOUR VISUALIZATION

Affirmations are positive statements that reinforce your goals. When you repeat your affirmations to yourself in a deeply relaxed state, you are practicing self-hypnosis. Affirmations can reinforce your intentions to increase your stress resistance, organize your time better, improve the quality of your relationships, find a

---

● EXERCISE

PRACTICING VISUALIZATION FOR SUCCESS

1. *Set your visualization goal.* How can visualization help you? What do you want to achieve?

2. *Devise an image to represent the goal behavior.* Keep the image clear and simple. If you want to eat less junk food, for example, you might target a behavior such as your morning visit to the doughnut shop. You could imagine yourself taking a different route in the morning or walking by the doughnut place without going inside. Replace the behavior you want to get rid of with a better one. Maybe you take along a bagel to eat instead of the doughnut. You imagine going right past that doughnut shop and being happy with that most delicious bagel. You can also visualize yourself as a leaner person, looking and feeling the way you would like.

Here's another example. One stress management student wanted to quit losing her temper and yelling at her two children. She had just completed a workshop series on effective parenting and learned how important it was to use her anger wisely. She also began to see that the more she yelled, the less her children listened, and the more angry she became. During her visualization practice, she visualized herself with her two children, the anger at their behavior welling up inside her. She pictured herself taking a few deep breaths, controlling her voice, and dealing with the rivalry directly but calmly. She imagined herself remaining calm and detached despite the flaring tempers of her children.

3. *Practice visualizing your image, making it as real as possible to all your senses, just as you did with the special place exercise.* Many students begin their visualization with the special place practice, and then move on to visualize their other images. As you focus on your image, maintain that passive, noninvolved attitude you have been using in the other relaxation exercises. This can be hard if the image elicits strong emotions! Try to achieve an objective attitude toward the image. Simply view it with your mind's eye and trust that the results will come.

---

satisfying job, and so forth. Here a few guidelines for writing effective affirmations from *Creative Visualization* by Shakti Gawain (1978):

1. Phrase affirmations in the present tense, as though your goal is already achieved. You must focus on your goal's potential for present reality and not think of it as something that will happen later, or later may never come. "I choose healthful foods" has more influence than "I will be thinner by springtime."

2. Phrase affirmations in a positive way, affirming what you want. "I set priorities and manage my time well" is more effective than "I won't procrastinate anymore." Say these statements to yourself. Can you feel the difference? The first is reaffirming. The second almost shakes a finger at you, reminding you of your previous bad behavior. It calls you to focus on what you *don't* want.

3. Keep affirmations simple and direct. An affirmation should be "a clear statement that conveys a strong feeling; the more feeling it conveys, the stronger the impression it makes on your mind" (Gawain, 1978, p. 24). Avoid affirmations that get lost in too many words and details.

▲ ACTION PLAN

MEDITATION AND VISUALIZATION

Use the following questions to help you make a plan for practicing meditation and visualization, and use the log to record your practice.

1. How could meditation and visualization practice be most beneficial for you? Which techniques seemed most interesting or useful to you?

2. Choose the best time for daily practice.

3. Where will you practice? How will you avoid interruptions?

4. What problems (real or perceived) might encourage you to skip your meditation and visualization practice? Describe how you might deal with each problem.

Practice Log

Date	Time	Meditation/Visualization Technique	Notes

4. Create affirmations that feel right to you. We each respond differently to a given affirmation statement, just as we all respond differently to visual images. If the wording of an affirmation sounds stupid or silly, it won't be believable and will be rejected by your deeper mind.

5. As you practice your affirmations, keep in mind that you are creating something new, not redoing what currently exists. Adopt the attitude that you accept what currently exists while creating a better future. This prevents you from getting stuck in a conflict with your present reality and again focusing on what you do not want.

6. Affirmations are not intended to repress negative feelings. Just as you observe your thoughts and feelings during mindfulness meditation, so too do you observe your feelings during visualization. Even negative thoughts and feelings have an important message that must be acknowledged.

7. When repeating your affirmations during relaxation, try to believe them, even if only for a few moments.

Try writing some affirmations of your own. Here are some examples of affirmations students have used in the past (several adapted from Gawain):

"Every day in every way I'm getting better and better."

"I love and appreciate myself just as I am."

"I have everything I need to relax and enjoy my life."

"Everything is just the way it is supposed to be."

"I communicate clearly and effectively."

"It's okay for me to have fun and enjoy myself, and I do!"

"I enjoy everything I do."

"I make good decisions, and my higher self is guiding me in everything I do."

Gawain notes that people who connect their affirmations to spiritual beliefs reap greater benefits, just as Benson found that meditation was more effective for those who called upon a higher power. If you are not comfortable with the word *God*, or a specific spiritual figure such as Christ or Buddha, try a term such as higher self, divine light, or the light within me.

> *The light of God surrounds me, the love of God unfolds me, the power of God flows through me. Wherever I am, God is, and all is well.*

SUMMARY

1. Meditation refers to a variety of techniques that include some sort of mental focus to alter one's mental state.
2. Like other relaxation techniques, meditation has been associated with the prevention and treatment of many stress-related disorders.
3. Meditation practices are as old as recorded history and are found in almost every religion. Western scientists became especially interested in meditation in the 1960s.
4. Transcendental meditation teaches the meditator to focus on a special mantra, or phrase, during meditation.
5. Herbert Benson introduced a secular meditation technique that he called the Relaxation Response. It mimics transcendental meditation except that

meditators select their own meditation mantras rather than being given mantras by their teachers.

6. Meditation practice elicits the physiological relaxation of resting homeostasis. Meditation is associated with alpha brain waves, which are indicative of a relaxed, meditative state.

7. Most forms of meditation include the following elements: (a) a quiet environment, (b) a comfortable sitting position, (c) a mental focus, (d) physical relaxation and calm breathing, (e) a passive attitude, and (f) regular practice.

8. In mindfulness meditation, meditators simply try to keep their awareness in the present moment, using the breath as their focus. The goal of mindfulness meditation is to observe the process of thought itself.

9. Visualization combines use of the imagination with a meditationlike focus.

10. Hypnosis is one type of visualization that combines deep relaxation or a trance-like state with suggestions made by the hypnotherapist.

11. Autogenic training was created by Johannes Schultz, a Berlin psychiatrist, who noted that people coming out of hypnotic trances reported specific physical sensations, such as warmth and heaviness in their arms and legs. Schultz found that visualizing these sensations could induce a state of relaxation.

12. Biofeedback training uses instruments that measure physiological variables such as muscle tension to give people information, or feedback, on their relaxation efforts. Biofeedback instrumentation can speed the mastery of relaxation techniques by helping people monitor their physiological responses.

13. Programmed visualization is a form of creative visualization in which a person focuses on an image designed to achieve some specific purpose, such as relaxation, behavior change, athletic performance, or healing.

14. Receptive visualization is similar to mindfulness meditation, in which a person simply becomes aware of ideas and images that emerge during the visualization session.

15. Affirmations are positive statements that reinforce one's goals. When repeated to oneself in a deeply relaxed state, they serve as hypnotic suggestions.

REFERENCES

Achterberg, J. *Imagery in Healing*. Boston: New Science Library, 1985.

Achterberg, J, and GF Lawlis. *Bridges of the Bodymind*. Champaign, IL: Institute for Personality and Ability Testing, 1980.

Albright, GL, JL Andreassi, and AL Brockwell. Effects of stress management on blood pressure and other cardiovascular variables. *International Journal of Psychophysiology* 11: 213–217, 1991.

Alexander, CN, GC Swanson, MV Rainforth, TW Carlisle, CC Todd, and RM Oates, Jr. Effects of the Transcendental Meditation program on stress reduction, health, and employee development: A prospective study in two occupational settings. *Anxiety, Stress, and Coping* 6: 245–262, 1993.

Alexander, CN, MV Rainforth, and P Gelderloos. Transcendental Meditation, self-actualization, and psychological health: A conceptual overview and statistical meta-analysis. *Journal of Social Behavior and Personality* 6: 189–247, 1991.

Barber, TX, NP Spanos, and JF Chaves. *Hypnosis, Imagination, and Human Potentialities*. New York: Pergamon Press, 1974.

Beauchamp-Turner, D, and DM Levinson. Effects of meditation on stress, health, and affect. *Medical Psychotherapy* 5: 123–132, 1992.

Benson, H, with W Proctor. *Beyond the Relaxation Response*. New York: Berkeley Books, 1984.

Borysenko. J. Foreword to J Kabat-Zinn, *Full Catastrophe Living*. New York: Delta, 1990, pp xv–xvii.

Brown, BB. *Between Health and Illness.* New York: Bantam Books, 1984.

Brown, BB. *New Mind, New Body.* New York: Bantam Books, 1974.

Collings, GH, Jr. Stress containment through meditation. *Prevention in Human Services* 6: 141–150, 1989.

Cox, RH. Intervention strategies. A Monat and RS Lazarus (eds). *Stress and Coping.* New York: Columbia University Press, 1991.

Davis, M, ER Eshelman, and M McKay. *The Relaxation and Stress Reduction Workbook.* Oakland, CA: New Harbinger Publications, 1995.

Deepak, KK, SK Manchanda, and MC Maheshwari. Meditation improves clinicoelectroencephalographic measures in drug-resistant epileptics. *Biofeedback and Self-Regulation* 19: 25–40, 1994.

Delmonte, MM. Expectancy and response to meditation. *International Journal of Psychosomatics* 33: 28–34, 1986.

Delmonte, MM. Meditation and change: Mindfulness versus repression. *Australian Journal of Clinical Hypnotherapy and Hypnosis* 11: 57–63, 1990.

Denney, MR, and JL Baugh. Symptom reduction and sobriety in the male alcoholic. *International Journal of the Addictions* 27: 1293–1300, 1992.

Edmonston, WE, Jr. *Hypnosis and Relaxation: Modern Verification of an Old Equation.* New York: Wiley, 1981.

Fergusson, LC, AJ Bonshek, and M Boudigues. Transcendental Meditation and five factors relevant to higher education in Cambodia. *College Student Journal* 28: 103–107, 1994.

Gaston, L, J-C Crombez, M Lassonde, J Bernier-Buzzanga, and S Hodgins. Psychological stress and psoriasis: Experimental and prospective correlational studies. *Acta dermato-venereologica* 156: 37–43, 1991.

Gawain, S. *Creative Visualization.* New York: Bantam Books, 1978.

Gelderloos, P, HJ Hermans, HH Ahlscrom, and R Jacoby. Transcendence and psychological health: Studies with long-term participants of the Transcendental Meditation and TM-Sidhi Program. *Journal of Psychology* 124: 177–197, 1989.

Green, E, and A Green. *Beyond Biofeedback.* New York: Dell Publishing Co., 1977.

Green, EE, AM Green, and D Walters. Biofeedback for mind-body self-regulation: Healing and creativity. *Fields Within Fields . . . Within Fields* 5: 131–144, 1972.

Greene, Y, and B Hiebert. A comparison of mindfulness meditation and cognitive self-observation. *Canadian Journal of Counselling* 22: 25–34, 1988.

Greenspoon, J, and J Olson. Stress management and biofeedback. *Clinical Biofeedback and Health* 9: 65–80, 1986.

Hudesman, J, P Beck, and CM Smith. The use of stress reduction training in a college curriculum for health science students. *Psychology: A Quarterly Journal of Human Behavior* 24: 55–59, 1987.

Ikemi, A, S Tomita, M Kuroda, Y Hayashida, and Y Ikemi. Self-regulation method: Psychological, physiological and clinical considerations. *Psychotherapy and Psychosomatics* 46: 184–195, 1986.

Jones, M. Multimodal treatment of irritable bowel syndrome. *Medical Psychotherapy* 2: 11–20, 1989.

Kabat-Zinn, J. *Full Catastrophe Living.* New York: Delta, 1990.

Kabat-Zinn, J. *Wherever You Go There You Are.* New York: Hyperion, 1994.

Kabat-Zinn, J, AO Massion, J Kristeller, LG Peterson, KE Fletcher, L Pbert, WR Lenderking, and SF Santorelli. Effectiveness of a meditation-based stress reduction program in the treatment of anxiety disorders. *American Journal of Psychiatry* 149: 936–943, 1992.

Kaplan, KH, DL Goldenberg, and M Galvin-Nadeau. Tie impact of a meditation-based stress reduction program on fibromyalgia. *General Hospital Psychiatry* 5: 284–289, 1993.

King, TI. The use of electromyographic biofeedback in treating a client with tension headaches. *American Journal of Occupational Therapy* 46: 839–842, 1992.

Laselle, KM, and TT Russell. To what extent are school counselors using meditation and relaxation techniques? *School Counselor* 40: 178–183, 1993.

Ornish, D. *Dr Dean Ornish's Program for Reversing Coronary Heart Disease without Drugs or Surgery.* New York: Ballantine Books, 1992.

Pearl, JH, and AF Carlozzi. Effect of meditation on empathy and anxiety. *Perceptual and Motor Skills* 78: 297–298, 1994.

Rice, PL. *Stress and Health.* Belmont, CA: Wadsworth, 1992.

Sachs, BC. Stress and self-hypnosis. *Psychiatric Annals* 16: 110–114, 1986.

Schultz, JH, and W Luthe. *Autogenic Training: A Psychophysiological Approach to Psychotherapy.* New York: Grune and Stratton, 1959.

Seaward, BL. *Managing Stress.* Boston: Jones and Bartlett, 1997.

Shapiro, DH, Jr. A mode of control and self-control profile for long-term meditators. *Psychologia* 35: 1–11, 1992.

Sharma, MP, V Kumaraiah, H Mishra, and JP Balodhi. Therapeutic effects of Vipassana Meditation in tension headache. *Journal of Personality and Clinical Studies* 6: 201–206, 1990.

Shaw, RM, and DM Dettmar. Monitoring behavioural stress control using a craniomandibular index. *Australian Dental Journal* 35(2): 147–151, 1990.

Shellenberger, RD, J Turner, and J Green. Health changes in a biofeedback and stress management program. *Clinical Biofeedback and Health* 9: 23–34, 1986.

Simonton, OC, S Matthews-Simonton, and JL Creighton. *Getting Well Again.* New York: Bantam, 1978.

Smith, G. Meditation, the new balm for corporate stress. *Business Week*, May 10, 1993, pp 86–87.

Soskis, DA, EC Orne, MT Orne, and DF Dinges. Self-hypnosis and meditation for stress management: A brief communication. *International Journal of Clinical and Experimental Hypnosis* 37: 285–289, 1989.

Sothers, K, and K Anchor. Prevention and treatment of essential hypertension with meditation-relaxation methods. *Medical Psychotherapy* 2: 137–156, 1989.

Stanton, HE. Hypnosis and rational-emotive therapy—A de-stressing combination. *International Journal of Clinical and Experimental Hypnosis* 37: 95–99, 1989.

Thackwray-Emmerson, D. Stress and disease: An examination of psychophysiological effects and alternative treatment approaches. *Counselling Psychology Quarterly* 1: 229–234, 1988.

Thackwray-Emmerson, D. The effect of self-motivation on headache reduction through biofeedback training. *Medical Psychotherapy* 2: 125–130, 1989.

Ulett, GA, and DB Peterson. *Applied Hypnosis and Positive Suggestion.* St. Louis, MO: CV Mosby, 1965.

Wallace, RK, and H Benson. The physiology of meditation. *Scientific American* 226: 85–90, 1972.

Wenger, MA, and BK Bagchi. Studies of autonomic function in practitioners of Yoga in India. *Behavioral Science* 6: 312–323, 1961.

Zika, B. The effects of hypnosis and meditation on a measure of self-actualization. *Australian Journal of Clinical and Experimental Hypnosis* 15: 21–28, 1987.

Glossary

Note: Terms defined in this glossary appear in boldface in the text.

Abstinence: With reference to substances commonly abused (such as alcohol), abstinence refers to no use at all.

Abuse: With reference to substances commonly associated with addiction and negative health effects (such as alcohol), abuse refers to use that hurts or endangers users or those around users.

Acquired immune deficiency syndrome (AIDS): A disorder caused by the human immunodeficiency virus (HIV) and characterized by certain indicator diseases such as Kaposi's sarcoma, fungus diseases, and others. These indicator diseases result from the decreased immunocompetence resulting from the HIV infection.

Adaptive coping: Responses to stress that have generally positive effects and help reduce feelings of stress.

Addiction: Enslavement to a practice or substance that is physically or psychologically habit forming to the extent that cessation of the practice or substance causes intolerable withdrawal symptoms.

Adipose tissue: Body fat.

Adrenal cortex: The outside layer of the adrenal glands, the adrenal cortex secretes two families of hormones: the mineralocorticoids and glucocorticoids.

Adrenal glands: Endocrine glands located on top of the kidneys. The adrenal glands are really two glands: the adrenal cortex and the adrenal medulla.

Adrenal medulla: The inner portion of the adrenal gland, the adrenal medulla secretes epinephrine (adrenalin) and norepinephrine (noradrenalin).

Adrenocorticotropic hormone (ACTH): A hormone produced by the pituitary gland that stimulates the adrenal cortex to release glucocorticoids and mineralocorticoids.

Aerobic exercise: Activity that significantly increases metabolic rate for prolonged periods of time (15 minutes or longer).

Aerobic fitness: Sound physical state of the body's cardiovascular and energy production systems, a benefit of aerobic exercise.

Afferent nervous system: Nerve cells that receive information from the external and internal environment and conduct this information to the brain.

Aldosterone: A mineralocorticoid secreted by the adrenal cortex. Aldosterone causes the kidneys to retain sodium and water, which increases blood volume and consequently, blood pressure.

Alpha wave: Brain-wave form (indicative of the brain's electrical activity) that is associated with a calm mental state, as recorded on an electroencephalograph.

Anal canal: The last inch of the rectum; stools exit through the anus.

Anorexia nervosa: An eating disorder characterized by suppression of appetite, self-starvation, and extreme weight loss.

Antidiuretic hormone (ADH): A hormone secreted by the pituitary gland during the stress response. Antidiuretic hormone is also known as vasopressin. It causes water retention and contraction of peripheral arteries, thus raising blood pressure.

Arteries: Blood vessels that carry blood from the heart to the rest of the body.

Atherosclerosis: A process in which the walls of medium and large arteries become lined with plaque, composed of fat, cholesterol, and other substances.

Atherosclerotic plaque: A grayish-yellow mound of tissue that forms inside an artery in the process of atherosclerosis. The plaque is composed of cholesterol, cells of the artery lining, and other substances.

Atria: The two upper chambers of the heart (in humans) that push blood into the two lower chambers, the ventricles.

Autogenic training: A relaxation technique developed by Johannes Schultz in the 1930s. Autogenic training teaches a person to relax by imaging sensations of warmth and heaviness in the arms and legs, calm and regular heartbeat and breathing, warmth in the solar plexus, and a cool forehead.

Automatic thoughts: The continuous stream of phrases, pictures, and images that make up a person's conscious thoughts.

Autonomic nervous system (ANS): A branch of the efferent nervous system that sends messages from the central nervous system to nonskeletal systems such as the circulatory, respiratory, digestive, urinary, and endocrine systems.

Beta-endorphins: Chemical messengers that are similar to opioids in structure and function.

Body composition: The proportion of a person's body made up of fat, as opposed to fat-free mass.

Body Mass Index: Weight (in kilograms) divided by height squared (in meters) (kg/m^2).

Brain: Organ of the central nervous system, composed of a mass of nervous tissue.

Brain stem: Oldest and deepest part of the brain, containing structures that automatically regulate essential life functions such as breathing, heart action, and digestion via the sympathetic and parasympathetic branches of the autonomic nervous system.

Bulimia nervosa: An eating disorder in which large volumes of food are consumed and then purged from the body by vomiting, use of laxatives, or other means.

Catecholamines: The hormones epinephrine and norepinephrine, secreted by the adrenal medulla.

Calorically dense: With reference to food, high in calories.

Carbohydrates: A compound containing carbon, hydrogen, and oxygen atoms that is a common constituent of foods. Examples of carbohydrates include sugars, starches, and dietary fibers.

Cardiovascular fitness: Sound physical state of the body's cardiovascular and energy production systems, a benefit of aerobic exercise.

Catecholamines: Collective name for the hormones epinephrine and norepinephrine.

CD4 lymphocytes: White blood cells that are destroyed by the human immunodeficiency virus.

Central nervous system (CNS): Brain and spinal cord.

Cerebral cortex: The outer layer of the brain that includes areas associated with thought, judgment, memory, sensation, motor control, and other emotional and intellectual processes.

Challenge: A personality characteristic of hardy individuals, as theorized by Kobasa and colleagues. Challenge refers to the ability to view demands as challenges to master rather than obstacles to be overcome.

Co-dependency: A situation in which one person feels he or she is responsible for the behavior and problems of others, especially a family member or partner.

Cognitive intervention: Techniques that change people's stress response by helping them change the way they think about stress and stressors.

Cognitive restructuring: Consciously changing one's self-talk and perceptions to alleviate stress.

Cognitive therapy: Using cognitive intervention techniques in a clinical psychotherapy setting.

Commitment: A personality characteristic of hardy individuals, as theorized by Kobasa and colleagues. Commitment refers to a deep connection to and a valuing of things such as family, friends, career, community, and so forth—as opposed to alienation from social and community ties.

Complex carbohydrates: Commonly known as starches, complex carbohydrates have larger molecules than simple carbohydrates, or sugars, and tend to be broken down and absorbed more slowly.

Compulsive overeating: An eating disorder characterized by an inability to control or stop eating and often by binging and rituals that involve food preparation and consumption.

Control: A personality characteristic of hardy individuals, as theorized by Kobasa and colleagues. Control refers to a belief that one's actions affect the outcome of problematic situations.

Coping: Anything you do, including changing cognition, to deal with a stressor or feelings of stress.

Controlled use: With reference to substances commonly abused (such as alcohol), controlled use refers to safe and appropriate use of a substance.

Cooldown: The period at the end of an exercise session in which exercise intensity is gradually decreased to allow the body to adjust to a resting state.

Coronary arteries: Arteries that carry blood containing oxygen and nutrients to the heart.

Coronary artery disease: Atherosclerosis occurring in the coronary arteries, compromising blood flow to the heart.

Corticosterone: A glucocorticoid hormone released by the adrenal cortex during the stress response.

Corticotropin-releasing hormone (CRH): A hormone released by the hypothalamus that stimulates the pituitary gland to release adrenocorticotropic hormone (ACTH).

Cortisol: A glucocorticoid hormone, also known as hydrocortisone, released by the adrenal cortex during the stress response. The most abundant glucocorticoid, cortisol is responsible for about 95 percent of glucocorticoid activity.

Cortisone: A glucocorticoid hormone released by the adrenal cortex during the stress response.

Cross-reactivity: The theory that the physiological response to one type of stress may be reduced by training the body to recover from a different type of stress. For example, repeated exposure to exercise stress may help a person recover more quickly from emotional stress.

Cytokines: Substances produced by both the immune system and the brain that may act as or interact with central nervous system neurotransmitters.

Dental plaque: Debris that adheres to tooth surfaces, formed by bacterial action on food particles.

Diastolic blood pressure: Pressure in the arteries while the heart is "resting" between beats.

Diencephalon: An area of the brain composed of the thalamus and hypothalamus.

Differential relaxation: A state in which a person is contracting only those muscles necessary to accomplish the task at hand while keeping other muscle groups relaxed.

Direct coping: Taking action to change or eliminate a stressor. Problem solving is the most common form of direct coping. Synonymous with problem-focused coping.

Disordered eating: Refers to a continuum of problems with body image and food that run from mild, such as occasional dieting, eating binges, and some concern about being overweight, to severe, characterized by clinical eating disorders.

Duodenum: The part of the small intestine adjacent to the stomach. The duodenum is a common site of ulcers.

Efferent nervous system: Nerves that conduct messages from the central nervous system to the rest of the body.

Electroencephalograph (EEG): An instrument that measures the electrical activity of the brain.

Emotion-focused coping: Thoughts and behaviors one can use to reduce the stress response, to feel more relaxed. Synonymous with palliative coping.

Endocrine: Refers to the endocrine system and its hormones.

Endocrine system: The system of ductless glands that secrete hormones.

Endothelium-derived relaxing factor (EDRF): Substance released by arteries that makes arteries expand to increase blood flow.

Epinephrine: A sympathomimetic hormone secreted by the adrenal medulla.

Esophagus: A hollow muscular tube that carries food from the mouth to the stomach.

Essential hypertension: Hypertension not caused by an underlying disease—about 90 percent of all cases.

Eustress: Stress associated with positive stressors, such as travel, vacations, holidays, and parties.

Exercise: Physical activity performed for the express purpose of improving physical fitness.

Flexibility: Range of motion in a joint.

Free fatty acids (FFA): A substrate that can be used by cells to produce energy. Free fatty acids are released from triglycerides—molecules used to store fat.

Gastrointestinal (GI) tract: The digestive tract that runs continuously from the mouth to the anus and includes the esophagus, stomach, small intestine, and large intestine.

General Adaptation Syndrome (GAS): Hans Selye's theory about the health effects of chronic stress. When exposed to chronic stress, an animal exhibits three stages of adaptation. Initially, the fight-or-flight response occurs, which Selye called the *alarm reaction.* As exposure to the stressor continues, the animal will develop some resistance to the stressor. Selye referred to this period as the *stage of resistance.* The stage of resistance continues until the stressor stops or until the animal's resistance is worn down, at which time it enters the *stage of exhaustion.*

Gingivitis: Gum disease.

Global self-esteem: A person's general sense of self-worth.

Glucagon: A hormone released by the pancreas in response to low blood sugar.

Glucocorticoids: Hormones secreted by the adrenal cortex, including cortisol, corticosterone, and cortisone.

Health behaviors: Actions that affect one's health, including eating and exercise habits, smoking, alcohol use, sleep patterns, and so forth.

Hemoconcentration: A condition in which the formed elements of the blood become more concentrated due to a loss of plasma (the watery part of the blood).

High-density lipoproteins: A class of lipoproteins associated with a decreased risk of artery disease. Lipoproteins contain lipids and proteins, and transport lipids in the aqueous environment of the blood stream.

Human immunodeficiency virus (HIV): Virus that causes acquired immune deficiency syndrome. HIV may remain latent for many years but eventually causes a decline in immune function.

Hypertension: High resting blood pressure.

Hypoglycemia: Low blood sugar.

Hypothalamus: An area of the brain important in the control of many physiological functions. The hypothalamus controls the autonomic nervous system, regulates the pituitary gland, and secretes several hormones and other chemical factors.

Immune system: The various physiological cells and organs that help to protect a person from disease. The immune system is composed of the lymph nodes and vessels that run throughout the body and carry immune cells; the spleen, thymus gland, and bone marrow, which manufacture immune cells; and the various immune cells circulating in the blood and lymph.

Inflammatory bowel diseases (IBDs): A group of diseases, including ulcerative colitis and Crohn's disease, characterized by an inflammation of the colon.

Insomnia: Problems sleeping, such as taking a long time to fall asleep, awakening frequently during the night, or awakening too early in the morning.

Insulin: A hormone released by the pancreas in response to rising blood sugar. Insulin allows blood sugar to enter the body's cells to be stored or used for energy.

Irrational beliefs: Ideas that are not logical and are impossible to achieve but nevertheless are guiding forces in one's life; they contribute to low self-esteem and feelings of anger, anxiety, and depression. An example of an irrational belief is that one must do everything perfectly.

Large intestine: The part of the digestive tract that carries wastes from the small intestine to the anal canal.

Leukocyte: A type of white blood cell that attacks foreign invaders.

Limbic system: An area of the brain composed of the thalamus, hypothalamus, part of the cerebral cortex, and other structures. The limbic system is involved with motivation, emotion, and memory.

Lipids: Dietary fats and oils.

Low-density lipoprotein (LDL): A class of lipoproteins associated with increased risk of artery disease. Lipoproteins contain lipids and proteins, and transport lipids in the aqueous environment of the bloodstream.

Lower esophageal sphincter: A tight band of muscle between the esophagus and the stomach that relaxes during swallowing but then prevents stomach contents from backing up into the esophagus.

Macrophage: A type of white blood cell that engulfs foreign particles, such as bacteria, and stimulates the production of other factors important in the immune response.

Maladaptive coping: Attempts to deal with stress that may seem to help initially but lead to more problems later.

Millimeters of mercury (mm Hg): Unit of blood pressure measurement, referring to the distance a column of mercury rises in a tube for a given pressure.

Mineralocorticoids: Hormones released by the adrenal cortex during the stress response. Mineralocorticoids help control fluid and salt balance.

Muscular endurance: The ability to sustain muscular contractions for a given period of time, usually 30 seconds or more.

Muscular strength: The amount of force muscles can exert in a short period of time, often measured by how much weight can be lifted in a given position.

Negative problem orientation: Psychological perceptions that inhibit problem-solving ability.

Nervous system: Brain, spinal cord, and the peripheral nerves that travel from the spinal cord to all parts of the body. It is the job of the nervous system to coordinate all parts of the body so that they work together.

Norepinephrine: A sympathomimetic hormone secreted by the adrenal medulla and a neurotransmitter.

Nutrient dense: A term describing foods that supply a lot of nutritive value per calorie.

Osteoporosis: A disease in which bones gradually become weaker due to the loss of bone mineral.

Overload: Condition that occurs when the body is asked to do more than it is accustomed to doing. Overload may result from increasing the distance, pace, intensity, resistance, or duration of exercise.

Overnutrition: The consumption of too many calories, especially fat and sugar, which contributes to obesity and other chronic diseases.

Overuse injuries: Injuries that usually result from improper training techniques and doing too much too soon.

Palliative coping: Thoughts and behaviors one uses to reduce the stress response, to feel more relaxed. Synonymous with emotion-focused coping.

Parasympathetic nervous system: A branch of the autonomic nervous system whose effects are associated with the relaxation response, including physiological processes that conserve and restore energy.

Perfectionism: An irrational need to do everything perfectly.

Peripheral nerves: Nerve tissue that is not part of the central nervous system.

Peripheral nervous system: All nerve tissue that is not part of the central nervous system.

Peristalsis: Successive rhythmic contractions of the smooth muscle that forms the lining of organs such as the digestive tract.

Physical activity: Any activity that involves physical movement.

Pituitary gland: A small endocrine gland attached to the hypothalamus.

Platelets: Blood cells that aid in clotting. Platelets are not true cells as they lack a nucleus.

Positive problem orientation: Psychological perceptions that enhance problem-solving ability.

Problem-focused coping: Taking action to change or eliminate a stressor. Problem solving is the most common form of problem-focused coping. Synonymous with direct coping.

Problem solving: Methodically looking for ways to change or eliminate a source of stress.

Progressive relaxation: A relaxation technique developed by Edmund Jacobson in the 1920s. In progressive relaxation, a person alternately contracts and relaxes muscle groups to become aware of the difference between feelings of muscle contraction and muscle relaxation.

Proteins: Food components made from amino acids. Amino acids supply energy and molecules for many other physiological uses.

Psychoneuroimmunology (PNI): The study of the interrelationships of the three systems that serve as communications networks in the maintenance of health: the nervous, endocrine, and immune systems.

Psychophysiology: The study of the relationship between psychological and physiological functions.

Relaxation response: Opposite of the fight-or-flight response, the relaxation response refers to resting homeostasis and a state of mental and physical relaxation.

Resistance training: Exercise that requires exertion of force against a resistance, such as elastic bands or weights.

Reticular formation (RF): An area of the brain that scans sensory information making its way to the brain and evaluates its importance, selectively relaying information deemed relevant and short-circuiting information that seems unnecessary.

Risk factors: Variables associated with a person's probability of developing a given disorder or circumstance, such as heart disease.

Saliva: Fluid produced by the salivary glands that moistens and breaks down food in the mouth.

Selective abstraction: Focusing on certain characteristics in the environment while overlooking others.

Self-concept: One's general image of oneself in the broadest sense.

Self-talk: The continuous stream of phrases, pictures, and images that make up a person's conscious thoughts.

Simple carbohydrates: Commonly known as sugars, simple carbohydrates are relatively small carbohydrate molecules that are broken down and absorbed quickly compared to complex carbohydrates.

Sinoatrial node: A mass of cardiac cells that works as the heart's pacemaker.

Small intestine: A long tube that is part of the gastrointestinal tract and in which food is digested and absorbed. The small intestine carries food from the stomach to the large intestine.

Smooth muscle: Type of muscle located in the walls of internal organs such as the digestive tract.

Somatic nervous system: A branch of the efferent nervous system, the somatic nervous system sends impulses from the central nervous system to skeletal muscles.

Sphygmomanometer: Blood pressure cuff used to measure blood pressure.

Spinal cord: Part of the central nervous system, the spinal cord is a mass of nervous tissue that runs from the brain stem through the spine and from which the peripheral nerves originate. The spinal cord conducts information between the brain and the rest of the body.

Stomach: A saclike organ that digests food.

Stress: Feelings of anxiety and physical tension that occur when people perceive that the demands placed on them exceed their abilities to cope.

Stress management: Intentionally intervening in one's stress cycle to change sources of stress and reduce one's stress response.

Stressor: Anything that causes stress, real or imaginary.

Stress response: The physical and psychological response to a stressor.

Stroke: Destruction of brain tissue because of damage to the blood vessels that supply the brain. Stroke may be caused by atherosclerosis in the arteries supplying the brain or by bleeding into the brain because of a break in a blood vessel.

Sympathetic nervous system (SNS): The branch of the autonomic nervous system that is activated during the fight-or-flight response. The sympathetic nervous system speeds up those functions necessary for immediate survival and suppresses functions such as digestion that are not necessary for immediate survival and can be temporarily postponed.

Sympathomimetic: Having an effect similar to that of the sympathetic nervous system.

Systolic blood pressure: The pressure in the arteries at the moment blood is ejected from the heart as it contracts.

Temporomandibular joint (TMJ) syndrome: A disorder characterized by facial pain, headaches, earaches, and dizziness. The temporomandibular joint connects the upper and lower jaw.

Thalamus: An area of the brain that integrates and relays sensory information to the cerebral cortex. The thalamus helps interpret sensations of pain, temperature, and pressure and is involved in emotion and memory.

Thyroid gland: An endocrine gland located in the throat. The thyroid gland secretes thyroid hormones.

Thyroid hormones: Hormones secreted by the thyroid gland, including thyroxine (T4) and triiodothyronine (T3).

Thyroid-stimulating hormone (TSH): A hormone released by the pituitary gland that signals the thyroid gland to secrete thyroid hormones.

Thyrotropin-releasing hormone (TRH): A hormone secreted by the hypothalamus that causes the pituitary gland to release thyroid-stimulating hormone.

Thyroxine (T4): A hormone secreted by the thyroid gland.

Training effect: The physical changes that occur in response to an exercise program.

Triglycerides: Fat storage molecules found in foods and fat cells.

Triiodothyronine (T3): A hormone secreted by the thyroid gland.

Tunnel vision: Focusing on certain characteristics in the environment while overlooking others.

Type A Behavior Pattern: Personality characteristics identified by cardiologists Friedman and Rosenman that are associated with increased risk of heart disease.

Values clarification: The process of defining and evaluating one's values and understanding the influence they have on one's decisions.

Vasopressin: A hormone secreted by the pituitary gland during the stress response. Vasopressin is also known as antidiuretic hormone. It causes water retention and contraction of peripheral arteries, thus raising blood pressure.

Ventricles: The two lower chambers of the heart (human) that receive blood from the atria and pump it to the lungs and the rest of the body.

Very low-calorie diet (VLCD): Diet that is very low in calories, usually less than 1,000 calories per day.

Warm-up: A period of time at the beginning of an exercise session in which movements are performed at a relatively low intensity to gradually prepare the body for more vigorous exercise.

Weight-bearing exercise: Exercise in which the bones must support weight or exert force against resistance. Walking is considered weight bearing as the bones must bear the weight of the body, as opposed to swimming in which exercise is relatively weightless.

Weight cycling: Repeated cycles of weight loss followed by weight gain.

Wellness: A philosophy/lifestyle based on the idea that the lifestyle choices one makes throughout the years have an important influence on one's mental and physical well-being. Wellness means doing what one can to maximize personal potential for optimal well-being and to construct a meaningful and rewarding life.

Photograph and Cartoon Credits

Name Index

Acevedo, M. C., 192
Achterberg, J., 53, 344
Adams, J. L., 93, 107
Adler, A., 119
Adler, T., 193
Ahlscrom, H. H., 338
Alamada, S. J., 43
Alberti, R. E., 168
Albright, G. L., 349
Alexander, C. N., 335, 336
Allred, K. D., 305
Alser, K. B., 61
Amirkhan, J. H., 87, 88, 89
Anchor, K., 335
Anderson, B., 329
Anderson, C., 50
Anderson, G. E., 69, 73
Anderson, S. C., 267
Andreassi, J. L., 349
Antonucci, T. C., 279
Arapakis, M., 159
Ardell, D. B., 11, 76, 77, 117
Argyle, M., 239
Armstrong, D., 210
Aspinwall, L. G., 279
Atkinson, R. H., 135, 145
Avinir, O., 243
Aycock, D., 168, 261

Bagchi, B. K., 336
Bahrke, M. S., 212
Baker, K., 240
Balodhi, J. P., 335
Banken, J. A., 255
Barber, T. X., 345
Barefoot, J. C., 300
Barrett, D. C., 54
Baucom, D. H., 255
Baugh, J. L., 349
Baumeister, R. F., 279
Bean, R., 288
Beauchamp-Turner, D., 338
Bechtel, L., 81, 246, 247, 250, 259
Beck, A., 245, 259
Beck, J. R., 116
Beck, P., 349
Beery, R. G., 150

Bellingham, R., 117, 119, 308
Benedict, A., 212
Bennett-Goleman, T., 247
Benson, H., 30, 242, 255, 318, 335, 336–337, 337, 340
Berger, B. G., 167, 208
Bernstein,. D. A., 325
Beswick, G., 279
Betz, N. E., 167
Bhagat, R. S., 90
Bjork, R., 230
Black, D. R., 96, 238
Blakemore, R., 91
Blanchard-Fields, F., 89
Blankenship, J., 163, 263
Blankstein, K., 151, 279
Blascovich, J., 277, 282
Blissett, S. E., 240
Block, J., 240
Blumenthal, J. A., 208, 211, 300
Bobko, P., 113
Boden, J. M., 279
Bohachick, P., 318
Bonner, R. L., 91, 259, 267
Bonshek, A. J., 335
Borkovec, T. D., 321
Borysenko, J., 255, 344
Bouchard, C., 200
Boudigues, M., 335
Bowden, J. D., 160
Bowden, M. L., 318
Bower, B., 280
Brack, G., 89
Braiker, H. B., 260
Brannon, L., 53, 55, 193
Brehm, B. A., 200
Bresnitz, S., 240
Bridges, M. W., 45, 53
Britton, B. K., 113, 143
Brockwell, A. L., 349
Brodsky, A., 151
Brown, B. B., 336, 344
Brown, J., 279
Brown, J. D., 208, 240
Brown, L., 163, 263
Brown, R. D., 208, 212
Brown, R. T., 147, 152

Brown, S., 160
Brownell, K. D., 183, 194, 195, 196, 200, 201
Budd, M., 255
Buhrfeind, E. D., 246
Bukowski, C., 146
Bulbulian, R., 211
Burack, J., 54
Burda, P. C., 167
Burg, M. M., 300
Burish, T., 168, 318
Burka, J. B., 150
Burnis, J. J., 267
Burns, D. D., 144, 152, 266
Burt, C. D. B., 246
Butler, R. W., 257
Butterfield, P. S., 259, 267
Buunk, B. P., 282
Byrne, B. M., 277, 282
Bystritsky, A., 255

Campaigne, B., 196
Campbell, J. D., 277
Campbell, S. M., 194
Cannella, K. A. S., 168, 261
Cannonito, M., 236
Caplan, M., 168, 279
Cardozo, S. R., 267, 299
Carlozzi, A. F., 338
Carr, D. B., 210
Carver, C. S., 38, 285
Cassel, J., 158
Cassileth, B. R., 53
Castillo, S., 192
Castonguay, L. G., 255
Cataldo, M. R., 235
Chamberlain, K., 258, 308
Chang, E. C., 255
Chapman, E. N., 273
Chapman, L. S., 117
Chaves, J. F., 345
Chesney, M. A., 45
Cheung, S-K., 255
Chir, B., 23
Chrousos, G. P., 25
Clark, A., 288
Clark, N., 191, 192, 204
Clemes, H., 288

365

Subject Index

Note: Page numbers followed by a *t* refer to tables, and those followed by an *i* refer to illustrations.

2043